A CORNER OF A FOREIGN FIELD

RAMACHANDRA GUHA

A CORNER OF A FOREIGN FIELD

The Indian History of a British Sport

PICADOR

First published 2002 by Picador
an imprint of Pan Macmillan Ltd
Pan Macmillan, 20 New Wharf Road, London N1 9RR
Basingstoke and Oxford
Associated companies throughout the world
www.panmacmillan.com

ISBN 0 330 49116 4

3 5 7 9 8 6 4 2

A CIP catalogue record for this book is available from
the British Library.

Typeset by Intype London Ltd
Printed and bound in India by Replika Press Pvt. Ltd., 100% EOU
Plot No. 310 EPIP, HSIDC, Kundli 131 028

for Shekhar Pathak

and his *Pahar*

It is a dreadful pity when a beautifully spacious generalization is upset by one or two simple facts.

Neville Cardus

Contents

RELIGION
RIOTS MINUS THE STABBING

NATION
HISTORY'S RESIDUES

List of Illustrations

The illustrations that I have chosen for this book are either rare and difficult to obtain or illustrate the cultural rootedness of cricket in India. I have not reproduced pictures of Test match crowds or of contemporary cricketers such as Sachin Tendulkar, judging that the reader would already be familiar with them.

1. Cricket in Bombay, as depicted by the London *Graphic*, 1878. (H. D. Darukhanawala, *Parsis and Sports and Kindred Subjects* (1934), copy in the author's collection.)
2. The Parsi touring team to England, 1886. (The Anandji Dossa Collection © Cricket Club of India, Mumbai.)
3. Expatriate cricket in the Himalaya, *c.* 1890. (Courtesy of Sunil Khilnani.)
4. Villagers playing cricket in the Himalaya, *c.* 1894. (F. J. St Gore, *Lights and Shades of Hill Life in the Afghan and Hindu Highlands of the Punjab: A Contrast*, 1895.)
5. Palwankar Baloo, 1904. (J. M. Framji Patel, *Stray Thoughts on Indian Cricket* (1905), copy in the author's collection.)
6. The Palwankar brothers. (Anandji Dossa Collection © Cricket Club of India, Mumbai.)
7. C. K. Nayudu, outside the London Zoo, 1930. (Courtesy of Mrs Sumati Bagchee.)
8. An advertisement for cricket balls and bats, 1932. (From *The Field*, a monthly sports magazine then published from Madras, issue of October 1932, copy in the author's collection.)
9. The Muslim team that won the Bombay Quadrangular tournament of 1934. (From *Indian Cricket*, December 1934, copy in the author's collection.)

Preface

NINETEENTH-CENTURY ENGLAND gave the world the railroad, electricity and the theory of evolution, but also football, rugby and hockey. The major team sports were all invented in one island, as were the popular racket games of badminton, table tennis and tennis. Men have raced and punched one another since the invention of fire, but it was Englishmen who gave athletics and boxing their modern forms. Only two of the great games of humankind are not of English origin: basketball, which was patented in New England in the 1890s, and golf, the contribution of the Scots across the border.

Early modern England has verily been the 'games-master' of the world.[1] Of all the sports they gave birth to, cricket is the one which the English themselves recognize and uphold as their national game. In its origins a rural sport which was once hugely popular in the villages of southern England, in the nineteenth century cricket was made part of the life of the industrial towns. The rules of cricket, and still more its ethos, most fully embodied the self-image of the Victorian elite, its aspiration to set moral standards for the rest of humanity. In 1851 the West Country parson James Pycroft suggested that

> The game of cricket, philosophically considered, is a standing panegyric on the English character: none but an orderly and sensible race of people would so amuse themselves. It calls into requisition all the cardinal virtues, some moralist would say. As with the Grecian games of old, the player must be sober and temperate. Patience, fortitude, and self-denial, the various bumps

of order, obedience, and good humour, with an unruffled temper, are indispensable. For intellectual virtues we want judgement, decision, and the organ of concentrativeness – every faculty in the free use of all limbs – and every idea in constant air and exercise. Poor, rickety, and stunted wits will never serve: the widest shoulders are of little use without a head upon them: the cricketer wants wits down to his fingers' ends.[2]

Cricket is a game of finesse and skill; it lacks the element of physical contact and occasional brutality that marks football and rugby. Less subtle games might be played by Italians and Germans, but cricket, Pycroft insisted, 'is essentially Anglo-Saxon. Foreigners have rarely, very rarely, imitated us. The English settlers and residents everywhere play at cricket; but of no single club have we ever heard [that] dieted either with frogs, sour-kraut or macaroni.'[3]

Numerous clubs have since dieted on curry and rice. Cricket was taken up in the white Dominions, as the good parson expected, but its most dramatic conquests have been among excitable and intemperate Asiatics. They have played and watched and talked cricket with a verve and intensity that would have amazed, and perhaps dismayed, the game's Victorian chroniclers. Indeed, the case can be made that as a *national* sport Indian cricket has no parallel. There may be more money in American basketball, and as much passion in Brazilian soccer. It is the weight of numbers that makes Indian cricket bigger still, with money and passion being multiplied by the 500 million who partake of it.

When India became free, some Anglophobe nationalists called for the game to disappear along with its promoters, the British. In this they were spectacularly unsuccessful. What was previously an urban sport has penetrated deep into the countryside. Indigenous games like *kabaddi* and *kho-kho* never had a chance, but cricket has also vanquished sports like hockey, where India was once the acknowledged world leader. The doings of the national cricket team are followed all over the country. The best players enjoy the iconic status otherwise reserved for Hindu gods and film stars. Their faces peep out of highway billboards; on television they commend all kinds of consumer products. The Bombay batsman Sachin Tendulkar is perhaps the best-known Indian, as well as one of the richest. There are pamphlets and books about him in his native Marathi, and in Hindi and Tamil too. When Tendulkar is batting against the Pakistani swing-bowler Wasim Akram, the television audience exceeds the entire population of Europe.

How did this most British of games become so thoroughly domesticated in the sub-continent? This book provides the answer. It is not so much a history of Indian cricket as a history of India told through cricket and cricketers. It is woven around biographies of men of influence, such as C. K. Nayudu, the first truly mass hero of sub-continental sport, each of whose sixes was interpreted as a nationalist answer to the British Raj. I have written of two famous English cricketers, Lord Harris and D. R. Jardine, whose time in India, now forgotten, complicates what we know of their character and of their Empire. Harris and Jardine were Oxford men, as was Abdul Hafeez Kardar, a cricketer who was also an ideologue, and through whose life one can read the coming into being of the nation of Pakistan.

Plenty of politicians stalk these pages too. At various times, cricket drew into its fold India's first Prime Minister, its last Governor-General, and its first two Presidents. Muhammad Ali Jinnah and Indira Gandhi make cameo appearances. Surprising connections are established between cricket and the most venerated of Indian politicians, Mahatma Gandhi, as well as the most feared, Balasaheb Thackeray.

But the book's most heroic character is a cricketer and politician now forgotten by both cricket and politics. He is Palwankar Baloo, a slow left-arm bowler of low-caste origin who led the Hindus to some famous victories against the Europeans of Bombay, and who took more than 100 wickets on the first All India tour of England, in 1911. Baloo, I argue here, was the first great Indian cricketer and a pioneer in the emancipation of the Untouchables. His career in cricket and politics stretched from 1895 to 1937. My narrative starts half a century before he began to play and comes down to the present. The book is about much else, but it is Baloo's story that, in more senses than one, is its centre-piece.

For the social historian, mass sport is a sphere of activity that expresses, in concentrated form, the values, prejudices, divisions and unifying symbols of a society. The importance of sport to the modern world is manifest in the pervasive use of sporting metaphors in popular discourse. Why is it that a new and conspicuously successful party in the land of Mussolini and Michelangelo has called itself Forza Italia, or Goal! Italy? Or that a controversial law in the US state of California is justified in terms of a baseball metaphor, 'Three strikes and you are out'? Or indeed, that when faced with a political crisis, generations of British Prime Ministers, Tory, Labour and Liberal, take cover in the language of cricket, and speak of playing with a straight bat on a sticky wicket? And how is it that since the end of the First World War there has been only one Kaiser in German society, and he a footballer, Franz Beckenbauer?

These are questions that should in theory interest historians, but in practice they do not. Or at any rate, not often enough. For the study of sport, in its cultural and historical context, is an underdeveloped field in most countries, my own not excepted. There is an *International Journal of Sports History*, some of its articles are of a very high quality, but these focus for the most part on the practice of sport, the background of its players and patrons, the evolution of its associations and tournaments, and on how it pays or does not pay for itself. I do not myself support the placing of sports history (or indeed, other emerging fields such as environmental history and women's history) in a ghetto of its own. In my view, the attempt should rather be to use ignored or previously marginal spheres, such as sport or gender or environment, to illuminate the historical centre itself.

The American writer Jane O'Reilly has remarked that the 'one nice thing about sports is that they prove men do have emotions and are not afraid to show them'.[4] It is also, as this book shows, the one nasty thing. For the cricket field was both a theatre of imperial power and of Indian resistance. The career of Palwankar Baloo illuminates the operations of that unique (and uniquely dreadful) human institution, caste. The disagreements between Hindus and Muslims before 1947, and between India and Pakistan since, have thrown a long shadow across the playing-fields of the world.

The commercialization of modern cricket and the corruptions that have come in its wake have led some commentators to speak wistfully of a time when this was a 'gentleman's game'. In truth, there was no golden age, no uncontaminated past in which the playground was free of social pressure and social influence. Cricket has always been a microcosm of the fissures and tensions within Indian society: fissures that it has both reflected and played upon, mitigated as well as intensified. The cricketer or cricket lover might seek to keep his game pure, but the historian finds himself straying, willy-nilly, into those great, overarching themes of Indian history: race, caste, religion and nation. To the dismay of some of my friends, this has become a book on cricket which does not focus exclusively on runs, wickets and catches, on epic innings and exciting matches. The making of modern India is its theme, with cricket serving merely as a vehicle, as my chief source of illustrative example.

RACE

DOMESTICATING A GAME

1. The Homesick Colonial and the Imitative Native

THAT ACUTE OBSERVER of the conqueror's ways, Nirad Chaudhuri, once remarked that to the Englishman abroad literature was his wife and sport his mistress.[1] Books and games provided the twin consolations by which he came to terms with an alien – and potentially hostile – culture and climate. Living in Calcutta in the 1830s, 'stifled with the stench of native cookery and deadened with the noise of native music', Thomas Babington Macaulay sought refuge in Plutarch's *Lives* and the histories of Herodotus.[2] A generation later, Winston Churchill spent an oppressively hot summer in southern India reading the works of Macaulay.[3] Their more philistine colleagues, meanwhile, escaped the alienness of this land through sport.

The first mention of cricket in India dates to 1721, when British sailors played a match among themselves in the port of Cambay. 'When my boat was lying for a fortnight in one of the channels,' wrote one of the players, 'though the country was inhabited by the Culeys, we every day diverted ourselves with playing Cricket and to other Exercises, which they would come and be spectators of . . .'[4] The admirals and generals knew their men to be prone to homesickness. Thus, as one pioneering cricket historian put it,

> our soldiers, by order of the Horse Guards, are provided with cricket grounds adjoining their barracks; and Her Majesty's ships have bats and balls to astonish the cockroaches at sea, the crabs and turtles ashore. Hence it has come to pass that, wherever Her Majesty's servants have 'carried their victorious arms' and legs – wind and weather permitting – cricket has been played.[5]

Sport, like the Flag, first established itself along the coast of India before making its way into the untamed hinterland. The early records of Indian cricket – the first hat-trick, the first tie, the first century – all relate to military men. The first cricket club outside Britain was the Calcutta Cricket Club, founded in 1792 in the bridgehead of British power. The club played in the ample Maidan that skirted – and still skirts – Fort William, the 'manly exercise of cricket' followed in the evenings by dinner and dances where the cricketers 'might try their ability in another way'.[6] Twelve years later the club sponsored a 'Grand Match of Cricket' between Old Etonians and a team drawn from the lesser members of the East India Company. This match was notable for two firsts: the first hundred scored on Indian soil (by Robert Vansittart), and the first bets placed in India on a cricket match. The Old Etonians defied the odds – two to one against them – to win by an innings.[7]

Also in 1792 is the first evidence of cricket in Madras, courtesy of a painting of that date made by the Daniells.[8] Meanwhile, the game was taking root in the third of the great port cities of the Raj. Thus the *Bombay Gazette* of 6 October 1825 carried a cheerfully exhortative announcement under the heading 'Cricket Revived':

> We at all times feel infinite pleasure in announcing amusements, which tend to counteract the effects of this enervating climate by rousing the spirits from apathy, and the physical powers from that feminine indolence, which is generally rewarded with premature old age, 'skin hanging in drapery, and muscles reduced to pack-thread'.
>
> The cricket players are now preparing to resume their exercise for the cold season and several, grand matches between men in the Queen Royals, from the famed counties of Hampshire, Sussex and Kent, are on the [cards] . . .
>
> A meeting will take place tomorrow at four o'clock, on the ground near the Racket Court, and the play will continue at the same hour, on every succeeding Thursday throughout the cold weather.
>
> Tents, it is understood, are to be pitched for the accomo-

dation of ladies, and as the cricketers are all to be dressed in an appropriate uniform, we anticipate one of the most gay and animated scenes that has ever graced our island.[9]

Cricket and other sports were, as this excerpt suggests, a source of much comfort to the expatriate Englishman. By their means he could impose order on the essential randomness of the country he had come to rule over. There was always, in India, the fear of death by war or disease. 'Two monsoons', it was said, was all the colonial could reasonably expect to live through. Here sport came to be a consolation, through which the expatriate could re-create memories of life in England. Note that this early announcement of cricket in Bombay uses the phrase 'our island'. Through their entertainments the British could imagine that they had even brought their country with them.[10]

It appears that in the beginning the British had no intention of teaching the natives to play cricket. They had invented the game at Home and played it in India as a welcome retreat from the utter strangeness of life abroad. The forum by which the retreat was effected was that other British invention, the social club. These clubs were set up in the cities and cantonments, and sometimes in the wilderness too. The local club provided the main focus of the exile's social life. It generally 'boasted of very few books', but provided space in which to play and drink afterwards. Some Anglo-Indians were so devoted to their club that they refused to go back to England after retirement. They built a home near the club, spent the days in its library and the evenings in the bar, and instructed their heirs that they wished to be buried somewhere within striking distance of the eighteenth green.[11]

The racial exclusivity of the colonial clubs was complete and long-lasting (in most cases, they stayed all-white until the transfer of power in August 1947).[12] The 'life and work of the majority of the members', wrote a luminary of one such club,

required them daily, and in an increasing degree to mix with their Indian fellow-subjects, not only in work or business, but also socially . . . and it was surely not asking too much that a

man might have, after his day's work, a place where he could
for an hour or two take his ease in the society of men of his
own race, and those whose habits and customs were the same
as his own.[13]

An American writer visiting the great imperial summer capital, Simla,
saw the club as 'the last resort of a colony shut off from the metro-
politan forms of amusement'. It was 'intended to provide an afternoon
of undiluted nonsense for those who don't care as long as they
enjoy themselves'. The activities of the club in Simla, he commented
sarcastically, 'resemble very closely some of the adventures of the Don
Quixote de la Mancha: such as charging the windmills, sheep, tent
pegs, etc.; but there are some less dangerous items; to wit, egg and
spoon, cricket ball and affinity races.'[14]

Places such as the Calcutta Cricket Club and the Madras Cricket
Club provided English food and English entertainments. The wine
may have been French, but the only concession to India was the
commonly used suffix, gymkhana, which derived from *gend-khana*,
or ball-house.[15] The games played by the gymkhana's members were
all of English origin: whist, billiards, tennis and, above all, cricket.
In contrast to those other sports cricket was collective, longer lasting,
and rather more ceremonial. The slow stateliness of the walk to the
wicket, the interruptions between balls and overs, the graceful clothes
that the players wore, the greenness of the grass, the understated
gaiety of the lunch and tea intervals – all these made cricket an
extended escape from India, from its chatter, its dirt, its smells and
its peoples.

The rulers would play, and the Indians serve. These respective
roles were neatly delineated in a description of the Calcutta Cricket
Club, *circa* 1840:

On the cricket arena stand two spacious tents, not, however,
like the paltry affairs bearing that name in England, but lined
with fancy chintz, furnished with looking glasses, sofas and
chairs, and each player's wants, whether it be a light for his
cigar, iced soda-water, or champagne, supplied by his turbaned

attendant. . . . The natives do not enter at all into the spirit of the game.[16]

In the port cities of Bombay and Calcutta, with their well-staffed clubs and easy access to equipment from England, 'the cricket of the exile assimilate[d] to the cricket played in the land of the free'. Elsewhere, to play the game required skilful improvisation. One memoirist has left a charming account of how cricket came to the ancient Burmese capital of Mandalay. A group of bored officers, posted there in the 1860s, instructed their Tommies to get packing material from the regimental store. This was converted into a matting wicket, while discarded fish-netting was made into a cricket net. However, there was only enough netting to go behind and on the off-side of the wicket. The leg-side was wide open, and 30 yards away lay 'the historical lake into which King Thebaw and his enterprising little child-wife Soup-i-lat popped all their cousins and aunts who stood in the way of the succession to the throne'. The rules of the game thus forbade any hitting to leg. Otherwise, there would have been 'a second tragedy' if the officers had lost their only cricket ball in the lake into which King Thebaw had sunk his relatives.[17]

For civilians serving in lonely outposts the odd game of cricket with their nearest (white) neighbours was much looked forward to. One officer, posted with the Salt and Akbari Department in the arid Tamil country, recalled a series of matches played between his department and a team of artillery officers visiting from Madras. The visitors were all English, but for the hosts an 'octet of [cricket-illiterate] aborigines' were compelled to join the three resident officials of the Salt Department. Other aborigines were set to work levelling the ground and preparing a pitch. A strip of coconut matting was laid on top, and the Englishmen had their cricket, far from Heaven and further from Lord's, 'where never in the world's history it had been played before, and almost certainly never been seen since'. After the match the civilians wrote to the armymen apologizing for their lack of hospitality, blaming it on the absence of a Fortnum and Mason in the neighbourhood.[18]

The self-conscious exclusiveness of expatriate cricket is vividly brought out in a chapter of A. G. Bagot's *Sport and Travel in India and Central America*. These recollections of an old Army officer were published in Macmillan's Colonial Library in 1897, although the sport they speak of was played some forty years previously. Cricket, remarks Bagot,

> is acknowledged to be the national game par excellence of Eng-lishmen. Wherever they may be, north, south, east, or west, sooner or later, provided a sufficient number are gathered together, there is certain to be a cricket match; and climate has little or no effect on their ardour, for you will find them playing on the burning sand of the desert with as much zest as if it was the best possible pitch in the Old Country; and even an expedition to the North Pole is not considered complete without a consignment of bats, balls, and stumps.

There follows a description of a cricket tour in the India of the 1850s, a journey by a regimental team to a station in the interior. Their enjoyments were varied. When a covey of snipe was spotted, the train carrying the soldiers was stopped for an hour, to allow them to disembark with their guns and come back after killing a few birds for the pot. The matches were exciting, often won or lost in the last over. After play ended billiards was played and whisky drunk. A donkey was placed in the camp-bed of a colleague who was the last to leave the bar. These English games, however, almost fell victim to an unknown Indian. For 'on that tour', remembered Bagot,

> I nearly got into serious trouble, for I was within an ace of slaughtering an unoffending baboo, whose curiosity got the better of his discretion. I was practising at a net, around which was gathered a select little crowd of native gentlemen, who, though warned more than once not to come too near, kept on gradually edging in and making their remarks, 'Arre dheko, etc.' ['See, see!'], till at last I got a half-volley fair to square leg and the ball landed the leader plumb centre, which doubled him up into a ball and he was carried off in a moribund condition. Of

course it was quite unpremeditated on my part, and a pure accident, but they were all very indignant, and vowed that they would have me in the lowest dungeon, and, if my friend had 'handed in his checks', as our American friends call it, I verily believe they would have had a real good try for it. Happily, however, after about an hour or so he came round, and matters began to assume a more roseate hue; but he did not come anywhere near the practice nets again, and I fancy the game of cricket fell considerably in his estimation.

From Bagot's account, it seems that in both city and country the Indian had no feel for cricket at all. At this time 'the native mind had not grasped the delicacies and intricacies of "yorker", "longhops", and "half volleys", but were rather apt to look on a cricket match as proof of the lunatic propensities of their masters the sahibs, and to wonder what possible enjoyment they could find in running about in the sun all day after a leather ball'. In the great city of Calcutta, where Bagot was once stationed, the only Indian with a connection to cricket was the club's official

'Fecknee waller', or thrower, who was by no means bad practice; very straight and very fast, of course with no break and little variation of either length or pace, but with six annas on the wicket, apt to be very deadly if you did not play with a straight bat. Many a rupee has he had out of me in the old days, and would doubtless do so again if he is still in the flesh; but, beyond that, and being a tolerable field on emergency, provided the ball did not hit his legs, he was useless. Batting with him was an unknown science, and one he did not care to learn. He threw and earned his 'talub', picking up unconsidered trifles also in the way of tips, and there his cricket ended. His day's work over, I have no doubt that over his hubble-bubble he was wont to dilate on the folly of the sahibs to an admiring circle of his fellow-countrymen.[19]

This is a narrative of mutual distaste. The sahib thought the natives unfit to bat or field, although they might bowl – after a fashion –

for a wage and tips alongside. He also thought that the Indian believed *him* to be a fool to play cricket.

In retirement, the old colonial generally looked back on the club as the high-point of his life in India. When, in 1964, a cricket club in southern Calcutta came to celebrate its centenary, a former member wrote feelingly of 'My Days of Enjoyment at Ballygunje'. When the invitation came to contribute to the commemorative souvenir, said Bernard Owens,

> In my mind's eye I saw again the morning scene, faithfully enacted over the years. It is 11.10, and the game starts at 11. The roller has been harboured by the mali's hut besides the Store Road gate, and two small children with their nannies are playing on it. The bell has rung to take down the nets. Stragglers of both sides, clad in multi-coloured blazers, carrying cricket bats, are leisurely crossing the ground. A few early spectators are choosing chairs and points of vantage. Old friends are greeting each other, and there is anticipation in the air. The bearded Khansamah, turbaned, his imposing girth set off by, and resplendent in, the cummerbund worked in the club colours, has already served some early customers.
>
> By 11.20 two umpires from the batting side have been requisitioned, the fielders appear tossing the ball from hand to hand. The wicket keeper, who has forgotten his box, dashes to join his comrades, and the openers, rehearsing the shots they fondly hope to make, eventually reach the wicket. The scorers push their table into the sun, and the game is on.[20]

This remembrance relates to the 1920s, when Indians had begun clamouring in numbers for political independence. It was written nearly two decades after they had attained that independence. Yet for this member the Ballygunje Cricket Club was a corner of a foreign field that would be forever England. True, play did not start on time – the tropics promoted leisureliness – but the game's idiom and its actors were recognizably English. Only the groundsman who rolled the pitch and the bearer who mixed the drinks were not. Another recollection in the same volume underlines how Indians had, strictly speaking, no part of the cricket itself. 'I was at Ballygunje', remembered A. A. Leslie,

> when George Craik hit a ball out of the ground on the Old Ballygunje Road side. A tikka gharry was passing with the coachman fast asleep. The ball dropped in the gharry, but it did not wake the coachman and the horse went on quite unconcerned. The gharry was chased by chokras and the ball retrieved by one who demanded a rupee for its return.[21]

A post-colonial critic would go to town on these stereotypical views of the lazy and grasping native. What should interest us, however, is not how the native is represented but where he is placed. It thus appears that the Indian might roll the pitch or serve the whisky. He might even watch cricket and (at a price) retrieve the ball or throw it for the sahibs to bat back. He was not expected to *play* the game.

But he would.

THE FIRST INDIANS to play cricket were the Parsis of Bombay. This community of fire-worshippers had fled their native Persia after the coming of Islam, and settled along the coast of western India. They took easily to trade and commerce, professions viewed with disdain by the high-born Hindu. They spoke the language of the land, Gujarati, but clung tenaciously to their faith. By the time the British came the Parsis were already well established in the coastal towns of Bharuch, Ankleshwar, Surat, and Navsari.[22]

The Parsis were a 'comprador' class, who allied themselves with the British to great mutual benefit. They began as merchants and commission agents and in time graduated to the law and the colonial civil service.[23] When Bombay emerged as a centre of power they gravitated towards it. The Parsis, writes Eckehard Kulke, 'poured out of Gujarat into Bombay to the same extent that Bombay became more important as a port and economic, administrative and cultural centre'.[24] Commerce and culture brought them closer to the rulers than any other Indian community. 'After the advent of the British in India', remarks one chronicler, 'the dormant qualities that lay concealed in the Parsi bosom . . . obtained free scope.'[25] Some Parsis made huge killings in the China opium trade. Far quicker than the Hindu or the Muslim, the Parsi took to Western dress, Western music and the English language. With his 'elastic and fascinating character, half oriental, half occidental',[26] he took readily to cricket, too.

The origins of Indian cricket – as distinct from cricket in India – lie in an expanse of green ground at the southern end of the island of Bombay, acres of open space now broken up into half a dozen pieces and ringed by those colossal works of colonial Gothic: the High Court, the University, St Xavier's College and the Victoria Terminus. A hundred and fifty years ago the roads and buildings did not exist, and the grass was continuous. This ground was just outside the walls of the fort of black basalt within which the city's first settlement lay. In 1772, fearing attack by the French, the British levelled and completely cleared the area outside the fort's walls, to provide a clear range of fire. By the turn of the century the threat from the French had receded. Meanwhile the population of the fort, white as well as brown, had grown steadily. The acres of green grass now found more creative peacetime uses.[27]

The area was known to the Army as the Parade Ground, to the English civilian (and his lady) as the Esplanade, and to everybody else as the Maidan. From the early 1800s the natives flocked to the Maidan in search of exercise and recreation. In a city sited on a long but narrow sliver of land, it was the only place to which they could go (Indians, especially urban Indians, are not partial to the sea). A Parsi memoirist wrote that a stranger visiting the grounds in the middle of the nineteenth century could

> at a glance view how the undulating stretch of the verdant meadow was dotted all over by groups of persons, young and old, but almost [all] of the sterner sex, engaged in their daily social amenities of diverse varieties. He would view small groups

of men squatted on China mats, either in a square or circle, averaging from six to ten. . . . The squatting groups would be seen merrily playing games of cards. . . . Others would be noticed playing either the *dam* (draughts) or chess. . . . A little further to the north might be seen parties of youngsters either playing the old but most popular form of 'gilly danda' (a kind of Indian cricket still holding its own in villages outside the cities) or the game of 'Asookh Mahasookh', a sort of physical exercise in which the feet were mostly in evidence, though the employment of hands was not less to be discerned when in the act of bowing and balancing on a single leg while the other was uplifted a few inches from the ground.[28]

European soldiers played cricket on the northern end of the Esplanade, with bats and ball imported from England and with their ladies in attendance. They soon found their imitators. Parsi boys were playing cricket here as early as the 1830s, 'their chimney-pots serving as wickets and their umbrellas as bats in hitting elliptical balls stuffed with old rags and sewn by veritably useful cobblers'.[29] These cricketers wore not the regulation trouser-and-shirt but traditional attire. The pioneer Parsi cricketer 'went to the wicket with a white band around his forehead, giving him the air of the inmate of some hospital, and a still whiter apron dangling from his waist, which was encircled by the sacred thread of his faith'.[30] Even so, cricket was a more challenging game by far than *gilly danda*. There are two materials of the Indian game: a thin stick 3 feet long and a smaller piece of wood the size and shape of a banana. Its objects are likewise crude: to hit the twig as far as one can with the branch. Cricket, by contrast, is a game of immense possibilities, in artistry, technique and dramatic interest far superior to anything previously played on the subcontinent.

For Parsi boys in search of entertainment, cricket would very easily supplant *gilly danda* and *asookh mahasookh*. The implements, to begin with, were of their own making, and the turf was not as smoothly cultivated as they would have wished. As one chronicler colourfully put it, it was on a 'broken, irregular and rough ground overgrown with coarse grass' that 'the pioneer Parsee cricketers were content to learn their alphabet of the noble English game, and their lot certainly does not appear to have been enviable'. For 'the inconvenience arising from bad ground was vastly increased by other circumstances'.[31] From sunrise to sunset, one chunk of the Maidan was occupied by Muslim dyers, who spread out long strips of cloth coloured with indigo. Cricket balls occasionally wandered on to the drying cloth, which led to fights when the dyers threatened to confiscate them. More damagingly, a flying ball once struck the wife of a European constable out on her evening walk. After this incident, the Parsi cricketers were temporarily banned from the Maidan.[32]

About the year 1848 the Parsi boys, now men, founded their first club, the Oriental Cricket Club. This dissolved itself in two years, to be replaced by the Young Zoroastrian Club, still going strong 150 years after its inception. The Young Zoroastrians were funded by the emerging business houses of the Tatas and the Wadias. The club's prime mover, however, was one Hiraji Gosta, also known as Kuka Daru. He charged his members 2 annas a month; those who found this beyond their reach could pay 1 pice for every day they practised.[33] The Young Zoroastrians played every day on the Maidan, disregarding the English journalist who wrote that they presented a 'comic sight', playing the game 'in their strange accoutrements of *Bandis* and pyjamas'.[34]

At least thirty Parsi clubs were formed in the 1850s and 1860s, named for Roman gods and British statesmen: Jupiter, Mars, Gladstone and Ripon, for example. The emerging Parsi bourgeoisie welcomed the growth of cricket for strengthening their ties with the overlord and for renewing the vitality of a race that had lived too long in the tropical sun. One eminence, Sir Cowasji Jehangir, Bart, advertised in the community paper, *Rast-Goftar*, that he would distribute cricket kit free to anyone who cared to ask for it.[35] Another, Sorabji Shapoorji Bengalee, C. I. E., endowed a prize for the best Parsi club. His grant generously allowed for a band to be in attendance during the matches, for tents to be pitched for the convenience of the players, and for food to be provided for them and for spectators as well.

These prize matches, held annually between 1868 and 1877, enormously consolidated the Parsi interest in cricket. Individual achievement meshed nicely with community solidarity. Thus, when the Zoroastrian Cricket Club won the tournament in 1869, it distributed its prize money of 100 rupees as follows: 25 rupees for a newly constructed Parsi gymnasium, 20 rupees for Parsis recently impoverished by cholera, 5 rupees for the poor box, 20 rupees to buy bats for its ablest players, and 30 rupees reserved for the club's kitty. S. S. Bengalee's gift worked marvellously in overcoming any residual inhibitions that the orthodox had as regards the English game. As one observer remarked, 'old folks that were always denouncing "ball-bat" were seen in the forenoon wending their way to the cricket ground, and basking there in the sunshine, witnessing the prize-matches'.[36] The conservatism of culture was easily vanquished by the spirit of competition.

2. Searching for Space

THE FIRST PARSIS to play cricket remain anonymous, but not the first Hindu. His name was Ramchandra Vishnu Navlekar, and he entered the field in 1861.[1] Five years later he helped form the Bombay Union Cricket Club, its membership restricted to men of his Prabhu caste. Meanwhile, the Hindu students of the Elphinstone High School were competing with their Parsi fellows to catch the attention of their cricket-minded Principal, H. P. Jacob. In 1877 some Marathi students of the school founded a Hindu Cricket Club. At first, this had only a handful of members, each paying 2 annas a month. The financial base of the club was assured when the Gujarati Hindus, who were prosperous traders, joined in. The membership slowly increased, and with it a rise in the quality of their cricket.

The Parsis took to cricket in imitation of the rulers. The Hindus, in turn, were spurred by the Parsis. The students who formed the Hindu Cricket Club claimed they were 'shabbily treated' in the supply of bats and balls, the English schoolmasters making sure that these first reached their favoured subjects. The Hindu boys played in *dhotis* and without shoes, and made 'all the mistakes of novices'. The Parsis were 'much more advanced than they', owing 'to their greater imitation of everything European'. However, the 'progress of the Parsees made the Hindus only more ambitious and wistful', determined to start their own teams and play the game in proper clothing and with the correct techniques.[2]

As these clubs came up, one by one, players made their way with bat and ball to the Maidan, still the only large open space available for recreation. Dozens of cricket matches were played here every weekend. 'There is no more agreeable sight to me', remarked a famous Parsi Mayor of Bombay, 'than of the whole Maidan overspread by a lot of enthusiastic Parsi and Hindu cricketers, keenly and eagerly engaged in this manly game.'[3]

At first the Europeans thought little of attempts by their subjects to take to their national game. An Army regiment, after pressure was put on it, agreed to play against a Parsi club, but as 'Officers with Umbrellas versus Natives with Bats'. This distaste was ecumenical. Thus a Bombay journalist wrote sneeringly of some Hindu players that 'their kilted garments interfered [when batting] with running, and they threw the ball when fielding in the same fashion as boarding school girls'.[4]

The criticisms stung, and reforms were effected. The *dhoti* and the *dagli* were abandoned in favour of cream flannels. The wickets were watered and rolled, and the grass on the outfield cut down to 3 inches. Sporting firms imported all the necessary equipment: bats with handles made of single and double cane, in sizes fit for adults and for children; Duke's balls, double and triple seam; leg-guards, shoes and wicket-keeping gauntlets of 'superior quality and well venti-lated'; batting gloves ('best imported, vulcanized, tubular India rubber') and bags for carrying cricket kit, these made of 'strong green cloth', with leather binding and brass locks besides; and stumps and cricket nets with poles and ropes to put them in place. Those who could not afford these English products made do with serviceable imitations produced by local craftsmen.[5]

By the 1870s the card-players and dyers had disappeared from the Maidan. But the Europeans remained. In June 1875 they formed the Bombay Gymkhana, which consolidated, into a single institution, separate polo, cricket, football and rifle clubs run for and by whites. With the Governor of Bombay as its patron, and the Chief Justice as its Secretary, the Gymkhana could count on pulling a string or two. A lease was swiftly signed between the promoters and the government, allowing the Gymkhana the exclusive use of some 4,575 square yards of previously open land, to be converted into tennis courts, a cricket ground, and buildings 'of such construction as will admit of easy and speedy removal'.[6]

There were, at this time, a little over 7,000 Europeans in Bombay, out of a total population of 650,000. The Bombay Gymkhana kept out all Indians but also whites of uncertain pedigree, such as the petty tradesman and the soldier without a commission. Including wives and children, the club would have had not more than 3,000 members. Less than half of 1 per cent of the city's population had thus taken over one-quarter of the Maidan. Indians were welcome as sweepers and cooks and, very occasionally, as cricketers. For in response to a request from the Parsis, the Gymkhana agreed in 1877 to play a two-day match against them. It is just possible that this invitation was a consequence of a munificent bequest to the Gymkhana by the Parsi potentate, Sir Cowasji Jehangir. Sir Cowasji paid for the furnishing of the club pavilion, although he knew this would not buy him a membership.[7] Still, it would not hurt when the time came for him to ask for trade concessions. And it might, in this case, also have allowed his co-religionists the chance of playing against the British at their own game. The scene is finely described by the *Bombay Gazette*:

> Yesterday the match of the Parsees against the Gymkhana was resumed at eleven o'clock. The day was peculiarly hot, and it says much for the devotion both of the Parsees and their opponents to the noble game of cricket that they bore the heat and burden of the day with so much enthusiasm. There was a large number of spectators. Hundreds of natives, chiefly Parsees, were gathered beneath the trees that skirt the cricket-ground – surely with its brilliant verdure and splendid surrounding buildings one of the liveliest in the world – and in the Gymkhana tents there was a numerous company of Europeans. In the afternoon the ground bore a singularly lively appearance. Thousands of natives took up a position wherever they could get a glimpse of the players, and whenever a hit or a catch was made, they yelled with an enthusiasm that bespoke much for the future of cricket among them in Bombay. Near the Parsee tent, the Parsees

were packed as closely as herrings in a barrel, the front rank being composed of an interesting collection of small boys dressed in their best-coloured silk trousers, and the second and other ranks of a crowd in which the white head-dress of the Parsee priests was as conspicuous as a white man among a lot of black men.

The Gymkhana tent was crowded and a number of gentlemen were very well content to lie upon the grass, at the risk of being covered with ants, though from the remark one victim made, who found himself alive with these little pests, we fancy they had no reason to enjoy the cricket match. Catching a handful, he laughed a demoniacal smile of triumph as he said, melodramatically, 'Hah! Hah! my torments, I can kill more of you than you can of me', and thereupon he slew his thousands. We were glad to see several European ladies on the ground. The match throughout was contested in the most friendly way, and it shows the levelling and humanising tendencies of cricket that the Parsees were as much applauded from the pavilion for particular exhibitions of good play as the Europeans were.[8]

IN THIS CONTEST OF 1877 the Parsis had played better than expected. They led on the first innings, and although the Gymkhana recovered strongly the match was evenly poised when stumps were drawn. The Parsi bowlers had not yet switched to the new over-arm style, but were accurate and fast nevertheless. Their outcricket was outstanding. 'The Parsee fielding was remarkably good', remarked the *Times of India*, 'while the return of the ball was very quick.'[9] The match was repeated the following year and seemed set to become an annual event. Indeed, the news of Parsi proficiency even reached the Mother Country. In August 1878 the *London Graphic* ran an illustrated feature on Bombay cricket, commenting that 'the Parsees, who have for long shown themselves superior to the prejudices with which other Indian races are more or less fettered, have come out quite strong as cricketers'. The newspaper passed on the rumour that a Parsi cricket eleven might even tour England. 'We have already received several severe drubbings in the cricket field from our Australian cousins, perhaps next we are destined to be knocked (cricketically) into a cocked hat by the descendants of the Fire Worshippers of Persia.'[10]

Meanwhile, back in India, the discriminatory tendencies of Empire had come to clash directly with the levelling tendencies of cricket. The agents of disruption were the European polo players. Until 1879 they had played in the Marine Lines, which lies west of the Maidan, abutting the sea. But in that year their club merged with the mother Gymkhana, and the polo players migrated to it. Two days a week they played polo on the unenclosed part of the Maidan. After the final *chukka* they tethered their ponies outside the Bombay Gymkhana and went inside for a rub-down and a drink.

The coming of the polo players led to a bitter protest by the native cricketers. Their struggle to evict polo from the Maidan provides a fascinating window on the cultural life of Empire, and demonstrates how quickly and how energetically Indians had made cricket their game. Remarkably, the battle of European polo versus Indian cricket has escaped the notice of previous historians.[11] It would have escaped me too, had I not chanced upon a contemporary account in the library of the Lord's Cricket Ground. The book lay in an unused corner of that great library – away from the glass cases containing works on cricket at Home and in the favoured Dominions (Australia and South Africa), and in the bottom of an open shelf marked 'other countries', a dull green binding concealing its original cover.[12]

Shapoorjee Sorabjee's *A Chronicle of Cricket Among Parsees and The Struggle: European Polo versus Native Cricket*, printed in 1897, is (as the title suggests) actually two books bound in one. They are the work of a participant observer, a man who played cricket on the Maidan, who wrote petitions to get rid of polo from the Maidan, and who was a political theorist of some originality besides. Shapoorjee begins his account by noting that the Bombay Gymkhana would not allow polo to be played on its premises. They protected their own cricket ground, while encouraging members to spoil turf tended and used by others.[13] Season after season the condition of the Indian pitches grew worse, leading to numerous injuries as batsmen were hurt by rising balls.

An early complaint against polo was recorded by the Parsi newspaper *Jam-e-Jamshed*. In July 1879 it carried a communication from an anonymous cricketer, which described how the polo players enclosed their playing area with black flags, prohibiting native cricketers from playing within its boundaries. Notably, the riders did not observe their own rules, straying outside the field in chase of the puck and into the midst of a cricket match. European ladies also drove their carriages on to the cricket field to get a better sight of their men. Thus 'nearly two-thirds of the parade ground is occupied by Europeans to the great inconvenience of the school-boys wishing to play cricket'.[14]

Two years after this report, Shapoorjee Sorabjee wrote a letter of protest to the Bombay Gymkhana on behalf of the Persian Cricket Club, of which he was the Secretary. The Polo Secretary of the Gymkhana sent back a terse reply, saying that since they came to the Maidan only twice a week, 'the native cricket community have therefore their full share of the ground'. Ten days later the Secretary of the Gymkhana also informed Shapoorjee that polo would continue as before.

Denied justice lower down, Shapoorjee now aimed for the top. Signatures were solicited, and on 27 October 1881 a petition signed by 460 cricketers, Parsis as well as Hindus, was dispatched to Sir James Ferguson, Governor of the Bombay Presidency. The petitioners first submitted that

> ever since the introduction of the noble game of cricket among the natives of Bombay nearly twenty years ago, they have been uninterruptedly in the habit of playing on the Esplanade known as the Parade Ground.
>
> That there are more than 500 young men of all ages and of all castes who pursue this healthful sport on the Parade Ground,

where alone they are permitted to play and which is the only
suitable ground for cricket.

The document then rehearsed the recent history of the ground. The
Bombay Gymkhana had been granted the Maidan's southern portion,
but steadily enlarged its territory until it controlled almost one-third
of the area, railed and roped off to all but its European members.
Following this encroachment, said Shapoorjee and company, the
native cricketers 'have been obliged not only to betake themselves to
ground less suited to cricket, but also to pitch their wickets so close
to one another that anything like a free play of the game is impossible'.

Then, to compound matters, came the polo players, who after
the formation of the Gymkhana moved to the Maidan for one reason
alone, that they 'prefer to be within reach of the comforts and
conveniences provided by the Gymkhana buildings'. The petitioners
thought it just

> a little unfair that the comforts and conveniences of the half-a-
> dozen gentlemen, who generally play polo, should be preferred
> to the necessary healthful recreation of over five hundred native
> youths, still for the sake of the respect due to the ruling race and
> to high officials and rather than trespass upon your Excellency's
> valuable time, Your Petitioners would cheerfully forego their
> games for two evenings a week, were it not for the fact that the
> polo ponies completely ruin the turf and render the ground
> unsuitable for cricket. Your Petitioners need scarcely remind your
> Excellency in Council how much good cricket depends upon
> the state of the turf, and if any proof of the fact were wanted it
> would be furnished by the circumstance that the [Bombay]
> Gymkhana carefully preserves its own cricket field from being
> trampled upon by the ponies and even by passers by.

This petition was drafted four years before the formation of the
Indian National Congress. Like the Congressmen, these sportsmen
were skilled in the use of the English language, the language of the law
and the idiom of British justice. How could you practise democracy at
home and deny it abroad, asked the nationalists. How could you

keep your turf protected and make us play cricket on ground so manifestly unsuited to it, asked the cricketers. They began, as they had to, with deference, but ended with a direct challenge to colonial authority. 'Under the conditions above narrated', concluded the petition,

> and in such consideration of the necessity for healthful exercise and recreation such as cricket affords to the young men of this over-crowded city, your Excellency in Council will be pleased to request the Bombay Gymkhana to play polo on some other spot, or to allow your Petitioners to play among themselves on the ground at present reserved for the exclusive use of the Gymkhana cricketers and which is much too large for their requirements.

The petitioners thus daringly moved from opposing polo on the Maidan to demanding a piece of the Bombay Gymkhana. It is not clear whether the petition was ever read by the Governor. His Secretary cleverly directed it to the Army, under whose formal control the disputed land lay, and from whose ranks the polo players came. On 25 November 1881 Shapoorjee's men were sent a brusque answer signed by the Assistant Quarter-Master General: 'The Brigadier General considers the Native cricket players must remain satisfied with being allowed the use of the parade ground for 5 days in the week and that the polo players be permitted to play on the remaining two.' To this Shapoorjee provides a striking gloss, when he says that the answer showed 'nothing of the sportsman spirit', but 'everything of a warrior trained up to carry things at the point of the bayonet'. It was 'evidently meant to summarily silence the weak voice that was just endeavouring to be heard'.

Undaunted, the cricketers addressed another petition to the Governor on 27 March 1882, where the facts were once more stated, and the conclusion drawn even less deferentially than before. Because of polo, said this petition,

> hundreds of native cricketers are forced to be crowded into a

small space with all its disadvantages of imperfect and cramped play and to run the risk of being often hurt by balls both flying about in close proximity and unexpectedly breaking and bounding on account of the unevenness of the ground. And all this only because half a dozen gentlemen of the Gymkhana may play polo for about three-quarters of an hour two days in the week and some gentlemen of the Gymkhana may occasionally play cricket.

This time the petition was not returned to the Army, the Government writing back that 'instructions will be issued to permit the Native Cricketers to use the Esplanade Parade ground, when not required by Government for military or other purposes'. On 13 April 1882 the Public Works Department issued a formal resolution stating that native cricket would have precedence over European polo. The Government was of the opinion that the cricketers' petition 'contains a substantial grievance'. It noted that a portion of the Esplanade had been 'permanently alienated' for the exclusive use of the Bombay Gymkhana, and that the public were excluded from the 'portion of the Esplanade reserved for military purposes' for two afternoons a week. The Bombay Government now conceded that 'this is improper'. The use of the ground, continued the Resolution, 'ought not to be vested in any officer and the Military Department should now be informed . . . that the allocation of the unenclosed part of the Parade Ground in favour of a limited club cannot be permitted, and that Government, in the interests of the public, reserve to themselves the disposal of the ground when not required for military purposes'.

We have here, very clearly, a tussle between the civil and military arms of the Raj. When necessary, the Esplanade would be handed over to the Army for the parades held twice or thrice a year or when troops needed to be billeted on their way to or from the Afghan Wars. But to play polo on a regular basis, twice a week, could not be considered a 'military purpose', even if all the players had King's Commissions. For, as the Resolution's last sentence ran, 'a dozen gentlemen cannot expect to have the open spaces of such a city as Bombay kept for their personal gratification'.[15]

To mark their triumph, 250 cricketers met on 22 April when they thanked the Governor, thanked Dadabhai Naoroji – the great Parsi scholar and social reformer who had taken up their case – and appointed a committee to reward their ringleader suitably. Six months later, at a well-attended meeting at the Framjee Cowasjee Institute, Shapoorjee was presented with a watch, watch-guard and locket 'bearing adequate inscription'.

The polo players took their defeat badly. As Shapoorjee, their chief adversary, put it, 'not to have an upper hand in such a matter where the most powerfully influential European gentlemen . . . were on one side, all hot-burning with the fire of prestige, and the weak and pigmy cricketers, with absolutely no influence or importance on the other, was too much for the Bombay Gymkhana to put up with'. By the previous Government Order the polo players had been forced to relocate to the Cooperage, about a mile and a half further south. Loath to ride the distance to their club after the game was over, they sought to return to their old field. In May 1883 the Polo Secretary of the Bombay Gymkhana forwarded a petition to the Governor 'signed by certain inhabitants of Bombay'. This stated that 'in addition to those who actually engage in the game of Polo, there is a large number of persons who, as spectators, take the greatest interest and derive the greatest enjoyment from the game'. Since, in their view, 'the only open space of sufficient size and in other respects suitable for Polo is the Parade Ground', they asked the Government to cancel its Resolution of 13 April 1882, so as to 'again permit that game to be played on the ground referred to, on two evenings of the week, in the same way as it had been for many years previously to the passing of the Resolution above quoted'.[16]

That consummate petition writer, Shapoorjee Sorabjee, had met his match. Note thus the crafty reference to citizenship (the polo players were 'inhabitants of Bombay' too), to the weight of numbers (we may be twelve players, but we attract many more spectators), and above all, to tradition and precedent, to a return to the situation as 'it had been for many years previously'. Shapoorjee himself scoffed at the claim that polo was a sport of the people. There were not many spectators, he said, when polo was played at the Cooperage ground. Admittedly, a larger number of citizens did watch polo when it was played on the Esplanade, but 'only because the ground lies on their way home from office; and they would stop there as well watching polomen careering as a monkeyman exhibiting'. In any case, the 'interest and enjoyment of outsiders in polo were never dreamt of before, but came apparently to be evolved, by some disingenuous process, out of the circumstances of the cricketers' petition to Government'.

So it did seem, but unfortunately by May 1883 a new Governor was in place, who appears to have been more sympathetic to the military, and to his race. On 30 May a resolution was passed allowing polo to be played *once* a week, and also in the morning of the Brigade holiday.[17]

It is not clear whether the reduction in the frequency of polo was prompted by respect for native cricket, or the increasing cost of ponies, or the decreasing presence of skilled horsemen in a city that was now a centre of commercial rather than military authority. The cricketers protested anyway, pointing out that the resumption of polo violated the Government Resolution of 13 April 1882. The Government replied that since polo was played less often, the Indians should withdraw their complaint. Then in April 1884 a fresh Resolution was passed allowing polo to be played on Tuesdays and Fridays, first 'until the annual matches have been played off', and later, through an amendment, 'until further notice'.[18] The status quo had been comprehensively restored. This, commented Shapoorjee,

> was the final and finishing blow dealt, it may be justly said,
> in darkness in the long protracted process of gradually wiping
> out the Government Resolution favourable to the cricketers:
> and thus ended the guerilla warfare successfully conducted on
> the strength and support of prestige and influence as the all-

pervading elements on one side, against the just cause of grievances of the uninfluential cricketers on the other.

The Europeans were triumphant. The Polo Secretary of the Gymkhana, N.S. Symons, wrote to the *Times of India* asking its readers not to 'allow the preposterous notion to take root that a few young Parsee cricketers are going to be allowed to oppose the whole European community and jostle the Europeans off the Esplanade, whether at polo or anything else'. But the struggle continued. The Parsi paper *Rast Goftar* suggested in September 1885 that the newly established Bombay Presidency Association take up the complaint of the 'hundreds of Native youths' whose cricket had been interrupted or displaced 'for the convenience of about ten European polo players'. Six months later, it returned to the subject. 'The encroachment made by European players of polo on the Esplanade play-ground', remarked the paper, 'has nearly driven out from it thousands of Native youths who used to play there.' A Parsi cricketer, Jehangir Pestonji, dashed into a polo pony while running after a ball and had to be taken to hospital. 'It is to be regretted', said the *Rast Goftar*, 'that no spacious play-ground has been reserved for the use of the rising generation of Natives.'[19]

Strikingly, the otherwise loyalist Parsi establishment was solidly behind its cricketers. True, there was the odd rat, such as the past Secretary of the Parsee Cricket Club who wrote a letter to the Bombay Gymkhana disassociating himself from the petition against polo, terming it 'a rash and badly advised act'. But other members of his club had signed the petition. The native cricketers also drew comfort from the support of Dadabhai Naoroji. In April 1884 the reformer was one of eight prominent Indians invited to help the Executive Engineer demarcate the polo ground. Naoroji declined to attend the meeting. The Government, he said, had refused to answer the 'chief objection' against polo, that 'it spoils the ground for cricket badly'. He also wondered why 'the native cricketers themselves, though one of the interested parties, are not to be asked to send any representatives to the conference, to have their side as fully heard as that of the Gymkhana'.

In his account of *The Struggle: European Polo versus Native Cricket*, Shapoorjee wrote contemptuously of the 'earth hunger' of the Bombay Gymkhana. By his calculations, the Esplanade covered 180,000 square yards all told. Of this the Bombay Gymkhana 'permanently and exclusively' used about 35,000 square yards. When polo was played they took up an additional 60,000 square yards for the game, but another 15,000 square yards, between the polo field and the Gymkhana, were also rendered unfit for cricket. In all, he calculated, polo and parades and the like colonized this space for 155 days a year. Thus for five months

> native cricketers of all the different communities combined use only about half the amount of ground, the other half being used by the comparatively insignificant number of the European Gymkhana players. This in itself may be readily owned as rather not fair. But this is not all: during the remaining 210 days or 7 months of the year the ground, rough and rugged as it is made by polo playing, is . . . a source of danger to the limbs and bones of the ever apprehensive and hampered native cricketers.

In this continuing contest for space there was a curious irony. For polo itself is of Indo-Iranian origin, at some distant remove an 'indigenous' sport of the Parsis and the Hindus, whereas cricket is in its origins and culture very much a British game. However, in nineteenth-century Bombay polo ponies were beyond the reach of the Indian, while cricket provided a ready, sociable and relatively cheap source of recreation in a crowded city. And so the Asian game played by Europeans became the emblem of patrician power, and the English sport indulged in by natives the mark of plebeian resistance.

BETWEEN 1879 AND 1883, the years of the 'struggle' against polo, no cricket matches were played between the Parsis and the Bombay

Gymkhana. A compromise was somehow reached, and in 1884 the matches recommenced. The following year the Parsis asked to be allowed to appoint one of the umpires. Until this time both umpires had been British, generally soldiers, a class the Parsis had especial reason to distrust. Back in 1878 a soldier-umpire had called their best bowler, Rustom Gangar, for throwing. Over-arm bowling was just then coming into its own, and disputes were frequent about which deliveries were 'fair' and which were not. The Parsis, however, maintained that Gangar's action had not been questioned before. When, in 1885, they suggested that each side appoint one umpire, they received a stiff answer. 'As regards the umpires,' wrote the Secretary of the Bombay Gymkhana, 'you must allow us to provide them as usual. They will be gentlemen, members of the Club. It is our rule to appoint the umpires on our own ground and we cannot deviate from it.'[20]

The competence and credibility of English umpires would remain an object of contention. For the moment, the Parsis pocketed the insult, focusing on the cricket. That winter they invited a Surrey professional, Robert Henderson, to prepare them for a planned tour of England. What Henderson taught we do not know, but when he went Home he was given a splendid send-off. 'On his departure from Bombay he was decorated with wreaths of flowers and provided with a painted cocoanut to throw into the sea to ensure calm in the event of rough weather – an exceptional mark of Parsi respect.'[21]

Henderson's wards soon followed him to England. Before they left, they were addressed by the great Parsi lawyer Pherozeshah Mehta. Mehta reminded the players that the object of their visit was

> a very modest one. Cricket, as you know, is the national game of England. It has taken root among the Parsee community, and as artists go to Italy to do homage to the great Masters, as pilgrims go to Jerusalem to worship at a shrine, or as students in the Middle Ages went to the chief seats of learning in places where science and philosophy had made their home, so now the Parsees are going to England to do homage to the English

cricketers, to learn something of that noble and manly pastime
in the very country which is its chosen home.[22]

The aims were modest, and the results more modest still. In the
summer of 1886 the Parsi cricketers travelled all across England,
playing against teams representing clubs and towns, but not the first-
class counties. The tourists lost nineteen matches and drew eight.
Their sole victory came against Lord Brassey's side at Normanhurst,
a patron and venue otherwise unknown to the history of cricket.
Elsewhere the Parsis were outplayed and, it appears, overawed. Their
main bowler took to playing with a skull-cap with the placatory word
GOD written over it in big letters. The trip, in the words of one
historian, 'proved a cricketing and financial failure'. But the Parsis
did play at Lord's against the greatest of all cricketers, Dr W. G.
Grace. And they were entertained at Cumberland Lodge in Windsor
Park by a son of Queen Victoria.[23]

The Bombay Hindus, meanwhile, were making steady progress
in *their* cricket. A nobleman of Kutch, Rao Shri Khengari, endowed
three prizes for the best Hindu cricketers of the year. In 1882 the
Hindu Cricket Club defeated a British team, the Carlton Cricket
Club. The following year the Bombay Gymkhana agreed to play
against a 'Hindu XVI'. Then, in 1886, an enterprising member
printed a nineteen-page booklet entitled *Rules and Regulations of the
Hindu Cricket Club*. This outlined five classes of members, distinguished by how much money they would contribute. Rules were
drafted for the appointment of the Cricket Captain, and for the
constitution of Match and Apparatus Committees.[24]

This booklet was clearly inspired, or rather provoked, by the Parsi
tour of England in 1886. As ever, the Parsis were a step or two ahead.
A Parsi Gymkhana was formed, which elected the fabulously wealthy
Sir Jamsetjee Jeejebhoy as its President. On 6 October 1886 the new
Gymkhana wrote to the Governor, Lord Reay, asking for a grant of
land 'on terms similar to those accorded to the Bombay Gymkhana'.
The 'game of cricket', it said, 'has for some time been very popular
among the young men of our community. But unfortunately owing

to want of suitable arrangements or other deterrent causes, almost all the young men, as they leave the school and college and enter upon their chosen walks of life, have found it impracticable to continue to engage in this favourite pastime.'

Polo, one supposes, must have ranked high on the list of 'other deterrent causes'. The 'elderly leading men of our community', the letter continued, had raised enough money for the construction of a pavilion and the levelling of the ground. Two hundred members had joined the Gymkhana, and other Parsis would pay up once the institution 'finds a local habitation'. The petitioners had their eye on a site of 20,000 square yards, located on the Esplanade itself, between the Waudby and Cruickshank Roads. This site would do nicely for a cricket ground, a pavilion and two tennis courts, allowing for a 'more systematic cultivation of out-door games'. Then, the letter concluded, 'the energies of the Parsi youths will be better directed and wholesome results as to their physical and moral tone will be obtained'.[25]

The first note on this letter, by an unnamed official, insisted that 'no encroachment on the parade ground can be permitted'. A further note was more helpful. 'Might not the land on the Kennedy Sea Face be also made available for cricketers until it is required for building purposes?' it asked. This land 'would require some levelling for cricket – but a club would do that'.[26]

This seemed, at the time, to be a master-stroke. The Esplanade was already the site of competing uses and claims. Moreover, it lay in the exclusive southern part of the city, close to where the British lived and worked. But so long as the Bombay Gymkhana had its grounds here it would invite imitators. Technology now stepped in to save the Government from embarrassment. Thus the Parsis were neatly deflected to the Kennedy Sea Face, land newly reclaimed from the ocean, lying a mile or two west of the Esplanade. By a Government Resolution of 24 February 1887 the Parsis were sanctioned a plot on the Sea Face, 'on the same terms as that held on the Esplanade by the Bombay Gymkhana'. The Resolution added: 'All expenses in connection with its preparation and execution will be borne by the Parsi Gymkhana.'[27]

The caveat was unnecessary, for within the ranks of the Parsis were men who could buy out the Government of Bombay. Money was easily forthcoming for the levelling of ground and the construction of a pavilion. As the new Parsi Gymkhana took shape, its members were choosing a team to tour England in the summer of 1888. In 1886 the Parsis had been grievously handicapped by including only those men who could pay their way. Now a more carefully chosen sixteen made the trip. By far the best player was Dr M. E. Pavri, who was already known as the 'W. G. Grace of the Parsis', on account of their shared profession and the Indian's own skills with bat and ball. Pavri claimed 170 wickets on tour, for a niggardly 12 runs apiece. The overall results were more gratifying as well. Of thirty-one matches played, the Parsis won eight, lost eleven and drew the rest. Those dozen drawn matches were, it seems, in part due to the efficacy of prayer. When pushed into a corner, with eight wickets down and several hours of play left, the visitors got down on their knees and 'invoked the help of the elements'. This being England, a thunderstorm invariably came to their rescue.[28]

Unhappily, this tour also 'proved an uncompromised failure in a pecuniary sense'. However, the passages to England and back had added greatly to the experience of the Parsi cricketers. Henceforth their cricket would have a less *ad hoc* quality. The various little clubs still played on the Esplanade, but when time came for the community's team to be chosen the elect moved over to the Parsi Gymkhana, with its well-cropped wicket and its outfield untouched by ponies' hooves. The Gymkhana sponsored the side, but the annual match had still to be played on the Europeans' turf. In 1889 the Parsis won a famous victory over the Bombay Gymkhana. In a low-scoring game the home side were left with 53 runs to make in the fourth innings. M. E. Pavri bowled beautifully and made astute field placings, and the Europeans were all out for 50. 'The tact, judgement and skill they had exhibited in that match', crowed one schoolmaster, 'removed for ever the stigma that [the Parsi cricketer] could not play an uphill game.' The ordinary Parsi was more expressive. After the match concluded, a band of youths, 'elated by their success, improvised a Zoroastrian flag and hoisted it'. The elders hastily intervened, for 'Parsee loyalty would not allow this and clamoured for the Union Jack'.[29]

Greater triumphs were in store. In the winter of 1889–90 the Middlesex cricketer G. F. Vernon brought a team of amateurs out to India on a cricket tour. The side included Lord Hawke, captain of the Yorkshire County Cricket Club, but otherwise could not be judged a first-class side. They still played cricket of a quality not generally seen in India. By the time Vernon's side came to Bombay they had won six matches and drawn a seventh. They then thrashed the Bombay Gymkhana by an innings. On 30 January 1890 they started their match against the Parsi Gymkhana, this advertised as being for the 'Cricket Championship of India'. Days before the match the Bombay Government made two announcements that had a bearing on Parsis in general and on their sporting skills in particular. The first announcement was the appointment, as the Province's next Governor, of the famous England cricket player Lord Harris. The second announcement authorized the admission, for the first time, of Parsis into a 'Volunteer Corps', a step on the road that led to full admission into the ranks of the Army, so far denied to the Parsis as they were not deemed 'martial' enough. Now Parsi young men could become Volunteers if they passed a language test and were willing to 'wear the uniform and conform to rules and regulations'. The *Bombay Gazette*, the voice of official record, said it would not raise 'any awkward questions concerning the physical qualities and the *morale* of the Parsis to be admitted. It then patronizingly added: 'The name of Rustum, nevertheless, still lingers in the race, and with the name there must be something of his virtues.'[30]

This, perhaps, was exactly the spur the Parsi cricketers wanted. Play started at the surprisingly late hour of noon, and at the end of the first day the match was well poised. The visitors had been dismissed for 97, with Vernon making 45 not out. The Parsis, in reply, were 80 for 9 at the close. The *Bombay Gazette* had this to say on the proceedings so far:

> Those who had seen the immense improvement in Parsee cricket fully expected that they would give a good account of themselves, but it is safe to say that the most sanguine did not expect that they would come off as well as they did yesterday . . . [T]he fielding of the Parsees was all but perfect – as good at any rate as that of their opponents.[31]

The following morning the Parsis declared at their overnight score. The Englishmen went into bat again, and were sent packing one by one by M. E. Pavri, who took 7 for 34 as the visitors crumbled to 61 all out. Set 79 to win, the Parsis lost their first five wickets before 40 runs were on the board, but in the end won by four wickets. This time the *Bombay Gazette* was not so gracious. 'Had Mr Vernon not been run out', it commented grumpily, 'the game might possibly have gone differently.' It allowed that this was indeed a 'most significant victory', but put it down

> to the difference between the cold weather temperature of Bombay and that of the upcountry stations where the English team had previously played. Thursday and yesterday were exceptionally hot days for the time of year, and the Parsees, standing on their native heath, had that fact in their favour.[32]

The match between the Parsi cricketers and the touring Englishmen was the greatest sporting contest in the history of Bombay. A decade later, the home captain, J. M. Framji Patel, recalled how 'the city went mad on the game'. Business came to a halt for two days, as a crowd in excess of 12,000 streamed to the Bombay Gymkhana. This ground,

> the scene of many international contests, presented a most animated and picturesque sight; almost all the varied nationalities of the great city were represented there. The canvas tents pitched on the western side of the ground were closely packed with the *élite* of Bombay Society, Indian and European. The dark-eyed

daughters of the land for the first time mustered strongly. The Parsee priests in their white garb invoked the aid of the 'Asho Frohers' to secure victory to the Zoroastrian arms. The schoolboy managed to take French leave. . . . The 'man in the street' was out enjoying his holiday, and in tiers of five and six deep the eastern and northern boundaries of the ground were closely packed by impatient sightseers. Some perched themselves (to get a good view of the game) on the trees surrounding the enclosure. In fine, it required the brush of a Rubens to translate such beautiful sights into colours.[33]

After the match had ended and the Parsis had won, a less appreciative account of the crowd was penned by an English observer, Captain Philip Trevor. 'The crowd that demonstrated at the close of the match', he wrote,

was more attractive to the artist than to the administrator. Few of us who saw it will forget that surging, lowing, multi-coloured throng. Its reproduction defies the pen and the brush. But the faces of those who composed it wore, in too many cases, an ugly expression. Of that vast multitude not a thousand knew the name of the thing they were looking, not a hundred had even an elementary knowledge of the game of cricket. But they were dimly conscious that in some particular or another the black man had triumphed over the white man, and they ran hither and thither, gibbering and chattering and muttering vague words of evil omen. I was in the tent of the Byculla Club when the end came, and the head of one of the largest firms in Bombay said to me, 'I know nothing of cricket and I care less, but I could have collected a lac of rupees on the ground to prevent this, if money could have prevented it.'[34]

This was not an over-reaction. Europeans as well as Parsis regarded the cricket result as a blow to the prestige of Empire. As Framji Patel put it, 'the imaginative and emotional Parsee youth felt for a day or two that he was the victor of the victors of Waterloo'. One Zoroastrian went further back still. 'Nahavand has been avenged,' he muttered, this a reference to the infamous defeat of the Parsis at the hands of the Arabs in AD 641.[35] On both sides of the racial divide, men of position moved in to restore order, to make sure that dangerous meanings were not read into the outcome of a mere cricket match. The Chief Justice, Sir Charles Sergeant, sent a gracious note of congratulation to the victors. Meanwhile the Ripon Club, a bastion of the well-heeled and loyal Parsi, threw a celebratory dinner for the cricketers, with a string band in attendance. Mr Dodabhoy Framjee, who presided, began with a toast to the Queen Empress. As the *Times of India* reported, Dodabhoy Framjee expressed the hope that the guests of the evening

> would take their victory modestly, and instead of being flushed with success, would strive ever to gain greater proficiency in the game (Cheers). He regarded the instinctive fondness of the Parsees for the national game of Englishmen as a proof of their aptitude for cultivating the national spirit of Englishmen – i.e., their courage, their manliness, their perseverance, and their coolness under adverse circumstances.[36]

The reception and representation of this match starkly revealed the communal competitiveness that, more than anything else, was to drive the progress of cricket in colonial India. Thus the *Bombay Gazette* called for a resurgence of European cricket in answer to the Parsi challenge: 'there is no reason', it remarked, 'why something of the prestige of the [Bombay] Gymkhana eleven in the old days should not be won back . . .' It recalled the dark warning of a high colonial official that 'tennis would some day be the ruin of [European] cricket in Bombay'.[37] The Parsi establishment, meanwhile, asked its cricketers to take note of the Indians behind them, namely, the Hindu cricketers who would be both inspired and provoked by their achievement. As the community newspaper *Rast Goftar* put it:

> The other races of India are following in their wake, and will, no doubt, do all in their power to emulate the example of their

neighbours, and, therefore, there should be no resting on their oars – we are not here simply talking about cricket – if the Parsis were to maintain their predominance, unchallenged and unsurpassed.[38]

3. Claiming the Heartland

By THE LATE NINETEENTH CENTURY Bombay had emerged as the first city of Indian cricket, a position which, with only the odd hiccup, it has comfortably maintained since. But the game was also taking root elsewhere. Wherever the British settled, in ports and plantation towns, they started clubs and gymkhanas to steal time away from the natives, to play their own patented games among themselves. Outside the club walls the natives would imitate them. In Calcutta, where the low-born preferred football, the gentrified Bengali, or *bhadralok*, took more readily to cricket. Early patrons included the Princes of Natore and Cooch Behar. A better player than either was Sarada Ranjan Ray, the W. G. of Bengal, a bearded opening batsman, the serving Principal of Vidyasagar College, and the future great-uncle of the film-maker Satyajit Ray. The spread of the game was also aided by the intrepid Parsis, one of whom, M. Framji, became the first Indian professional cricketer when he took employment with the Calcutta Gymkhana in 1878.[1]

Moving south, we have the Madras Cricket Club, set up in 1846, with its lovely ground at Chepauk, on land acquired from the Nawab of the Carnatic. Indians could not play at Chepauk but they could watch. A precocious spectator was Buchi Babu, a Telugu-speaking boy who was taken in a pram by his English nanny to see the Madras Cricket Club play. Buchi Babu was the grandson and heir of M. Venkataswami Nayudu, who had made a handsome fortune as the *dubash*, or commission agent, of the firm of E. I. D. Parry's. In the garden of the family's spacious Mylapore bungalow Buchi Babu played cricket, at first with his grooms, later with other children of high-born families. These boys started the Madras United Cricket Club, which was to play against, and occasionally defeat, the English club across the way. For years to come Indian cricket in Madras was dominated by the Brahmin and Nayudu families of Mylapore.[2]

Cricket was brought to the ancient city of Poona by the army which conquered the Peshwas and then themselves set up camp there. In the Cantonment stands the Poona Club, with its tree-ringed ground where cricket has been played continuously for 120 years. Across the river, on the Indian side of the city, cricket commenced in the old *kabutar khana*, or pigeon loft, of the Peshwas. Then came the plague of 1896, which took a toll of lives but gave a curious opportunity to those it spared. Fearing contagion, the residents of the crowded *peths* moved to temporary shelters outside the town, near where Poona University now stands. Open space lay on all sides, beckoning young boys to set up stumps and play strokes not feasible in the lanes of the old town.[3]

One of these refugees from the plague was Dinkar Balwant Deodhar. Years later, the greatest of Poona cricketers recalled how he came to play the game. Their parents were torn and depressed by the epidemic, by the loss of kin and the loss of livelihood, but, Deodhar remembered, the children

> only wanted the happy monopoly of open air life and uninter-
> rupted games, sports, competitions. We played 'cricket' in those
> camps and pitched our wickets in any field anywhere, sometimes
> even in a garden surrounding a villa of a wealthy gentleman
> who was generally without love for sports. The trees were our
> stumps, a broken fir plank our bat and a rotund – never mind
> if it was oval – piece of wood served us as a ball.
>
> With such equipment we played, and quarrelled, and frisked
> and gambolled like calves let loose on a village green. And we
> became as active, agile and fighting fit. Even when there was no
> plague epidemic to 'help' us we marched daily with our 'bats'
> and 'stumps' dangling awkwardly in our hands to play on open
> spaces wherever we found them.[4]

The kind of Indian who took to cricket varied enormously by region and community. A Parsi cricketer had once written, in a fit of self-congratulation, that

> It is the opinion of many teachers that the Parsee boy takes to cricket as a duck takes to water. The Hindu is slow in learning it, but once attracted by the game he goes on improving. The Mahomedan boy prefers his marbles to bat and ball.[5]

This might have been true of Bombay, *circa* 1890. In some other cities the game was dominated by high-caste Hindus. And in still others the game was genuinely multicultural. One such was Karachi, the port city a few hundred miles up the coast from Bombay. The history of cricket in this old Sind town can be plotted through a little memoir by one G. A. Canser, the autobiography of a now unknown cricketer that has these charming opening lines:

> Born in Karachi on Thursday the 23rd May 1878 with a silver spoon in the mouth. I soon grew up in strength and sinews. In 1884 I entered the C. M. S. Anglo-Vernacular School. . . . In 1888 I was admitted into the C. M. S. High School . . . Here I saw cricket for the first time and I took fancy to the most scientific game. As my dear father was one of the oldest landlords in Karachi and each year he either bought some immoveable property or built one, I implored him to ask the carpenters to make cricket bats for me. I also soon introduced myself into the school cricket team. . . . The naked love for the King of Games grew so strong that at the age of 10 I started my own team in the Lyari [river] bed . . .

Canser, from his own account, was a player and patron of cricket, but also the game's proselytizer and its ideologue. Fortunately, with his passion came his father's purse. The cricket-mad boy 'bought a complete set of stumps, cricket balls and all' and started a Hindu Union Cricket Club, many of whose members were 'stalwart Marhattas'. This team soon graduated from the river bed to a regular field. At its height the club had forty-four members, each paying a monthly subscription 'ranging between 9 pices and two rupees according to their means'. Canser naturally picked up the shortfall; his reward the job of captain and a place high up the batting order.

For many years the Karachi Hindus played on a plot of vacant land with houses around it. But a campaign started by Canser's family newspaper persuaded the Government to acquire and demarcate a large open space and reserve it for cricket. On these various grounds the Hindus played matches against teams of other Indians and, occasionally, against Englishmen. Canser speaks of a contest against a team of the Royal Field Artillery, 'whose lovely captain made it a point to pour a full jug of beer into my mouth before he would accept my challenge for a match'.

An intriguing aspect of these memoirs is the harmony between Hindus and Muslims. Canser speaks of how when his team practised, the cricket ball would often be struck into the compound of a fabulously rich merchant named Mohammed Ishaq. 'The camel-men would hide the ball, but Mr Mohammed Ishaq rebuked them all along and the ball was instantly delivered over.' For these and other acts of kindness – such as placing 100 camels at the disposal of Hindu pilgrims – the merchant was blessed with a son, Ghulam, who became the leading fast bowler in Sind, and whose 'most successful cricketing career has always been a matter of the greatest pride to the oldest Young Hindoos'. Again, Canser recalls the matches his team regularly played with a side drawn wholly from the Gujarati Muslim sect of the Bohras. The Bohra captain, Ghulam Hussein 'Galia', was Canser's closest friend in cricket: 'We two were so thick with each other and had so much confidence that any questionable decision of any Umpire, Mr Galia's or my decision, always prevailed.'

In turn-of-the-century Karachi the sharpest animosities were between Hindus and Parsis: the two communities were rivals in business, in the professions, in politics – and on the cricket field. Fifty years after the event, Canser writes of how hard he had to work to become the first non-Parsi in his school eleven; then, the 'best batsman' prize was denied him by the Parsi headmaster as it would dent 'Parsi prestige', to maintain which two prizes were awarded that year, so that a Parsi could get at least one. It seems that Canser's driving ambition was to get the better of the Parsis at this British sport. He published an essay entitled 'Hindus in Cricket Circles', which urged his community to work harder in drawing level with the Parsis. The leading Hindus of Karachi, he wrote, 'were culpably indifferent to physical culture, and it grieves one to find so many lawyers, Government servants, and merchants driving around in pomp and show and living the lazy life of an epicure'. He feared that if this continued, the 'general progress' of the Hindus 'in the race of life will be very slow and uncertain'. He then added, meaningfully, that 'the foremost position the Parsis now enjoy is due to their sportsmanlike habits no less than to their general push and pluck'.[6]

IN KARACHI, as in Bombay, the Parsis sought to 'catch up' in cricketing terms with the British; the Hindus, in turn, with the Parsis. The development of Muslim cricket, meanwhile, got an enormous boost with the setting-up of the Mohammedan Anglo-Oriental College in 1875. The name speaks of a happy hybridity, and the college's founder, Sir Syed Ahmad Khan, did indeed hope that the students would read the Quran before classes began and play English games after they had ended. In 1878 the Professor of Mathematics, Rama Shankar Misra, sponsored a cricket club, restricted to twenty-two members, who had to pay 3 rupees in advance. From this money came their kit and a snack of fried gram and biscuits, to be served after practice.

A Brahmin teacher began cricket at Aligarh, and it was an Englishman who was most energetically to promote it. This was Theodore Beck, who joined the college as its Principal in 1883, staying in the job until his death sixteen years later. As the historian of the college writes, 'although Beck himself was a complete "duffer" at the game, he made it a major part of his educational program. During his first year as principal he led the cricket team on a well-publicized tour of Punjab; spectators could see what Aligarh was all about whenever a match stopped for prayers.' Beck believed that cricket fostered self-reliance, physical vigour, courage and team-spirit: in a word, manliness. He always maintained that 'the reputation of the College depends to a very large extent on the success of our cricket and football elevens'.[7]

In 1887 Beck asked another Englishman, a Professor Wallace, to take over the running of the cricket club. When he joined, the uniform of the Cricket XI consisted of flannel trousers, a white shirt, a belt made of red towelling, and a Turkish cap. To this Wallace added an elegant black jacket with a border made of red satin. Adorned with the college monogram – embroidered in silk on its left pocket – the jacket had to be worn on all formal occasions inside and outside college. Their dress marked out the cricketers from the herd: as one envious student who never made it to the First XI commented, 'it made them look distinguished and dignified'.[8]

Another innovation of Wallace's was to have the names of all First XI members engraved on a board; rows of these, one for each year, were then hung on the walls of the Union Room. The intention was to elevate the cricketers to a status they would enjoy in an English public school of the time. Very quickly, the cricket team became the focus of the college's identity. Students who could, played; students who couldn't, cheered. Those still in college and those recently out of it both supported the Aligarh First XI with an interest that bordered on fanaticism. Consider this recollection:

> A one day match against a visiting team was going the way of the visitors. The home team had a huge total to chase and was running out of time. Everyone was visibly upset. I, Inayutullah, was a spectator. I was heartbroken and turned away to head for my room. Suddenly I noticed Aftab Ahmed Khan running from the field towards the Boarding House. Since the building was still under construction it comprised only a platform with a corner covered by tiles which used to serve as our Masjid. Aftab Ahmad Khan ran into this Masjid. I went closer and found

him to be facing West and praying hard. After a number of supplications he ran back towards the field . . .

Aligarh students loved cricket for its own sake, but also as a means to social advancement. Thus 'the good cricket players of our college have achieved popularity amongst the local Englishmen'. Proficiency in cricket helped students get jobs which their academic record would have denied them. Captains of cricket went on to become police officers, judges, and teachers. In Aligarh, which was famously loyalist, cricket allowed the Muslim gentry to come still closer to the Raj.

In the early 1890s the Aligarh cricketers defeated a side of visiting Parsis. Now, 'flushed by the vanity of our past successes', they decided to take on St Stephen's College, Delhi. A match was arranged in Delhi to coincide with the first Muslim Educational Conference.

The contest between these two prestigious colleges had a special edge. Set up by the Cambridge Brotherhood in 1881, St Stephen's was more catholic in its student body and its general orientation: unlike Aligarh, 'college' did not seamlessly merge into 'community'. A decent-sized crowd thus turned out to watch the match, which was played at the Company Bagh, just outside the walls of the old city. St Stephen's batted before lunch and scored 114. At the interval the Aligarh team went across to the great Jama Masjid to offer prayers. But after lunch they were themselves dismissed for a mere 76 runs. They walked disconsolately back to their quarters, accompanied all the way by a small bunch of *dilliwallas* asking them to go back to Aligarh and eat *gazak* (the sweet made of sesame seeds and jaggery for which their town was, and still is, celebrated). As one student recalled, years later, 'we found this a regrettable way to becoming famous but at our destination we had to face yet another punishment'. Word of their defeat had reached a eminent nobleman, Sir Syed Alia Rahmat, who was in Delhi for the Educational Conference. Like the cricketers, he was staying at the Anglo-Arabic College. When the boys reached the college Sir Syed told them he had ordered thirteen nose-rings, one for each of them: for by losing to St Stephen's they had proved they were girls, not boys.

This story is told in a charming memoir entitled *Aligarh ka Cricket*, written by an old student whose own interest in the game vastly exceeded his aptitude. But he also recalls his side's victories, against the Parsis at home and, on tour, against a side playing under the colours of the Maharaja of Patiala. After their team had won, students competed with one another to compose Urdu poems in its honour.

Another incident provides an insight into the complex hierarchy of colonialism, and how cricket could, on occasion, be used to sustain it. After Professor Wallace's death a bunch of old students gathered funds for a memorial. This took the form of a cricket pavilion, with a plaque outside dedicating it 'to the memory of P. M. Wallace, Esq., former Professor of the Club and President, Cricket Club'. The names of those who had contributed money were listed, and the British engineer who designed the structure was also thanked. Tragically, the memorial to Wallace was not as enduring as its sponsors had wished it to be. A later Vice-Chancellor invited the Viceroy of India to the college. As it happened, the visit of this most powerful Englishman coincided with a visit by the richest Muslim in India, His Exalted Highness the Nizam of Hyderabad. The Nizam announced a gift of 10,000 rupees to the college, to build a 'permanent structure in honour of the Viceroy'. Now, the honorand was a cricketer himself – a Cambridge Blue, in fact – and cricket was more or less the most important activity of the college. Thus the Vice-Chancellor decided to break down the Wallace Pavilion and replace it with a larger, grander, Willingdon Pavilion, whose inscription prominently bore the name of its patron, the Nizam of Hyderabad.

Through these stories, *Aligarh ka Cricket* speaks of how within a decade and a half of the introduction of cricket it had become a central activity of the college. The most venerated student at Aligarh was the cricket captain. By custom the captain always stayed in the same room – No. 13 S. S. East – a room chock-a-block with trophies and cups which was known as the 'Kaba' (shrine) of Aligarh cricket.

However, some patrons and parents opposed this deification of a foreign sport. Decades after Theodore Beck's death, a distinguished Urdu writer complained that in the Principal's reign

Cricket and football players were held in great esteem. Neither the teachers, nor the Trustees, ever gave a thought to encourage scholarship. Beck often used to say that Ranjit Singh [sic] (afterwards ruler of Bhawanagar [sic]) the famous cricket player was far superior to Dadabhoy Naoroji, the first Indian Member of the British Parliament. Mr Beck's favourite students were all players. Next to players were the students who realized subscriptions to the 'Duty Society'. The players were like the Europeans, the collectors of donations like Eurasians, the rest commanded as much respect as the common native. The latter were not considered worthy of any appreciation or encouragement. Literary giants like Maulvi Aziz Mirza and Khwaja Ghulam-us-Saqlain, though very high in the esteem of their fellow students, were an eyesore to the College authorities. If Maulana Muhammad Ali was respected it was because of his brother Shaukat Ali who was a famous Cricket Captain.[9]

As cricket was being more thoroughly domesticated, as it came to replace indigenous sports like *gilly danda* and *kabaddi*, as, in sum, the game became more completely Indian, there arose also critical voices of dissent, who would see in their countrymen's love of cricket evidence only of an unhealthy subservience to the values and culture of the foreigner.

THE SOCIAL HISTORY of Indian cricket suffers from one enormous disadvantage: that we, as a people, have a criminal indifference to the written record. Consider this tale told by the Secretary of the Elphinstone Cricket Club, one of the first Hindu clubs in Bombay. When asked by his fellow members to read the annual report, which contained the scorecards of the season, he replied: 'Brothers, I wrote the report on the wall of my house for permanency, but unfortunately my father got it whitewashed and the report along with it.'[10] Likewise, a Muslim cricketer wrote that 'of the growth and development of Aligarh University Cricket, it must be admitted with regret, that we do not possess any written records which could throw light on the subject'. He continued: 'The action of time and the vandalism of man are two great enemies which play havoc with ancient records and relics of antiquity. One of these things has certainly been responsible for the disappearance of our old records.' This was written in 1940, or less than a century after cricket came to Aligarh.[11]

The early history of Bombay cricket is moderately well documented. Among the things borrowed by the Parsis from the British was a regard for facts; in this particular case, facts that were to their advantage. A tiny community numbering fewer than 100,000 was motivated to preserve the records of their cricketing prowess. But they were inhibited from writing about their fellow Indians. In his *Stray Thoughts on Indian Cricket*, J. M. Framji Patel apologized for devoting only four pages to the Hindus: 'I wish I could write more about up-to-date Hindu cricket, but in that case I should be poaching on the preserves of my friend, Mr Telang, who, like a R[i]shi, has long contemplated writing a history of Hindu cricket.'[12] This was a mistake, for Telang's book never appeared. Like a Rishi, the Hindu sportsman would operate only in the oral tradition.

There are three good little books written on Parsi cricket, printed in 1892, 1897 and 1905 respectively. Otherwise, there is little for the historian to go by. To plot the growth of cricket in India, to sense which Indians were playing the game and why, he must search for stray references in club souvenirs, cricketing memoirs, Government files, old newspapers and travellers' accounts. These tell us that, apart from the centres already mentioned, by the turn of the century the game was making fair progress in Bangalore, Lahore and Nagpur. (Returning to Lahore from Allahabad in February 1889, Rudyard Kipling was perplexed to find Punjabi boys infected with 'cricket mania'.)[13] These were all towns that were to become cities, each with a community of Europeans to inspire and challenge the native. Other towns that took quickly to cricket were Indore, Baroda and Patiala, capitals of princely states that were closely allied to and socially imitative of the Raj.

In England cricket had begun in the countryside and slowly

moved to the towns. In India it was from its origins an urban game.
One reason for this, perhaps, was caste: how would one select a
village eleven satisfactory to Brahmin and Untouchable alike? A
second reason was visibility, the fact that one had to be in the
proximity of Englishmen to see cricket before playing it oneself.
A third reason was that it was only in the towns that the British
successfully imposed their own ideas of time. At least in India, the
playing of organized sport required the prior acceptance of a secular
calendar. The *raiyat* working to the agricultural calendar could not
take time off whenever he so chose. Nor could the worker or the
babu, but by the terms of his contract he at least had his evenings
and his Sundays free. These would be devoted to cricket or football
or hockey. Inevitably, it was the cities with the densest concentration
of workers and clerks, Bombay, Calcutta and Madras, that became
the three original centres of Indian cricket.

Altogether the most surprising reference to cricket that I have
come across is in a book of 1895 by F. St J. Gore entitled *Lights and
Shades of Hill Life in the Afghan and Hindu Highlands of the Punjab*.
This is a shikar memoir by an Oxford man, and cricket appears
glancingly, when the author is camped in Manikaran, in present-day
Himachal Pradesh. Manikaran was then known for its Siva temples,
its hot springs and its ibex. (The ibex have now disappeared and the
cultivation of high-quality marijuana has replaced them.) Cricket has
never formed part of the advertised pleasures of Manikaran, or of the
state in which it lies. Himachal Pradesh was one of the last entrants
to the National Cricket Championship, the Ranji Trophy, and it
competes for the wooden spoon only with its Himalayan neighbour,
Jammu and Kashmir.

The European *shikari* who visited Manikaran a hundred years
ago was not allowed into the temple, but he could take the waters.
'There is no doubt', he concluded, 'that, with the help of Hindu
Providence and a good cake of soap, the Manikarn water is very
efficacious in relieving one of superfluities of all kinds.' Thus cleansed,
he set off for a walk. His 'surprise was unbounded' when, 'on turning
the corner of a chalet in this alpine village', he

came across a game of cricket in full swing! I could hardly believe my eyes. Yet there it was, with bats roughly cut from an old plank, the regulation three stumps of rather unorthodox lengths, and a ball made up of a hard lump of rag. It was the Manikarn school (I won't say 'eleven', for I don't suppose there was that number of boys in the school altogether) spending their half-holiday in the enjoyment of the noble game. The ground, it is true, was not large, for the cliffs rose steep on one side and the torrent roared fiercely on the other; but a few square yards of level ground had been squeezed in between two chalets, and there the game proceeded with much vigour, one of the fielders spending most of his time on the shingle roofs, that always afforded a safe run from a well-placed hit.

The hunter was so pleased at his discovery of the 'sporting element of Manikarn' that after their game had concluded, he extemporized an athletics competition, with 2-anna pieces as prizes. His description of the 100-yard sprint is priceless. The course, he writes,

> was indeed not quite level, for it consisted of a race to bring me a leaf off a bush that grew some sixty yards up the steep cliff; but at the word 'Jao!' they were all off. Grown men, lads, and urchins – up they went in less time than it takes me to write it, leaping from rock to rock like a herd of chamois, as nimble as cats; and as for their descent, there seemed only a cloud of dust and a shower of stones down the mountain side, out of which the eager winner darted forward and thrust the leaf into my hands amidst the shouts of the excited villagers.

That the hillman could run and jump like a goat was scarcely a surprise. That he would play cricket was. How did the game come to Manikaran? The traveller believed that

> the game had, no doubt, been taught by some Assistant Commissioner to the teacher, and he, in coming up here to this out-of-the-way village, had brought it with him, to the great delight of the boys.

Having established, if only to his own satisfaction, how cricket came to Manikaran, the *shikari* continued:

> It is pleasant to notice the care that is given to stimulate such rational amusements for young India. In no country in the world do the boys stand more in need of the open manliness that is fostered by honourable competition in outdoor games, and I could not help wishing that the young Englishman who, at some time or other, started the game in Kulu, had been present; he would have been amply rewarded for the time and trouble he had given in sowing the seed, in the sight of its growing and flourishing up in this odd distant corner of the world.[14]

All this – the 'time and trouble' taken to nurture cricket at 'some time or other' by 'some Assistant Commissioner' – was pure speculation. More likely, the village teacher, or perhaps one of the boys, had seen the game played on a visit to the imperial summer capital of Simla, located just a few high valleys away. Judging by what we know of Bombay or Madras or Calcutta, the progress of cricket in Manikaran would have owed itself to native emulation rather than European proselytization.[15]

F. St J. Gore's interpretation of how cricket came to a remote valley is entirely characteristic of the time, of the late nineteenth century, the high noon of Empire. In the beginning cricket was played by the colonist to *get away* from the coolie. But the coolie took to the game nonetheless. In time he asked to play matches against the rulers. It made sense now to see this eagerness as a confirmation of the imperial mission, a pleasing sign of the brown man's readiness to absorb British values. Slowly, the rulers convinced themselves that they had actively preached the gospel, that they had taught Indians to play cricket. The British, it was now said, *converted* the Indian to cricket, to thus bind him more firmly, and more happily, to their rule. What the hunter wrote about the hill peasant was anticipated, nine years earlier, by a British journal commenting on the 1886 Parsi cricket tour. 'The visit of a team of native Indian cricketers', wrote *Cricket Chat,* is an event of no small significance, not only from the standpoint of cricket, but also from the political point of view. Anything which can tend to promote an assimilation of tastes and habits between the English and native subjects of our Empress-Queen cannot fail to conduce to the solidity of the British Empire, and if only for that reason this latest development of cricket, the zeal for which the natives of India are working to secure proficiency in the chief as well as the best of our sports, cannot be over-estimated.[16]

4. The Empire of Cricket

THE GREAT CAMBRIDGE historian G. M. Trevelyan once remarked that if the French nobles had been in the habit of playing cricket with their tenants, their châteaux would not have been burnt in 1789. In the English countryside the pleasures of the game helped obscure the distinctions of property and class. The hours spent together on the field bound the cottagers more firmly to their squire, more so if he happened to be a good cricketer himself.[1]

Cricket began in England as a rural sport, but by the nineteenth century its chief centres were towns and cities. Some townsmen played, and many others liked to watch. In 1864 had begun the County Championship, contested by sixteen teams, each with its own ground and cadre of devoted fans.[2]

Unlike its great rival, soccer, cricket had a following that spanned all sections of society. The men who played competitive football were almost without exception members of the working class. So were their fans.[3] At the other end of the spectrum, rugby and tennis were unashamedly elitist sports. Only cricket seriously incorporated both high-born and low. Thus three or four public school or Oxbridge men figured in most county elevens. They were known as 'gentlemen', and in theory played for fun. Their more numerous colleagues, who played for a wage, were known as 'professionals'. There were separate dressing-rooms for the two classes, and separate gates in and out of the pavilion. On tour they roomed separately. The amateurs were usually batsmen, whereas the wage-earners could both bat and bowl. By custom it was always a 'gentleman' who was captain of the county side, a policy of affirmative action that was bitterly resented by the more qualified professionals.

The relationship of the two classes was a curious combination of deference and defiance. In public the working cricketer paid respect to his captain, but behind his back often mocked him. The professionals disliked the amateurs for their snobbishness, and delighted in getting them out. A lovely story tells of an elegantly dressed Oxford undergraduate being bowled first ball by an ex-miner from Yorkshire. When the batsman, en route to the pavilion, complimented the bowler on the delivery, the answer he got was 'Aye, but it were wasted on thee.'[4]

In the 1870s and 1880s, at the time when Indians were acquiring a taste for competitive cricket, the two great gentlemen cricketers of England were George Robert Canning, later the 4th Lord Harris, and Martin Bladen, later the 7th Lord Hawke. Born in Trinidad in 1851, the son of the island's Governor, Harris played cricket for Eton and Cambridge before captaining England against its arch-rival, Australia. For many years he was also cricket captain of his county, Kent. Hawke, who was nine years younger, studied at Eton and Oxford before assuming the captaincy of the most successful county side, Yorkshire. He also appeared, on occasion, for England. Both were competent batsmen but would not have played for their country or led their county had it not been for their class.

Hawke and Harris were each to become President of the Marylebone Cricket Club (MCC), the most powerful body in English and world cricket. With one or two other such men they decided how much professionals would be paid, how long their contracts would be, what kind of menial work they might get in the winter, and which, when summer returned, would be picked to play for England. Such was their power and influence that they were known with a mixture of awe and derision as the Archbishops of Canterbury and York.[5]

So far as one can tell, Hawke moved only between his estates and his cricket. But Harris was a paid-up member of the Conservative Party and an intimate of its grandees. When the time came to appoint

a new Governor of the Bombay Presidency he was chosen for the job
by the Prime Minister, the Marquess of Salisbury. The appointment
owed itself to personal friendship and political obligation, but perhaps
cricket also played a part, for five years previously the Indian National
Congress had been formed. This was at first a club of educated
Indians, but its courteously worded petitions concealed a fierce desire
for a greater say in their own affairs. In the circumstances, Harris's
past as a cricketer was not irrelevant to the job in hand. A colonial
administrator was required, above all, to cultivate contented subject-
hood among the peoples of the British Empire. The history of cricket
showed the way. Much as the lord of the manor once played on the
village green with his tenants, much as the gentleman successfully
commanded the loyalty of his professional flock, the imperial proconsul would use sport to bind the Indian to the Empire.

Lord Harris had a longstanding family connection with India.
His great-grandfather, the 1st Baron, was the son of a Kentish curate
who used the surest route to upward mobility within the Empire: the
Army. After serving in the United States he came to India in 1788.
Eleven years later General Harris played a key role in the defeat of
Tipu Sultan, ruler of the Carnatic and one of the most defiant
opponents of British expansion. After this battle Harris received his
'just share of the prize-money'. In time, he was elevated to the peerage,
becoming Baron Harris of Belmont and Seringapatam. His son, the
2nd Baron, was wounded at Waterloo and ended up as a Lieutenant
General. The 3rd Baron, the cricketer's father, studied at Eton and
Oxford, and later served as the civilian Governor of Trinidad
and Madras.[6]

The cricketer himself lived in Madras as a young child, cared for
by an Indian bearer after his mother died. At thirteen he was sent to
Eton. A quarter of a century later he returned to India. The years in
between had been spent in the serious pursuit of cricket. His political experience was trifling, this a worry to at least one anonymous
Englishman, whose poem about Harris, entitled 'I'm Going to
Bombay', featured this telling verse:

In Cricket I shall lose a *'pal'*
An *'keen* regret is mine;
But in a *palankeen* I shall
Find comfort most divine!
Or, seated in my *bungalow*,
I'll puff my nargileh.
(I hope I shall not *bungle, oh!*)
I'm going to Bombay.[7]

Harris arrived in India in the summer of 1890 and stayed for almost five years. His period in the sub-continent has since acquired almost mythical status. Writers both English and Indian have credited him with achievements somewhat beyond his deserts. One Viceroy even claimed that 'cricket was first actively started in this country largely through the influence of that fine British cricketer, the late Lord Harris'.[8] Likewise, that much-loved cricket writer A. A. Thomson believed that Lord Harris 'pioneered and fostered' the game in India: indeed, he 'gave to cricket the same sort of unselfish service as his forebears of several generations had given to civil and military administration in India'.[9] And a recent work of reference calls Lord Harris 'perhaps the greatest administrator and "missionary" in the history of cricket', adding that while Governor of Bombay he 'was a great patron of the game'.[10]

Back in 1911, in a majestic and marvellously illustrated work dedicated to King George V and designed to celebrate 'the rise and progress of the game throughout the Empire', the Oxford historian Cecil Headlam claimed that no one did more than Lord Harris to further the development of cricket in India. The cricketer-turned-Governor, wrote Headlam, demonstrated that 'much friction between the Europeans and natives in India might be abolished by bringing the rulers and the ruled together by means of sport'.[11]

There seems to have been some plagiarism at work, for a decade previously the great Parsi cricketer M. E. Pavri had written that 'it was [Harris's] personal example that gave great impetus to sports of all kinds in Bombay . . . Lord Harris, as a sage statesman, at once saw that much of the friction between the Europeans and the Natives of India could be got rid of by bringing the rulers and ruled together by means of sports.'[12] In 1905 J. M. Framjee Patel dedicated his *Stray Thoughts on Indian Cricket* to the ex-Governor of Bombay 'in grateful remembrance of a high-minded and sympathetic ruler and a generous and genuine sportsman, who, during his Governorship of Bombay, zealously encouraged physical culture amongst the people and proved a true FRIEND AND PATRON of Indian Cricket and Parsee Cricket in particular'. Likewise, in a history of Indian cricket published in 1929, Wahiuddin Begg wrote that 'while Governor of Bombay (1890 to 1895) he took special pains to improve Indian Cricket and did a lot to invigorate interest of the game among all classes of people. In fact, Lord Harris is regarded as the "Father of Indian Cricket" and Indian Cricketers shall remain ever grateful to him.'[13] After all this it comes as something of a surprise to read in a book by the Madras writer N. S. Ramaswami of 'Lord Harris who, as Governor of Bombay had played *a* part in the development of Indian cricket . . .'[14]

That indeterminate 'a' is an open invitation to the historian. What then does the contemporary record, as distinct from later accretion, tell us about Lord Harris, his time in India, and cricket?

NATIVE CRICKET, of course, was already well established in Bombay at the time of Lord Harris's arrival in the city. There were dozens of clubs in operation. The Parsis had a representative Gymkhana, and the Muslims and Hindus were working towards theirs. The Bombay Harris came to had numerous enthusiastic cricketers. Some were even skilled. What they all needed, desperately, was space.

At first, Harris seems to have been keener to play his own cricket. Governor's House in Bombay lies in a large wooded estate on Malabar Hill that slopes spectacularly down to the sea. The terrain does not permit the laying of a cricket pitch. But the first officer of the Presidency had another property 100 miles away in Poona, that lay on level ground (this was Ganeshkind, now the home of the University of

Poona). A third place at his command was in the hill resort of Mahableshwar; this too had facilities for cricket. Soon the Governor was at work building a team of his own and recruiting players for it. One such, on deputation from the Indian Army, was the great Hampshire batsman Major R. M. Poore.

Weeks after he arrived in India, Harris refused to grant an appointment to a group of social reformers.[15] The messy business of politics and administration did not much attract him. Nor, it seems, did the hot and sticky climate of Bombay. From early in his stay he showed a marked preference for his other homes. Thus in July 1890 we find him in Mahableshwar, promoting a cricket match between European ladies and European gentlemen. When the monsoon hit the hills he moved to Poona. Driving through the city, he saw a cricket match in progress. He stopped his carriage, watched the play for a while and later sent the native cricketers two bats and 'a note in his own handwriting wishing it [the team] prosperity and success'.[16]

The following summer the Governor's concern for Indian cricket was put sternly to the test. On 18 June he was sent a petition signed by over 1,000 cricketers, which first outlined the unhappy history of polo on the Bombay Esplanade before asking him to ban it in consideration of the interests of his own favourite sport. The native cricketers had not forgotten their successful eviction of the polo players back in 1883. The invaders had later returned, but the arrival of a new and cricket-mad Governor now gave fresh hope. As ever, their draughtsman, Shapoorjee Sorabjee, chose his words carefully. 'That your petitioners are fully aware', said the document, 'that a renowned cricketer like your Excellency will fully feel the weight of such a grievance'. It continued:

> That your petititioners fully believe that your Excellency is fully aware that even in England there are vast grounds reserved for cricket alone, and the very idea of the turf being spoilt by the polo ponies would not be for a moment tolerated by the authorities.[17]

This was sharply put, and rightly so. Would His Excellency, in his

capacity as President of Kent Cricket Club, allow polo to be played
on the St Lawrence ground in Canterbury? More than his prede-
cessors, this Governor must have known the difficulties and hazards
of playing cricket on turf broken up by pounding hooves. The
petition was (naturally) leaked to the press, who added their own
words of recommendation. The Governor had been speaking of the
need for better sporting facilities for schoolboys, and a few weeks
previously had opened a gymnasium for Parsi boys. Thus, when
the cricketers' complaint reached its office, the widely read *Bombay
Samachar* asked the Governor to respond sympathetically to it

> as the sport of cricket has been growing quite popular among
> school-boys, who have little to resort to in the shape of physical
> exercise, and their habitations are situated in quarters close to
> or round the Esplanade, while the polo players, who are very
> few and wealthy will not be much inconvenienced by resorting
> to another piece of ground.

'His Excellency being a keen cricketer', added the *Jam-e-Jamshed*,
'must recognize the fact that the same place cannot be suitable for
cricket as well as polo.' Harris, it said, should ask the polo players to
return to their original home, the Cooperage.[18]

Shapoorjee and his supporters seem to have overlooked the fact
that, like all of us, Harris had multiple selves. He was a cricketer but
also an Englishman – *an Englishman in India*. The Governor's staff
forwarded the petition to the polo players, who sent back a forceful
reply. This gave particulars of other open spaces in the city and their
unsuitability for polo. The new laws governing polo, they reminded
the Government, mandated that the field had to be exactly 300 yards
long and 200 yards wide. The Cooperage and the Marine Lines were
too small, the Oval was long but narrow, the Wellington Lines were of
an irregular shape. The Kennedy Sea Face was large enough, but 'the
soil is principally sand with a rotten subsoil and it would be impossible
to play polo on it at any time of the year'. On 5 July the Private
Secretary to the Governor wrote back to the cricketers. Enquiries had
been made, he said, which revealed that there was no ground suitable

to polo in Bombay other than the Esplanade. He had 'been directed by his Excellency to say that he is glad to find amongst cricketers in Bombay the same spirit of generous concession to the convenience of those who pursue other sports and pastimes than cricket, as he ventures to think is observable amongst cricketers all the world over'.

Harris thus adroitly twisted cricket's idea of 'fair play' to ask a thousand cricketers to allow their game to be spoiled by a dozen polo players. The Indian cricketers had hoped that the Governor's own well-advertised love for their game would win over the claims of race and Empire. When these hopes were disappointed, their leader, Shapoorjee, offered this bitter and brilliant commentary:

> The whole 'spirit of generous concession' was expected by Lord Harris from one side only – the native cricketers – and none at all from the Gymkhana gentlemen, who sent their men to play polo on the native cricketers' ground to the entire destruction of its turf and surface and kept their own cricket ground for their cricketers safe and untouched not only by their polo ponies but even by the native cricketers! A remarkably curious appreciation of justice and 'generosity' Lord Harris had![19]

Even as he was turning down the native cricketers, Harris was preparing for some cricket of his own. He had invited his old Eton friend, Lord Wenlock, the current Governor of the Madras Presidency, over to his estate in Ganeshkind. 'Bingy' Wenlock planned to bring down an eleven composed of his officers and civilians, which after a week's practice would play against Harris's team. Cricket during the day and dances by night were in any case how the Bombay Governor spent his time in Poona. The Etonians' plans, however, were disrupted by the non-arrival of the monsoon. In Madras famine threatened, and Lord Wenlock had to cancel his programme. The *Kaiser-i-Hind*, a bilingual paper of standing, said that if Wenlock had not abandoned the trip, Harris and he

> might have been overwhelmed with the taunts and jibes of friends and foes alike. . . . Playing high antics as devils and angels

and then rushing off 700 miles to indulge in the pastime of
wood and leather like truant boys are certainly not the means
by which a Government could be carried on efficiently or by
which a Governor could achieve a reputation. But, possibly, in
these days of sporting and dancing administrators it is not
expected that anything like reputation, unless it be on the cricket
field or the dancing floor, could be achieved. . . . With scarcity
bordering on famine in Madras, the departure of Lord Wenlock
to Poona to play cricket with His Excellency Lord Harris would
have been characterized as out-Neroing Nero himself.[20]

In truth, it was not only high-born Englishmen who found cricket
a diverting distraction from life in India. Thousands of Indians did
as well. Some of these had gathered in the Islam Gymkhana, an
institution which now advanced a claim for a ground of its own.
Muslim cricket in Bombay had been pioneered by the Lukmani and
Tyabji families. These patrons of cricket were, like their Parsi
and Hindu counterparts, Gujarati-speaking merchants with cash to
spare. The Tyabjis, a progressive family rich in scholars and judges,
helped establish a Muslim cricket club in 1883. By 1890 this was
calling itself a 'Gymkhana', in line with the European and Parsi
institutions of that ilk. The Governor, Lord Reay, was approached,
but he evaded a decision, saying he had soon to demit office. In
September 1891 the campaign was renewed. The Secretary of the
Gymkhana wrote to the Secretary of the Public Works Department
applying for an allotment of land on the same terms as the Bombay
and Parsi Gymkhanas. 'The want of an institution of this kind for
the Mohomedan community', he remarked, 'is keenly felt, and a
bonafide desire to establish and maintain such an institution exists
in the community.' Members had joined up and donations were
flowing in. All that was now wanted was land to prepare a pitch and
build a pavilion. 'Considering the encouragement', concluded the
letter, 'which the present and former Governments have at all times
given to the cause of Mohomedan education and advancement and
to their social and moral progress the Committee earnestly hope that

this request will receive the favourable consideration at the hands of His Excellency's Government.'[21]

This letter sparked off a series of notings on file by officials opposed to the proposal. The land reclaimed from the ocean had been vested in the hands of the state, and Governments, whether colonial or nationalist, are always loath to cede any part of their properties. Moreover, the Kennedy Sea Face might later come in handy for the construction of offices or barracks, or a race-course. The trouble was the existence of precedent. In July 1892, when the file finally reached Lord Harris in Ganeshkind, the Governor commented that he did not see how 'we can refuse a piece of ground to the Mahomedan Gymkhana on the sea face'. The Bombay and Parsi Gymkhanas had been given leases of public land virtually free, noted the Governor, and

> we can be certain that in a short time we shall get a similar application from some Hindu Gymkhana, and so the ball will go on rolling. . . . I don't see how we are to refuse these applicants; but I will steadfastly refuse any more grants once a Gymkhana has been established under respectable auspices by each nationality, and tell applicants that ground having been set apart for their nationality they are free to take advantage of it by joining that particular club.[22]

In the last week of September a plot next to the Parsi Gymkhana, and of the same dimensions (425 feet square), was alloted by Government to the Islam Gymkhana. The rent was nominal, 12 rupees per annum. The news was carried in the *Bombay Gazette* in its issue of 23 September. The same evening, as Harris had predicted, the semi-active Hindu Cricket Club convened a meeting of its members. They 'could bear to be surpassed no longer'. When donations were called for, a Gujarati merchant, G. P. Jivandas, agreed to contribute the colossal sum of 10,000 rupees towards the construction of a Gymkhana. Two of his relatives promised 5,000 rupees between them. With the money in hand, fifty-five Hindu cricketers sent in a letter to the Secretary of the Public Works Department:

We, the members of the Hindu Cricket Club and other Hindu gentlemen interested in outdoor games, Indian and European, beg to approach you with our humble request that you will be pleased to recommend to Government that a piece of ground may be allotted to us near the Parsee Gymkhana on the Kennedy Sea Face at least equal in extent to that allotted to that Institution if not a quarter more owing to our numerical superiority, on the same conditions and terms on which similar plots have been granted to the Parsee and Islam Gymkhanas in that neighbourhood.[23]

In sport, as in politics, the Hindus would ask for more. They were granted the land, but of strictly the same size as the Parsis and the Muslims. The Government engineers measured and marked out a site, preparatory to handing it over for levelling and construction. The plot lay next to that granted to the Islam Gymkhana, which was itself adjacent to that occupied for some years now by the Parsis. The Parsis, meanwhile, were busy practising for their most important match yet. They had played annually against the Bombay Gymkhana, and had often won. They had defeated Vernon's team too. For years they had sought the privilege of playing a European team chosen from the entire Presidency. This request had previously been denied, but now the Parsis saw a fresh opportunity in the political success of their leader Dadabhai Naoroji. In the summer of 1892 Naoroji had been elected to the British Parliament. He stood on a Liberal ticket, and was the first non-white ever to enter the House of Commons. The Governor of Bombay was constrained to send him a letter of congratulation, but his real feelings were expressed in a private letter to the Secretary of State. 'I am very disgusted at Dadabhai Naoroji getting elected to the House,' commented Lord Harris. 'Why England should elect natives I can't for the life of me see: they can't govern themselves. Why should they govern us? This man is of the priestly class, I believe, the class as a rule, I don't say that he does, who wash themselves night and morning in cow's urine.'[24]

In the wake of Naoroji's election to the British Parliament the

Parsis renewed their request to play a representative European side. Their wish was granted, and the match fixed for the last week of August 1892. Much interest centred on the possible participation of His Excellency himself. The Parsi paper *Jam-e-Jamshed* urged him to play in this inaugural match. Since Harris was a good cricketer, it said, and in the habit of playing with and against British soldiers in Poona, 'he ought to have no objection to join a well-known match against Natives'. In cricket contests, added the paper, 'no distinction is observed between the rich and the poor. Royalty and nobility are seen playing cricket with poor shepherds and poor tradesmen'.[25]

Harris declined the invitation, and the match was rained off anyway. He then offered to host a substitute fixture at Ganeshkind. This the Parsis won by three wickets. Would they have won if Harris had played? And why did this still active cricketer decline to appear in the match? Was it the worry that failure – a first-ball duck, shall we say – would have publicly undermined the authority of his office and his government?

IN THE WINTER OF 1892–3 the other great lord of English cricket came calling. Hawke had been to India before, as a member of G. F. Vernon's touring side of 1889–90. Now he brought along a side of twelve amateurs, of whom the most distinguished by far was F. S. Jackson. Also a Yorkshireman, Jackson made his reputation early: he took so many wickets at Harrow that a new composition was added to be sung at school assemblies, 'A Gentleman's a'bowling'. When he came to India he had just been appointed Captain of Cambridge (he would, in course of time, become a conspicuously successful Captain of England as well).[26]

The tourists first played three matches in Ceylon, and then one against the Gentlemen of Madras, an all-European side. In this latter game F. S. Jackson hit a six out of Chepauk, a graceful hit into the tennis courts that was to be remembered for years. One of his opponents, E. H. D. Sewell, wrote of this shot that while he had seen many sixers in his day none was 'the equal of this one for easy, effortless acquisition. The ball seemed to be persuaded over those trees, not hit.'[27]

From Madras Lord Hawke's team moved west and then north. Sporting railway companies had granted them first-class passage at half-price. They played a match apiece in Bangalore and Poona, and eventually reached Bombay in Christmas Week. At the Victoria Terminus the cricketers received a splendid reception. The Governor was represented by three of his ADCs, and plenty of Parsis were also in attendance. The cricketers were garlanded and then escorted outside the station. The Governor had thoughtfully sent four carriages, three drawn by pairs, the fourth, meant for Lord Hawke, drawn by four bays with postilions. It was what one would do for an old friend and cricketing comrade. Harris must have been quite unprepared for the reaction of the Hindu press, which now suppressed its own love for cricket in pursuit of a nationalist agenda. The *Native Opinion* remarked that the reception

> speaks highly of the condescension of Her Majesty's representative here in showing respect to a [fellow] nobleman of the realm. But the public generally will misunderstand the whole affair. To them the reception accorded will appear to invest the team with every political significance and make them think that even the reception of cricket teams is as sacred a function of the Government as the reception of the Viceroy or that of any Prince of the Royal Blood. One may admire Lord Harris' love of manly sports, but there is every chance of its being misunderstood by people when it goes beyond certain limits.[28]

Less polite was the *Mahratta* of Poona, the journal founded and edited by the radical nationalist Bal Gangadhar Tilak. 'Even the advent of a Viceroy or a three-headed monster', it commented caustically,

> could not have created so much interest. Only one thing was missing to complete the pomp of this princely reception, namely

the firing of guns. Lord Harris might have liberally ordered guns to be fired in honour of the event, eleven in number, one for each member of the team! An official levée and a municipal address will be quite appropriate! The fun of the matter, however, apart, may we ask who is to pay all the expense that will be incurred on the occasion. A special bungalow has been engaged at great cost near Government House and there will, of course, be the usual balls and fetés; but whence will the money come from? Will it come from Lord Harris' pockets or the Government treasury?[29]

Meanwhile, there was cricket to be played. The Bombay Gymkhana hosted a match between the Parsis and the tourists. F. S. Jackson had sun-stroke, and without him at his best the Englishmen were humbled by 109 runs in a low-scoring game. The following week a return match was played at Ganeshkind. Jackson was fit, and the weather was more English. Although the Parsis fought hard they were defeated by a narrow 7-run margin. Jackson scored a vital 39 in the first innings, bowled effectively and also took two brilliant one-handed catches. The unbeaten record of the Parsis had been dented, and their disappointment was manifest. It was said that Zoroastrian women watching the match 'wept like babies'.[30]

As notable – if less public – was the reaction of the host. Harris had shared the disappointment of Hawke's men on their Bombay defeat. When they won the return match Harris wrote to Bingy Wenlock that 'I'm awfully glad about it: for they were very down poor boys.' 'The second match was a real good one', he remarked, 'and we won because the Parsis had to make the runs, and played tame, and because they let us get seventy [in the] 1st innings before they put Writer on. I've always thought him their best bowler, but took care never to tell them.'[31] The partisanship is striking, for the Governor of the Bombay Presidency would be expected to be impartial, to support the Parsis even.

WATCHING LORD HAWKE's team play made Harris itch to organize some cricket of his own. In the first week of 1893 he wrote to his friend the Governor of Madras, suggesting he invite the Bombay Europeans in the summer. Harris said May was the best time for lawyers, as also for players from the Public Works Department and the Railways – 'the rest would be all soldiers who can of course get away: so that we could without doubt put in a fair team in that month'. 'The best plan', he continued,

> would be for your captain to write to the Cricket Secretary, Bombay Gymkhana, and invite Bombay to play the Madras Presidency and ask what time would suit. The Secretary would reply May and you would say then it must be played at Ooty, and we would fall in. This will keep you and I out of the business, which after the previous experience will be discreet.

Wenlock's own capital, Madras, fairly boiled in May. Hence the scheme to meet in Ooty, 7,000 feet up in the hills, a piece of Little England with its own golf-course, clubs and flower-laden bungalows. For reasons of state, Harris suggested that the co-conspirators themselves should not take the field. Anyway,

> I know I couldn't play at that altitude: get headaches very easily at 4,000 ft if I do any sustained movement; besides which I am just as happy looking on as playing now.
>   I am rather assuming that you would like us two drinking rums, one out of a box, the next the real Simon Pure.

In the last week of January Harris wrote to Wenlock with the news that the Viceroy had sanctioned his trip to Ooty. 'So if you still want us (I don't know whether you mayn't have another famine at hand) the only question is what is the latest date in May that is safe' (that is, before the monsoon broke). He would, he said, 'come down by sea to Calicut, which would be both economical and cool, as HM presents me with a yacht whenever I want one. I don't see why I should spent money on railways.'

A fortnight later, a reply from Wenlock in hand, Harris confirmed plans to arrive in Ooty from Calicut on 20 May, stay a week, and then return to Bombay by rail. The idea clearly was to have a great party with his Etonian friend, to recreate as best they could the climate and character of Home, by sipping rum on the Nilgiri Downs, dispensing advice and patronage while watching twenty-two Englishmen play a singularly English game.[32]

HISTORIANS OF INDIA have long been divided by their verdict on Empire: was it, on the whole, a benefit or a cost to the people of the sub-continent? Even the most diehard anti-imperialist, however, would allow that some of the men who ruled India worked hard and had brains besides. This was certainly true of the elite cadre of the Indian Civil Service, who had to come through a savagely competitive exam, and who served decades in the sub-continent. One cannot be so certain of the qualities of the political appointees who came and went after serving a term or two as Governor of a Province. Lord Harris's own temperament and orientation are, I think, best captured in a table he once sent Lord Wenlock, summarizing the liquor drunk in a single year in his Poona home:[33]

Number of bottles consumed
in Government House in 1890–1

Champagne	2,414
Claret	1,123
Hock	368
Sherry	411
Port	271
Liqueurs	144
Brandy	123
Whisky	545

It is as well that the *Mahratta* did not get hold of these figures. They reveal not only Harris's unfittedness for his job but also his desire to get away from India and seek comfort in the company and pleasant amusements of his race. One must not fault him unduly, however. He could run a county cricket club with assurance, the MCC even. But his Prime Minister had now placed him in charge of the Bombay Presidency, a territory several times larger than England, with more people than in England and stranger people too. Would he not escape it all to play cricket and drink port in Poona?

In the summer of 1893 bloody riots broke out in Bombay. Hindus were butchering Muslims, and Muslims Hindus, while the Head of Government was living convivially in Ganeshkind. When he finally arrived in the capital, it was because of a cricket match. He did make a show of helping to restore the peace, driving through the streets for an hour, but by this time the riots had subsided in any case. The following morning he was back in Poona. The press comment on this abdication of responsibility was unforgiving. A moderate Parsi journal suggested that the Governor should have come down by special train the day the riots erupted, 'visited the disturbed parts of the town the same evening and spoken words of comfort and sympathy to the suffering people and pacified the excited people by personally addressing them'. That gesture, said the paper, might have forestalled the escalation of violence which actually occurred.[34] 'While the riots caused serious mischief in the Presidency town', noted the *Gujarati,*

> His Excellency the Governor was playing cricket at Poona. He paid a flying visit to Bombay on the ninth day of the riots; and he has come down again and is to spend five days in witnessing cricket matches! Nothing is more disappointing than that a Governor should be so indifferent to the welfare of the people entrusted to his care and so much given to seeking pleasure.[35]

Harris's negligent attitude contrasted with that of his predecessor, Lord Reay, who had rushed to Surat when fire broke out there, comforted the victims' families and instituted measures to prevent further fires from breaking out.[36] The Bombay riots of July 1893 were quickly followed by clashes between Hindus and Muslims in other towns. The Governor did not visit these places either. 'As for

Lord Harris', commented a Marathi weekly printed in the inland town of Satara, 'he appears from his doings to be an inert marble statue with stuffed ears, holding in his hands a bat and ball'.[37]

THE SUMMER AFTER the Bombay riots, the Governor was, as usual, in Mahableshwar. Business again called him down to the city, business altogether more pleasurable than mediating between rival camps of rioting natives. A new cricket ground and pavilion had been built at the Hindu Gymkhana, and he was asked to commission it. The premises of the Islam Gymkhana had been formally opened some months before. As it happened, Harris was then away in England. The offer to inaugurate the Hindu Gymkhana was one he could scarcely refuse.

The Pavilion of the Bombay Hindus cost 15,000 rupees, the construction done 'gratuitously' by 'Mr Babaji Gopal, the well-known Hindoo engineer'. At its opening, on 5 May 1894, Harris led a star cast of notables present, including the Chief Justice, Parsi millionaires and Muslim merchants. The Hindu Gymkhana had chandeliers placed in the pavilion, while the grounds were aglow with electric lights. The whole place was decorated with banners, flags and bunting.

Opening the proceedings, Goculdas Tejpal, President of the Provisional Committee of the Gymkhana and a Justice of the Peace, said this was 'the first instance in which the Hindoo community have taken so decisive a step towards the development of physical exercise amongst the members of their community'. He regretted that Lady Harris was not present, but thanked her Lord, 'the typical representative of the British nation', for 'coming down from the bracing weather of Mahableshwar to Bombay at this sultry time of the year'.

Next the Secretary, R. R. Daradhar, read out a report on the march of Hindu cricket. In 1877, the year the Hindu Cricket Club was established,

the physical exercise in which the Hindus of the city participated was the exercise with dumb-bells, wrestling, *atia-patia, gili-dandu.* But it must be admitted that a very small number, indeed, participated in such exercise, and it was considered derogatory to do so. The Hindu students of those days gave scarcely any thought to the development of the body.

A 'new era' dawned with the creation of the Hindu CC, a club started by Marathi boys which 'gained a great acquisition of strength by the accession of several Gujarati members'. These Gujaratis reached deep into their pockets to help build the Gymkhana. By 1893 the membership had risen to 246. With a rise in funds also came a rise in the quality of cricket. In 1887, the Hindus first beat the Bombay Gymkhana, and three years later even defeated the all-powerful Parsis.

After Daradhar had finished his report, he called upon Master Dwarkadas, son of the club's patron, the late Goverdhandas Parmanand Jivandas, to hand over the key of the pavilion to the chief guest. The key was large and made of silver, with an engraving on the handle 'worked in relief on gold ground representing the mythological legend of Hanuman, the Hindoo deity, presiding over athletics, endeavouring to jump at and seize the sun as soon as he was born'. Harris opened the pavilion with the key, and made his own speech. He was pleased that before he left India he could open one of the new Gymkhanas. The Muslims and Harris could not find a mutually convenient date, and so he was 'very glad to have an opportunity of opening this one, for from the very first days of my sojourn in Bombay I was anxious to see some more organised efforts than were then apparent for the encouragement of athletics'. He complained that it was 'rather a tendency of cricket clubs in this country to be satisfied with very small numbers'. He told a story of a native cricket club that came to play at Ganeshkind, which had only eighteen members in all. 'When I suggested that they should amalgamate with some other neighbouring club, they would not hear of it and seemed quite satisfied with themselves.' Harris hoped that the establishment of the Hindu Gymkhana would 'eradicate this tendency among Hindoos and that it will form a nucleus towards which all lovers of athletic sports in the community will be attracted . . .'

How might the Hindus improve their game? 'Up to the present time here in India', remarked the English cricketer, 'you have had scarcely anything to do with professionalism . . .' But 'men who do not consider a payment for playing beneath them are necessary for proficiency'. These professionals would set the example of good style for the young to emulate. Harris returned, in conclusion, to the theme of unity.

> I hope in the course of years to hear that this club has succeeded in absorbing many of those little clubs that are split up over the parade ground, the result of which will be to form a strong club and to provide good players and hold their own both amongst players here and in meeting members of the Bombay Gymkhana.

Is it too conspiratorial to see in this recommendation a desire to finally clear the Parade Ground of native cricketers?[38]

WHEN THE TIME came for Lord Harris to leave Bombay, some loyalists sought support for a memorial. So extreme and intense was the commentary on this proposal that an enterprising publisher made up a book of newspaper extracts, entitled *Opinions of the Indian Press on Lord Harris's Administration and the Hollowness of the Permanent Memorial in his Honour by his Friends and Admirers*. The introductory note claimed that 'never during the last hundred years has a Governor of Bombay been so sternly criticized and never has he met with such widespread unpopularity on account of his administration as Lord Harris'. A memorial to the Governor, remarked the *Kaiser-i-Hind*, would be an 'exaltation of exalted failure'. It grimly recalled the riots of 1893, when 'His Lordship refused to leave his cricket ground and come down to Bombay'. Unaware of 'the real conditions of the city, he regaled himself at Ganesh Khind till the occasion of a cricket match, five days afterwards, brought him to Bombay to take an hour's drive through those streets which were the scene of anarchy and bloodshed'.[39] The *Mahratta* suggested that if money was raised,

> we beg to offer the following suggestions with reference to the shape which the memorial should take:
>
> 1. One colossal cricket bat with Lord Harris kneeling in a reverential attitude before it.
> 2. One colossal hammer which Lord Harris is engaged in vigorously applying on a lute representing the harmony between Hindus and Mahommedans.[40]

Lord Harris's record as a colonial administrator has thus far been a well-kept secret.[41] Meanwhile, his contributions to the development of Indian cricket have been vastly exaggerated. Although the odd native team was invited to Ganeshkind, he almost never played against them. He would not appear in the Presidency match either. On the field and off it, he preferred the company of fellow colonials. Indeed, had he played cricket more often with or against Indians, he might have been less disliked. His encouragement of Lord Hawke's team against the Parsis must be seen as a breach of trust. Again, in the matter of the Islam and Hindu Gymkhanas he was merely reactive. These Gymkhanas had been formed before he came, and they drew nourishment from decades of active cricket-playing among members of their communities. Harris did not – as some commentators have claimed – 'grant' them land on his own, but agreed to their request when he sensed there was no way out. Indeed, these grants might also have been motivated by the wish to keep other space in the city clear for the ruling race. Certainly, Harris was unwavering in his support for European polo over native cricket.

Even in the realm of cricket, Harris would not interfere with imperial practice, which dictated that while Europeans could on occasion play with Indians they must never publicly dine with them. A liberal English journalist who watched Lord Hawke's team play the Parsis was appalled at the blatant segregation off the field. The cricket ground was divided into two sections, one for the Europeans and one for the natives, and no native dared to be seen in the European Section. Joking apart, it was a case of black and white. When the luncheon hour arrived, the English team went off into the Gymkhana club-house, and the Parsees went off to their tents and messed alone.

The captain of the Parsi team happened to be a Cambridge graduate, but in Lord Harris's Bombay this man and his colleagues 'were not allowed to break bread with the Englishmen or to enter any English club, merely because their skins were dark'.[42]

A decade after he left Bombay, Lord Harris was asked to write the introduction to Framji Patel's *Stray Thoughts on Indian Cricket*. 'I was never impressed with Parsee batting,' he remarked here,

the best of them were liable to throw away their wickets by some rash stroke, due I expect to excitability. To wear down good bowling, and patiently wait for many overs for a run here and a run there, is easier for the phlegmatic Anglo-Saxon than for the excitable Asiatic.

Nor was he much impressed with Indian politics. British administrators had been charged with following a policy of *divide et impera*, but, noted this former Governor, 'there is no need for the British Raj to try to divide; the natives of India do that most effectively of their own motion . . .' Although Indians would by nature divide, England, by means of the games it brought here, would unite. 'I am thankful', said the Governor,

to be able to feel sure that England has done much, very much for India; and one of the many good things she has done has been to introduce a manly game which is open to poor as well as rich, which needs no prize beyond honour, and by its simple merits can enlist the support and countenance of the wisest men of each religion and each caste.

Sentiments akin to these also appear in Harris's autobiography, published in 1921, a chapter of which is devoted to his time in India.

This delicately side-stepped the question of politics, focusing on the cricket. There was a nostalgic evocation of his ground at Gane-shkind:

> The surroundings were charming, everything as green as in an English spring for some weeks. The Deccan hills looming up in the distance, a ground which sloped away slightly on three sides from the pitch, and a few red-coated *chokras* (little boys) on the boundaries to run after the fours, a small party of guests, and the band combined to make the ground and its surroundings very typical of cricket in England.[43]

Outside this little protected slice of turf the Indians played their cricket. Their progress was slow. 'It is in the matter of patience', remarked Harris magisterially, that 'the Indian [cricketer] will never be the equal of the Englishman.' 'Notwithstanding their multitudes', he added, 'I doubt if they [the Indian cricketers] are going to turn out a team of all India as good as the best of our county clubs.'

Harris followed a long line of colonials who played cricket in India chiefly as a means of consolation and chiefly among themselves. When the Indians started playing the game it was natural to patronize them. But they played in ever-increasing numbers nonetheless. The colonial now came round to the view that sport would more firmly bind ruler to ruled and, with luck, Hindu to Muslim as well.[44] This belief was absorbed by Harris, and superbly articulated in a passage of his autobiography:

> That cricket is going to stay in India there cannot be a shadow of doubt; it has taken hold all over the country, and *chokras* can be seen playing in every village with any sort of old bat and ball that they can lay hands on. I should hope that it will do something to get over any racial antipathy; for instance, it must, I think, bring the several races together more and more, in a spirit of harmony that should be the spirit in which cricket is played. Unquestionably, it arouses excitement and enthusiasm, and extreme ambition that one's own side should succeed, but it also ought to lead to friendliness, and that is what is needed

in India. East will always be East, and West, West, but the crease is not a very broad line of demarcation – so narrow, indeed, that it ought to help to bring about friendly relations.[45]

The idea that sport would promote racial harmony, and thus confirm the continuity of Empire, came naturally to British administrators in India. It was an idea that even the Parsis found hard to swallow. In the middle of Lord Harris's Bombay tenure, the *Rast Goftar* had written that

> it is the nature of things that the two races cannot coalesce. 'The grand free-masonry of cricket' may be a bond of brotherhood between people of the same race, but it is little more than an expression of conventional politeness when it is used in connection with teams formed of two entirely different nationalities.[46]

This comment appears to have been inspired by a lecture on the history of Parsi cricket delivered a fortnight earlier. This had alluded, inevitably, to the struggle of cricket versus polo. Surely, asked the lecturer, Manekji Kavasji Patel, 'surely the ingenuity of talented Englishmen should be able to devise some means of relieving the native cricketers from the hardship of playing on dangerously uneven ground'. The English were famous for their love of freedom: 'even women in England have discovered that they have what are called rights, and yet the Gymkhana polo players have been depriving native cricketers twice a week of their right of utilizing the Esplanade ground for cricket'. Patel insisted that there was 'no natural inequality between natives of India and Anglo-Indians'. He quoted from a speech of October 1892 by the dean of Western Sanskritists, Professor Max Müeller, which said that the feelings of strangeness between 'the white man and the dark man' were 'a disgrace to every one who harbours it'. 'What words of profound wisdom!' commented the Parsi lecturer. 'What a subject for contemplation to those who govern India in the Queen's name! If all Anglo-Indians were as sympathetic and liberal-minded as the learned Professor, there would then be no necessity for maintaining a costly militia for the defence of India . . .'[47]

That Parsi loyalist, J. M. Framji Patel, also drew attention, in his own gentle way, to the gap between British ideals and Imperial practice. 'Polo is sectional, cricket is catholic,' he says, but from remarks made elsewhere in his book it appears that even cricket was not catholic enough. 'Just the thing that will help Indian cricket', thought Patel, would be a 'cosmopolitan' team, composed of Hindus, Muslims, Parsis and Englishmen, to go on a cricket tour of the high centres of power, Simla and Ooty. That tour might even lead to the creation of 'a Cosmopolitan Gymkhana, where the whole army of caste prejudices and racial antipathies may be clean bowled evening after evening, and universal brotherhood come out triumphant in the end. Will not European cricketers take the lead in starting such a gymkhana?' Of course they wouldn't. But where conscience failed science might succeed. 'How I ardently wish', remarked the Parsi cricketer, 'that in this age of new inventions some one would invent a chemical preparation, or some such thing, which would convert a black face into a fair one, and cut the Gordian knot for all time!'[48]

The hollowness and hypocrisy of the Empire of Cricket were, as one might expect, bluntly exposed by Shapoorjee Sorabjee. I may be permitted a last, extensive excerpt from his book:

It is as complaisantly as frequently said that cricket levels down all sorts of differences, brings together men of different grades, and binds them all in a friendly union. These expressions emanate from self-delusion either on purpose, or for policy, or out of ignorance or thoughtlessness. . . . There is but one small particle of truth there *viz.* that all positions are forgotten or forgone so long as the game is afoot. So far as we have been able to see in Bombay cricket has not been able to alleviate the pangs of feelings on the one side, or the display of supercilious- ness or misguided use of influence on the other; nor has it been able even to check the daily widening of the gulf. Though the European Gymkhana and the Parsees have played, and cordially too, many a game at cricket, that circumstance has never been able to induce even a sympathetic consideration from the former, who, carefully keeping their own cricket ground untouched by the shadow of a polo-pony, continue to cut up the turf and make notches and holes in the cricket ground of the latter by polo-playing. Self-interest has too strong a hold upon them and actuates them to act in the manner they do. Where interests clash the struggle is inevitable all the same in cricket as in other human affairs.[49]

CASTE

Up from Serfdom

5. Working with Leather

THE REPUBLIC OF INDIA has twenty-eight states, but the India of the British once had only seven constituent parts. These were the three great Presidencies of Bengal, Bombay and Madras, and the four smaller units of the Punjab, the United Provinces, the Central Provinces and Berar, and the Northwest Frontier Provinces. The Presidency of our own focus, Bombay, commanded more than 1,000 miles of coast-line. Starting from Sind, in present-day Pakistan, it moved southwards through Gujarat and Maharashtra, then skirted the Portuguese colony of Goa to include the northern districts of what is now the state of Karnataka.

The area directly controlled by the British was interrupted by a patchwork of princely states which were economically and politically subordinante to the Raj. But 1,000 miles from north to south and 300 or 400 miles from east to west were the rough extent of the Bombay Presidency. This was a territory of sub-continental size and continental diversity. Within it were mountains, deserts, floodplains, arid scrub and rainforest. Looking closer, one might find 500 species of birds or 5,000 varieties of rice. The people of the Presidency included hunter-gatherers, farmers, shepherds, fisherfolk, artisans and priests. They spoke Kannada, Urdu, Gujarati, Marathi, Konkani, Telugu, Tamil and a variety of lesser tongues.

This great Presidency took its name from an island city that was at once its centre of commercial, political and cultural power. At the time of which we speak, the turn of the nineteenth century, Bombay was the most prosperous port in India, and a centre of finance and industry. It housed the Presidency's only High Court, and its sole

University. Bombay acted as a beacon for those who sought to study, or trade, or labour for a fairer wage than was paid in the countryside. A Gujarati or Kannadiga wishing to become a journalist or lawyer or doctor would migrate to Bombay. It was also to this city that one would come to pursue a career in cricket.

Not, of course, if one had already established oneself as a cricketer at Home. Thus when Lord Harris came to Bombay in 1890 he had little idea of the cricket played there, or indeed of the diversity of the Presidency over which he had come to rule. One suspects that he did not take kindly to this diversity, as reflected in the character and appearance of the migrants who lived in the city. Certainly he seems to have sought only to escape, to work and play in the enclosed and racially exclusive settings of Ganeshkind and Mahableshwar.

This part of the book traces the journey to Bombay and beyond of a man I regard as the first great Indian cricketer. His origins and later life make a complete contrast to the English cricketer whose acquaintance we made in the preceding chapter. Palwankar Baloo, to give the man his name, has been ignored by cricket writers, whose own narratives usually begin with the first official Test played by India, against England at Lord's in July 1932. Stranger still, he is unknown to the burgeoning field of Dalit (Untouchable) scholarship as well. Older works suggest that Baloo was the first Dalit public figure in western India, and an early hero of Dr B. R. Ambedkar, the great lawyer-scholar and leader of the Untouchables. But more recent works, written in the wake of Ambedkar's posthumous emergence as a leader more widely worshipped in contemporary India than Mahatma Gandhi or Jawaharlal Nehru, do not care to mention him at all.[1]

Yet he was once very well known. Consider a little thirty-page biography of Palwankar Baloo, published in Poona in 1959 as part of a series of Marathi tracts with the running title *Kahintari Navech Kara!* (*Do Something Distinctive!*). Priced at half a rupee, these booklets were aimed at school and college students presumed to be in search of role models. The subjects were chosen for having 'gone outside the rut of normal life', for making a name through courage and innovativeness. The tracts were short enough to be read within thirty minutes. Of the forty titles listed in the series, twenty were about Maharashtrians, twenty about people from other parts of India or the world. The publishers did not, of course, commission tracts on men like Shivaji or Tilak or Gandhi or Einstein, whom one could worship but certainly not emulate. The subjects written about included Marathi pioneers of theatre, printing, education, history and the cinema. They included a progressive Marathi poet, a wealthy and successful Marathi lawyer, and the first circus promoter in Maharashtra. From elsewhere in the sub-continent came the hockey player Dhyan Chand, architect of India's Olympic victories in 1928, 1932 and 1936; the first of our great modern painters, Raja Ravi Varma of Kerala; and the myriad-minded Bengali, Rabindranath Tagore.

More interesting perhaps was the choice of foreigners. There was Spartacus of Rome, described simply as *A Slave who Revolted.* There was Michelangelo, the *Unequalled Sculptor,* and Benjamin Franklin, the diplomat and scientist remembered also for *The Art of Cultivating Good Qualities.* There was a pamphlet on Captain Cook, *Girdling the Oceans for his Country,* and another on Lawrence of Arabia, that *Great Organizer of Military Campaigns.* From the world of technology came the builder of the Suez Canal, the *Monumental Architect* Ferdinand Lesseps. And finally, moving from the heroic to the pragmatic, there was a study of Woolworth, the founder of the chain store, entitled *Buy Anything Here.*

In this exalted company was to be found the name of Palwankar Baloo. The pamphlet on him, written by the Poona cricketer and broadcaster Bal J. Pandit, was entitled *Khada Kheladu* (True Sportsman).

P. BALOO made his home in Bombay in the winter of 1896–7. In November 1996, exactly 100 years later, I came to the city to seek out his traces. The first step was to look for clues in the telephone directory. This listed seven Palwankars. I rang them up one by one. I would introduce myself as a historian, and ask whether they were related to a family of once famous cricketers who carried their name. The fourth or fifth call elicited a positive answer. Yes, said the person at the other end, I am related to *those* Palwankars. He then invited me to come and visit him.

The following morning I got on a train to Thana, where the relative of Baloo lived. In the coach I allowed my historian's mind to roam fancifully backwards. More than anything else, more than the Congress Party and more than cricket even, it is the railway that has united India, carrying people and goods and letters and cheques from one corner of the country to another. There are some 60,000 miles of track in the sub-continent. This day I was, so to say, back where it all began, for the first ever railway journey in India was made between Bombay and Thana in the summer of 1853.

One scholar who recognized the significance of this inaugural journey was Karl Marx. In an essay published in the *New York Daily Tribune* of 8 August 1853, the London-based freelance journalist wrote that the introduction of the railways in India would bring 'results [that] must be inappreciable'. Transport by train would break up the 'self-sufficient *inertia* of the villages'. By fostering ancillary enterprises it would become 'truly' the forerunner of modern industry' in India. The railway would reduce military expenditure and help extend irrigation. The social consequences would be incalculable. 'Modern industry, resulting from the railway system', wrote Marx, 'will dissolve the hereditary divisions of labour, upon which rest the Indian castes, those decisive impediments to Indian progress and Indian power.'[2]

I knew these words well, for I had taken my doctorate in that redoubt of intellectual Marxism, Calcutta. In the train to Thana I thought of them again, especially for what they said of the caste system. Marx predicted that the railways would undermine caste by promoting industries and by promoting travel. As the railway carriages were segregated only by race, within their own compartments high-born and low-born Indians had to sit and eat together. I was now travelling along the railway that had inspired Marx's speculations, on the tracks of a cricketer who was himself an early challenger to the orthodoxies of caste.

The train reached Thana and I disembarked. The road I took ran through the old market, with shops on the ground floor and homes on the first, their sloping roofs covered with the burnt clay tiles so typical of the West Coast. It was a scene out of the nineteenth century. The road, narrow and curving, went down a hill to end in a modern railway colony. This is where Mr Palwankar lived.

Within five minutes of entering his home my mood had changed. Mr Palwankar of Thana was a bespectacled little man, dressed in an ill-fitting pyjama-and-shirt combination. He was related to Baloo, but not closely. My knowledge of Baloo's life, meagre as it was, still exceeded his. He did say, however, that there was another Palwankar whose connection to the cricketer was closer than his: as he put it, 'Unka rishta *aur* nasdeek hai.' This man lived in Bombay, and he would try to find out his whereabouts. If I rang the next day he might have something to report.

The following morning I rang as instructed, and was provided with the number of a 'K. V. Palwankar' who lived in Dadar. A further phone call brought forth a further invitation. The trip this time was shorter – a fifteen-minute taxi ride from Worli to Dadar T. T. – and the results dramatically different. This Palwankar looked like a sportsman: lithe and trim, dressed in smart trousers and a smarter shirt, his moustache twirled upwards like a cavalry officer's. This was Baloo's nephew, no less, son of his younger brother Palwankar Vithal. He had grown up in his uncle's house, grown up in the glow of Baloo's achievements, and of his scarcely less talented brothers. For a whole morning he spoke and I gratefully took notes. When I finally took my leave he asked me to wait, disappeared into his bedroom, and came out again with an old book, bound in black, its pages loose. 'This is my father's Marathi autobiography,' he said, 'you can take it.' I said that I would go to the market nearby, photocopy the book, and return it. 'No,' he said, 'you take it – now your need is greater than mine.'

It was an extraordinarily generous gesture. The book, Palwankar

Vithal's *Maze Crida-Jivan* (*My Sporting Life*) was published in 1948, in a print-run of perhaps 1,000 copies. I had not seen it cited anywhere, which I thought must be a consequence only of the cosmopolitan cricket historian's lack of knowledge of Marathi. But later, when I met the writer Bal J. Pandit in Poona, I learned that this biographer of Baloo had never heard of the book either. Now, Pandit had played first-class cricket and was a famous Marathi commentator besides. He lived in a city that was the acknowledged centre of Marathi literature, a city of scholars and bookstores and libraries. How was it that when, in 1959, he came to write his lovely little book on Palwankar Baloo he was not alerted to this larger volume by Baloo's brother, published only eleven years previously?

Soon after it was published, Vithal's memoirs seem to have vanished from cricketing consciousness. Books have a short shelf-life in India in any case, and perhaps 1948 was a particularly bad time to publish the autobiography of an old cricketer. For the previous year the country was freed and partitioned. There were now new cricketing heroes, who made their runs and took their wickets in official Test cricket, playing for and sometimes winning matches for their sovereign and proud nation. These men were written about in the newspapers and magazines, and in books that appeared under their names. Their stories had erased from popular memory the stories of older cricketers who played when India was not a country with a distinctive flag and currency, when, indeed, India had no Test team of its own.

THE NAME 'PALWANKAR' denotes the bearer's place of origin, the village of Palwan, on the Konkan coast, north of Goa, a land washed by the sea and watered by the monsoon, celebrated for its fish and its Alphonso mangoes. In rural Maharashtra people of all castes, when asked to assume a 'surname' (a category that did not exist before the British came to India) simply take the name of their village and add a suffix. Thus Palwankar means 'of the village of Palwan'. There might even be Brahmins with this name, but we know that Palwankar Baloo was a Chamaar, a caste that lies almost at the bottom of the Hindu social hierarchy. The caste's name comes from the Sanskrit word for leather, 'charman', and the people of the caste work with leather, as tanners and dyers, and as the makers of shoes, bottles, tents and saddles.

The Chamaars, wrote one authority, 'are by birth doomed to illiteracy' and a 'lamentable and abject poverty'. They undertook tasks vital to the clean castes, yet despised by them. 'Economically the Chamar is a most valuable element in the population, and his function is the rough toil and drudgery of the community.' In the 'traditional' Indian village the Chamaar is

> regarded with loathing and disgust by the higher castes. . . .
> Except when it is absolutely necessary, a clean-living Hindu will
> not visit his part of the village. The author of *Hindu Castes and
> Sects* says that the very touch of a Chamar renders it necessary
> for a good Hindu to bathe with all his clothes on. The Chamar's
> very name connects him with the carcasses of cattle. Besides, he
> not only removes the skins from the cattle that have died, but
> also he eats the flesh. The defilement and degradation resulting
> from these acts is insurmountable.[3]

For the Chamaars, as for other Untouchable castes, the advent of British rule allowed a means of escape. The adventurous and skilled among them could abandon the village to seek employment in the towns and cities of the Raj. In some professions, indeed, their past was an advantage. Caste Hindus would not work in ammunition depots and gun factories, whose bullets might use the grease of the sacred cow. But the Chamaars had no such inhibition. They would, when they could, flock to the cantonments and factories set up by the British in western and southern India after their defeat of the Peshwas in 1818.

Palwankar Baloo was born in July 1875, in the town of Dharwad, deep in the Deccan Plateau and at least 500 miles south-east of his native village. His father worked there but soon after his birth appears to have taken a job in Poona. He was employed in the army; one account suggests that he worked in the ammunition factory in the suburb of Kirkee, another claims that he was a sepoy in the 112th Infantry Regiment.[4] It was in Poona that Baloo and his younger brother Shivram learned to play cricket, with equipment discarded by army officers. The boys also went, briefly, to school, but soon withdrawn to help augment the family income. Baloo's own first job was at a cricket club run by Parsis. Here he swept and rolled the pitch, and occasionally bowled to the members at the nets. For this work he took home 3 rupees a month.[5]

In or about the year 1892 Baloo moved a step upwards, from the Parsi cricketers of the city to their European counterparts. These were congregated in the Poona Club, set up a few years previously in a wooded estate known as Edwardes Gardens. The club, typically, has no documents of its history, except for the original lease agreement signed between its promoters and the Bombay Government in March 1886. This granted, for a period of ninety-nine years and an annual rent of 13 rupees and 12 annas, an area of almost 14 acres for 'various annexed means of public recreation and amusement'. The 'public' meant, of course, the white public, but the state placed limits even on its chosen elite. Lessees could build on the land or mould it as they wished, but lessors reserved the 'liberty to search for, dig and carry away minerals and to sink all necessary pits and shafts and to make and erect all necessary erections, machinery, roads and other conveniences and things for the purpose'.[6]

No gold was ever found on the premises, and what digging was done was for sporting purposes alone. When I visited the club, in July, during the monsoon, the trees were in leaf and the cricket ground was in prime condition. The original pavilion, built in the 1880s, overlooked play from wide mid-wicket. It is a charming little stone building, with coloured pillars on the verandah and a shingled roof. In 1999 I could walk into the pavilion unchecked, but I don't suppose Palwankar Baloo ever entered it himself.

At the Poona Club Baloo had his salary increased to 4 rupees a month. His duties included rolling and marking the pitch, erecting the nets and, when required, marking the tennis courts as well. To these routine tasks was later added an altogether more pleasurable one: bowling to the members. It was, it seems, a Mr Tross who first encouraged Baloo to bowl to him. He might, after play ended, have seen the ground boy bowl a ball or two into an empty net, and recognized his talent. Baloo had taken as his model a Captain Barton, a left-arm bowler with a smooth, flowing action. Soon Baloo was bowling on a more or less regular basis to the members of the club, valuable practice for the matches they would play against other teams of expatriates.[7]

At this time, the leading English cricketer of Poona was Captain J. G. Greig. He was known as 'Jungly', because that was how his forenames, 'John Glennie', sounded if spoken quickly.[8] Greig was a small man with supple wrists and quick feet. A master of the square cut, for years he was regarded as the best white batsman in India. Like other small men – Don Bradman and Sunil Gavaskar most obviously – he had an appetite for runs that was gargantuan. Framji Patel wrote that

> you will never catch Captain Greig napping, even after he has made his hundred. He is always on the *qui vive*. He goes on piling up his big score without fatigue. His pose at the wicket is ideal, giving him a full view of the bowler's hand, as well as of the flight of the ball, which as a rule he watches with 'feline insistence'. He is quiet, but deliberate. For his small stature he has any amount of courage, resource and staying power.[9]

Every day Greig would arrive at the Poona Club an hour before anybody else, and command Baloo to bowl to him. Thus he would perfect his technique, and thus the Indian would improve his bowling. There is a nice story, undocumented but therefore all the more appealing, that Greig paid Baloo 8 annas for every time he got him out. At this rate, if the bowler was successful once a week he would have doubled his salary each month.

Baloo once told his son that although he had bowled for hundreds of hours at the Poona Club, not once was he given a chance to bat.[10]

In India, as in England, batting was the preserve of the aristocratic elite. One consolation was that by adding bowling to his other duties Baloo had his salary tripled. And his control of spin and flight was honed to perfection by the thousands of balls bowled to Jungly Greig and his less gifted colleagues.

Like his ancestors, Palwankar Baloo came to make a living working with skill and care upon a piece of leather. Slowly, word of his talents with the cricket ball reached the 'native' part of the city. There was a pioneering Hindu club, which sought to challenge the Europeans of Poona. Should they call upon the services of the Chamaar bowler? The question divided the Hindu cricketers. Some Telugu members were keen to include Baloo, whereas the local, Marathi-speaking Brahmins were not. At this stage J. G. Greig jumped into the fray. He gave an interview to the press suggesting that the Hindus would be fools to deprive themselves of Baloo's services. It was not that Greig had the instincts of a social reformer – his commitment to his race was scarcely less strict than the Poona Brahmin's commitment to his caste – but, rather, that he wished to test his skills against his net bowler in the fierce heat of match competition.

In the event, Baloo was invited to play for the Poona Hindus, but at a price. On the field the upper-caste cricketers touched the same ball as he, but off it they observed the ritual taboos. At the tea interval, that ceremony sacred to cricket, Baloo was served the liquid outside the pavilion, and in a disposable clay *matka*, while his colleagues drank in white porcelain cups inside. If he wished to wash his hands and face, an Untouchable servant of the club took a kettle out into a corner of the field and poured water from it. Baloo also ate his lunch off a separate plate, and on a separate table.[11]

But he took plenty of wickets all the same. Due chiefly to Baloo's bowling the Poona Hindus defeated the Poona Europeans and other local sides as well. On one celebrated occasion they visited the inland town of Satara, to play against its white-only Gymkhana. The hosts had instructed their groundsman to roll the wicket for a week, so that it would blunt Baloo's spin. Baloo still took seven wickets, and his team won easily. In one account the bowler was then serenaded on an elephant through the streets of Satara. In another account he was garlanded at a public function on his return to Poona, the garland lovingly placed around his shoulders by the great scholar and reformer Mahadev Govind Ranade. It was also Ranade who told his fellow Brahmins that if they could play with Baloo, they must drink tea and break bread with him too.[12] A little later, Baloo was praised at a public meeting by a Brahmin nationalist even more celebrated than Ranade, Bal Gangadhar Tilak. This, writes one chronicler, created 'a stir, because in those days a person from the backward community did not have an honourable place in society'.[13]

These gestures by Ranade and Tilak have to be viewed against the growing assertiveness of the lower castes. Back in 1873, Jotiba Phule had begun his Satyashodak Samaj, which opposed Brahmin dominance in the name of the 'brotherhood of man'. Himself from the *mali*, or gardener, caste, Phule was a remarkably gifted thinker and organizer whose life's work was to inculcate a sense of dignity and solidarity among the lower orders. Whilst he knew and liked Ranade, Phule found him and his organization – the Sarvajanik Sabha – timid in its approach to social reform. In May 1885 Phule wrote to Ranade that the Brahmin reformers had 'not the courage or guts to grant willingly or openly human rights . . . to those who have been deprived of them'. Their forefathers had looked upon the Sudras and Atishudras (Untouchables) as slaves, and 'the miseries and sufferings through which the Shudras and Atishudras had to go for ages and have to experience now in their life cannot be imagined by the wise-acres who make useless casual speeches at such meetings'.[14]

The challenge of Phule and his ilk very likely lay behind the belated Brahmin recognition of the Chamaar bowler. In any case, just as the Poona orthodoxy were opening out towards him, Baloo chose to move with his family to Bombay. One reason for this was the plague of 1896, which was especially severe in Poona; another was the attractions of cricket at the centre. At first Baloo worked in Bombay with an Army unit, and also played for the newly commissioned Parmanandas Jivandas Hindu Gymkhana. This institution had been in two minds whether to admit him. The cricket captain, Kirtikar, naturally wanted to augment his bowling attack. All the same, he got his way only after 'pacifying a few Gujerati members as regards his [Baloo's] admission'.[15]

In this, the last decade of the nineteenth century, there were dozens of active cricket teams in Bombay. Where Parsi clubs were generally demarcated by locality, Hindu cricketers sorted themselves out on the lines of caste and region. Consider the names of some clubs established in the latter decades of the nineteenth century: Gowd Saraswat Cricket Club, Kshatriya Cricket Club, Gujarati Union Cricket Club, Maratha Cricket Club, Telugu Young Cricketers.

The smaller communities in this city of migrants also formed their clubs. These included the Mangalorian Catholic Cricket Club (for émigrés from the southern port town of Mangalore), the Instituto Luso Cricket Club (for those coming to the city from Portuguese-ruled Goa), and the Bombay Jewish Cricket Club.[16]

A different category of clubs was those sponsored by companies and banks. Cricket teams were run by Thomas Cook, Forbes, Forbes and Campbell, the Bombay Gas Company, the Bank of Bombay, and the Army and Navy Stores. These were heterogeneous in their membership, with employees of various Hindu castes playing on the same side as Muslims and Christians, under the leadership of a senior manager, almost always an Englishman. One active club of this kind was run by the Bombay Berar and Central Indian Railway. It was this company that gave Palwankar Baloo a job, at the suggestion of its manager and cricket captain, a Mr Lucas.[17]

Baloo played for the BBCI Railway in inter-office matches, but otherwise for the PJ Hindu Gymkhana. Every Sunday, thousands of cricket lovers flocked to the Kennedy Sea Face, where matches were simultaneously held in the three Gymkhanas. The Muslims, at this time, still lagged behind. But the most terrific excitement attended contests between the PJ Hindu Gymkhana and leading Parsi teams such as the Baronet Cricket Club. There were large crowds ringing the ground, five or ten rows deep, with the overspill accommodated on the railway overbridge that linked the Gymkhana to the nearby

Churnee Road station. The scene was made more vivid by the near-
ness of the sea. There was no Marine Drive then, and as a participant
in those games recalled, 'the waves often used to beat over the rocks
and enter the cricket ground'.[18]

The statistics of those matches are lost to history, but one may
safely assume that Palwankar Baloo took plenty of wickets. From very
early on he was regarded as the bulwark of the PJ Hindu Gymkhana.
One of his formidable opponents, Dr M. E. Pavri of the Baronet
CC, described him as 'one of the best native bowlers. A left-handed
medium-pace bowler with an easy action. Has both breaks and a curl
in the air and has a lot of spin on the ball. The most deadly bowler
on a sticky wicket. May be called "Rhodes" of India. A sound bat
and an active field.'[19]

Baloo's control was phenomenal, and his variations subtle. 'His
pace was medium,' recalled a Bombay journalist, 'but he could bowl
from a very slow to a really fast one and send them by round to full
over-arm action. He manipulated an amazing change of flight in the
ball and set the batsman always guessing in each delivery, which was
always different.'[20] From across India, a Calcutta cricketer who had
observed Baloo at close quarters remarked that he was

> A fine left-hand bowler, who possesses marvellous stamina.
> Breaks from both sides. Has the easiest of deliveries. Seldom
> tires. Can bowl all day long. Keeps an excellent length. Never
> sends down a loose delivery. Understands the game thoroughly.
> Places the field to a nicety, catches come [to the fielders], they
> have not to go in for them. Decidedly a 'head' bowler.[21]

M. E. Pavri had called Baloo the '[Wilfred] Rhodes of India'. From
this description he seems rather to have been a left-handed S. F.
Barnes, to take another hallowed name from English cricket's Golden
Age. From what I have read it seems clear that Palwankar Baloo was a
spinner of great skill and subtlety, a worthy forerunner of such world-
class Indian slow left-arm bowlers as Vinoo Mankad and Bishan Bedi.

WHILE BALOO was making his name as a bowler on the cricket fields of western India, a Prince from the region was batting to glory in England. His name was K. S. Ranjitsinhji, and in his cricketing career he experienced hurdles not entirely dissimilar to those of his Chamaar contemporary. 'Ranji' was a Rajput who studied at the public school for princes, Rajkumar College, Rajkot, before going up to Jesus College, Cambridge, in 1891. In his first two years he was not given a trial at the University ground, Fenner's, on account only of the colour of his skin. He played his cricket on Parker's Piece, Cambridge's version of the Bombay Maidan, the venue of dozens of pick-up matches over the weekend. Word of the centuries he made there reached F. S. Jackson, who had been appointed captain of Cambridge for the 1893 season. In the winter of 1892–3 Jackson toured India with Lord Hawke's team, and saw for himself that brown men could bat and bowl to good effect. On his return home he gave Ranji a trial, which led to the Indian playing against Oxford in the University match of 1893.

From Cambridge Ranji went on to play for Sussex. In the county seasons of 1894 and 1895 he scored prodigiously, and when the Australians toured in 1896 there was a popular campaign to include him in the England side. Opposing the Indian's inclusion was our old friend Lord Harris, now President of the MCC. Harris argued that only 'native-born' cricketers should be eligible for selection. This, depending on how you look at it, was either rank hypocrisy or outright racism, for Harris had been born in the West Indies himself. Ranji was not chosen for the Test played at Lord's, the ground over which Harris presided, but then the Lancashire committee expressed their desire to see him play at the Test they were hosting at Old Trafford. The Australian captain, G. H. S. Trott, sportingly said that his team had no objection whatsoever.

The reader interested in the details of Ranji's epic debut at Old Trafford, the hundreds he later scored on tour for England in Australia, the records he broke in county cricket, the distinctiveness of his batsmanship and the quality of his fielding, shall find them in the two very fine biographies written by Alan Ross and Simon Wilde respectively.[22] Here, let me offer only two quotes by contemporaries. The first comes from a professional cricket writer who was once asked to be Ranji's 'ghost'. 'It was not only that Ranjitsinhji made runs,' wrote this man,

> it was the style in which he made them. The craft of a Bismarck or a Chamberlain, the dexterity of a Cinquevali, the strength of a swordsman – so well-directed was it – were all incorporated in his batting. He was a wizard of the bat, an artist in run-getting, a general in resource.[23]

The other tribute comes from the pen of the Scottish scientist and polymath Patrick Geddes. Like the majority of his countrymen, Geddes was indifferent to cricket, preferring soccer. This, as far as I know, is the only reference to the game in his vast and varied corpus of work. 'Prince Ranjitsinhji', says Geddes,

> is most welcome: he has done us no end of good; he has raised the popular esteem and respect for India in the man in the street more than a new Buddha would have done. We admire him like the Saxon Ivanhoe overthrowing the Norman champions at their own tournaments.[24]

Ranji himself was an arch-loyalist, who cared little for the political aspirations of the ordinary Indian. In 1897, the year after his spectacular Test debut, he published a large book on the evolution of cricket in England. It has been suggested – although without much concrete evidence – that his Sussex team-mate C. B. Fry wrote some or most of it. At any rate, the book appeared under Ranji's name, and he must at least have read and approved of its contents. Issued in the sixtieth year of Queen Victoria's reign, it was entitled *The Jubilee Book of Cricket*, and 'dedicated by her gracious permission to Her Majesty the Queen-Empress'. Separate chapters on bowling, batting and fielding were followed by extended appreciations of cricket in the public schools and at Oxbridge. There was no mention of cricket in India, or elsewhere in the colonies. The book ended with a paean to the role played by cricket in the formation of the British

character. Queen Victoria, thought Ranji, must take some credit for
this, for 'there is no part or condition of her loyal subjects' lives
which may not fairly be called upon to prove its right to be regarded
as one of the blessings Her Majesty may associate with her happy
occupation of the throne of England'.[25]

Ranji played cricket for Sussex and England in the summer, but
came back to India in the winter. The Jam Saheb, or Ruler, of
Nawanagar had no sons, and had designated Ranji, a fellow Jadeja
Rajput, as his successor. But a favourite concubine was pressing the
claims of a child of hers, allegedly also the Ruler's. The main reason
for Ranji's annual trip was to keep alive his claim to succeed to the
throne, to pressure the British Resident – who would ultimately
decide the case – not to recognize the other, illegitimate, claimant.

In the winter of 1897–8 Ranji did not come home, for he
was touring Australia with the MCC team. In five Tests he scored
457 runs, including a superb 175 in the Sydney Test. The following
winter there was no MCC tour, so the Prince came to India instead.
In Bombay the PJ Hindu Gymkhana threw a lavish reception for
Ranji. An address was presented to him in 'an artistically designed
silver casket representing a cricket set, the bat being made as to
contain the address and the ball to represent the earth on which
England, India and Australia were prominently shown to signify the
countries where he had distinguished himself in cricket'.[26]

Winter is the season when cricket is played in the sub-continent.
Between 1895 and 1900 Ranji did play a few matches in India every
year. His English biographers, understandably, do not write about
them, but at least two of these matches have been recorded for
posterity by an interested party. In the winter of 1898–9 Ranji
appeared for Kathiawad against Zalawad at Rajkot. Playing by invitation for the latter team was Baloo. The slow left-arm bowler must
doubtless have heard of the address recently offered to Ranji by the
PJ Hindu Gymkhana. Although he played for the Gymkhana, Baloo
would not, for reasons of caste and class, have been in the hall when
the ceremony to honour Ranji was taking place.

But the two were to meet shortly thereafter, and on the cricket field. Zalawad defeated Kathiawar by 10 runs, and it was Baloo who dismissed Ranji. Ten years later the two came up against one another in Calcutta. Baloo was playing for the Maharaja of Natore's team, while Ranji, recently crowned Jam Saheb, was helping out his fellow Rajput potentate, the Maharaja of Jodhpur. After scoring 20, 'Baloo's deceptive ball eluded Ranji's bat and the umpire immediately raised his finger. He was out lbw, and walked straight back to the pavilion.'[27]

These triumphs became part of family lore, told and retold, finally finding their way into print by way of Baloo's brother's memoirs, published a full fifty years after that first encounter in Rajkot. Knowledge of a third such triumph comes by way of an impartial witness, D. B. Deodhar. As a young boy Deodhar walked across the river to the Poona Club to see Ranji bat. But the Prince made only a handful, being caught at slip off Baloo.[28] These hearsay accounts carry a strong whiff of credibility, for one would except an attacking batsman, such as Ranji was, to be out leg-before-wicket or caught at slip to a high-quality slow left-arm spinner like Baloo.

Now, K. S. Ranjitsinhji was unquestionably the first great cricketer of Indian origin. But he always maintained that he was in essence an 'English cricketer', for it was in that country that he learned and played most of his cricket. England versus Australia, not Jodhpur versus Natore: that was the contest he would choose to remember.[29] If one rules out Ranji, claimants to the title of the first great Indian cricketer include the early Parsis, men like M. E. Pavri, for example, or B. D. Gagrat, another fine all-rounder, or the bowler R. E. Mody – known, after a famous Surrey cricketer, as 'the Richardson of the East' – or the big hitter B. C. Machliwalla, 'the Parsee Jessop'.[30] An earlier Parsi champion was the fast bowler Hiraji Kostao, who is said to have 'bowled with such precision and judgement as to sweep clean away a two-anna piece placed upon the bails; no wicket-keeper could stand within twenty yards of the wicket to stop his underhand balls, such was their force and fury; and woe to the batsman who got any of them on his shins, he would be lamed for life'.[31]

This description is taken from Manekji Kavasji Patel's history of Parsi cricket. But Patel then adds that 'these and other feats of strength and skill attributed to him [Kostao] make a large demand upon our credulity'. More reliable records exist of the skill and subtlety of the Hindu bowler of a later generation who might justly be called the 'first great Indian cricketer'. The case for Baloo is further developed in the chapters that follow.

6. The Game Goes On

FOR ALL THE PROGRESS made by the Hindus, the Parsi cricketers stayed a step or two ahead. The highlight of the Bombay cricket season, *c.* 1900, was unquestionably the Presidency Match, played over three days in September between the Europeans and the Parsis. J. M. Framji Patel wrote in tones of characteristic effusion that this annual encounter was regarded as the

> Indian Derby. People go to see it, just as the Greeks went to their Olympic games, or the Spaniards go to witness the bull fights in Madrid. These annual encounters are the test matches of India. The 'fights for the ashes' are as keenly contested out here as are those between England and Australia. In Lord Harris' own words, 'those who have seen a Presidency vs. Parsee match on the maidan at Bombay, ten thousand natives of India looking on with the keenest interest at an English game, must recognize that there are qualities in the game of especial merit'.[1]

The sides were evenly matched: of the first nineteen matches the Parsis and Europeans won eight apiece, with three being drawn.[2] The venue was always the Bombay Gymkhana, but home advantage was neutralized by the overwhelming preponderance of natives in the crowd. 'The element of national superiority', remarked Framji Patel, 'is at the bottom of the great excitement with which the results are watched.' However, the comparison with the Derby was not entirely appropriate, for that show was restricted to the adults. Here, by contrast, it was boys under eighteen who provided most of the noise: 'it is the Parsee lad from school, who, by his clamours and claps, by his shrieks and whistles from tree-tops and from behind the much outraged boundary lines, lends such life and such hullaballoo to the Presidency Match that gradually all dignified Bombay comes out in wonderment to see what the maddening show is'.[3]

In 1895 a Bombay Schools Athletic Association was formed. This was dominated by Parsis, which might explain why, when an inter-school cricket tournament was begun the following year, it was played for the Harris Shield. Earlier still, in 1893, St Xavier's had played Elphinstone in the first recorded match between colleges. Both teams were composed almost exclusively of Parsis. In 1896 a team of Zoroastrian students challenged the crack Parsi Gymkhana, losing by a mere 7 runs. The community's cricket renewed itself, generation by generation, delighting the veteran M. E. Pavri. These 'sturdy young Parsi Collegians', he wrote, 'are every day infusing fresh blood and spirit into the rather torpid limbs of present Parsi cricket and re-invigorating its worn-out sinews'.[4]

In 1900 the colleges of the Bombay Presidency competed for the first time for the Lord Northcliffe Shield. The Elphinstone College team, with ten Parsis aboard, won easily. The success was repeated the next year, whereupon the College decided to test its mettle against teams from outside the Presidency. Fourteen Elphinstonians, a dozen of them Parsi, were chosen for a long tour through northern and eastern India in the winter of 1901–2. They visited Delhi, Ajmer, Allahabad and Calcutta, combining cricket with education, visiting tombs and palaces and thrashing the local colleges and clubs, returning to Bombay 'with a bag full of victories and an unbeaten certificate'.[5]

These young Parsi men saw themselves as pioneers, taking the game to parts of India where it had not been played before, or at least not played with the same skill and assurance as in their home town, Bombay. One tourist has left a charming account of their visit to the most sacred of Indian cities, Benares. The train that took the cricketers from Allahabad was packed with pilgrims of another kind, 'enthusiastic sinners with their naked skin smeared with ashes and paints, in which not all the waters of the Holy Ganga or even

Neptune's ocean could impart a look of cleanliness'. After a day uneasily spent in such company the Parsis reached

> the holy city of the Hindoos, the home of a thousand temples and the resort of millions of pilgrims every year. We were perhaps the only company of travellers that alighted at the sacred city for such a mundane and modern purpose as cricket. And really cricket did appear curiously out of place amidst the hoary surroundings. The discussion of L. B. W. and the shouts of 'Hows that' did indeed sound queer within the hearing of the bells of a hundred ancient temples, in the close vicinity of the old world *Yates* and *Sanyasis* and *Acharyas*, construing and expounding the *Vedas* and *Puranas* and amidst fierce devotees distorting their bodies in self mortification. It is no wonder therefore, that we were stared [at] with some amount of curiosity by the crowd at the station.[6]

It is no wonder, either, that the Bombay cricketers defeated the boys of the local Queen's College by an emphatic 152-run margin.

THE 1901–2 TOUR of the Indo-Gangetic Plain was the first of several undertaken by the Elphinstone College cricket team. In other years they went to Kutch, to southern India, even to Ceylon. The published account of these tours attaches the distance covered – by train mostly – in each case. A mere 1,100 miles were traversed during the Karachi tour of 1905, but as many as 3,238 miles during the Great Eastern Tour of 1911.

As cricketing missionaries, however, the Parsis still had to take second place to the British. In the winter of 1902–3 a team of English cricketers toured India, the first such enterprise since the visit of Lord Hawke's men ten years before. The side called itself Oxford Authentics, but was liberal enough to include a few Cambridge men. The team's wicket-keeper was the historian Cecil Headlam, already the author of widely read histories of Nürnberg and Chartres and later the editor of the papers of the imperial proconsul, Lord Milner. Headlam wrote a book on the tour, whose title was redolent of the century that had just passed: *Ten Thousand Miles through India and Burma: An Account of the Oxford University Authentics' Cricket Tour with Mr K. J. Key in the Year of the Coronation Durbar.*

Landing in Bombay, the tourists spent two weeks in the city before calling on the expatriate communities in the south, at Secundera-bad, Bangalore, Madras and Trichy. They then proceeded via Calcutta to Delhi and the Darbar organized in that city to commemorate the Coronation of King Edward VII. Although the King himself was absent, the Darbar had been conceived by the Viceroy, Lord Curzon, as a great spectacle, announcing to loyal Indians the advent of their new monarch while signalling to the seditious the British determination to rule.

From Delhi the Oxford Authentics struck deeper into northern India, visiting the capital of the Punjab, Lahore, as well as the premier towns of the United Provinces: Aligarh, Agra, Allahabad, Lucknow and Kanpur. The Indian leg of the tour ended with a week's shooting in Kashmir, the cricketers returning home via Rangoon.

I suppose these English tourists might be compared to the classical Indian musicians who nowadays visit the United States. The singer or sitar player emulates the cricketer in travelling to give comfort and solace to isolated communities of expatriates in a foreign and forever strange land. Thus the Oxford Authentics played cricket, but they also shot, fished and socialized. The happiest times were when play and pleasure combined, as when they played the Gentlemen of India at Allahabad. This side was chosen from all over the country, but only from amongst the ruling race, at this stage the only cricketers in India to qualify seriously for that definitive appellation, 'gentlemen'.

To be fair, the Oxford Authentics also played against native cricket teams. These included the Anglo-Mohammedan College at Aligarh, whom they beat comfortably, and the Parsis of Bombay, to whom they lost. For the first time a representative side of Hindus was chosen to play against a touring team. The match was played at the Bombay Gymkhana, but only five of the Hindus were from the city. Three others came from distant Madras, and a fourth from Kamptee, near Nagpur. The Englishmen had much the better of a drawn match, the sole Hindu to acquit himself well being our Chamaar hero, Palwankar Baloo. He claimed five wickets, and would have got more had it not been for sloppy fielding. Baloo also top-scored in the Hindus' second innings. Notably, the grant of a match to the Hindus was resented by some Parsis, who 'barracked them disgracefully when in the field or at the wicket'.[7]

Headlam's text awaits discovery by the legion of US-based literary critics who make a living by scrutinizing the works of dead European males. Take, for instance, the account of how he dealt with a *babu* who took his time to issue a railway ticket. Headlam kicked the *babu*'s stool with his riding-boot, and

> in a second it capsized, and my Aryan brother capsized with it. Never shall I forget the look of astonishment and awe upon the faces of his gaping underlings, never the look of fear and injured pride upon the countenance of that sprawling and obese black gentleman. Without saying a word he got up and bowed, and deferentially led the way to the ticket office. In two minutes I had got my tickets and paid for them.

Or consider the account of the great Darbar itself, its attending crowd of Maharajas and plebeians hushed into a 'silence of respect and awe' by 'the order of military discipline, of British method and British policing, a thoroughly Western form of celebration'. 'Such lessons of order', thought the cricketing observer, 'so learnt and so impressed, are the justification of our rule in India.'[8]

As a historian, Headlam placed cricket in its proper context among the last and most benign influences of imperial rule. 'First the hunter, the missionary, and the merchant', he wrote,

> next the soldier and the politician, and then the cricketer – that is the history of British colonization. And of these civilizing influences the last may, perhaps, be said to do least harm. The hunter may exterminate deserving species, the

missionary may cause quarrels, the soldier may hector, the politician blunder – but cricket unites, as in India, the rulers and
the ruled. It also provides a moral training, an education in
pluck, and nerve, and self-restraint, far more valuable to the
character of the ordinary native than the mere learning by heart
of a play by Shakespeare or an essay of Macaulay . . .'⁹

Here, if stated more evocatively than anywhere else, is the familiar
thesis of the 'Empire of Cricket'. 'The growing enthusiasm of the
natives of India for cricket', added Headlam, 'will, in my opinion,
soon result in producing quite first-class teams among them.' Yet the
imperialist held less hope for the future of European cricket in India.
The white-only teams his team met were inferior to the Parsis, a state
of affairs Headlam attributed to the climate – 'you [i.e. Europeans]
do not want a game which keeps you out in the midday sun' – and
the time taken for the cricket – 'you want a short game, because
India [for the Englishman] is a land of work – of increasingly hard
work'. He predicted that among the colonists, at any rate, polo, the
game of kings, would oust cricket, the king of games. For 'polo you
can begin when the heat of the day is over, and it enables you to get
your exercise and enjoyment in time to turn up at the club – that
essential feature of Indian life – and to see your friends before
dinner'.¹⁰

This was an astute assessment of the declining skills of European
cricket in India, when viewed against the corresponding improvement
of native (and especially Parsi) cricket. There was a lesson here for
the future planning of tours such as the one just finished. 'It has
been the invariable fate' of visiting sides, comments Headlam,

> to lose their first matches in Bombay, and it is to be hoped that
> in future any touring team will benefit by the experience of
> Mr Vernon's, Lord Hawke's, and Mr Key's elevens, and take
> their Bombay games at the end instead of the commencement
> of their tour; otherwise, against a keen side in full practice like
> the Parsees, they are bound to give a false impression of their
> powers.¹¹

The maintenance of imperial dignity required that visiting English-men were given a fair chance of defeating teams of Indian cricketers.

FROM THE BEGINNING OF the twentieth century, Bombay's pre-eminence in Indian cricket was energetically challenged by the rulers of princely states. This class of Indians has been reviled by historian and novelist alike, portrayed as utter and contemptible wastrels, squeezing their subjects and spending their money on women, wine, jewels and trips to Europe. The picture, true in its broad details, needs to be qualified. Without the Maharajas and Nawabs, Indian classical music might never have survived into the twenty-first century. Nor, perhaps, would Indian cricket.

One of the earliest and most consistent of the princely patrons of cricket was the family of Patiala. Around 1900, the Maharaja, Rajendra Singh, built a splendid stadium named after himself. He recruited an English coach, the Surrey and England professional Walter Brockwell – a *Wisden* Cricketer of the Year in 1895 – to train him and the young nobles of his court. Perhaps advised by Brockwell, the Maharaja appeared on the playing-field without his customary turban, an economical sun-hat serving in its place. This brought forth an agitated protest from the priesthood, who 'implored him, in the name of the Sikh religion and people, to put on the head-gear of his race'.[12]

While a leading state of the Sikhs, Patiala was puny and poor in comparison to such great chiefdoms as Mysore, Hyderabad or Travancore. Those other Maharajas were known for their patronage of the arts, education and music; so Rajendra Singh sought pre-eminence instead in sport. Richard Cashman has discovered the names of the Patiala cricket eleven which played against the Calcutta Rangers in December 1898. Here are the names as Cashman lists them, a list which, as he rightly points out, 'underline[s] both the quality of the team and its cosmopolitan character':

W. Brockwell	*Surrey Professional*
H. Mistry	*Parsi, leading Indian all-rounder*
Prince Ranjitsinhji	*English Test batsman, Rajput*
Maharaja of Patiala	*Sikh prince*
B. Billimoria	*Bombay Parsi*
Badeshi Ram	*Hindu*
Mr H. Priestly	*English amateur*
J. T. Hearne	*Middlesex professional*
Mehta	*Parsi bowler from Karachi*
Manzoor Mahomed	*Muslim*
Williams	*European or Anglo-Indian (?)*[13]

With or without his turban Maharaja Rajendra Singh of Patiala was a batsman of ability. His son and grandson were also to be fine cricketers. Other Princes, such as the Maharajas of Kashmir and Alwar, had no talent and chose imperiously to disregard it. Naturally, the cricketers in their employment cultivated their vanity. The Maharaja of Kashmir, for example, liked to bat but disdained the game's lesser arts. When his team was in the field he would be in his *puja* room, where he would remain until a telephone message came advising him that it was now his turn to bat. A car, then still a rarity in India, brought the Maharaja to the ground, where pads and gloves were reverentially put on him by his valets. The Maharaja would walk on to the pitch, his hands on his helpers' shoulders. The bowlers were instructed, and paid, to bowl a series of slow long hops and full tosses, these deftly aided by the fielders' feet across the boundary line. In time the scorer would announce that the Maharaja had reached his century.[14]

Once, at the Mayo College in Ajmer, this Maharaja of Kashmir found himself sitting next to the immortal Ranjitsinhji. Both were patrons of a school meant to make English gentlemen of the sons of the Rajput nobility. 'Ranji, apne kabhi anda banaya?' asked the Maharaja ('Ranji, have you ever scored a duck?'). 'Bahut baar' ('Very often'), answered the great batsman. 'Maine kabhi nahin banaya' ('I have never scored a duck'), responded Kashmir. Silence prevailed, but

then the enormity of his achievement hit the unvanquished soul.
Calling the Principal to his table, he announced: 'Aaj school band
kar do aur baccho ko chutti de do' ('Close down the school today
and give all the kids a holiday').[15]

Other Princes, more sensibly, paid for better players to play under
their colours and were content to watch themselves. Famous patrons
of cricket included the rulers of the states of Bhopal, Baroda, Holkar,
Udaipur, Jodhpur, Dungarpur, Cooch-Behar and Natore. The last-
named had one overwhelming ambition: to defeat the all-European
Calcutta Cricket Club. One year he put together a side of top-class
Hindus, including the wicket-keeper K. Seshachari from Madras, the
fast bowler H. L. Sempre from Karachi, and Palwankar Baloo and
his brother Shivram from Bombay. His side won, but the colonists,
as ever, took their defeat without grace. After the match the captain
of the Calcutta Cricket Club asked Natore how many 'gentlemen'
there were in his side, insinuating there was no honour in Indian
professionals defeating a side of English amateurs.[16]

Almost half a century later, a boy who was present at this match
recalled its two heroes: Baloo, who dismissed most of the English
batsmen, and the wicket-keeper Seshachari, who helped him get them
out. The one, as we know, was born a lowly Chamaar; the other a
Tamil Iyengar, into that most exclusive and arrogant of Brahmin sub-
castes. They made a deadly combination, with the bowler inducing
the edges and misjudgements, the wicket-keeper effecting the catches
and the stumpings. Recalling their appearance under Natore's colours,
Romesh Ganguly wrote of a Baloo over that it contained 'six deliveries
– each a different menace and yet looking as harmless as the morning
dew on a grass blade'. More vivid still was the recollection of his
accomplice,

> the cricket colossus, Seshachari, dark and forbidding, in his stand
> in close vicinity behind the stumps. The fastest ball would not
> remove him from his place of operation so near to the batsman's
> citadel. He crouched low and I wondered if the bails would
> not be disturbed from their cradle on top of the stumps by

the volume of air let out by his lungs which I thought had the capacity of bellows. He reminded me of the sinister hill that hangs over the edge of a plain. I noticed some of his finger-tips were somewhat crooked. What made them so? The question intrigues me even today![17]

Also playing for the Natore XI versus the Calcutta Cricket Club was Palwankar Shivram. Seven years younger than Baloo, Shivram was a hard-hitting batsman, a useful medium-pace bowler and an outstanding fielder. Taller than his brother, and powerfully built, his trademark was a black belt that he wore around his waist. Understandably, we know far less of his early years in the game. But we do know that by 1906 he was regarded as one of the eleven best cricketers of his religion. For in February of that year, he was chosen with his brother to play for the Hindus against the Europeans of the Bombay Presidency.

The Hindus, growing in confidence, had first challenged the Parsis to a representative match. The Parsis refused, but the Europeans sportingly agreed to step in. For their eleven the Hindus chose six players from Bombay, including Baloo and Shivram, and five from outside, one being the incomparable Seshachari. They had hoped that K. S. Ranjitsinhji would play for and captain them, but he refused. In fact, as the match was being planned Ranji was finishing a little booklet for a British audience on 'how to play cricket'. This contained some patronizing comments on his countrymen. He acknowledged their enthusiasm: Indian club cricketers, he wrote, 'certainly do not suffer from lack of practice – they are literally always at it, in addition to a match every Sunday during the season and on many week-days also'. But he was not so sure of their skills. 'The game is making strides in my native land,' he remarked, 'but progress is slow.' In particular, 'bowling is a weak spot in Indian cricket'. He then made gracious mention of two or three Indian cricketers, *all Parsi*.[18]

Ranji was sceptical of Hindu cricket, but the Parsis were positively hostile. The *Bombay Gazette* predicted that when the Presidency played their newest challengers the crowd would be mostly made up of those who wished them to lose, and lose badly: 'That there will be a large number of Parsis to witness the match goes without saying, for who would forego the pleasure of seeing the Hindu cricketers passing through the interesting ordeal of playing in the midst of a large crowd of spectators mostly unsympathetic.' Recalling how the Parsis had booed and heckled them when they played the Oxford Authentics in 1902–3, the paper warned the Hindus to 'beware of your enemies. Attempts will be made to frighten you. Do not be nervous. Go and do your humble best and, if you fail, the blame will not be yours.'[19]

The week before the great game, a dress rehearsal took place in the shape of a match between the Bombay Gymkhana and the BBCI Railway. The Gymkhana was all-white, but the Railway team had four Hindus, four Parsis and three Englishmen. A large crowd turned up to see the contest-within-the-contest: J. G. Greig versus Palwankar Baloo. The Chamaar bowler got several wickets, but the military man made an unbeaten century.

The auguries for the Hindus were not good. It appeared that the best batsman on the other side had the measure of their best bowler; the years of practice at the Poona Club were paying off. For the big match the PJ Hindu Gymkhana called for a medium-pace bowler from Poona, Erasha, whose work with the ball Greig did not know as well. There was tremendous interest in the game, partly sporting, partly political. This was the first time the biggest community in India would play the most powerful, and at a sport greatly beloved of both.

The match inevitably carried nationalist overtones, for at this time – 1905–6 – the Indian National Congress was renewing itself under two leaders from western India, Gopalkrishna Gokhale and Bal Gangadhar Tilak. Across the country, in Bengal, the *swadeshi* movement has just been launched. Patriotic entrepreneurs had set up factories to compete with British capital. Radicals urged the boycott of foreign goods. Bonfires were being made of cloth made in the mills of Manchester.[20] In the last week of 1905 the Congress had met in the holy city of Benares, where the Bengali delegates urged a countrywide spread of their campaign. Tilak's paper, *Kesari*, agreed with the Bengalis. 'It is not so manly to resign onself to one's degraded position', it remarked, 'or to sit weeping in the house like women, but it is our duty to strive strenuously to remove the causes of our misfortune.'[21] Another Marathi paper asked for India to be granted Home Rule. Indians, it said, 'should fearlessly speak out their minds to their rulers without mincing words'.[22]

Interestingly, in this winter of 1905–6 the Prince of Wales was on an extended tour of India. Large parties were thrown in his honour, where he was introduced to local notables eager to be seen with him and shake his hand. The visit was intended to confirm the continuity of British rule. Some Indians were not impressed. One Marathi writer thought that 'the salaams and salutes, the banquets and fêtes, the expressions of loyal sentiment and homage' that the Prince had received from a 'chosen few' were 'little representative of the nation's feelings'. A second claimed that 'the tour of the Prince of Wales through India has not created a hundredth part of the stir and excitement caused by the *swadeshi* movement'.[23]

In this climate, the Hindu-European encounter was to test afresh the theory of the Empire of Cricket. Would its outcome be congenial to the loyalist or to the anti-colonial radical? As one letter-writer noted, all the Bombay newspapers were showing great interest in the forthcoming cricket match except a Parsi-owned journal 'which generally is the loudest at the time of Parsi–Presidency fixtures, but is most reticent today'.[24]

The three-day match was played at the Bombay Gymkhana ground from 8 to 10 February 1906. The *Gazette* listed the match in its day's events, sandwiched between the First Criminal Sessions and the Municipal Corporation on the one side, and the annual dance of the ex-students of St Mary's School and a show of Harmston's Circus on the other. In its assessment of the two teams the paper praised Baloo, of course, and said of Shivram that 'he is Mr Baloo's brother and that is enough. He must keep up the reputation of the first bowler of India, his brother. Much is expected of his smartness in the field.'[25]

The Hindus batted first and posted a decent score of 242, Baloo contributing 25 and his brother 24. Much to the disappointment of his admirers the 'Little Man' (Greig) was bowled by Erasha for 11. Erasha had figures of 6 wickets for 77 runs, Baloo had 3 for 41, and the Europeans were all out for 191. In their second knock the Hindus made 160 (Baloo 11, Shivram 16 not out). The rulers needed 212 to win. As they began their innings on the last day the play was 'marked with a deal of excitement and enthusiasm. Large throngs of people of every denomination – even larger than the previous two days – lined the ropes and greeted every stroke with loud ovation.'

The European challenge relied heavily on Greig. He began well, and had got to 27 when he was stumped by Seshachari off Erasha. The stumping was described in terms of justifiable pride by a newspaper from the wicket-keeper's home town, Madras. The batsman lunged, it said, 'and with a movement, meteoric in its quickness', Seshachar had stumped him. It was 'a superb piece of stumping worth going miles to see'; with it 'to all intents and purposes the match was won'. In the end the Europeans crumbled to 102 all out, with Baloo and Erasha each taking five wickets. In fact, the two bowlers bowled in tandem from the start of the innings to its end.[26]

The press commentary on the match result was vast and predictably varied. Listen, first of all, to the verdict of the voice of the Establishment, the *Bombay Gazette*. This conceded that it would have liked the Presidency to win, but generously congratulated the Hindus all the same. The European cricketers had found 'foemen worthy of their steel, possessing not only the instincts of cricketers, but of true sportsmen also'. One comment was most telling, a sideways crack at the Parsis: 'Had the Hindus been beaten by as much as they beat us, their enemies would have exulted, and all hope of making the Hindu-Presidency an annual fixture would have been delayed perhaps for a decade.'[27]

Hear next the moderate nationalist voice, as represented by the Bombay-based weekly, the *Indian Spectator*. This paper asked for justice from the rulers, but in restrained tones, deploring the shouts of the agitators. In its editorial on the match the *Spectator* suggestively remarked that 'the result gave an artistic touch to the interesting "fixture": the Hindu poets represent Rama and Arjun as having been vanquished by striplings because it is the unexpected that always heightens the effect of a story'. The journal then quoted an unnamed scholar who had been 'glad to see that the young [cricketers] had made a brave show. But he was still more gratified to find that they had displayed yet greater bravery by lunching with their European rivals and thereby furthering the cause of Indian social reform.'[28]

The result was welcomed with surprising restraint by the *Mahratta* of Poona, a paper which in mood and tone was generally at the other end of the nationalist spectrum. The victory, it said, 'should give a fillip to the cause of Hindu cricket and eventually to the cause of physical education generally in the Presidency'.[29] The feelings of the radicals were better expressed by the *Tribune* of Lahore. This paper run by Punjabi Hindus had to wait three days before reports of the match were brought to it by the Frontier Mail. When the news came the paper had to range very far indeed in search for a suitable comparison. It finally settled upon another recent victory of Asia over Europe, that of Japan against Russia on the battlefield. The Hindu cricketers had apparently been as dignified in victory as their Japanese military counterparts. They had behaved 'with the noble self-restraint which characterized the Japanese over the fall of Port Arthur and all the subsequent victories which attended their arms, victories the like of which history has never recorded . . .' Through the three days of the match the Hindu cricketers 'did not play to the gallery; they were neither bumptious nor ostentatious; they did not think it necessary to appeal to the umpire every two minutes or to indulge in buffoonery'. But were the result to have been reversed, suggested the *Tribune*, then the English cricketers would have been vulgar and ostentatious in victory – mimicking 'the perfect pandemonium into which hoary England had been converted by modern Britons over the relief of Mafeking' (this being a reference to the patriotic hysteria which overtook Britain during the Boer war).[30]

Comments such as these recall the warnings of a military officer who had the ill-luck to witness another famous cricketing victory of brown over white: by the Parsis against Vernon's team in December 1890. He warned that while the British may appear to be 'as firmly in our Indian saddle as ever', it was 'as well that we should win and not lose whatever matches we play with natives'. For 'we rule in India by conquest, by strength, by prestige, and we cannot afford that these three bonds of empire should be loosened even through the medium of so trivial an affair as a game of cricket'.[31]

The *Tribune* interpreted the cricketing victory as a sign that a subdued and suppressed Asia was shaking off its shackles. Other papers welcomed it as a victory over caste prejudice. As the *Indian Spectator* had noted, during the three days of the match the players of both sides dined together, the European with the Hindu and the Brahmin with the Chamaar. The way to this unprecedented intermingling had been previously cleared by the decision of the PJ Hindu Gymkhana to allow Baloo and Shivram entry not only into its cricket field but into its café as well. Now, the course of the match and the contribution to the Hindu victory of the Baloo brothers provoked a long leading article in that respected voice of Hindu liberalism, the *Indian Social Reformer*. By 'openly interdining' with low-castes, it said, the Hindu Gymkhana would 'destroy for good' the 'silly barrier of pollution by touch'. The 'history of the admission of these chamar brothers in the Hindu Gymkhana', continued the *Indian Social Reformer*, 'is a credit to all and has done far more to liberalize the minds of thousands of young Hindus than all other attempts in other spheres'. Indeed, the triumph of cricket over caste was

a landmark in the nation's emancipation from the old disuniting and denationalizing customs. This is a conscious voluntary change, a manly moral regulated liberty, not, as in [the] railways [where members of different castes had willy-nilly to sit with each other], a compulsory change. . . . Hindu sportsmen of Poona and Bombay have shown in different degrees that, where national interest required, equal opportunity must be given to all of any caste, even though the offer of such opportunity involved the trampling of some old prejudices. . . . Let the lesson learnt in sport be repeated in political, social and educational walks of life. Let all disuniting and denationalising customs in all high, low or lowest Hindus disappear and let India cease to be the laughing-stock of the whole world.[32]

In March 1907 a return match was scheduled between the Europeans and the Hindus. Again, this was prefaced by a fixture between the BBCI Railway and the Bombay Gymkhana. Baloo took five wickets and his side won, in front of a large crowd: for the Railway XI 'being a composite one a large number of native cricketers had assembled to witness the match'.[33] Many more still turned up for the bigger match. Tents were pitched on the southern and western aspects of the Gymkhana ground, while a large number of spectators simply stood under the shade of trees on the Waudby road. This time the natives won more emphatically still, by a margin of 238 runs. A rising young batsman, M. D. Pai, scored a hundred, and Baloo took a staggering 13 wickets in the match (and scored a fifty besides). The Europeans had to make in excess of 300 in the last innings; again, they could win only if Jungly Greig played a good hand. But before he had scored he was bowled by Erasha. At first Greig refused to go; he thought that wizard of a wicket-keeper, Seshachari, had skilfully (and illegally) disturbed the stumps. The Hindu captain, Chunilal Mehta, then showed Greig that the stump was reclining *backwards*, which meant that the ball had struck it directly, without any aid from the wicket-keeper. Greig grumbled, but he had to go.[34]

That year, the *Mahratta* recovered its voice, and sarcastically thanked 'the sportsmanly instincts of the Englishmen who have these two years allowed the Hindus to stand on the same level with their rulers and sometimes to defeat [them], if nowhere else, at least on the cricket grounds'.[35] The *Mahratta* was founded and edited by the radical agitator Bal Gangadhar Tilak. The years of these cricket matches, 1906 and 1907, were also the years in which Tilak was wresting control of the Indian National Congress from his great Poona rival Gopalkrishna Gokhale. The one asked for, nay demanded, political freedom – '*Swaraj* is my birthright,' he thundered – the other believed that social reform must precede it. The editor of the *Indian Social Reformer*, K. Natarajan, was of the Gokhale school, in keeping with which he stressed the lessons for caste emancipation of the cricketing victories. The *Tribune* of Lahore was run by an associate of Tilak's colleague, the comparably fiery Lala Lajpat Rai: thus, like the *Mahratta*, its reading of sporting matters was to be principally political.[36]

At the time, the Hindu cricket victories of 1906 and 1907 were the subject of a great deal of popular attention. They were seen variously as a triumph over caste prejudice and an assertion of a suppressed national spirit. Intriguingly, triumph on the cricket field attracted attention in a manner that political sloganeering and social uplift could not. As one nationalist paper sarcastically remarked, 'the Anglo-Indian papers are full of praise and congratulations for the Hindus, who, by defeating them at their national game, appear to have raised themselves in the estimation of the European public to an extent which no other qualification on their part could have done'.[37]

In the India of the Raj the Hindus were the dominant religious grouping in numerical terms. Unlike the Parsis or the Muslims, the Hindus – or at least influential sections among them – were opposed to the continuation of colonial rule. The ideologues of cricket – Lord Harris, Cecil Headlam and their ilk – liked to believe that their sport would serve to unite ruler and ruled. In truth, sport was used, especially by the Hindus, to highlight the gap between British precept and British practice. For, as the *Mahratta* suggested, it was the height of hypocrisy for the rulers to meet Indians on equal terms on the cricket field and to deny them equal rights in other spheres.

The *Mahratta's* remarks anticipate the criticisms of colonial duplicity made, also in the context of sport, by the liberal British newspaper, the *Manchester Guardian*. In 1913–14 *The Times* had expressed its opposition to inter-racial boxing, this when the black boxer Jack Johnson was the reigning world heavyweight champion.

The *Guardian* perceptively remarked that what the voice of the English Establishment most dreaded

> is that Johnson should be matched against an Englishman. In that case, as they feel, the Englishman might be beaten; indeed, he almost certainly would; and they fear that this would make negroes uppish in British Africa. . . . The negro might then begin to extract from *The Times* and adapt to his own case the great anti-suffragist argument that the only proper basis of the right to vote, and to political power generally, is personal physical strength. Bombardier Wells, the anti-suffragists argue, ought to have a vote, and Mrs Humphrey Ward ought not, because – to put it briefly – Bombardier Wells could knock out Mrs Humphrey Ward when it came to fisticuffs. It is feared that the Kaffir might adopt this philosophic doctrine and begin to argue that if Jack Johnson or Sam Longford were to knock out Bombardier Wells the negro's title to political power would similarly be established.[38]

We have here early intimations of a debate that was to be replayed, with regard to different games and different countries, throughout the twentieth century. *The Times* and Lord Harris wished to 'keep politics out of sport'. But, as boxing in pre-civil rights America or cricket in colonial India so clearly revealed, divisions in society would inevitably seep into sport and, by way of sport, into politics.[39]

IN THE EARLY YEARS of the twentieth century, there was a bitter falling-out between the Hindus and the Parsis. The reasons for this rift are lost to history, but we know that it was so serious that the PJ Hindu Gymkhana had even passed a resolution prohibiting matches with Parsi cricket clubs.[40] The Parsis, for their part, refused to play against a representative Hindu side in 1906. But in 1907, and after their rivals had twice beaten the Europeans, the two sides worked out a truce that paved the way for a novel, three-way annual contest.

This tournament was known as the Triangular, and was restricted
to players of the Bombay Presidency. It was played in the middle of
September, at the fag end of the monsoon. With the wickets green
and the sky overcast, the conditions were reminiscent of England. In
the five years that the tournament was held the Europeans won thrice,
and the Parsis twice. The outstanding individual performer, however,
was Palwankar Baloo. In the five matches he played between 1907
and 1911 he took 40 wickets at less than 10 runs apiece.[41]

The Triangular tournament was keenly looked forward to by the
cricket lovers of the city. The fans were partisan: when either
the Hindus or the Parsis were playing the Europeans, 'the crowds
of the other community showed unmistakably by their cheers that
they wished that the sister Indian community was defeated'.[42] When
the two Indian sides met, feelings were more intense still. Spectators
used mirrors to reflect rays of sharp sunlight on the other side's
batsmen. Each community had a special, derisory name for the
other. Parsis called Hindus 'Tatyas'; Hindus answered by calling Parsis
'Kakdas', which derived from *kauva*, or crow, and referred to the
Zoroastrian practice of leaving their dead to be eaten by birds.[43]

Years later, one fan, V. J. Divecha, vividly recalled his first Hindu–
Parsi encounter. His father had bought him a ticket and given the
boy an extra 6 annas to buy lemonade and *chana* (gram). There was
standing-room only, but for a 2-anna bribe Divecha was allowed by
a vendor of aerated water to stand on a pile of empty boxes. Sepoys
patrolling the boundary line, clad in blue uniforms and yellow
turbans, marched to schoolboy shouts of 'Left, right! Left, right!' All
through the match the Parsi players and their fans acted as if they
would win. The Hindus, batting first, were dismissed for a mere 65.
One batsman, bowled first ball for a duck, was so disconsolate that
he walked away from rather than into the pavilion. Baloo took a pile
of wickets, but the Parsis led handsomely on the first innings. Eventually they won by four wickets. As the Hindu supporters walked off
the ground, the Parsis mockingly called out, 'Pahilas khai' ('Did you
see that?'). A Parsi classmate told Divecha that it would take the
Hindus fifty years before they would beat their rivals at cricket.[44]

Shivram also played for the Hindus in the Triangular, as, from 1910, did a third brother. This was Palwankar Vithal, born in 1886, and sent by Baloo to the cricket-minded Elphinstone High School. Vithal was a graceful right-hand batsman with a penchant for the cover drive. While watching his brother play against the Oxford Authentics in 1902, he was greatly impressed by the visitors' fielding. Other Indians did not catch or throw like the English, but Vithal resolved that he would.[45]

After leaving school Vithal accepted a job with the Greater Indian Peninsular Railway, where Shivram already worked. The youngster scored a sheaf of centuries in club cricket, and was chosen to play for the Hindus in the 1910 Triangular. The following year an All India Team was due to tour England. From January 1911 trial matches were held in Bombay, for aspirants from all over the country. The selectors were seven in all – two Muslim, two Hindu and two Parsi, with the venerable Jungly Greig in the chair. This ecumenism was reflected in the team finally chosen. They included six Parsis, three Muslims (all from Aligarh), and five Hindus. The captain, however, was a Sikh, the twenty-year-old Maharaja Bhupendra Singh of Patiala, just installed on to his *gaddi* by the Viceroy, Lord Minto.[46]

Despite the strong recommendation of the English coach supervising the trials, Palwankar Vithal was deemed too young to be sent to England. Baloo, of course, was chosen, and Shivram was nominated first reserve. The day before the ship was to leave a player from Kashmir dropped out, and Shivram had hurriedly to gather his gear and other effects. That same evening, 4 May 1911, a farewell was organized for the players at the Orient Club. Presiding over the event was the tour's main organizer, that great servant of Indian cricket, J. M. Framji Patel. The tour, he said, was in the nature of a pilgrimage, with the Indians going to worship at the Home of Cricket. He asked each player to eschew their traditional fatalism in favour of 'scientific organization and method', to practise and train regularly and 'thus try to be worthy of the trust reposed in him by his countrymen'. Framji Patel concluded with a loyalist flourish: 'Let the providential alliance of India and Britain be cemented', he remarked, 'with the lasting and enduring ties of one peace-loving King-Emperor, one beautiful language, one victorious flag, and last not least one grand Imperial game.'[47]

The touring team of 1911 was handicapped at the start. Framji Patel had tried hard to secure the participation, as captain and batsman, of Ranjitsinhji, 'the greatest cricketing asset of the country'. But Ranji was now the Jam Saheb, or Ruler, of Nawanagar, and he declined pleading the pressures of State (notably, he also declined to contribute money to meet the tour's expenses). Two fine Bengali players did not attend the trials – one, a Brahmin, was warned by his family that he would be ostracized if he crossed the 'Kala Paani', whereas the other, an Untouchable bowler named Phaguram, was refused leave by the club where he served as the groundsman.[48] The curious composition of the selection committee must also have forced some unhappy compromises. Typically but not, in the case at hand, unfairly, the Hindus felt that far too many Parsis had been chosen.

In England the Indian captain was not often to be found with his team. Patiala played a match at Lord's, and one or two more, but for the most part he was active on the London social circuit, partying and going to the races (there were many parties to attend that summer, for a new King had just ascended the throne). The captain's absence was a blow in purely cricketing terms, for this particular Prince was a first-class batsman, and in social terms, for while he was away the side divided into Parsi and Hindu factions. Patiala also took his five servants with him wherever he went. This did not matter much, except that His Highness also insisted on having close at hand his secretary Keki Mistry, who at this time was perhaps the best of all Indian batsmen. Without Patiala and Mistry the tourists' batting was desperately ill-equipped to handle English wickets and English professional bowling. This showed in the results. Fourteen matches were played against the recognized English counties, of which two were won, ten lost and two drawn. Of the other matches, against such second-class teams as Ulster and the North of Scotland, the Indians won four and lost five.

The singular success, from the Indian point of view, was the bowling of Palwankar Baloo. He took 114 wickets at an average of 18·84 runs per wicket, and would easily have claimed 150 wickets had he had more support in the field. The scorecards of the tour tell a tale that is truly uplifting. Three early matches were played against Oxford University at the Parks, the Marylebone Cricket Club at Lord's and Cambridge University at Fenner's. On these three great grounds, redolent with cricket history, trod this Untouchable from Palwan who in terms of social background was as removed from the High Table as one could possibly be. But he could bowl. Against Oxford Baloo claimed 5 wickets for 87 runs, against the MCC he took 4 for 96 (his wickets including two county captains and an England Test player), whereas at Cambridge he returned the superb figures of 8 for 103.

Baloo enjoyed success against all the top county sides. He claimed 7 for 83 against Lancashire, 4 for 127 against Yorkshire, 4 for 74 against Warwickshire, and 4 for 100 against Surrey. (In these matches the home team usually got to bat only once.) And when the Indians beat Leicestershire by 7 wickets, Baloo's figures were 5 for 92 and 6 for 93. He got a mere six victims in the only other victory, against Somerset, but made up somewhat with a strokeful 55 in his side's second innings. The real match-winner on this occasion was younger brother Shivram, who scored 113 not out as the visitors scraped home with one wicket standing. For the tour as a whole, Shivram stood third in the batting averages, scoring 930 runs at an average of over 27 per innings. He was, said one observer, 'the most promising of Hindu batsmen'.[49]

Back in 1904, the Parsi patron Sir Dorab J. Tata had begun negotiations on Baloo's behalf with the English county Surrey, who needed a left-arm bowler. That plan fell through, but when Baloo finally came to England he impressed more than one county. Indeed, he received several offers to stay in England and play as a professional. In the summer of 1911, he was already thirty-six and a little past his best. He also suffered from synovitis, swelling of the shoulder, an affliction brought on by being over-bowled. His performance was outstanding as it was. What might he have done without a sore shoulder and had he been five years younger? In an interview with the *Times of India*, Baloo 'modestly declared that he was not satisfied with the work he himself did with the ball and very rightly wished that the team had been sent six years ago when he was in his best form'. But his comrade Seshachari told *The Hindu* that Baloo 'is so good that he is good enough to play for any county'. The respected English critic E. H. D. Sewell commented likewise that Baloo 'is a bowler most of our counties would be very glad to have in their eleven'.[50] His performance was truly exceptional. In the ninety years since Baloo returned home, only one other Indian bowler, Vinoo Mankad in 1946, has claimed more than 100 first-class wickets on a tour of England.

Overall, the Indian team of 1911 had performed much below expectations. In its retrospective of the tour a Bombay paper made the usual excuses: 'Climate, food, constant travelling, want of practice, a limited number of men to choose from in case of need – all these were unfavourable conditions against which the team had to fight'[51] – a long list of difficulties, not all of the writer's invention, yet one man, Palwankar Baloo, was able to rise above them.

According to one source, at the Orient Club's function to wish the team God-speed only Baloo and Shivram were not honoured with garlands.[52] But when the Indian cricket team returned to Bombay on 15 September in the steamship *Salsette*, there must have been garlands aplenty for its acknowledged hero. We know, for instance, of a function organized by the Depressed Classes of Bombay to felicitate Baloo. The community's pride was entirely justified, for this erstwhile Untouchable had far exceeded the Brahmins and Muslims and Parsis and Princes who accompanied him to England. At this function, the *manpatra*, or welcome address, for Baloo was written and presented by Bhimrao Ambedkar. The future draughtsman of the Indian Consti-tution was then a promising college student. This, according to the *doyenne* of historians of Untouchability, Eleanor Zelliot, was the first public appearance of the man who was to become the greatest of all lower-caste politicians and reformers, and a figure of surpassing importance in modern Indian history.[53] By virtue solely of his deeds on the cricket field, Baloo had become a hero and inspiration to countless Untouchables. And the young B. R. Ambedkar was one of them.

7. Baloo's Struggle

ON A VISIT TO the United States in 1907, the Parsi industrialist Jamshedji Tata asked for an audience with President Theodore Roosevelt. Tata had just started the first steel mill in India and doubtless wished to explore the American market for his product. His request was granted, but when he met the President that sporting-minded man greeted him with these words: 'And how is Parsi cricket getting along?'[1]

Parsi cricket was getting along perfectly well and – although the American would not know it – so was Hindu cricket. This was the work principally of one family, the Palwankars. By 1910 Baloo and Shivram were joined in the Hindu team by their brother Vithal. Meanwhile, the youngest brother, Ganpat, was studying for a bachelor's degree at Elphinstone College, his fees paid by brother Baloo, but he would play cricket too. In January 1912 he was the undoubted star of the college cricket tour of Northern India. When the visitors defeated the famous Mohammedan College in Aligarh, Ganpat top-scored in both innings, with 58 and 40. And in a drawn match against the Maharaja of Patiala's XI, played at Rawalpindi, Ganpat claimed two wickets, effected two catches, and scored a brilliant century besides. Ganpat Palwankar played 'cricket of the highest class', remarked the college cricket historian. 'It was not the sum of his runs that was so much appreciated as the style in which they were obtained, for he employed a variety of strokes and his batting was perfect and true.'[2]

That same year, 1912, the Muslims were admitted into the annual Bombay tournament, which thus became a Quadrangular.

The Muslims were pleased with the invitation, perhaps too pleased. They chose as their captain a man, Dawood Nensey, who was 'really at home with a knife and fork', for 'those days lunching with the British Sahibs was of great moment'.[3] (The others, one hopes, were chosen for their cricketing skills alone.) The entry of the Muslims made the tournament more attractive to its large and steadily growing audience. The Triangular was known in the vernacular as the *tirangi*, or the contest of three colours; now it became the *chowrangi*. These names nicely reflected the diversity of social interest, with each colour attracting its own band of devoted fans.

Played in the month of September, the Quadrangular was referred to as a 'great annual treat' for the citizens of Bombay and as 'the great international contest between the four leading cricket communities of western India'.[4] The cricket season began in June, with a drama-filled build-up towards its main event. First came the friendly matches, played between clubs and office teams. These were followed in July and early August by two-day practice matches between the four denominational Gymkhanas. The well-attended local matches, though 'interesting in themselves, are yet all played with an eye on the great international tournament, which dwarfs them all'.[5]

The players who scored runs or took wickets in these warm-up games were placed on a short-list by their respective Gymkhanas. They were joined in mid-August by cricketers specially invited from other parts of India. Promising Muslim cricketers came from Aligarh and Kashmir, and Parsis from Surat and Hyderabad. The Europeans and the Hindus, however, were restricted to players from the Bombay Presidency alone (this restriction was not lifted until 1916). The cricketers assembled for practice at the nets, watched over by their selectors. The newspapers carried the letters of fans urging the selection of their favourite players.

A week before the Quadrangular matches the physical preparations began. The wicket of the Bombay Gymkhana was watered and rolled and its outfield trimmed. The pavilion to the south of the ground was meant exclusively for Europeans, but spacious tents were erected on the other sides for followers of rival teams. Then, at last, came the matches, these watched by an absorbed and intermittently vocal crowd of about 20,000, and written up by papers small and big, Gujarati, Marathi, English and Urdu. Aside from the acclaim of the fans there was also money and cups to be won, paid for by merchants and Princes of the different communities.

After the tournament ended the papers carried extended post-mortems in their columns, the discussions to be duplicated in homes and cafés throughout the city. In the 1913 Quadrangular the Parsis lost to the Muslims, of all teams. Eight months later, at the annual general body meeting of the Parsi Gymkhana, the venerable J. M. Framji Patel suggested that this happened because of what the crick-eters had eaten the night before. Their team, he said, 'must particularly beware of taking the rich Parsi food' before their next representative match, 'as the effects of diet on nerves and senses cannot be too often drawn attention to'.[6]

In a happy coincidence, the inception of the Quadrangular in 1912 was followed in 1913 by the founding of the *Bombay Chronicle*. At this time the island city had many Indian-language papers, but the English press was dominated by British interests. The *Bombay Gazette*, once the official expatriate voice, was in terminal decline, its place being rapidly filled by the *Times of India*, a newspaper owned by Englishmen and strongly oriented to English tastes. Founded by a 'cosmopolitan Parsi' (Sir Pherozeshah Mehta) and funded by 'catholic Hindus', the *Bombay Chronicle* was a liberal nationalist alternative, offering the 'Indian' point of view to the city's growing middle class, the students, lawyers, merchants and bureaucrats who spoke Gujarati or Marathi at home but English with their friends or at work. From its inception the *Chronicle* was at the cutting edge of debates about adult suffrage, caste emancipation, Hindu–Muslim relations and the time frame of the British withdrawal from India. But it also carried stories and features about the arts and sport. There is no better place to study the emergence of the Bombay film industry, and no better source for the cricketing politics of the great Bombay Quadrangular.[7]

THE QUADRANGULAR was generally referred to as the 'Bombay Cricket Carnival'. But there is also a reference to it as 'a sort of a Roman forum'.[8] In truth, it was a mixture of both. Sport was both spectacle and contest, an outing with friends and family but also a vehicle for suppressed social ambitions. The noise level at the Quadrangular was terrific, far higher than in an English or Australian ground. Shouts and screams were accentuated by drums and bugles. Spectators sang songs, shone mirrors, flew kites and garlanded cricketers. Their enjoyment was huge anyway, but still more so if their man hit a six or if their team happened to win.

Perhaps the sharpest edge was reserved for the matches between Parsis and Europeans. 'Cricket is nowhere keener than on the Bombay Maidan,' observed E. H. D. Sewell in 1913,

> not even when Lancashire and Yorkshire have got to grips, or when Surrey are fighting the Blackheath superstition *plus* Blythe and the rest of Kent. Every Parsi lady in Bombay turns out in her best and most picturesque kit. The much-vaunted luncheon parade at the 'Varsity match is drab and drear compared with the Bombay maidan towards sunset on the day of a Parsi versus Presidency match.[9]

Some other contests were also loaded with meaning. When the Hindus played the rulers, their stakes were political as well as cricketing. Victory on the field meant a further fillip to national aspirations; defeat, a reluctant acceptance of British superority. (Once, after Baloo's team had defeated the Europeans, a nationalist paper suggested that 'if defeat had been the result, hardly a Hindu would have left unused the Hindu vocabulary of abuse'.[10]) And in Bombay, the rivalry between Hindus and Parsis could be vicious, for the two communities competed on the cricket field but also in the bazaar and stock market.

Within each of these contests there were individual match-ups that were keenly followed. One such was the battle between those two old stalwarts, Palwankar Baloo of the Hindus and J. G. Greig of the Europeans. At the time of the 1913 Quadrangular Baloo was already thirty-eight, but bowling as well as ever. Greig, three years older, was then serving as the Military Secretary to the Governor. He still took his cricket very seriously indeed. But when he came up against his old practice bowler he was quickly out to him, caught at slip by a ball that turned, the catch taken by the Poona youngster D. B. Deodhar.[11]

That year, 1913, Baloo was joined in the Hindu team by his brothers Shivram, Vithal and Ganpat. The captain, however, was the batsman M. D. Pai. Pai was felicitated by his caste association, the Gowd Saraswat Brahmin Mitra Mandal, for achieving the 'highest honour to which a cricketer can aspire'. In his reply, Pai thanked his community for the reception they had hosted for him, but added that 'the honour of captainship should have been given to his friend Mr Balu, he being the senior and experienced player in the team'.[12]

Pai had been on that 1911 tour, struggling with the bat while Baloo shone with the ball. Nonetheless, his remarks bespoke an extraordinary generosity. For in 1913 Mahatma Gandhi was still in South Africa, and the Hindu political elite was, by and large, still bound hand and foot to the Laws of Manu. An Untouchable cricketer of courage and skill could be chosen to play for the Hindus, but would he be made captain? Perish the thought, for the leader of a cricket team has to exercise his mind more often and more innovatively than a football or basketball captain. In this slow-paced sport it is the captain, not the coach or manager, who decides the order of batsmen, the order of bowlers and changes in the field. Intelligence and foresight were commonly held to be the preserve of the high castes. And Pai was a Brahmin while Baloo was a Chamaar. To appoint the spin bowler captain of the Hindus would symbolically upturn the hierarchy of caste. Admittedly, on grounds of talent and experience Baloo should long ago have been made the captain of the Hindus. Pai's speech to his caste-mates suggests that his team-mates would have found his elevation quite acceptable. But the merchants and lawyers who ran the PJ Hindu Gymkhana did not.

In June 1914 an editorial in the *Bombay Chronicle* commented that 'the services rendered by Baloo to Hindu cricket are worth their weight in gold, and it speaks volumes for the wonderful vitality of the man that after the lapse of more than two decades he is still their foremost bowler'.[13] The following month the paper carried an angry letter by one 'C. S. T.'. The previous year, said this disappointed fan, the Hindus had been robbed of a win by 'bad management and worse fielding'. 'There ought to be more permanent interest in Hindu cricket', said 'C. S. T.', 'in place of the spasmodic outbursts of frenzy which agitate the lovers of cricket.' The Selection Committee should make its choices early and play the chosen players together in practice matches. 'The choice of a captain', he added, 'should be a free one and that onerous post should be in the hands of the best and most competent man on the field.' The letter writer was plainly hinting at Baloo, whom he elsewhere called a 'sure thing', the Hindus' 'crack bowler who can always do some work of outstanding merit'.[14]

Although many Indians fought and died in the First World War, the country itself was untouched by the hostilities. Club and university and princely cricket prospered. The pool of talent from which the Quadrangular sides were chosen was deepened and widened. The Hindus began catching up with the Parsis, the Muslims with the Hindus. The Europeans, meanwhile, had allowed themselves to recruit cricketing professionals. Previously they had restricted themselves to the elite of Empire – Army officers, civil servants, planters and *boxwallahs* – cricketers who also qualified as members of the Club. But after three consecutive losses, for the 1915 contest they commandeered the services of Frank Tarrant, a superbly gifted all-rounder of Australian birth, who played for money in the English County Championship in the summer and coached the Maharaja of Patiala, also for money, in the winter.

In 1915 the Quadrangular was played at Poona, apparently on the insistence of the Europeans. They had lobbied hard for this, for, as one Indian critic sarcastically commented, in a Poona September 'the [social] season is in full swing with all its gaieties, the pitch is more like Home and the climate is less exhausting'.[15] The matches were played at the Poona Club, that old haunt of Baloo (and J. G. Greig). An early report suggested that all four Palwankar brothers were certainties. But when the side was chosen a week ahead of the

Hindu–Parsi match Baloo was not in it. Apparently a selector had asked him how he was, and the bowler, out of modesty, answered 'that he was not in his usual form but added that if he were selected he would gladly lend his services in the interests of Hindu cricket'.[16] This diffidence was used as an excuse to drop him.

The *Bombay Chronicle* now received numerous angry letters of protest suggesting that the Hindu selection committee had conspired to throw Baloo out. 'Now nobody will say that Baloo is quite the demon bowler he once was,' said one writer, 'but it cannot be denied that he is still a fine bowler, who is worth his place in any representative eleven.' The decision to dump him, remarked this correspondent,

> has been received with great and justifiable surprise by the supporters of Hindu cricket. Baloo has been the mainstay of Hindu cricket for more than a decade and a half and his services in the cause of Hindu cricket have been invaluable. By every right of ability, of seniority, and of the services rendered to his side, he should long ago have been appointed captain of the team. He has not only been denied that right but now he has been excluded from the team itself.[17]

Intriguingly, the day after the appearance of this letter the *Chronicle* carried an explanatory letter from the Hindu captain, M. D. Pai. 'I was strongly in favour of Mr Baloo's inclusion,' he wrote, 'but the hesitating reply of Mr Baloo showing his inability to keep up for three days forced the Committee to give him up.' The captain had urged that 'preference should be given to Mr Baloo, on whom I much rely as a bowler of sound and mature judgement'.[18] But his words were disregarded. That a captain should openly participate in a selection controversy was most unusual. Perhaps Pai felt Baloo's omission deeply, or perhaps he wished to forestall criticism in case his team performed poorly in the tournament.

What is notable about this controversy is the absence of any open allusion to Baloo's caste. Earlier that year Mohandas K. Gandhi had returned to India, but he had not yet found his political feet, and his views on Untouchability were yet to become an object of public debate. The Hindu cricket fan who was also a social liberal had thus to express his suspicions indirectly.

Although caste was certainly the main reason why Baloo was not made captain of the Hindus, it did not help that he was his team's main bowler. Batsmen are cricket's aristocrats, who monopolize attention and awards. Back in the 1950s the England batsman (and captain) Len Hutton was knighted. The half a dozen cricketing knights before him had all been batsmen too. The great Australian leg-spinner Arthur Mailey congratulated Hutton, then added: 'I hope next time it is a bowler. The last bowler to be knighted was Sir Francis Drake.'

Conventional wisdom holds that bowlers make poor captains. It is said that they are too absorbed in their own craft to pay proper attention to bowling changes or field placings. Batsmen, on the other hand, are free of personal responsibility when their own innings is over. The theory that batsmen make the best captains is an old one, and it is still widely accepted. The Hindu selectors who chose Pai over Baloo might very well have subscribed to it. One can imagine the progress of the discussion in the committee room: yes, he is wise and he is experienced; no, we do not really mind that he is a Chamaar; however, we must not further burden our main bowler. Pai, the Brahmin and batsman, would thus always win out over Baloo, the Chamaar and bowler.[19]

The Quadrangular began on 6 September with the Hindu–Parsi match. The following day's paper carried this surprising headline: 'Baloo playing after all'. A Hindu cricketer, S. M. Dalvi, had sportingly stood down in his favour. Public pressure had forced the inclusion of the popular hero. The Hindus won their first match, but lost in the finals to the Europeans. The inclusion of the plebeian Tarrant paid off: he scored an unbeaten half-century and also bowled well. No doubt the Europeans were encouraged by the presence throughout the match of the Governor of Bombay and his wife. Lord and Lady Willingdon sat through three full days, arising from their seats only to visit the various tents to be garlanded.

At the tournament's end, a published 'retrospect' said that while the crowds were good, they were not quite as large as in Bombay. The reporter identified Vithal as the best Hindu batsman, with Ganpat a close second. But J. G. Greig's batting, he remarked, 'has shown a marked falling-off since he took over the Military Secretary-ship; and what Government House has gained has been a loss to the world of cricket'.[20]

We can be sure that Jungly Greig read this and came to the 1916 Quadrangular determined to prove the critic wrong. As it happened this year, for the first time in its history, the tournament would miss Greig's old foeman, Palwankar Baloo. He was indisposed', and in his place came a young man from Nagpur making his first-class debut. His name was C. K. Nayudu and he came from a moderately well-to-do family – his father and uncle had been contemporaries of Ranji at Cambridge. When the boy took to cricket, the father contacted his friend for advice. Ranji asked the aspirant to follow three injunc-tions: 'Balla Seedha Rakho. Jore Se Maro. Aur Ghabrao Mat' ('Keep the Bat Straight. Hit Hard. And Don't Funk').[21]

Nayudu was a superb athlete, with a wiry, steely physique honed by hours at the local gymnasium. He was principally a batsman who hit hard, but also a useful bowler and excellent in the field. In this, his Quadrangular debut, his first scoring shot was a six. However, it was his bowling that was the cause of an incident that was to rock the tournament almost to its foundations. At this time, Quadrangular matches were supervised by an umpire from each team. The Hindu umpire for their match against the Europeans in 1916 was M. D. Pai, who did not play that year. Early in the European innings Pai gave Greig out stumped for a duck, off C. K. Nayudu's bowling. Greig, typically, contested the decision. He claimed that the bails had not been properly dislodged by the wicket-keeper. Both the non-striker and the European umpire at the bowler's end urged him to stay. Pai insisted that he was out, and Greig returned slowly to the pavilion. No sooner had he got there than he complained to the former Hindu captain Chunilal Mehta, who was watching the match. Mehta, a rising industrialist soon to be knighted, summoned the Hindu captain and Hindu umpire from the field. The game was held up for fifteen minutes while they told Mehta that in their opinion Greig had been fairly dismissed and there was no question of their allowing him to resume his innings.[22]

To stop proceedings because of a player's protest is a commonplace of contemporary football. In the context of an early twentieth-century cricket match it created a storm. The following day, the opposing points of view were carried by the *Times of India* and the *Bombay Chronicle* respectively. Whereas the English-owned newspaper suggested that Pai was incompetent, the *Chronicle* stood by its man. Pai told its reporter that 'nothing would deter him from independently and impartially performing the duties of an umpire'. In another interview, the Hindu captain, S. K. Diveker, said that Captain Goldie, the non-striker when Greig was dismissed, and Mr Cumber, the European umpire, had 'no right to challenge the decision, for an umpire's decision must in all cases be held to be final'.[23]

On the field itself Jungly Greig had the final word, scoring 55 not out in the second innings as his side won by six wickets. But the Indian press continued to dwell upon the stumping incident, which suggested to them that the English had no monopoly on sporting virtue. One Anglo-Indian paper, the *Advocate of India*, carried an article titled 'Hindu Umpires' Mistakes', which claimed that even in the previous year's tournament some of their batsmen had been wrongly adjudged leg-before-wicket. The *Advocate*, remarked the *Chronicle* bitterly, wrote 'as if the Presidency men had no legs at all'. Hindu pride had been hit hard by the aspersions cast against their umpires. As the *Chronicle* continued:

> If any of the Hindu batsmen had been wrongly given out by the Presidency Umpire and protested, the 'Advocate' would have been the first to proclaim that the Umpire was in a better position to judge, there could be no mistake and the protest was unseemly in the extreme. If it is, however, the decision of a Hindu Umpire against a Presidency batsman, that decision is wrong and only its reporter from the corner of the maidan can judge correctly.[24]

After the match Greig wrote a letter richly abusing Pai, which was forwarded with approval by the Bombay Gymkhana to its Hindu counterpart. The Joint Secretary of the PJ Hindu Gymkhana wrote back regretting that Major Greig 'should have thought it fit to have used the language that he has used with reference to the character of the Hindu Umpire'. 'My Committee', wrote the official archly, 'do not agree that Mr Pai with his well-known credentials could with any propriety be called a "Bad Umpire".' Pai, it said, was 'absolutely certain that Major Greig was out', and there was 'good reason to believe that there is a considerable body of outside opinion which bears out Mr Pai's opinion'. In any case, the Major's imputations were 'entirely opposed to the character of sport and are calculated to create general unpleasantness'. Indeed, 'if decisions are to be disputed in this manner no self-respecting gentleman would agree to take up the task'.[25]

Meanwhile, the Parsis had defeated the Muslims in the other semi-final. The second and third days of the final were washed out, but the first day's cricket was watched by a handsome crowd. Lord and Lady Willingdon lunched with the two teams. Afterwards, the Governor and his lady were taken by the President of the Bombay Gymkhana to the different tents, and 'were everywhere most enthusiastically received and profusely garlanded'.

With a world war on, the Quadrangular could still be presented as an affirmation of colonial rule. The Bombay Gymkhana would host the tournament and the Governor would graciously bless the teams. And the game was a British game anyway.

But the stumping episode had upset the apple-cart somewhat. A famous English cricketer, and a ranking Army Major to boot, had done what no sportsman was supposed to do: challenge an umpire. In its retrospect on the tournament, the *Bombay Chronicle* put it magisterially: 'The truly sportsmanlike procedure is to accept an umpire's verdict, once it has been given, and we must say that we have never before heard of such procedure as has been followed by Major Greig and others in connection with the incident.'[26]

Thirty years later, a participant in that 1916 match returned to

the controversy. Greig's insinuations against Pai, and the support
he received from the *Times of India* and the like, suggested D. B.
Deodhar, was

> a serious reflection on the sporting character of the communal
> series. The inborn and dormant prejudice as well as the superi-
> ority complex of the Britishers in India, was clearly brought out
> by this incident which showed that they thought us incompetent
> to get over our communal bias and prejudice.[27]

The superiority complex was manifest in ways large and small.
It was around this time – 1916–17 – that the Bombay Gymkhana
put up a notice during the Quadrangular commanding the Indian
cricketers to wash their hands and faces in a shed outside the pavilion. The reason given was that one or two Muslim players had, the
previous year, been noticed chewing *paan* while washing their hands
and had left behind red marks on the basin. Except for the week of
the cricket carnival the native cricketers were not allowed into the
pavilion anyway. The new notice, remembered one Hindu player,
was 'very insulting', and nearly sparked a boycott of the tournament.
Finally, the Parsi captain Dr H. D. Kanga persuaded the Gymkhana
to withdraw the prohibition.[28]

WRITING IN 1915, a man who had been both Bishop of Calcutta
and Headmaster of Harrow hoped that

> in the coming years games like cricket and football, which have
> long since proved themselves as effectual bonds of sympathy
> between Great Britain and her Colonies, may do much, and
> perhaps even more than any other agency, to unite the governing
> and the governed classes in India by a strong community of
> interest and admiration.[29]

This was the remark of someone who doesn't seem to have watched
any inter-racial cricket in India or, if he did, kept his ears and eyes

firmly shut. Contrast his hopes with this pithy verdict of a Bombay weekly, offered soon after the 1916 Quadrangular: 'Thirty years of cricket in Bombay have done more to infuse racial pettiness in us than anything else.'[30]

Although the parallel would not have occurred to its participants, the 1916 umpiring controversy recalled the famous battle over the Ilbert Bill in 1883. Then, a progressive Viceroy, Lord Ripon, had promoted a bill allowing Indian judges to try Englishmen (Indian defendants, of course, were appearing before English judges all the time). The English community in Calcutta erupted, and their cause was energetically taken up by Tories at home.[31]

Was an Indian qualified to pass fair judgement on an Englishman? Or would he be biased by race or incompetent by culture? By 1916 the Empire's subjects would not so easily accept the slur. Indians had been Senior Wranglers at Cambridge, Fellows of the Royal Society, ranking members of the once white-only Indian Civil Service. An Indian had even won the Nobel Prize for Literature.

1916, the year of the spat between Jungly Greig and M. D. Pai, was also a year of hectic political activity in India. It was in 1916 that Home Rule Leagues were started by Annie Besant and Bal Gangadhar Tilak. Waiting in the wings was Mahatma Gandhi, who had lately returned from South Africa and was searching for the soul of India in its villages, preparatory to moving into politics himself. In some places racial feelings ran high. In October 1916 the *Mahratta* ran a report of an incident where an Englishman had not allowed an educated Indian, a Rao Bahadur no less, into a first-class compartment despite his having a valid ticket. The paper said the rulers were 'seized with Nigger-phobia'. When Europeans 'travel in railways, they seem to imagine that all who are not of their colour or ilk should appear before them on bended knees'.[32]

Greig's refusal to accept the umpire's decision was a product perhaps of a batsman's natural reluctance to depart. But it might have been influenced by these wider trends, and by the fact that a world war was on and he was a Major, bound by his office to uphold the prestige and power of his race. Likewise, Pai's refusal to go back on his verdict was a product of old tensions on the cricket field, but also of newer challenges to the authority of the white man.

The controversy over the stumping was to introduce a revolutionary change in the way in which the game would be adjudicated. Once, both umpires in a Parsi–Presidency match were English. But from the inception of the Triangulars the Europeans had been made to accept at least one native umpire. Now, between the 1916 and 1917 Quadrangulars, the Bombay Gymkhana was forced against its will to accept the idea of 'neutral umpires'. The arbitrators in any Quadrangular match would henceforth come from the two communities not represented on the field of play. Thus, for example, if the Parsis were playing the Europeans, a Hindu and a Muslim umpire would officiate. This, so far as I know, was the first application of the principle in the sphere of cricket. Other international sports, football and basketball and suchlike, have always had referees from countries other than the ones playing. But cricket, until very recently, has relied exclusively on 'home country' umpires. The Bombay Quadrangular stands out as a pioneering exception.

Neutral umpires first made their appearance in the 1917 tournament. Another change was instituted the following year, when the Quadrangular was shifted from September to November/December. In four of its first six years the tournament's final match had to be abandoned due to rain. But winter in Bombay was dry and cool. When the matches themselves were extended to four days each instead of three, one could be reasonably assured of a result.

The rulers won the cricket tournament in 1918, the year they won a more consequential battle on the fields of Europe. German guns and airplanes they could deal with; but now, in their prize colony, they came up against an opponent using weapons altogether foreign to them. In the last years of the war, Gandhi began asserting himself in Indian politics. In the spring and summer of 1917 he organized his first *satyagraha* on Indian soil, on behalf of tenants working on indigo plantations owned by British firms in Bihar. The following winter he mobilized small farmers in Gujarat in a protest against high rates of land revenue. Then, in early 1918, he successfully mediated between striking workers and textile mill-owners in Ahmedabad.[33]

The success of these local struggles encouraged their leader to seek a larger stage. The British gave it to him when, in March 1919, they approved a report authorizing the trial without jury of anyone the Raj deemed to be 'seditious'. Some nationalists sent in petitions of protest against the Rowlatt Act (thus named for the chief author of the report), but Gandhi and his colleagues chose instead to organize strikes in the cities of India. Bombay, Delhi, Lahore and Calcutta were all shut down for days. Then Gandhi was detained while proceeding to the Punjab, and in that province itself two prominent Congressmen were arrested. The movement met a bloody end in an enclosed park in Amritsar, the Jallianwala Bagh, when a British General ordered his troops to fire on a crowd of unarmed demonstrators, killing several hundred.[34]

Gandhi's prestige had soared as a consequence of the Rowlatt *satyagraha*. A striking feature of the protests was the participation of Muslims. Inter-religious unity was furthered by Gandhi's decision to support the *ulema*'s call to protect the position of the Caliph of the Ottomans, who was threatened both by reform-minded Turkish politicians and by European powers. Thus began the so-called Khilafat movement, a series of joint Hindu–Muslim demonstrations between 1919 and 1922, designed to force the full restoration of the Caliphate.[35]

The hectic political developments of these years were to cast a long shadow over the cricket fields of Bombay. The events of 1917–19 had opposed the British on the one side to a common Hindu–Muslim front on the other. What then of the fourth participant in the annual cricket carnival, the Parsis? For the most part, they stayed on the sidelines. Prior to the coming of Gandhi, some Parsi lawyers had been among the most influential leaders of the Congress. But these liberal constitutionalists were uncomfortable with street protest, even if it was non-violent. Other Parsis were openly loyalist, coming together in December 1918 to build a memorial to the departing Governor of Bombay, Lord Willingdon. This proposal was bitterly opposed by Gandhian nationalists as well as by leading Muslim politicians such as Muhammad Ali Jinnah. The flamboyant loyalism of a few Parsis was to raise a broad question mark over the nationalism of the community as a whole.[36]

The Quadrangular of 1919, therefore, was played against a more complicated background than ever before. But it began with an old problem, the question of the Hindu captaincy. As in 1915, the Hindu selectors finessed the question by initially dropping Baloo. The *Bombay Chronicle* promptly labelled this a 'capital blunder'. This time the campaign seems to have been behind the scenes, but it was once again successful. Thus when the Hindus played the Parsis in the carnival's first match, Baloo was on the field. A crowd in excess of 10,000 'loudly cheered [Baloo] for his magnificent performance'. In one afternoon he dismissed the best Parsi batsmen, Kapadia and Vajifdar, and also defied his age by taking a leaping catch, one-handed, at point. To judge by the match report, the forty-four-year-old was bowling at close to his best: 'Baloo was making the ball turn. Sometimes he broke right across the wicket when he pitched on the leg stump. Sometimes he broke just sufficiently to hit the wicket. He could not be depended upon for the amount of breaking he was going to impart . . .'[37]

For the first time, the high schools and colleges of Bombay had morning hours only, to enable their pupils to contribute more fully to 'the cheering and counter cheering for their respective sides [which] make things so lively'. The crowd grew steadily through the match, as the Hindus marched towards their first outright victory over the Parsis. They eventually won by six wickets, a result made possible by Baloo's bowling and the batsmanship of C. K. Nayudu. The winning hit, by the captain, M. D. Pai, was made

> amid a perfect tornado of cheering, and before the two batsmen, Deodhar and Pai, could reach the Gymkhana pavilion, they were surrounded by an immense crowd of Hindu spectators, who shouldered the two men into the pavilion. Even after that, the crowds continued standing in front of the pavilion and calling

cheers for those members of the team who had contributed materially to their side's success. The cheering went on for nearly quarter of an hour, so great was the enthusiasm the great Hindu victory had evoked among their supporters.[38]

The Hindu supporters were over the moon. For they disliked the Parsis for competing with them in the textile trade and in the courts. They despised the Parsis for staying aloof from the recent anti-British protests. Above all, they resented the Parsis for their superior record on the cricket field. This, in twelve years of trying, was the first time the Hindus had defeated their rivals in the Bombay tournament.

Some days later, the PJ Hindu Gymkhana gave an 'At Home' for the victors. The Secretary spoke on behalf of the Gymkhana, and M. D. Pai and Palwankar Baloo replied on behalf of the cricketers. The players were all garlanded, and then joined the fans in listening to a concert by a celebrated singer of Hindusthani music.[39]

There was a match still to be played, against the Muslims, who had defeated the Europeans in the other semi-finals. The Hindus won the final by an innings, with Vithal scoring a century and Shivram and Baloo taking the wickets. On the second day of the match, a dinner was arranged for *both* teams at the Taj Mahal Hotel. And an eventual Hindu victory gave rise to little exultation. In the wake of the Khilafat campaign, Hindus and Muslims were like brothers: never before and – it has to be said – never since were the two communities on such terms of happy amity.

IN THE MONTHS leading up to the 1920 Quadrangular, Mahatma Gandhi began speaking out against the practice of Untouchability. Now the pre-eminent leader of the Congress, he used his enlarged pulpit to return to a theme that had obsessed him since his time in South Africa: the purification of Hinduism. Untouchability was 'a crime against God and humanity', he remarked in May 1920: 'My conscience tells me that Untouchability can never be a part of

Hinduism. I do not think it too much to dedicate my whole life to removing the thick crust of sin with which Hindu society has covered itself for so long by stupidly regarding these people as Untouchables.'[40] A short while later, writing in his journal *Young India*, Gandhi suggested that divine retribution had made Indians the 'pariahs of Empire'. Their subjection to the British, he claimed, was a consequence of their own oppression of the Untouchables. Non-cooperation with the rulers, previously seen as a purely political act, was now being redefined as a 'movement of intensive self-purification'. Upper-caste Hindus, Gandhi thought, 'must realize that if they wish to offer successful non-cooperation against the Government, they must make common cause with the *Panchammas* [Untouchables], even as they have made common cause with the Mussulmans'.[41]

At this stage, Gandhi was a defender of *varnashramadharma*, the division of Hindu society into endogamous castes with their own hereditary specialisms. But he considered the practice of Untouchability to be contrary to *dharma*; it was, he wrote in October 1920, 'an instance of the evil of extremism in Hinduism'.[42] His attack on the institution was to become more radical later on, but even at this stage his criticisms were to attract wide attention. Other Hindus had questioned the practice in the past, but they lacked Gandhi's political standing. When he spoke millions listened, among them a growing number of Hindu cricket fans in Bombay.

This year, as usual, there was a slow and stately build-up to the Quadrangular. The club and office matches were finished off in August and September: now the Gymkhanas took over. In the third week of October the PJ Hindu Gymkhana was playing a two-day match against a visiting side from Rajputana. On the first day news came in of the death of Palwankar Ganpat, of consumption. He was only twenty-seven. Play was abandoned for the day in his memory.[43]

Ganpat's death hit his three brothers hard, but they gamely continued to do what they were best at: playing cricket. The sporting public, Hindu or otherwise, saw in each Palwankar a distinctive combination of character and playing skill. Baloo was the patriarch, heavily built, his hair greying, but at forty-five still a high-class bowler.

Shivram batted doggedly down the order and bowled usefully with the new ball: in the field, he was recognized by the thick sash around his waist. Vithal was by this time the premier Hindu batsman: perhaps he had specialized in that aspect of the game at the prodding of his brothers, who knew that batsmen were cricket's pampered aristocrats. With Baloo and Shivram ageing, it fell to Vithal to uphold the family's honour. He did it with style: as a Parsi journalist recalled, when he batted Vithal always wore a green tweed hat, known to the fan as 'sanssouci'.[44]

The 1920 tournament was scheduled for the first week of December. In mid-November, the *Bombay Chronicle* ran a full-page feature on the preparations of the different teams, their chances and the likely response of the crowd. Frank Tarrant could not play that year for the Europeans, while the Parsis would miss their key fast bowler, J. S. Warden. However, the Muslims had cast their net wide, selecting players from Kashmir, Rajputana, Aligarh and the Punjab. As for the Hindus, the anonymous feature writer tastefully put the case for a long overdue elevation. 'It would not be out of place', he suggested,

> to give expression to the very widespread desire that exists among the Hindu public that the captaincy of the team should at least for once be offered to P. Baloo . . . No Hindu bowler could claim such a distinguished and sustained record of achievement in first-class cricket extending over a large number of years as he. . . . [S]heer justice demands that his long and splendid cricket career should be crowned with the leadership of the Hindu representative team before he finally retires from first-class cricket. He is still a good bowler, but wonderful as his constitution is, age must tell sooner or later, and in a couple of years perhaps international cricket would have seen the last of him. The desire given expression to above is not the result of any doubt as to the capacity of M. D. Pai. . . . Pai has proved himself one of the best captains the Hindus ever had, and he could still be next year's captain. But it would be doing bare justice to the greatest bowler the Hindus ever had if Baloo were offered

the captainship even once. One has not heard that Baloo cherishes the ambition of monopolising the position. He would, from what one hears, be quite content with holding the place for one year and would have no objection to playing under the leadership of anybody in future. In fact he has done this in the past and played under Pai, who in turn should not consider it *infra dig* to play under his great colleague.[45]

A week later the Hindu team was announced, with M. D. Pai as captain. Vithal and Shivram had been included in the eleven, but Baloo was dropped. Ten days still remained until the tournament was due to begin. In this waiting period Pai fell ill and withdrew from the first match, which was against the Muslims. The Hindu selectors now appointed D. B. Deodhar as captain. Deodhar was a fine player but, as it happened, a Brahmin and a batsman. The Gymkhana's decision was a subject of furious controversy amongst its rank-and-file. There 'was much discontent prevailing among the members of the [Hindu] Gymkhana over the repeated exclusion of Mr Baloo', reported one scribe: 'The trend of opinion among the bulk of the members who were present in the Gymkhana in the evening was that Mr Baloo should now be taken in the team and asked to captain it.'[46]

To the Palwankars, already bowed by Ganpat's death and Baloo's exclusion, Deodhar's appointment was a final, brutal blow. For both Vithal and Shivram were at least the equal in talent of the Poona cricketer: and they had been playing for the Hindus for years before he had. As Vithal recalled in his memoirs, when Pai fell ill, 'amongst the players of the team myself and Shivram were the most senior and considering our ability and skill it was our rightful expectation that one of us should have been chosen captain. Many members of the Hindu Gymkhana also expected the same'.[47] In disgust, they decided to stand down from the Hindu team. Their explanation, published in the papers the day the Hindu–Muslim match began, still makes compelling reading:

It need hardly be said [wrote Vithal and Shivram] that the claims of one of us are superior to those of Mr Deodhar, and the [Hindu Selection] Committee's decision can only be characterised as unsportsmanlike in the extreme, inasmuch as they have apparently been influenced by the caste and social and educational status of their selection rather than his achievements or seniority in the field of cricket, and as such the Committee's decision can only be taken as partial with a bias in favour of caste. Social or educational status has no place in sport, when the claims of a cricketer of lesser social status are admittedly superior. In the decision the Committee arrived at, this vital principle of all sport appears to have been lightly passed over, with the result that the claims of one of us have been brushed aside as beneath contempt. This sort of shuffling of claims by the Hindu Selection Committee has compelled us to withdraw from the Hindu Representative Team this year, much against our desire to add our quota to the achievements of the Hindu Cricket Team. In arriving at this decision [not to play] be it remembered that we feel very strongly the covert or overt insult levelled at us as belonging to the so-called depressed class as it amounts to a nullification of our claims for recognition for all time. That such matters as caste should be the determining factor in Cricket is more than we can quietly bow down to, hence our decision to stand down from the Hindu Team this year. The impartial cricket-loving public, we feel sure, will at once understand our position and exonerate us from all blame for the step we have thus deliberately taken as it was on a question of principle and self-respect.[48]

The sentiments were unquestionably their own, although the statement itself might have been drafted by a better-educated member of the impartial cricket-loving public.[49] A small section of this public regarded the withdrawal as a 'revolt against authority', but numerous others approved of the action, believing that as 'self-respecting men [Vithal and Shivram] could not have done otherwise'. Among the strikers' supporters were those who approved of Gandhi's wider struggle against Untouchability. A movement was afoot to collect funds for a purse to be presented to Vithal and Shivram. Contributions were to be sent to 'Mr Govindji Vasanji, the National Confectioner, either at Chira Bazar, Girgaum, or at the Grant Road Terminus'. Five hundred rupees, then a considerable sum, was collected in the first twenty-four hours.[50]

The Hindus won their match against the Muslims. The formidable Parsis were to be encountered next. Hectic parleys now commenced within the PJ Hindu Gymkhana. Their outcome was summarized in a banner headline printed the day the final began: 'PAI CAPTAINING THE TEAM: BALOO BROTHERS PLAYING'. M. D. Pai, now fit, was to captain, and Vithal, Shivram and Baloo were all to play. The decision to reinstate the strikers and to call upon their brother, remarked one journalist, 'though belated, is a sensible one and is undoubtedly a concession to public opinion'. Baloo, wrote the scribe, was at first inclined to reject the call: it was 'on the urgent intervention of friends whose love of Hindu cricket surpasses their love for the Committee and its ways, that Mr Baloo consented to play in today's match'. In fact, the Hindu Selection Committee was suitably conciliatory, as in this letter written by its Secretary, S. A. Shethe:

> Dear Mr Baloo,
>   I understand that you are hesitating to play though selected in the match against Parsis. I shall be obliged if you will kindly reconsider your decision and play. The interest of cricket will appeal to you as in the past.[51]

Honour was restored more fully when Baloo was appointed vice-captain. In what must certainly have been a pre-arranged move, Pai left the field while the Parsis were batting in the second innings. A sympathetic reporter commented on the 'excellent leadership' of Baloo, adding, 'he displayed fine judgement in the management of his side's bowling'.[52] The match itself had a suitably dramatic *dénouement*. The Hindus amassed a score of 428, with C. K. Nayudu scoring a century. They then dismissed the Parsis for 214, and asked them to follow on. Early in the Parsi second innings their captain, Dr H. D.

General view of the match

Cricket in Bombay, as depicted by the London *Graphic*, 10 August 1878. Judging by their clothes, this appears to be a match between Parsis and English soldiers.

The Parsi touring team to England, 1886, the first side of Indian cricketers to make a trip overseas.

Expatriate cricket in the Himalaya, c.1890. The only Indians in the picture appear to be the servants standing on the verandah of the 'pavilion'.

Villagers playing cricket in the Himalaya, c.1894. Note the makeshift bat and stumps, fashioned out of some nearby tree.

Palwankar Baloo, photographed by a fellow cricketer, c.1904. Baloo, an Untouchable who bowled left-arm spin, was arguably the first great cricketer produced by India, and also a great hero and role model among the low castes.

Famous Palvankar Brotherhood

P. Baloo

P. Shivram

P. Vithal 1910.

P. Ganpat.

The Palwankar brothers, from a magazine published at the time of the Bombay Quadrangular Tournament of 1929. 'Did ever a family establish such a record?', asked one chronicler. His answer: 'Nowhere else does the history of cricket supply such a glorious page . . . One brother after another raising the Hindu cricket edifice higher and higher, spreading its brilliance all over India and beyond'.

C. K. Nayudu outside the London Zoo, 1930, with two Indore friends and the zookeeper. Nayudu towers above his colleagues, as he towered above other Indian cricketers who played with or against him. One of the Indore men asked whether the lion cubs would bite, and the keeper answered: 'No, but they might piss on you.' Nayudu seems unfazed by either possibility.

STUDY YOUR BATTING AVERAGE
with one of these Bats and Balls.

CRICKET Bat construction is an art, which requires expert workmanship, machinery and materials of the finest quality to produce bats of perfection.

We have these three essentials *plus* the advantage of an English Expert in Cricket.

OUR OWN MAKE BATS

The Buffering
Rs. 15, 18, 25 and 30 each.

The Perfecta	Rs. 20-0
The Resista	„ 18-0
The Tropical	„ 16-0
The Oriental	„ 13-0
The Madras Special	„ 8-0
The Practice No. 1	„ 5-8
The Practice „ 2	„ 4-8

ENGLISH CRICKET BATS.

GUNN AND MOOR'S

Nonjar, Cannon Selected, Specially selected Autograh, Extra Special and Star, prices **Rs. 16 to 33 each.**

GUNNER BROWN'S

J. B. Hobb's selection X, XX, XXX and XXXX. **Rs. 20 to 31 each.**

Rapid Scorer (Gradidges oiled in England). **Rs. 25 each.**

We also stock Wisdon's Cricket Bats.

CRICKET BALLS.

THE Perfecta Cricket Ball is made after the same principle as the best Western makes, the Leather is dyed through. Guaranteed for shape, weight and size ... **Rs. 5 0**

The Togo, another very good ball	...	„ 4 0
The Pokoo, second to Togo ...	...	„ 3 8
The Oriental—The most popular ball in India, can be used for matches as well as practice		„ 2 8
The Rangroot Cricket Ball ...	...	„ 2 4
The Special Practice Ball ...	...	„ 2 0
The Popular	...	„ 1 12

Please consult us for your requirements. You will find us cheaper and better.

Telephone : 2734.

Head Office : SIALKOT.

Uberoi LIMITED.

22, MOUNT ROAD, MADRAS.

Factories: SIALKOT.

Largest Manufacturers of Sports Goods in the East.

An advertisement for cricket bats and balls made and sold in India, 1932. Sialkot, now in Pakistan, remains an important manufacturing centre for cricket equipment.

Kanga, was injured and taken to hospital. The ninth Parsi wicket fell after lunch on the final day, and, assuming their side had won, the Hindu fans streamed onto the ground with garlands. As they reached the pitch the umpire drew their attention to Dr Kanga, who was slowly emerging from the pavilion, a runner alongside him. The crowd reluctantly withdrew to the boundary's edge, where they stayed for the next two hours as the last wicket pair of Kanga and Elavia played out time to draw the match.[53]

THE STRUGGLE OVER the Hindu captaincy anticipated, by nearly forty years, the campaign to have a black man chosen as captain of the West Indies cricket team. The West Indies played its first Test matches in 1928; for the next three decades it was axiomatic that a white man, and a white man alone, could be the team's captain. Such remarkable cricketers as Learie Constantine and George Headley had to be content with being 'led' by fair-skinned sportsmen of demonstrably inferior skill. In his playing days Constantine had protested against this discrimination. He continued to speak out after he retired, joined by such men as the great historian and revolutionary C. L. R. James. It was James who was in the forefront of the campaign which, in 1960, resulted in Frank Worrell's appointment as the first black captain of the West Indies.[54]

The career of Palwankar Baloo also anticipated, by half a century and more, the much-memorialized breakthrough into major league baseball of Jackie Robinson. Only in 1947 would the American public accept racially mixed teams in sport: but already, in 1896–7, the Hindus of Poona and Bombay were made to accept an Untouchable cricketer. Like Robinson after him, Baloo broke through a previously impenetrable social barrier as much by force of personality as by sporting skill alone.

Modern sport has been steeped in social discrimination. Think of Jim Thorpe in 1912, whose medals were taken away from him because the men who organized the Olympics could not abide the idea of a Native American winner. Or of Jesse Owens, whose four gold medals in the 1936 Berlin Olympics were all won in front of a hostile crowd of Nazis, the Führer included. Today, a similarly successful American athlete would, on return, be taken straight to the White House, the audience with the President to be followed by rewarding meetings with Ted Turner and Bill Gates. But in the racially divided thirties, Owens's extraordinary achievements were ignored by the press, the white public and the politicians. No job was forthcoming: indeed, the returning hero was reduced to racing against horses for a living.

The most awful stories of discrimination in sport come from apartheid-ruled South Africa. Cricket historians know of Dik Abed, the gifted Cape Coloured who could not play for his country, and of Basil D'Olivera, who emigrated in time to become a citizen of England and an England cricketer. My own favourite – if that is the word – story concerns the great golfer Sewsunker Sewgolum. An Indian South African from a poor family, Sewgolum was a one-time caddie who played with a unique grip, left hand below right. After years of trying, he was finally allowed to join the professional circuit. One of his first triumphs was in the 1963 Natal Open. The award ceremony was to be held on the eighteenth green, but just before it began the skies opened. The function was hastily shifted indoors, to the clubhouse. The problem was that by the rules of the day no dogs or coloured men were allowed into the building. With imperial disregard, the organizers held the ceremony anyway, *without* the star participant. The speeches were made and the lesser prizes given away to the white golfers who had earned them. Sewgolum stood wet and shivering outside, waiting for a club flunkey to deliver to him his own medal and cheque.[55]

The battles fought by Owens, Robinson, Worrell and Sewgolum were fought before them by a now unknown but truly heroic family of Indian low-caste cricketers. From 1895, when Baloo first began playing competitive cricket, the Palwankar brothers had struggled to be included in mixed teams, struggled to be served tea and cakes in the cups and plates used by their fellows, struggled to be rewarded with the leadership status their achievements had called for. The 1920 Quadrangular was their most substantial social victory to date. In the wake of Gandhi's movement, the cricket-loving public had generously supported the revolt of Vithal and Shivram. Following the revolt they had been honourably reinstated, and so had their revered elder brother. The Hindu reactionaries were forced to retreat, while a sympathetic Brahman, M. D. Pai, had conspired to allow an Untouchable to lead, if only part of the time, a multi-caste cricket team. The next chapter takes up the struggle's final phase, the full-time subversion on the cricket field of the ancient and divinely sanctioned hierarchy of caste.

8. Vithal's Triumph

A BENGALI HISTORIAN once complained that had Mahatma Gandhi not assumed control of the Indian national movement, football rather than cricket would have become the country's national sport. The shorter game was popular in Calcutta, the city which witnessed the first major protests against British rule. But the Mahatma decisively moved the centre of politics from Bengal to western India, where cricket dominated. This shift in political power, the Bengali argued, also led to a shift in cultural influence. Hence cricket became India's most avidly patronized sport.[1]

Did Gandhi ever play or watch cricket himself? The biographies that I have read do not mention the game, indeed any game. A cricketer does, however, figure fleetingly in his autobiography. When Gandhi first went to England as a student, in 1889, one of the three letters of introduction he carried was to his fellow Kathiawari, Prince Ranjitsinhji.[2] We do not know whether they met. In any case, it was only after Gandhi left London, in 1891, that Ranji moved to Cambridge to make his name on its playing fields.

The only evidence of a Gandhian interest in cricket that I know of is contained in a newspaper essay of 1958 by the Gujarati journalist Harish Booch. Booch had just met one of the Mahatma's classmates at Alfred High School, Rajkot. This man, Ratilal Ghelabhai Mehta, remembered Gandhi as 'a dashing cricketer' who 'evinced a keen interest in the game as a school student'. He was, it seems, 'good both at batting and bowling', and had an uncanny understanding of the game's uncertainties as well. Mehta spoke of a match they had watched together as schoolboys, played between Rajkot city and

Rajkot cantonment. Apparently, 'at a crucial moment in the match, as if through intuition, Gandhiji said a particular player would be out and hey presto, that batsman was really out!'[3]

These recollections were offered ten years after the death of Gandhi, more than seventy years after the event he predicted, and to a journalist hungry for a new angle to a ruthlessly written about figure. Both interviewer and interviewee were, it appears, a trifle apologetic about the revelations. After Mehta had praised Gandhi's skill at batting and bowling, he added: '*Though* he had an aversion for physical exercise at school, as he pointed out in his autobiography'.[4]

Cricket might not have affected Gandhi, but Gandhi certainly affected cricket. He never watched Baloo bowl or Vithal bat, but his campaign against Untouchability emboldened the Palwankars and their followers to fight more openly for their rights. They were encouraged further when, immediately after the 1920 Quadrangular, Gandhi insisted that 'the Hindus owe it as a duty to make a determined effort to purify Hinduism and eradicate this practice of untouchability. I have said to the Hindus, and say it again today, that till Hindu society is purged of this sin, *swaraj* [freedom] is an impossibility.'[5]

These remarks come from a speech made at Nagpur on 25 December. The following day, the annual session of the Congress commenced in the city. The Nagpur meeting witnessed a bitter battle between liberal constitutionalists who urged moderation and radical agitators who wished to launch a countrywide movement of 'non-cooperation'. Already, in the summer of 1920, Gandhi had launched a boycott of the colonial courts. He now wished to extend this to the 'renunciation of [all] voluntary association with the Government'. His supporters included his Khilafat colleagues, the brothers Muhammad and Shaukat Ali. His opponents in Nagpur included Chittaranjan Das, from Bengal, and Muhammad Ali Jinnah, from Bombay. Crucially, the vast majority of the 14,000 delegates were for non-cooperation. So enamoured were they of their leader that they shouted down his rival Jinnah, their screams and taunts chasing him away from the podium and from the Congress itself.[6]

After Nagpur social reform took a back seat to politics. Gandhi had promised *swaraj* in one year, and for the first quarter of 1921 it seemed a likely possibility. Schools and colleges run by the Government were bereft of students. The working class was on strike in many towns and cities: according to official figures, there were 396 strikes in 1921, involving 600,000 workers and a loss of 7 million workdays. Peasants in Gujarat stopped paying taxes: so did peasants in the United Provinces. Hill tribes in northern Andhra violated the forest laws. Merchants in coastal Sind downed shutters for weeks on end. The protests transcended the bounds of class and locality. Meanwhile, the union of non-cooperation and Khilafat promoted an unprecedented fraternization between Hindus and Muslims. Orthodox Brahmin families asked *mullahs* to dine in their homes. Muslim women in purdah invited Gandhi to address them. The 'climax was reached when Muslims refrained not only from eating beef, but even from sacrificing cows on the sacred day of Id'.[7]

Then, in August, a rebellion broke out in Malabar, where long-victimized Muslim tenants rose against Hindu landlords and the colonial state which protected them. Offices and telegraph stations were burnt, some landlords killed and some others forcibly converted. Several *taluks* passed out of governmental control into the hands of newly formed 'Khilafat Republics'. Marxists viewed the uprising as a lower-class revolt against the elites. But Gandhi sensed that in the popular mind the clash might get cast in religious terms. He was in Sylhet when the Moplahs rose, and quickly took a train across India to Malabar. The Army, which had got there before him, would not let Gandhi enter the affected areas. Nonetheless, in his speeches and writings he urged the promotion of 'Hindu–Muslim unity at all hazards'.[8]

In the midst of all this, the Prince of Wales had planned a Royal Tour of India. He was due to arrive in Bombay on 17 November and travel around the country, accepting addresses and making speeches. One of the early events on the programme was the Bombay Quadrangular. In any case, the Governor graced the cricket carnival each year. The Prince's presence, the organizers thought, would give the tournament a more elevated stamp still.

After this proposal was made public a torrent of letters descended on the offices of the *Bombay Chronicle*.[9] When the Ali brothers were in jail, wrote a man styling himself 'Earnest Non-Cooperator', when a holy Shankaracharya was behind bars, when women were being harassed in the Punjab, above all when the great Mahatma had called for a boycott of the Prince's visit, he would 'appeal to all the players – Hindu, Mahommedans and Parsis – to think twice before taking part in this match'. 'Earnest Non-Cooperator' hoped the public would follow them: 'Taking into consideration all that is going on in our country I think everybody should think to keep himself aloof from the "Tamasha".'

A Muslim patriot agreed that 'this is certainly not the time to take part in merriment'. He requested his 'Muslim brothers to retire from this year's matches', for the 'Hindu and Parsi players to follow their example', and for the spectators also to 'refrain from visiting these matches'. A Parsi journalist wrote to complain of the decision of community elders to present a welcome address to the Prince of Wales, this 'notwithstanding the dissentient note rightly struck by some thousands of Parsis'.

These ordinary folks were joined by L. R. Tairsee, a textile mill-owner and office-bearing Congressman who was Vice-President of the PJ Hindu Gymkhana. Tairsee asked the cricket fan to boycott the Quadrangular and to send the money thus saved to the Congress Committee's Malabar Relief Fund. This would be 'killing two birds with one stone'. Among the first to send in his ticket money was the confectioner Govindji Vassanji, who the previous year had organized a public fund for Vithal and Shivram.

Some nationalists were convinced that the Prince of Wales's visit was deliberately made to coincide with the Quadrangular. 'Where else', asked Manilal Vadilal, 'can those Loyalists get an Indian crowd twenty thousand strong to cheer the Prince, and make a show that he is enthusiastically received?' To go to the cricket was to play into the hands of the Loyalists. At this 'critical stage' of the freedom struggle, said Vadilal, it did not become the patriot to 'spend our time and energy after such games'.

The boycott was, however, opposed by the sports correspondent of the *Chronicle*, known to us only as 'Onlooker'. He professed sympathy with the sorrows of the nationalists, but 'as a true lover of sport' trusted 'the authorities concerned will not make the big blunder of abandoning the tournament. Politics have hitherto not been introduced into the field of play in any country, and I hope for the good name of Indian sport that it will not be introduced now.' Relations between England and Ireland, 'Onlooker' pointed out, were by no means ideal, yet they played football against one another. In any case, the Prince of Wales was to watch only one afternoon of the Quadrangular. Why was it necessary to boycott the entire tournament?

Here was a classic preview of later controversies: over cricket visits to apartheid-ruled South Africa, for example, or the boycott of the Moscow Olympics after the Soviets had invaded Afghanistan. Is sport a vehicle for politics, indeed, is it not irremediably political? Yes, said 'Earnest Non-Cooperator' in 1921, and President Jimmy Carter in 1980. Or is sport above and beyond politics? Yes, said 'Onlooker', yes, said the sponsors of rebel tours to South Africa, and yes, said the British athletes who defied the Americans to go and run in Moscow.

In 1921, despite the excitement of non-cooperation and the Prince's visit, the cricketing public had not wholly forgotten the Palwankars. On 12 November, days before the tournament began, the *Chronicle* printed a letter asking why M. D. Pai had once more been appointed captain ahead of one of the brothers. A controversy was averted when the Maharaja of Patiala expressed a desire to play for the Hindus, encouraged, one suspects, by the hope of a handshake with the Prince of Wales. And if Patiala played he had, of course, to be made captain.

When the matches commenced dozens of fans stayed away, sending their ticket money to the Malabar Fund instead. But other fans filled their place. An added attraction this year was the presence of three great English cricketers: Wilfred Rhodes, George Hirst and

C. B. Fry. The Yorkshire duo had come to India to coach, while Fry had come to party and shoot with his friend Ranji. Their participation in the Quadrangular was eagerly canvassed for by the Bombay Gymkhana. In the first match, the Yorkshiremen vanquished the Hindus almost by themselves. While Hirst took seven wickets, Rhodes claimed eight, and also scored a masterful 156 as his side won by an innings and plenty. One of the fielders marvelled at the sure defence and precise placement of Rhodes's strokes: batting of this quality, he remarked, had not been seen in India before.[10]

The Hindu–European match ended on 16 November. The following day the Prince of Wales arrived in Bombay. A black flag demonstration was successfully kept away by the police, but the frustration at not having shown the flags found expression elsewhere. That night a large portion of the city was in darkness, as street lamps had been smashed by protesters. Police clashed with people in Gandhi caps and *khadi* coats. Striking mill-hands pitched in on behalf of the Congress volunteers. The rioting continued, non-stop, for three days. Indian turned against Indian, non-cooperator against cooperator, Hindus and Muslims on one side versus Parsis, Jews and Christians on the other.[11]

Gandhi was in Bombay, en route to Bardoli, in Gujarat, to flag off a no-tax *satyagraha*. He saw little of the violence, but reports reached him of the destruction of property and the attacks on cooperators. Disgusted, he issued a statement saying that the 'reputation of Bombay, the hope of my dreams, was being stained'. He suspended civil disobedience, and announced that in penitence he would fast for twenty-four hours every week.[12]

While the rioting was in full flow the Prince of Wales had escaped to Poona. But peace was restored, and the Prince returned. Remarkably, while the rioting was on, the Parsis had played and defeated the Muslims. On the 21st they lined up again to play the Europeans in the Quadrangular final. About 10,000 spectators were present when the Prince of Wales arrived at the ground. He was met by the Governor and the President of the Bombay Gymkhana. He watched play for about fifteen minutes and then came down to have tea with the players. He was also introduced to the Presidents and Secretaries of the four Gymkhanas. After tea the Prince went into the field, faced a few balls from the Parsi bowler J. S. Warden, and departed. His Royal Highness, reported the *Bombay Chronicle*, 'received a great ovation, the spectators being particularly enthusiastic when he got to the field of play'.[13]

Appositely, the Europeans won the final, again by an innings. Rhodes, Fry and Hirst made the runs, and Rhodes and Hirst took the wickets. Imperial honour had been shaken, but in the end restored. Before the tournament began, there had been intimations of a 'demonstration against the Prince from various tents which may spread to the audience on the Maidan'.[14] This might yet have happened, had the Hindus been playing the final, when the tents would have been packed with their supporters.

IN FEBRUARY 1922 a police station in a small northern village was torched by the non-cooperators. Twenty-two constables were burnt alive. Gandhi immediately called off the movement. A suspicious Government arrested him nonetheless. The Mahatma was sent to Yeravada jail, near Puné. It was in that city – known to the English as Poona – that the 1922 Quadrangular was played. For this reason perhaps the *Bombay Chronicle*'s coverage was disappointingly brief. But three weeks before the matches began it suggested that 'P. Baloo stands every chance of being the captain of the Hindoo team in view of his sound and thorough experience extending to many years of cricket tournaments.' Since Vithal and Shivram were also in fine form, the paper thought 'that the Hindoo team this year will be as strong as any participating in the Quadrangular'.[15]

The captain and players were to be chosen by the local sponsors, the Poona Hindu Gymkhana. The city was a conservative one, and its Hindus, by and large, never had time for Gandhi. Unlike the members of the PJ Hindu Gymkhana, the Brahmins of Poona were not convinced that Untouchability was altogether a bad thing. The

Poona Hindus chose S. M. Dalvi as captain, and Vithal and Shivram went on strike again. The Hindus won their first match, narrowly, and had now to play the Parsis in the final. A compromise was attempted, whereby M. D. Pai would be appointed captain and Vithal and Shivram would agree to return. But Pai refused to play ball, and the brothers stuck to their guns. A complete nonentity, Dr Prabhakar, was asked to lead the Hindus. The Parsis, by contrast, were at full strength. Expectedly they won by a handsome margin.[16]

The press comment on the Hindu defeat was curious. Before the final the *Chronicle* said that the 'Hindu team will hardly be representative without a trio [the Baloo brothers] whom everybody will miss'. Afterwards it suggested that if the defeat 'will only serve to shed more light on this *faux pas*, real or imaginary, the moral which distills out of this year's tournament will have been sufficiently emphasized'.[17] The *Mahratta* of Poona appears to have drawn a different moral from disunity and defeat. 'We do not know what exactly was the apple of discord', it remarked,

> but it is more than probable that it must have been the captainship . . . [We] do not mean to put one caste against one another, but our idea is that the healthy spirit of rivalry kindled by such inter-communal games must be maintained at a high level. We congratulate the Parsis on their deserved success and wish that the Hindus will make up their deficiency and will not allow their private grudges to hamper their efficiency.[18]

This, to me, reads like a back-handed criticism of Vithal and Shivram. The *Mahratta* wanted them to suppress their 'private' grudges in the interests of the community. Someone who saw the Hindu failure in a different light was the radical playwright B. V. ('Mama') Varerkar. The sidelining of Vithal and Shivram in the 1922 Quadrangular inspired him to write a remarkable play on the bloody intersection where the politics of cricket met the politics of caste. Entitled *Turungachya Darat (At the Gate of a Prison)*, the play was written in the weeks following the Quadrangular, and first peformed at the New Imperial Theatre in Bombay on 1 February 1923.

Described as a 'staunch Congressman with leftist sympathies', 'Mama' Varerkar had no university education and prided himself on this. He worked in the Postal Service but was dismissed after organizing a union of its workers. Then he turned his hand to writing plays. He was, noted one literary historian, 'very severe against Poona writers and particularly against what he calls the *Kesari* clique' (the *Kesari* being a sister paper of the *Mahratta*).[19]

Varerkar's play *Turungachya Darat* has three acts: the first is set in Puné two weeks before the 1922 Quadrangular; the second in Bombay while the finals between the Hindus and the Parsis were being played in Poona; the third, also in Bombay, the day after the Hindus' ignominious defeat. The characters are clearly divided on how they perceive the stranglehold of caste. The hero is a progressive Brahmin named Sanjeev, who is heir to a banking fortune. Until he turns twenty-one, the fortune is held in a trust handled by his deceased father's friend, Sarjerao, a duplicitous Maratha from Poona who is President of a depressed classes mission but nevertheless practises Untouchability at home; and by Chamarz, the manager of the bank, who was born a Chamaar but was taken to England as a servant and assumed an Englishman's accent and appearance. A Chamaar who appears as himself is Santu, the maker of Sanjeev's shoes.

The central female character is Johara, a great classical singer and courtesan. Her caste is unknown; as she says, she is above caste and has relations with Hindus of all castes. Sanjeev, who is married to a Brahmin girl named Sudha, learns music from Johara without seeking her sexual favours. The third female character in the play is a young singer from the untouchable Mahar caste, Jini, who is adopted by Johara.

In the play's first act, Sarjerao and Chamarz come to Sanjeev's house while Johara is teaching him music; as they linger, Santu is invited by Sanjeev into the living-room to deliver a pair of chappals. The trustee and the manager express their displeasure at the presence of the two outcastes, whereupon Sanjeev says he cannot stay in conservative Poona, but will move to Bombay.

The second act takes place in Johara's new Bombay home; she

has moved to this city with Sanjeev, as, at her suggestion, has Santu. Set up by a loan from the courtesan, the cobbler addresses Johara: 'Madam, how can I thank you? You showed me a new world by asking me to leave Puné for Bombay. In Bombay no one thinks twice about stepping into my shop. But in Puné: . . . it's better not to talk about Puné.'

Then Sanjeev and Sudha walk in. The young heir asks his wife to do *namaste* to the cobbler; she hesitates. Johara is provoked to tell the story of how the saint Ramakrishna Paramhansa cleaned the latrine of a sweeper (*bhangi*) to rid himself of caste prejudice. She speaks next of Mahatma Gandhi's adoption of a Mahar girl. His wife Kasturba at first objected, but now fed the girl with her own hand. Santu then adds an exemplary story of his own. One year, during the great Ganapati festival in Poona, the cobbler had made an idol of the elephant god and was proceeding to immerse it ritually in the water. But when he joined the procession he hesitated, wondering how his *ganesha* could go in with all the Brahmin *ganeshas*. Then, he recalled, a man with a red turban who looked like the deity of Pandharpur gently took his idol and set it alongside the *ganesha* representing the famous Brahmin locality, Vinchurkarwada. This Good Samaritan, said Santu, was none other than the *lokmanya*, Bal Gangadhar Tilak. But now Tilak was dead, and Untouchability had returned in full force to his city. Poona, once a house for Santu, had become a prison, its Hindu prisoners captive to their prejudices. Hence the cobbler had to move to Bombay.

The next visitors to Johara's home are Sarjerao and Chamarz. They have come to ask her to sing at a function to celebrate Sanjeev's twenty-first birthday, when he will also at last be able to take over his father's bank. It is here that Santu recognizes Chamarz as his long-lost younger brother, and tells him so. We also see Sarjerao coming round to more modern views, as when he touches Jini, the Mahar girl.

The final act takes place the day after the Hindu cricketers had lost to the Parsis in Poona. In Sanjeev's new Bombay bungalow, a grand party is in progress to celebrate his coming of age. The guests include Parsis and Muslims and Hindus of all castes. Here the 'white man' Chamarz publicly admits he is a Chamaar, to the acclaim especially of his brother Santu, who says that only when men of depressed castes become leaders in their own right can one say that society has reformed itself. In a general declaration against social prejudice, the caste-specific dresses of those present are exchanged in favour of that pan-Indian dress acceptable to all, *khadi.*

In the play's last scene, Chamarz reverts to his original name: Janu Nagu Chambhar.[20] He asks his new boss, Sanjeev: 'Will you accept a bank manager with this name?' Sanjeev answers: 'I like this name better than any other for my manager. Yesterday we made the very serious mistake of leaving out Vithal and Shivram Chambhar and lost in the Quadrangular cricket tournament. I do not want to lose in the battleground of life by leaving you out.'[21]

'MAMA' VARERKAR's play is structured around two central oppositions: the reform-minded Hindus versus the reactionary ones, and the catholic, open-minded city of Bombay versus the prison that was Poona. But like a good Gandhian, he held out possibilities of a change of heart. Sarjerao and Chamarz came clean in the end. And even the history of Poona allowed for exceptional periods, as when Tilak and his ilk were in the forefront of its political life.

Varerkar was inspired by the cricket field to make a more general statement on behalf of social reform. I do not know how his play was received, but it might very well have played a part in what was to follow. For at the next Annual General Meeting of the PJ Hindu Gymkhana, a vote of censure was passed against the selectors of the previous year's team. When the tournament came back to Bombay, in 1923, they set against the claims of tradition the call of the Mahatma, and the fact that in both 1921 and 1922 their team had lost heavily. Now the management of Hindu cricket in Bombay was dominated by *banias,* or merchants, who were perhaps more pragmatic and certainly less ideological than the Poona Brahmans.

Crucially, for the case in hand, Gandhi was himself a *bania*. The concerns of the members reached the selectors, who appointed P. Vithal as captain.[22]

A ten-year campaign on behalf of the Chamaar cricketers had finally succeeded. How would the new captain do? In the early matches the Hindus defeated the Muslims by an innings, while the Europeans prevailed over the Parsis. The rulers this year did not have Rhodes and Hirst, but were pretty strong all the same. They batted first, and sent the Hindus on a leather hunt. 'It was a marvel to many', wrote one reporter, 'that the Presidency were able to pile up runs like apples against the bowling which played such a great havoc on the Mahommedan only last week.' The Hindu team were irritable, and showed it. Their main bowler, S. M. Joshi, complained that he was being unfairly no-balled by the Muslim umpire. A friendly critic concurred: this umpire, he said, 'seemed to have left his glasses at home and gave himself up to absurd rulings'.[23]

The Europeans posted an impressive total of 481. The Hindu reply was built around a composed and assured hundred by captain Vithal. With Deodhar and Nayudu also scoring half-centuries they reached 475 all out. Three full days of cricket had passed, watched by a large and appreciative crowd. 'Every inch of space was occupied and the crowd at the tree end was at least ten deep. Every pavilion was full and hundreds were watching the game from house-tops, while some were perched on trees.' During the partnership between Vithal and Nayudu, wrote one reporter, the crowd clapped so much that the sound 'was similar to the sound of sea-waves dashing to the floor'. The captain's century brought forth a surge of 'maddening joy'.[24]

At the conclusion of the Hindu first innings only one day's play remained. The European captain, Travers, now suggested that since a result was impossible they might as well call it a draw. Vithal answered that since 20,000 fans had come to watch the match they must play it out. The Europeans went in again, and this time found S. M. Joshi on his best form. As he handed him the ball, Vithal told Joshi, in Marathi, that it was time to 'start Bhairavi'. The bowler was a fine classical singer, and Bhairavi is the last *raga* sung or played in a concert. Thus inspired, Joshi took 7 for 39 as the Europeans crumbled to 153 all out.[25]

From Vithal's description, Joshi appears to have been a right-handed Baloo. He took but four or five steps, recalled his captain, and 'the ball would reach the batsman slowly'. But 'as soon as it pitched, it would rise suddenly towards the stumps in such a way that even an expert and skilled batsman would get confused'. He turned the ball both ways, and bowled a well-disguised googly to boot. Like Baloo, he required 'an alert and quick wicket-keeper as well as an attentive and diligent fielder at long off or long on'.[26]

After S. M. Joshi's magnificent spell of bowling the Hindus required 162 runs to win. Two hours of play remained. Now Vithal played another master-stroke. Instead of the wicket-keeper–batsman J. G. Navle, a careful and orthodox player, he sent in the big-hitting C. K. Nayudu to open with K. G. Pardeshi. Nayudu smashed the bowling all over the park, and outside it. One six landed on the Bombay Gymkhana pavilion, another on the Waudby Road. Pardeshi also scored at a brisk pace. When Nayudu was dismissed 20 runs were left to get. The captain promoted himself, and hit three slashing boundaries as the Hindus won in a canter.[27]

In his memoirs, Vithal wrote that he would 'never forget the moment' when he hit the winning run. As the ball crossed the boundary,

> groups of spectators one after another jumped up from the tents and ran towards the wicket. A few among them carried both of us (Pardeshi and myself) on their shoulders to the pavilion, shouting joyously. On reaching the pavilion everyone rushed to shake hands with me. Many European ladies congratulated me saying 'O Vithal, well played, congratulations, Vithal'. The reason for these congratulations (as I came to know afterwards) was that they had taken a bet on the result of the match and had won against their own menfolk.[28]

This description is confirmed by the *Bombay Chronicle* report, which speaks of how 'at the end of the game a seething mass of humanity invaded the pavilion and expended their enthusiasm and exuberance of hilarity near the players'. Three thousand rupees were immediately subscribed for a Prize Fund. The donors, in these last days of the Khilafat movement, included Hindus as well as Muslims.

An editorial on the tournament in the *Chronicle* noted that

> the success of the Hindu team was largely due to the confidence which its captain inspired. The heartiest congratulations of all lovers of cricket are due to him and to his team and no less to the Hindu Selection Committee which did not allow a pernicious caste prejudice to come in the way of selecting the right man to lead the team.

The same issue contained the same sentiments expressed more evocatively by a letter-writer. 'The Hindus' brilliant victory', said Vijayashram, was

> due more to the judicious and bold step of the Hindu Gymkhana in appointing Mr Vithal, brother of Mr Baloo – premier bowler of India – who is a member of the Untouchable Class to captain the Hindu team. The moral that can be safely drawn from the Hindus' magnificent victory is that removal of Untouchability would lead to *swaraj* – which is the prophecy of the Mahatma.[29]

Vijayashram's letter carried the heading 'Hindus' Brilliant Victory and its Moral'. Three days later the paper printed a letter by P. R. Lele entitled 'Vithal's Victory'. The Quadrangular final, said Lele, while exciting and surprising in itself, also had 'a special interest attached to it from the Indian National point of view'. For *swaraj* would not come until the curse of Untouchability remained. The sporting sphere had been heavily tainted by prejudice, wrote Lele: 'The untouchable communities have supplied the best cricketers during the last eighteen years but not one year was an untouchable raised to the dignity of captainship of the Hindu team . . .' This year, at last, the prejudice was challenged, and the Untouchable captain responded by leading from the front. Vithal's victory, the letter-writer suggested, was moral and political rather than purely cricketing. 'The happiest event', he said, 'the most agreeable upshot of the set of matches was the carrying of Captain Vithal on the shoulders of Hindus belonging to the so-called higher castes. Hurrah! Captain Vithal! Hurrah! Hindus who forget caste prejudice! Mahatma Gandhi Maharaj ki jai!'[30]

Was Gandhi following all this? The *Bombay Chronicle* reached him every day, for the British jailors in Yeravada were, as jailors go, generous and decent people. Did he read the sports pages? Not normally, but in this case one of his cricket-minded followers might have alerted him to Vithal's victory. The *Collected Works of Mahatma Gandhi*, alas, are silent on this score. One wishes even more that we knew how the other Palwankars felt. Shivram, in fact, also played in the match, his last Quadrangular appearance. Baloo would have watched his brothers play and, at the end, basked in the fragrance of a victory that he had so long struggled for. Also in the crowd, perhaps, was the author of *Turungachya Darat*. That would have been apposite in more ways than one, for 'Mama' Varerkar's own middle name was 'Vithal'.

THE MOST CURIOUS REACTION to the 1923 Quadrangular was that of an English visitor to the city. Seeing the shouts and celebrations, he drew a conclusion designed only to comfort himself. The game of cricket, he remarked,

> has been the means of educating the youth of Bombay, of keeping the boys out of mischief, of helping the people to lead healthy lives, of narrowing the prejudices which existed between one community and another. The players have gradually become English in their habits; they wear the usual cricket flannels casting aside the loose flowing dhotee and the highly coloured shirt, different communities sit at the same tiffin table, enjoy

the same food, talk in cricket language – and cricket has taught all that.[31]

The traveller saw what he wished to see. But sport, as *we* have seen, did not so much promote *communitas* as act as a conduit for politics. Previous Quadrangulars had foregrounded the antagonisms of race and caste. In 1924 the question of religion raised its head for the first time. In its search for outstation talent, the PJ Hindu Gymkhana extended an invitation to P. A. Kanickam, a Tamil from Bangalore who was hitting hundreds and double hundreds in local cricket. Then they discovered that he was in fact a Christian, and withdrew the invitation. The *Times of India* gleefully reproduced a comment from the *Daily Post* of Bangalore, which spoke of how Kanickam's fellow townsmen 'rejoiced' at the invitation from Bombay and later 'grieved' at its withdrawal. The *Times* now added a gloss of its own:

> It is of course no part of our business to presume to interfere in such a matter, yet we should have supposed that having been born a Hindu, Kanickam's religious convictions would have been immaterial. In picking a European side, a man's religious creed would most certainly not influence any Selection Committee. If the obstacle is insuperable we can but say that it is a great pity and we offer our sympathies. We can only echo the sentiments of our Bangalore contemporary, and we hope yet to see Kanickam playing on a Bombay cricket field. When he does, you may be sure of a reception all the more enthusiastic, because his religious convictions have barred him from his communal team.[32]

This was both pompous and hypocritical. The European Selection Committee would not care whether a man was Protestant or Catholic, but they certainly knew the difference between white and brown. An Indian Christian, even if baptized at birth, would not have been allowed to enter the club, still less play for its team. Hindu caste prejudice found its own mirror reflection in the racial intolerance of the British.

P. A. Kanickam could not come, but the show would go on. In a two-column article on Quadrangular prospects, the *Bombay Chronicle* lavishly praised last year's hero. Vithal was 'perhaps the best Indian bat today. It is a treat to watch him drive the bowlers all round the wicket – especially on the off side. He is also a sure field almost everywhere but a marvel on the cover point.' It then moved on to the Muslims, whose Selection Committee was 'trying its hardest to efface the memory of last year's [innings] defeat against the Hindus. It has requisitioned a large number of old and new talents from up-country.'[33]

The Islam Gymkhana had invited twenty-seven men for their trials: seven from Bombay, the rest from Aligarh, Bhopal, Kashmir, Karachi, Hyderabad, Rajputana and the Punjab. A Muslim fan commended the Gymkhana for the initiative, but urged that the Selection Committee 'should make up its mind in selecting a real Captain for their team because a good captain is almost half the strength of the Eleven'.[34]

The Muslim captain, Abdus Salaam of Aligarh, was no Vithal, but he did have some greatly talented youngsters playing under him. They included A. U. Botawala from Rander, in Gujarat, a left-arm swing-bowler, and Syed Wazir Ali, a prolific opening batsman originally from Jalandhar in the Punjab who had come to notice while playing for the Aligarh Muslim University. Wazir scored 197 and Botawala claimed eight wickets as the unfancied Muslims beat the powerful Hindus to take away the championship for the first time.

The day after the final the Muslim Students' Union gave a dinner party for their victorious cricketers. A sitar recital by Barkatallah Khan was followed by the food, and then came the speeches. The man proposing a toast to the cricketers was the pre-eminent Muslim citizen of Bombay, Muhammad Ali Jinnah. The future founder of Pakistan was at this time an ambassador of Hindu–Muslim unity. Indeed, at a special session of the Muslim League, held at Lahore the previous May, he had insisted that 'India will get Dominion Responsible Government the day the Hindus and Mohammedans are united.

Swaraj is an almost interchangeable term with Hindu–Muslim unity.'[35]

Like his great rival, Gandhi, Jinnah had not distinguished himself on the playing-field. His first biographer, the New Zealander Hector Bolitho, tells a colourful story of how the boy Jinnah dramatically forsook native games for the foreign one. It seems that, aged fourteen, he thus addressed his mates: 'Don't play marbles in the dust; it spoils your clothes and dirties your hands. We must stand up and play cricket.'[36] The tale has not been repeated by Bolitho's successors. But unlike the Mahatma, Jinnah must have watched the game. For most of his life he was a Westernized Oriental Gentleman, who liked whisky, ham sandwiches and other things English. He was a member of the Bar, and a member of more than one club. Above all, he lived in Bombay, the home of Indian cricket. His fellow lawyers, his own junior among them, have written of the attractions of the Quadrangular, of how 'whenever there were big matches we [lawyers] would run away from court' and head for the Bar Gymkhana tent at the Bombay Gymkhana ground.'[37] It is more than likely that Jinnah went along to the cricket too.

That December evening in 1924, Jinnah spoke of the terrific popular following enjoyed by the tournament just concluded. Thousands watched, thousands more followed the games in the newspapers: 'even the judicial atmosphere in High Court, at the Bar, was stirred, taking the keenest interest' in the cricket. His side had won, but Jinnah was

> sure that even their Hindu brethren would rejoice in the Mahommedans' success, in a spirit of true sportsmanship. The cricket field had many lessons to teach in other walks of life. The brotherly feeling that prevailed throughout the play was no less remarkable and he hoped their Hindu brethren as sportsmen would no less be pleased . . . at the Mahommedans' winning the championship.[38]

At this time the Hindus of Bombay, both cricketers and others, could take a Muslim victory in the proper spirit. For one thing, it was their first win. For another, thus far they had more need to best the other teams in the competition. Indeed, in the tournament of 1925 the Hindus, led by Vithal, defeated the Parsis in the first round. Playing the Europeans in the final, they were behind by nearly 100 runs on the first innings. Eventually they were set a target in excess of 350, and got there with four wickets in hand, their captain scoring 97 not out. As he hit the winning run the spectators rushed on to the field. With some difficulty Vithal reached the players' pavilion, where one of the first persons to congratulate him was the Jam Saheb of Nawanagar, Ranjitsinhji.[39]

The following year the Quadrangular was played in September in Poona. The cricket fans of Bombay were denied their annual feast but, as one commentator wrote, 'perhaps the offices will have less cause to be satisfied as illness will not be so prevalent as usual in the period embracing this feast, and grandmothers will not require burial'.[40] It was the turn of employers in Poona to complain of absenteeism. Apart from those who bought tickets, hundreds of others flocked around the scoreboards specially erected at key intersections, which were updated every over by telephone.

The weeks before the Quadrangular were marked by rising tension between Brahmins and non-Brahmins in and around Poona. The Satyashodak Samaj printed pamphlets denouncing Brahmin arrogance. There were clashes between high and low castes in the villages. On behalf of the Poona Brahmins, the eminent mathematician R. P. ('Wrangler') Paranjype met the Governor to protest against what his community felt were 'scurrilous' attacks on them. One complaint was that it was being claimed that their beloved Ganapati was originally a god worshipped by non-Brahmins. Interestingly, Tilak's own former paper, the *Mahratta*, was now squarely on the side of the Brahmins.[41]

In post-Phule and post-Tilak Poona the caste boundaries were once again firmly drawn. But Vithal's recent successes meant that even the most hide-bound Brahmin had to accept him as captain of the Hindus. As in 1923 and 1925, the Hindus met the Europeans in the final. The key Hindu bowler S. M. Joshi was not playing, owing to a knee injury. In his place came L. Ramji, a fearsome fast bowler from Ranjitsinhji's hometown of Jamnagar, who bowled with a large vermilion *tilak* painted on his forehead. Played on a rain-affected wicket, the match was a low-scoring thriller. The Hindus conceded a first innings lead of 62, and eventually the Europeans were set a meagre 117 to win. Vithal made astute bowling changes, and despite the low target had a close-set field throughout. Ramji and Chandarana took early wickets while the European captain, A. L. Hosie, batted resolutely at one end. With less than 20 runs to get Hosie cut a ball hard, but D. B. Deodhar took a brilliant catch in the gully. This was the turning-point, for the Europeans then crumbled to 105 all out. At the end the losing captain had tears in his eyes.[42]

In four years Palwankar Vithal had led the Hindus to three victories. This last win might have given him the most pleasure, for it was a desperately close-fought match, a match played in reactionary Poona and at the ground where his beloved elder brother had slaved and bowled. Baloo was never allowed to enter the pavilion of the Poona Club, but it was in that pavilion that Vithal received the Quadrangular trophy. At the ground and afterwards, he received tributes aplenty. He and his men were fêted with At Homes and *pan suparis*, and even congratulated by the now conservative *Mahratta* for coming out 'with flying colours against the Europeans in a game native to them'.[43] Vithal was constrained to insert a collective acknowledgement in the newspapers; 'I have received a number of telegrams and letters congratulating the Hindu Team for their victory in the Quadrangular Tournament. It is not possible for me to write to each of them separately. I, therefore, hereby thank them for all their kindness and sympathy, and hope they will kindly accept it.'[44]

Vithal always underlined his debt to the eldest of the Palwankars. 'I must mention with respect and gratitude my brother Shri P. Baloo,' he once wrote: 'His advice and instruction were very useful and his deep knowledge about the game was always helpful to me.'[45] But Vithal was a real hero in his own right. His skill with the bat and his artful captaincy had won him a wide circle of admirers. In his memoirs, he writes of the affection he received from the Bombay public, and elsewhere too. He had certainly 'tasted the sweetness of popularity'. Once, when he was playing in Rajkot for a team sponsored by the Jam Saheb of Nawanagar, a crowd gathered round the players' tent asking: 'Where is Vithal? What does he look like?' At this Ranji himself asked him to stand on a table, and announced to the assembled fans: 'See! This is Vithal!' And in Calcutta the rush of fans screaming 'Esho! Esho!' ('Come! Come!') so unnerved him that he had to escape through the back door of his host Gymkhana.[46]

An impartial witness to Palwankar Vithal's terrific popularity was Vijay Merchant, who was himself destined to lead the Hindus and become India's leading batsman. A Bombay boy born to privilege, Merchant was in his early teens when Vithal was in his pomp. Years later, he recalled the impression the great Hindu stalwart had made on him:

> 'Vithal': a slim, alert, elegant personality with that well-known green tweed hat on his head and a gracefully held bat in his hand that would swing easily when he reached the wicket. . . . From thousands of cricket lovers there would come the spontaneous cry: 'there comes Vithal'.
>
> 'Vithal': the moment one heard the name . . . spectators would visualize all the grace and charm of Indian batsmanship. . . . With supple wrists, keen vision, perfect judgement of flight and agile footwork, Vithal had mastered the art of [batting]. He used to play his strokes with ease whether in front of the wicket or behind it. But one superb stroke of his that I cannot forget is the cover drive. Nowadays lot of effort and power goes into this stroke because of the off-side cordon. But due to his timing Vithal used to score more runs on this side of the wicket, effortlessly, through perfect coordination of wrist and leg movements. . . . He used to score fast because of his art of placing the ball in the gaps.[47]

The years of Vithal's triumphs, 1923 to 1926, coincided with the arrival on the political stage of Dr B. R. Ambedkar. Ambedkar had returned to India in 1923 with a doctoral degree from London. He had previously qualified for the Bar from Gray's Inn. While Vithal was leading the Hindu cricket team, Ambedkar was making a name at the Bombay Bar and, when the court was in recess, in politics. He travelled through the villages of the Deccan, seeking to build a base among the depressed classes. In his speeches Ambedkar would recall his own association with the first and greatest of the Palwankars. As a student and teacher in Bombay, he had 'looked at the solid fame of the Untouchable bowler with pride'. As a little-known lecturer in Sydenham College, he had organized meetings to felicitate the bowler and worked for his elevation to the city's Municipal Corporation. Now, as he sought to establish his credentials with the Untouchables of western India, Ambedkar would tell his audiences of his early attempts at promoting the proper recognition of Baloo's achievements.[48]

BY THE 1920s the stars of the Bombay Quadrangular came from all over the sub-continent. The European captain, A. L. Hosie, formerly of Oxford and Hampshire, was a *boxwallah* in Calcutta. The stylish Hindu batsman C. K. Nayudu, originally from Nagpur, was now a Captain in the Holkar State Army. Wazir Ali of the Muslims worked on the staff of the Nawab of Bhopal.

The development of cricket in the regions was helped by tournaments modelled on the Bombay *tamasha*. The highlight of the Madras cricket season was the Presidency Match, played between Indians and Europeans at the time of the Pongal harvest festival. From 1923 Lahore had an annual Triangular, played between Hindus, Muslims and Sikhs. A Central Provinces Quadrangular was instituted in Nagpur in the 1920s. Then there was the Sind Quadrangular, established in 1916 in Karachi (and to become a Pentangular in 1923), whose matches attracted upwards of 15,000 spectators.[49]

These variations on the Bombay pattern were influenced by local demography and relations of power. The Parsis were a fully fledged side in Karachi, their second city, as well as in Nagpur, but could not

form a team in Lahore. Definitions of 'community' were fluid. Thus
the Sikhs were willing to play as Hindus in Bombay, but not in
Lahore, which as recently as 1840 was the capital of their kingdom.
The Europeans admitted talented Eurasians in Madras, a province
known since the time of Sir Thomas Munro for progressive governance. They would even admit Indian Christians in Nagpur, a town
tucked away deep in the interior. This was in contrast to Bombay,
where the racial divide was sharp and unbridgeable.

These other cricket carnivals were also a vehicle for the playing
out of political rivalries. The meanings read into defeat and victory
reached far beyond the world of sport. Once, when a brilliant century
by C. K. Nayudu helped the Hindus to defeat the Europeans in the
finals of the Central Provinces Quadrangular, it was said that this
'proves only one thing, viz., that given equal opportunities, Indians
would be more than a match to Europeans in any field. In the
realms of science, law, literature, politics, art and oratory, individual
Indians have excelled the Britishers. In the realm of sports also, they
are proving as the equals or superiors of Europeans.'[50]

These animosities animated other sports too. An Englishman in
Bombay recalled a hockey match played in the prestigious Aga Khan
tournament in the mid-1920s, between a side of Indian Muslims and
a Railway side composed of Europeans and Anglo-Indians. No sooner
had the match started than coarse witticisms such as 'Show the niggers
your worth' could be heard from the Bombay Gymkhana enclosure.
As the Railway forwards moved towards the Muslim goal the cries
grew more feverish: 'Now is your chance! Buck up the Railway; thrash
the niggers'; these uttered by men and women alike. But when the
attack was repulsed and the Muslims scored first, their goal was met
in the Gymkhana pavilion by a 'dead silence'. When the Indian team
won the match by two goals to nil the whites were 'crestfallen'.
The man who wrote about this match, himself English, explained
the partisan attitude in these terms: 'Unfortunately, there is a certain
class of people in this country who think it is the proper thing to
call an Indian a nigger, and other disparaging epithets, whenever an

opportunity offers itself. They believe it very manly to show in public how they despise an Indian.'[51]

The progress of Indian sport was to be tested afresh in the winter of 1926–7, when a team of English cricketers came touring for the first time in more than twenty years. This was a high-powered side, officially sponsored by the MCC. Led by the current England captain, A. E. R. Gilligan, it contained six other Test cricketers, including such acknowledged stalwarts as Maurice Tate, Andrew Sandham and R. E. S. Wyatt. Arriving in Karachi in the middle of October, the MCC side left the sub-continent only at the end of February. They were worked ferociously hard, playing thirty-four matches in all, getting from one venue to the next by bus, boat and train.[52]

In late November the MCC reached Bombay, having already played in Sind, Rajputana and the Punjab. Cricket in this island city was now over a century old. In 1926 the Bombay film industry was in its infancy, so, for rich and poor, Hindu, Muslim and Parsi, cricket was still the most widely preferred form of recreation. Just as the MCC team reached India, a citizen moved a resolution at the City Improvement Board asking that 'mud-sports should not be held on the Maidan as they spoiled the cricket pitches of the numerous cricket clubs and deprived a very large number of the cricketing public the pleasure of regular open-air exercise'.[53] There is a curious echo here of that old battle against polo. Once, the cricketers fought off competition by the sport of kings; now, they wished not to be disturbed by working-class games like wrestling and *kabaddi*.

The visitors were to play as many as five matches in the home of Indian cricket. Weeks before they arrived, potential players began making their preparations, and potential patrons as well. The owner of Gazdar's Health Home, in Marine Lines, offered to place his expertise and appliances at the disposal of the local cricketers selected to play against the MCC. Equipment and instruction would be free. If the cricketers 'go through certain vigorous body-building exercises every day', said Mr Gazdar, 'they will be able to make a better stand all-round'.[54]

The MCC came to Bombay undefeated. Their first opponents in

the city were the Hindus. In its pre-match report, a nationalist paper, newly started, captured the feelings of its likely readers: 'The tents are pitched and the field set for the reception of the MCC on Monday next, and thousands are in their throes of anticipation. India expects Bombay to do its duty – to check the victorious career of the visitors.' Thus far only the Parsis had defeated visiting teams – Vernon's side in 1889–90, Lord Hawke's side three years later, the Oxford Authentics in 1902–3. 'Those were the palmy days of Parsi cricket,' commented the paper, 'but now we depend upon the Hindus to resist the invaders.'[55]

The day before the match, Palwankar Vithal gave an interview to the pro-Congress Marathi newspaper, *Navakal.* The Hindu captain said the strengths of the MCC team had been exagerrated by the media. True, they had some fine bowlers but there was no reason for panic. 'Let the MCC team come, and we will take care of the rest,' remarked Vithal. *Navakal* endorsed his sentiments, saying they would instil the necessary confidence in his men. The Hindus should be proud of their captain, said the paper. One reason they had lost in the past to the Parsis was the lack of a potent and self-confident leader.[56]

Twenty-five thousand people turned out for the first day of the tourists' match against the Hindus. They were well rewarded. Just before the close the visitors were all out for 363. The Somerset amateur G. F. Earle hit a rapid 130, with as many as eight sixes. The Hindus were a nervous 16 for 1 when stumps were drawn.

Already the cricket had been exciting enough. The following day, 1 December 1926, was more electrifying still. The Hindus started steadily but by the time they got to 84 had lost two more wickets, including their captain, Palwankar Vithal. C. K. Nayudu strode in briskly, and lofted his third ball on to the roof of the Gymkhana pavilion. While L. P. Jai blocked at the other end Nayudu went berserk. He had hit four sixes and got to 50 not out when play was stopped for lunch.

During the interval the news of the happenings at the Bombay Gymkhana spread through the city. Office workers headed hastily to

the Maidan by train. After lunch, writes one chronicler, 'every tree
was black with human spectators, every roof-top was occupied that
commanded even a partial or very distant view of the game'.[57] Even
if they saw little, the shouts they heard from inside the ground
confirmed that Nayudu was continuing where he had left off. Sixes
and fours poured off his bat as he reached his 100, then 150. Two
more drives landed on the roof of the Bombay Gymkhana. A high-
class attack led by four Test bowlers was completely demolished.
Nayudu was eventually out caught in the deep for 153. He had
batted less than two hours and hit 13 fours and 11 sixes, the latter a
world record.[58]

Each of Nayudu's boundaries was met by a colossal bout of
cheering. The roar of the crowd, wrote one observer, was so loud
that it must have unnerved the station-master of the Victoria Terminus, half a mile away. 'The hand-clappings and those hurrahs and
those shouts for [Nayudu's] shots were heavier for horizon than the
thundering sound of Punjab, Allahabad, Pioneer mails and what
not.'[59] That the Hindus were 7 runs behind on the first innings did
not seem to matter in the least. For, as E. L. Docker has written, the

> importance of the day lay in the emotional scene at the finish
> when outside the pavilion in the quickening dusk people began
> to gather in little groups craning their necks, straining every
> muscle to catch a glimpse of their hero, touch him, garland him
> with flowers, press gifts into his hand. How he had raised them
> up! What glories he had shown them![60]

With E. L. Docker, we may say that Nayudu's hundred was
Indian cricket's moment of arrival. The quality of the opposition and
the manner of its conquest were both unprecedented. Back in 1911
Baloo had got the better of accomplished English sides, but except
for his team-mates no Indian had seen it happen. And to the common
man (though not necessarily to the connoisseur) aggressive batsmanship is always more exciting than artful slow bowling. Nayudu played
the part and looked it too. He was lithe and handsome, a superb

athlete whose dancing footwork and six-hitting were of a piece with his brilliant outfielding and more than useful medium-pace bowling.

Thirty years later, someone who had bowled to Nayudu that day recalled his explosive innings of 153. R. E. S. Wyatt said that C. K.'s 'ability to drive good-length balls back over the bowler's head made it very difficult for bowlers to keep him quiet'. The Indian batsman's 'perfect poise, high backlift and long, pendulum swing brought beauty to his strokes'.[61]

The day after the match ended, a fan who could not even get to a tree-top in time wrote a bitter letter to the newspapers. 'S. S. S.' of Kalyan pleaded for 'A Glimpse of the Game for the Poor', for space within the ground for the thousands of 'poor people who cannot check their enthusiasm and whose purse is too lean to bear the price of a seat in rented tents'. These 'have no other alternative than to climb the trees around them and if fortune is not on their side to be a victim of a bad fall for a single glimpse of the game'. The tents for the paying public could remain, suggested S. S. S., but in between the tents open space might be kept for those with no money but plenty of interest, who were willing to stand huddled together to watch the game.[62]

Those who could pay, however, got close to their heroes in their off-duty hours as well. On Sunday, 5 December, the Hindu team was honoured at the Bombay Theatre, with the felicitation followed by a concert by Hirabai Barodekar, the 'world-renowned popular young songstress of gramophone name'. The tickets were priced at 15, 10, 5, 4, 3, 2 and 1 rupees, with a few available for 8 annas. An advertisement placed in the papers appealed, 'CITIZENS OF BOMBAY! ATTEND! ONE AND ALL!! ATTEND!!' This call to all citizens suggests that Muslims and Parsis were likely to share in Nayudu's triumph.[63] Another sign of an inclusive nationalism was that the featured singer, Hirabai Barodekar, was half Hindu, half Muslim.

The evening after the show at the Bombay Talkies, Nayudu and his team-mates were honoured at the Damodar Thakersee Mooljee Hall in Parel. Presiding over the function was the famous liberal lawyer, M. R. Jayakar. The cricketers watched a performance of *The*

Taming of the Shrew in Marathi, put on by the Social Service League, and later received medals on behalf of the jewellery firm of Narotham Bhawoo and Company. Only one person, C. K. Nayudu, received a Gold Medal, 'as a mark of appreciation by the Parel public, especially the clerks and operatives employed in mills and factories, of his splendid performance with the bat'.[64] Some days later, Nayudu was presented with a silver bat and a Triumph motor-cycle with an attached side-car, the gifts being made on behalf of 'friends and admirers of Hindu cricketers'.[65]

With no disrespect to Pavri and Mistry, Botawala and Wazir, Baloo and Vithal, C. K. Nayudu was the first Indian cricketer to be a popular hero, whose appeal transcended the barriers of caste, class, gender and religion. One did not need to have a cultivated interest in the art of cricket to recognize his achievements. Nayudu's display of fireworks was timed to perfection. To play an innings like that, against the English, in 1926, in Bombay, and on the Bombay Gymkhana ground, was to tap into all the sources of nationalist pride. What we know of the man suggests that Nayudu did not have any firm views on Raj and *swaraj*. Yet he would become, almost despite himself, an icon for all patriotic Indians.

After their match against the Hindus the MCC played against a mixed team of Parsis and Europeans. They were due next to play a Hindu–Muslim combination, which at the time seemed as natural as a Parsi–European one. The day before the match PJ Hindu Gymkhana hosted a sumptuous dinner for the visitors at the elite Willingdon Club. The Governor of Bombay led the cast of notables in attendance: others included the Jam Saheb of Nawanagar (Ranji), Sir Dorab Tata and Sir Ibrahim Rahimtullah. The President of the Hindu Gymkhana, L. R. Tairsee, said in his welcome speech that his organization had 'been able to bring about considerable social reform among Hindus. The doors of the Gymkhana were open to every Hindu including an Untouchable and the Gymkhana had thus been able, through cricket, to remove the barriers of caste.'[66]

The intent of Tairsee's remark was clear: that since high-caste Hindus had given Untouchables a fair deal, it was time for the British to start playing on equal terms with the Indians, in cricket and in politics as well. But some Englishmen were not even prepared to concede parity on the sporting field. The *Times of India* complained that three of the matches in Bombay had included Sunday play, something completely forbidden in England. Why should the organizers, it asked angrily, 'conclude that because they are in India there is no need to observe a rule that public opinion enforces at Home'? This outburst was used by the Indian press to do what it liked best: deliver a homily at its rulers. At Home we might be very orthodox, agreed the *Indian National Herald*, but abroad one must follow the rule: do in Rome as the Romans do. The European community in India had long played cricket, golf and tennis on Sundays: how come the *Times* had not previously objected to this? The new-found religious fervour, commented the *Herald* delightedly, was surely a sign of senility: 'The Old Woman, having devoted enough of her life to the cultivation of Mammon, is now taking on the role of Piety.'[67]

Meanwhile the cricket continued. Vithal led the combined Hindu–Muslim side in a drawn match marked by a spell of furious fast bowling by L. Ramji. Notably, the mixed Hindu–Muslim crowd cheered when the English batsmen were hurt by short balls; this, perhaps, a last flicker of the Khilafat movement, and stoked also by the fresh memories of C. K. Nayudu's remarkable innings. Their crude nationalism disgusted a liberal newspaper. 'We are told that cricket is the most civilizing of games,' it remarked, 'that it teaches us tolerance, but we looked in vain for those virtues in the people who jeered at the MCC batsmen when they were injured by dangerous balls.'[68]

In their next fixture the MCC easily defeated a Bombay Presidency XI. Vithal was supposed to play in this match but dropped out with an injured hand. Now came the contest everyone had awaited, between the MCC and an All India XI. The *Bombay Chronicle* confidently expected Palwankar Vithal to be named captain. Had he not led his side to three Quadrangular wins in four years? In the event, Vithal was included in the playing eleven, but the old Parsi batsman Colonel Keki Mistry was appointed captain. In all the side had six Hindus, three Parsis and two Muslims. The press now printed several letters of complaint on behalf of the Hindu captain, who 'could have been safely entrusted to guide the All India XI'.[69] Mistry was indeed a peculiar choice, for he was the wrong side of forty and had not played first-class cricket for years. He 'hardly deserves to be chosen captain', remarked one critic, for 'the essential duty of a leader is to have an extensive knowledge of the abilities of men in his team, and we wonder whether Colonel Mistry will be able to make a single move on the field without consulting Vithal at every point'.[70]

On the eve of the match Vithal dropped out, with a reported attack of malaria. Was this a silent strike? Vithal had captained the Hindus against the MCC, then a mixed eleven of Hindus and Muslims. He withdrew, however, from the Bombay Presidency side owing to an 'injured hand', and from the All India XI because of 'malaria'. Might this have been because of the choice as captain of the (European) L. Travers in the first case, and of Colonel Mistry in the second? Both Travers and Mistry were inferior to Vithal as batsmen and cricket tacticians, but were, of course, superior in social status. It is not inconceivable that the injury and illness were his way of declaring a protest.

Vithal's place in the eleven was taken by the Poona batsman, D. B. Deodhar. The MCC batted first and posted an impressive total of 362. In reply, the Indian openers Wazir Ali and Navle put on a century partnership. Four wickets then fell quickly (including Nayudu's), but Deodhar, in association first with Nazir Ali and later with Mistry, rallied the innings. He scored 148, his most productive shots being the cut and the drive. When the MCC score was passed the 'whole crowd went mad with joy and rang with cheers'. A Hindu boy ran on to the field and placed his cap at Deodhar's feet. Within seconds a Muslim boy did likewise. The European umpire, Mr Higgins, angrily kicked the caps away, but they were picked up and dusted by the Indian umpire, a Mr Davar. Higgins's kick alienated the crowd, who thought 'the action of the boys represented sincere unbiased admiration in its simplest form and certainly did not deserve such treatment'. The public and the press were mollified after play had ended, when the fielding captain, A. E. R. Gilligan, sportingly apologized for the 'highly reprehensible act' of his countryman.[71]

D. B. Deodhar was presented with a medal or two, but judging only by the press accounts, his innings did not receive half the acclaim that C. K. Nayudu's did. Nayudu's knock came first, always an advantage, and he hit huge sixes, whereas Deodhar played mostly along the ground. But taken together, these innings represented an assertiveness that was unprecedented in the history of Indian cricket. Two Indian batsmen had successfully taken on a near-full England side. Nayudu's knock had brought the Hindus to within 7 runs of the MCC score, while Deodhar had ensured that his side took the first-innings lead. Both matches were drawn honourably.

Indeed, after Bombay the MCC side had an easy time, winning most matches by an innings. They played against one other team styling itself as 'All India'. This was at Calcutta, and the home side included seven expatriate Englishmen. One must not, however, read too much into this. It was simply that the hosts for this match, the all-white Calcutta Cricket Club, were also the hosts for the MCC tour as a whole.

THE FINE DISPLAYS against Gilligan's side of 1926–7 made some Indians think of forming a body that could do for their country what the MCC had done for cricket in England. Some provinces, in preparation, formed cricket associations. Some patrons thought of sending a representative Indian side to tour Australia. The move was wisely squashed by Frank Tarrant, who pointed out that the game had reached such a high level in his country that the best Indian side would make a very poor showing indeed.[72]

So, for the moment, the Quadrangular remained the pivot of the Indian cricket season. In 1927 the Europeans won for the first time in six years, helped by the superb swing-bowling of the Oxford Blue R. J. O. Meyer. Meyer claimed a staggering twenty-eight wickets in two matches, and his antics alternately entertained and horrified the crowd. In the final against the Muslims he chased a stray dog, brought it down expertly with a rugby tackle, and handed it over to a policeman. Later, he was garlanded by a spectator, but proceeded to stamp vigorously on the present, to cries of 'Shame! Shame!' For this act Meyer also earned a rebuke from the *Bombay Chronicle*, which asked for 'judicial restraint of animal feelings on the cricket field at least'.[73]

The following year the tournament welcomed an even more celebrated newcomer. This was Ranji's nephew, K. S. Duleepsinhji, a batsman of genius who had just won his Cambridge Blue. When Duleep appeared in a practice match for the PJ Hindu Gymkhana against Dr Kanga's XI, 10,000 turned out on the Kennedy Sea Face to watch him bat. A few Hindus thought that by virtue of his pedigree he should immediately be appointed captain. In the end Vithal was retained. This, even for him, was a novelty: he had led many Brahmins but not, before this, a prince.

Duleep batted well but the Hindus lost to the Parsis. The latter team went on to beat the Europeans by 134 runs. Their hero was a little left-arm spinner named 'Jamsu' Jamshedji, who hid violin resin in his trouser pocket to keep his fingers supple. Three years earlier a well-known cricket writer had lamented the decline of Parsi cricket, which was 'in great need of due encouragement and support from the Parsi community'.[74] When they won in 1928, 'wild scenes of jubilation were witnessed after the match and the Parsi team was actually "mobbed" by the admiring crowds. Jamshedji, the hero of the day, was chaired and carried into the pavilion to the accompaniment of cheers.'[75]

Meanwhile, the political situation was warming up once more. A no-tax campaign had commenced in Gujarat, led by Gandhi's lieutenant Vallabhbhai Patel. An all-white commission to investigate India's 'future', led by Sir John Simon, was met everywhere by black flag demonstrations. The 1929 Quadrangular was thus played against the backdrop of a rising anti-British feeling. Some critics were nervous that the tournament was a threat to the unity of the nation-in-the-making. The Quadrangular, remarked one writer, 'is, to put it plainly, a communal tournament which in the best interest of absolute Nationalism need not exist'.[76] An old captain of the Hindus, now a leading industrialist, suggested that an Inter-Provincial tournament, for cricket teams representing the provinces of British India as well as the princely states, should replace the Bombay carnival. This would rid India's favourite sport of the 'communal character' with which it had come to be associated. 'Fortunately for us', remarked Sir Chunilal Mehta,

> this communal tension has not expressed itself very acutely so far, and it might be said that at least in regard to the two major communities in India, namely the Hindus and the Mohamma-dans, the feeling has been thoroughly sportsmanlike and friendly. But it is necessary to take action in time. . . . Instances have not been unknown in the past where feeling has run very high at matches between the Hindus and the Parsis, and between Euro-peans and non-Europeans.[77]

These reservations, for the moment, were not widely shared. The magazine that carried Sir Chunilal's article itself offered 100 rupees (then not a trifling sum) to any reader who accurately predicted the Quadrangular winner and their margin of victory.[78] The tournament was more popular than ever before, helped by the fact that all four teams had won the competition in the past five years. In the *Bombay Chronicle* a writer calling himself 'Short-Stop' published an evocative piece on 'The Cricket Fever'. As the carnival approached, he wrote, the city was swept by a

> furious epidemic. For nothing moves the placidity of Bombay as the premier sporting event of India. In London you have Poppy Day, New Year's Eve, the Varsity Boat Race, Epsom, the Test Matches. But in Bombay you go on working and clogging and grubbing the whole year round – except in Quadrangular week.

Nor was this frenzy of activity confined to those who played or watched the cricket. So tailors were busy with the necessary apparel for their clients; clerks, business-men, odd-jobbers pounce upon every opportunity of making a little money either by betting [on the cricket] or having a finger in the pie; [carriage-drivers] and school-boys shout themselves hoarse; grandmothers die; offices are empty on account of ill-ness; college rolls are never taken; briefless barristers rush up and down Waudby Road.[79]

It was, of course, school and college boys who were most maniacally gripped by the fever. A regular attendee at the Quadrangu-lars of the mid-1920s remembered the 'excitement that preceded the event of events, the gradual accumulation of all savings till it collected itself into one or possibly two ten-rupee notes'. In Quadrangular week 'trousers were especially well-creased'. The 'coat and tie were chosen with care'. A little eau-de-cologne 'was pinched from someone else's dressing-room'. Books were carried to the Maidan, 'just to make-believe that we really attended classes'. The memoirist wrote that he 'remembered Vithal, the "bhel", that new drink called "Vimto" and the plate of "samosas" '. Amidst all the preparations beforehand and the food and drink consumed at the ground there was space only for one cricketer's name: Palwankar Vithal.[80]

The question would remain: was the division of teams by race and religion productive of social tension? Some observers immediately threw the query out of court. It was mere 'tosh', remarked 'Short Stop', to suggest that 'communal cricket is bad for communal relations'. The fight, he insisted, is 'not between Hindu and Parsi or Christian and Muslim but between those who play "cricket" and those who do not'.[81] His sentiments were echoed the following day by 'Spectator', who pointed out that the game had captured

the fancy of all classes of society in Bombay. Right from the 20-rupee *hamal* [vendor], nay, even sometimes the one pie beggar, to the big-bellied *Shethia* [merchant] or the topied bureaucrat, all follow the fortunes of the different teams with zeal and enthusiasm: and what is more, although the tournament is run on communal lines, in cricket there is little or nothing of the communal spirit, and you see a Muslim applauding the hefty hit of Nayudu with the same enthusiasm as any Hindu.[82]

However, in 1929 no Indian would so readily applaud a sixer struck by an Englishman. Thus in this year's semi-final the Parsis played a close-fought encounter with the Europeans. The Parsis led on first innings, and had simply to play out time to qualify for the finals. At a crucial stage their key batsman, Bahadur Kapadia, played a ball into the close field. The European captain, A. L. Hosie, claimed a catch, which was negatived by the Hindu umpire officiating at the bowler's end. Hosie then appealed to the Muslim umpire at square leg, and when he concurred with his colleague, threw the ball down in disgust. For a while 'the game was suspended and unprecedented scenes prevailed in some of the tents'. Play was finally resumed, although 'anything but an amiable spirit existed between the teams'.[83]

As ever, a dispute on the field spilled over into the newspapers. The *Bombay Chronicle* thought that 'the attitude of the European captain under the rules and etiquette of cricket was rather queer'.[84] The *Times of India*, on the contrary, thought that Kapadia was out, and that the umpire had made a 'palpable error'. The paper also complained that the Parsis had played defensively, resting on their first-innings lead rather than going for an outright win. The headline said it all: 'Parsis in Final: Stonewalling "Ad Nauseam": Europeans' Brilliant Innings'. The attempt to play out time was a 'miserable display of cricket', a 'technical victory' which only demonstrated 'how the King of Games should not be played'.[85] It was a typical inversion: the *Chronicle* claimed that A. L. Hosie was unsporting for questioning the umpire; the *Times* answered that the Parsis were unsporting for stonewalling their way into the next round.

In the other semi-final the Hindus beat the Muslims by an innings. One letter published in the newspapers pointed to the continuing identification of cricketing prowess with religious pride, as well as, perhaps, to the growing social schism between the communities. The letter was written by 'Z. A. B.', probably Z. A. Bukhari, a gifted young scholar and broadcaster. Bukhari was angry that the Muslim selectors had chosen local 'freshers' in preference to experienced men from outside Bombay. 'When will the Mussulmans learn to send their best talent to the Quadrangular matches which have an importance of their own?' he asked. 'It will be regarded as a great *national* drawback on the part of the Mussulmans if in future they fail to send their best team to the field. It was far better not to have played at all than to have sent in a team without much stuff.'[86]

In the final the Hindus defeated the Parsis by five wickets. The spectators in the PJ Hindu Gymkhana tent 'distributed sweetmeats, taking particular care to feed the ladies'. Afterwards the Brahmin Sabha of Bombay gave an At Home to the victorious players. The main speech was made by the doctor–politician G. V. Deshmukh. Interestingly, he dwelled more on the semi-final in which the Hindus did not play. It 'is a matter of pride for us', he remarked,

> that Indian cricket triumphed and the Parsis won the match by their plucky play against one of the strongest teams put by the Europeans in the field. I know that the Parsi team is blamed for not showing the so-called sporting spirit by prejudiced, irresponsible and ignorant critics, in not throwing away their wickets in theatrical fashion. Besides, one would like to know what were the bowlers for on the European side.

For Deshmukh, the 'lesson of the cricket carnival is that given equal opportunities and encouragement there is no field of activity in life where an Indian be he a Parsi or a Mahomedan or a Hindu will not be a match for an European if not his superior'.[87]

Or, one is tempted to say, the lesson equally of the cricket carnival was that given equal opportunities and encouragement there was no field of activity in life where an Untouchable would not be a match for a Brahmin or a Bania or a Rajput, if not his superior. Sadly, the Hindu triumph in 1929 was one in which the Palwankars could not share. They might have been in the crowd, and special invitees also at the At Home, but this Quadrangular was the first where no Palwankar had played. Vithal was now forty years old, and a host of

promising youngsters was waiting to take his place. Notably, before
the carnival began, the unofficial voice of the Congress, *Navakal,* had
expressed itself strongly in favour of his retention. Vithal, it said,
had exemplary qualities of *savoir-faire* and fortitude, and had brought
the Hindus many victories in the past. It recalled the great match of
1923, when the Europeans had run up a huge total. When he went
to bat with the Hindus struggling, a fielder had taunted him that his
side had no chance. Vithal, in the paper's words, had answered: 'As
long as I am at the wicket, this match is mine'. Vithal was 'the
greatest captain the Hindus have produced', yet this year he had been
in poor form with the bat. When he did not score in the trial matches
he was not included in the Hindu side, of which D. B. Deodhar was
appointed captain.[88]

With Vithal dropped, the 'last of the Baloo family after years of
meritorious service has been unceremoniously driven from first class
cricket'. Thus wrote one 'R. V. M.', in a moving tribute to the
brothers, a tribute marked by deep knowledge of the game of cricket
and a subtle understanding of its sometimes brutal social context.
The Hindu team's announcement, he remarked,

> abruptly ends a thirty years' unbroken connection of the Baloo
> brothers with Hindu cricket. Nowhere else does the history of
> cricket supply such a glorious page. Thirty years and a single
> family. One brother after another raising the Hindu cricket
> edifice higher and yet higher, spreading its brilliance, along with
> their own, all over India and beyond.

The individual brothers were recalled one by one. First the patriarch:

> And what a proud record to contemplate! It was Baloo who
> began Hindu bowling as such. With what wonderful wiles did
> he accomplish single-handed the herculean task of putting the
> Parsi and European veterans out, only those knew who intelli-
> gently watched him doing it. Bowlers on the other side might
> come and go but Baloo plodded on for ever.

Then the younger siblings:

Baloo brought Shivram into the field and the best fieldsman
he became, with considerable bowling and batting powers in
addition. Then came Vithal. . . . He made his first appearance
at the Marine Lines Parade Ground, when the Parsi Parekh had
a hat-trick and Warden a century against the Hindus. Vithal,
however, was not one of the 'tricked' ones. He played with the
sweeping forward style that alone could withstand the fast
swerving left-handers of the Parsis. He wielded this weapon with
considerable effect and gradually stayed the rot year after year,
with centuries against the Mahomedans and the Europeans. To
his help then came Gunpat with his pretty style and quick
movements. There was thus a time when the Hindu team
included all the four brothers at one and the same time, and
people fondly called the Hindu side as 'Baloo brothers plus 7'.

R. V. M. now showed how sporting skill could vanquish social
prejudice:

Did ever a family establish such a record? Could a Hindu lover
of cricket having the least culture within him ever dream of
breathing against such pillars of Hindu cricket any ignoble reference to their caste? Could a Hindu cricketer think of them with
anything but respect? The late Pandharinath Telang, the Hindu
Jessop, noble-minded as he was, could never think of Baloo as
other than a dear comrade. Sir Chunilal [Mehta] never entertained any ugly thought of the Baloo brothers' 'depressed' class.

But society, it seems, sometimes moved more slowly than the cricketers. The final steps to the summit were the hardest:

Baloo though senior was deprived of the captainship. He soon
retired and the matter was hushed up. Shivram retired before
such a question could crop up in his case. Then it came to the
turn of Vithal. But time and again he was put down. His juniors
were thrust over his head. No wonder the Hindus failed –
miserably failed – yet the die-hards would not listen to justice
and reason. But the force of circumstances was too great and

after a lot of higgling, at long last, they 'liberalized' themselves
enough to throw the captainship at Vithal.[89]

The history of cricket does in fact have pages filled with the deeds
of brothers: the Graces of England, the Pollocks of South Africa, the
Chappells and the Waughs of Australia, the Hadlees and Crowes of
New Zealand, the Wettimunys of Sri Lanka, the Flowers of Zimbabwe, above all, the Mohammeds of Pakistan. In cricketing skill and
achievement the Palwankars of India were comfortably the equal of
them all. These other families, moreover, had to fight their demons
on the field alone, whereas the Palwankars were sinned against most
grievously by the society into which they were born. Why then are
they so wholly forgotten? One reason is that they played before India
became an 'official' Test-playing nation. Another is the unconscion-
able ahistoricism of the Indians, their disregard for documents,
records, remembrances and past heroes. While the Palwankars lived
and played it was all too different. Men like R. V. M. knew what
they were worth. Men like Dr B. R. Ambedkar knew it too. It is
high time that they were restored to their rightful place in the history
of Indian cricket, indeed in the history of Indian social emancipation.

RELIGION

Riots Minus the Stabbing

9. A Prodigal's Return

NEARLY TWENTY YEARS AGO, I took a flight from London to New York in the company of an English father and son. The father, aged about sixty, asked me sharp questions about Indian politics, but the son, aged thirty, did not even know where India was. Finally the father asked him, in exasperation: 'Have you heard of the British Empire?' He hadn't.

In truth, even in the heyday of Empire some educated Britons had no clue of the places over which they ruled. As late as 1930, for example, there was little recognition at Home of the spread of English recreations in India. In that year a London author published a guide-book for Indian students coming to England to study. This had chapters on English surnames, on the hobbies of the English boy, on Stratford-upon-Avon, Oxford, Bath, Cambridge, Christmas and English flowers. Each chapter contained a few pages of description and explanation followed by a list of questions to test the student.

Chapter 5 of this guide-book dealt with 'Cricket'. The author (perhaps a Surrey supporter) chose to set his narrative at the Oval, rather than Lord's. The chief features of the game were patiently described, and the list of questions at the end included such gems as: 'How may the wicket-keeper be distinguished from other players?'; 'How many players are there in a cricket match?'; and 'How many balls are there in an over, and who counts them?' Best of all was the chapter's last paragraph, which asked the Indian student:

> Has the game struck you as being rather slow and a little ridiculous in its solemn ritual? Perhaps it is. But to us, you

know, the proper playing of this game has become the canon for all right conduct, so that we can say nothing harsher of a man's behaviour than 'It's not cricket' or 'It's not playing the game'. But now the luncheon interval is being taken, so we will leave the ground and return again in a few weeks' time when you will have become more familiar with the game and have less difficulty in following it with interest. For I am sure that a little practice at the nets will soon turn you into an enthusiast as keen as the hardiest English boy.[1]

SOME INDIAN STUDENTS who came to England in the 1930s might not have known of Shakespeare, but there were none who did not know about cricket, none who had not played the game themselves. It was comfortably the most popular Indian sport, played in cities and towns across the country, on roads, beaches, mud and turf, and by all social classes. Since 1907 Bombay had hosted its great All India tournament, and there were plenty of local competitions to stoke and further an already considerable interest. Indeed, by 1930 India even had a formal association to coordinate its cricket, an Indian equivalent of the MCC.

The origins of the Board of Control for Cricket in India lie in a casual conversation that took place in Delhi's lovely Roshanara Gardens in February 1927. The participants were the MCC captain, A. E. R. Gilligan, the Maharaja of Patiala, and an ambitious Delhi businessman named R. E. Grant-Govan. To this select audience the visiting captain suggested that there should be a regular exchange of cricket visits between England and India. C. K. Nayudu's slaughter of his best bowlers in Bombay had convinced Gilligan that the erstwhile pupils could now play on more or less equal terms with their masters.[2]

Grant-Govan had a secretary, A. S. D'Mello, who matched him in ambition and had more energy besides. Born in Karachi in 1898, and of Goan extraction, D'Mello studied in England and returned to become a *boxwallah* in Delhi. Now he and his boss sent circulars to clubs in the different provinces, and followed up with personal visits. The upshot was the formation in December 1928 of the Board of Control for Cricket in India (BCCI), with Grant-Govan as founder-President and D'Mello as founder-Secretary. The first meeting was held in Bombay, a city that in usual circumstances would expect to house the new Board too. As one critic observed, 'If Indian cricket was born in Bombay, cradled in Bombay, and spooned and fed by Bombay to its present growth and strength, the home of the new Board must also be in the same parent city.'[3] However, the promoters knew that if they were to retain control it must be headquartered elsewhere. With money from the Maharajas and building permits from the civil servants, the President and Secretary set about the construction of a cricket ground in Delhi. The Board planned to locate its office in the ground's spanking new pavilion.

In May 1929, Grant-Govan and D'Mello travelled to London to participate in a meeting of the Imperial Cricket Council. Lord Harris, then seventy-eight, was President of the ICC. Now, in his one certifiable contribution to Indian cricket, he agreed to a tour of the sub-continent by the MCC in the winter of 1930–1, to be followed by a return visit in 1932.[4] India's standing had been enormously helped by the recent performances of its hockey players. In 1928 they had easily won the gold medal at the Amsterdam Olympics. This was followed by a successful tour of Europe in which one player alone, Dhyan Chand, scored seventy-five goals. A journalist accompanying the team recalled a conversation in a London pub, the gist of which seems to have been: 'Whatever the Indians might be unable to do [such as run their country], there is one thing they could certainly do, and by Jove, how! How they can play Hockey!'[5] The deeds of Dhyan and company helped Grant-Govan and D'Mello persuade the ICC that Indians might be able to hold their own in other sports as well.

The following winter the Cricket Board's twin promoters were in Bombay during Quadrangular week, seeking out hosts and sponsors for the tour of 1930–1. Early the following year, however, Gandhi decided to make one of his periodic interventions with the course of Indian cricket. On 26 January 1930 he led the members of the Congress in taking an 'Independence Pledge' on the banks of the river Ravi in Lahore. The pledge denounced the British for having 'ruined India economically, politically, culturally and spiritually'. To submit further to this rule was, it said, 'a crime against man and God'.[6]

Six weeks later, the master of civil disobedience began the slow, stately walk to the sea known as the Dandi March. The walk took twenty days, with public meetings held in villages and towns en route. A bemused adminstration made no move to stop Gandhi. On 6 April he reached the sea, aiming to break an archaic law forbidding individuals from making salt. As Gandhi picked up a fistful of salt he said he was 'shaking the foundations of the British Empire'. Following his example, volunteers in other parts of the country broke the salt and forest laws, picketed liquor shops and distilleries, and organized shut-down strikes. By the end of the year a staggering 60,000 Indians had been put behind bars.[7]

The MCC tour of India was hastily called off and so was the 1930 Quadrangular. For Bombay was a centre of nationalist activity, with daily bonfires of foreign cloth, marches in support of striking peasants, street-corner speeches and the display of exhortative posters. In October 1930 the PJ Hindu Gymkhana passed a resolution forbidding its team from taking part in the carnival. The other sides also withdrew, but some club cricket was allowed to be played. The newspapers carried reports of a match between the Bombay Gymkhana and a team of Indian Christians. The PJ Hindu Gymkhana also played a friendly tie against St Xavier's College. Appearing for the college was their present coach, the sometime Hindu captain, Palwankar Vithal.[8]

After a year in jail Gandhi was released, and made his way to the Viceroy's palace in New Delhi to parley on equal terms with the representative of the King-Emperor. In September 1931 he set sail for London to attend a Round Table Conference on India's future. Gandhi was the Congress's sole representative, but also attending were spokesmen for the Princes, the Sikhs, the Muslims and the

Untouchables. The last two were, from Gandhi's point of view, the real problem. The Muslims had stayed aloof from the latest round of civil disobedience. And the Untouchables were represented in London by the formidable B. R. Ambedkar. Ambedkar insisted that the Untouchables must elect their own legislators from a separate electorate in which caste Hindus would not participate. This, to Gandhi, was 'the unkindest cut of all'. The claims of the other minorites he could understand, but he thought he represented the Untouchables himself: 'I claim that I would get, if there was a referendum of the untouchables, their vote, and I would top the poll . . .'[9]

The conference failed, for the British were reluctant to devolve power to the provinces, and the Indians were fighting among themselves anyway. While Gandhi was away in London civil disobedience was resumed. Men like Jawaharlal Nehru and Khan Abdul Ghaffar Khan were put in jail. The new Viceroy, Lord Willingdon, was determined to replace his predecessor Lord Irwin's policy of indulgent understanding with stern repression. In January 1932, a month after his return, Gandhi was also arrested and sent to Yeravada.

While Gandhi languished in jail, the Indian cricket team to tour England was being chosen. Trial matches were organized at the Maharaja's grounds in Patiala and at the Roshanara Club in Delhi. Ranji was the chairman of the selection committee, but he had forbidden his nephew Duleep, already an England cricketer, to participate. Three promising Bombay batsmen, Champak Mehta, L. P. Jai and Vijay Merchant, withdrew from the trials in support of Gandhi and civil disobedience. Another Bombay batsman, P. Vithal, did play in the trials, but to no avail. In 1911 he was told he was too young and in 1932 he was told he was too old. Unlike his brother Baloo, Vithal would never play at Lord's. As an admirer bitterly remarked, he was thus 'stopped from going to Pandhari'. For the non-Maharashtrian these few and evocative words shall need a gloss. To prohibit this superb cricketer from playing at the Home of Cricket, suggested Vithal's friend, was akin to prohibiting the deity he had been named after from being present at the great shrine in Pandharpur built for his worship.[10]

The 1932 side nicely reflected the balance of communal interests: 7 Hindus, 4 Muslims, 4 Parsis and 2 Sikhs. The captain was the Maharaja of Porbandar, who, it was alleged, owned more Rolls-Royces than he had made runs. Mercifully, he played little on tour, and agreed to step down for the only Test match so that C. K. Nayudu could be captain in his stead. England won the Test, but not without difficulty. In other matches the Indians defeated as many as nine first-class counties. The undoubted successes of the tour were Nayudu and the fast bowling combination of Mohammed Nissar, from the Punjab, and Amar Singh, a former student of Gandhi's own school, King Alfred's in Rajkot. Nayudu, chosen one of *Wisden*'s Five Crick-eters of the Year, batted consistently well, never better than while making 118 against the MCC. It was in this knock that he hit a six of which it was said, 'the ball was last seen leaving the Home of Cricket in an easterly direction'.

The Indian cricketers, said one reporter, had made a better im-pression than had their politicians in 1931. Perhaps the 'English like sports better than politics, and it is just as well'. For 'what the Round Tablers might fail to achieve the Naidus alone might succeed'.[11]

Interestingly, two Indians appeared for their counties against the tourists. Duleepsinhji played for Sussex, and the Nawab of Pataudi for Worcestershire. Both had disdained to appear in the colours of All India, hoping rather to be chosen for that winter's tour of Australia by England. Both were selected, although Duleep dropped out through illness. While India was still ruled by the British such anoma-lies were possible. It is notable, though, that neither was asked to play for England against India in the solitary Test of 1932.

THE INDIAN CRICKETERS played their last match in England at Scarborough in the second week of September. While Nayudu and his men were on the ship home, the political climate was warming up once more. In response to Ambedkar's demands, the British Government announced a 'Communal Award', whereby Untouchables would be chosen for the legislature from a separate electorate composed only of themselves. Gandhi, in Yeravada, announced his decision to fast unto death in protest. He passionately believed that the Untouchables were part of the greater Hindu family, that upper-caste Hindus must make reparations for their treatment, and that any attempt, legislative or theological, to separate Untouchables from other Hindus would lead to civil war. An early reaction to the Mahatma's proposed fast was that of Palwankar Baloo. In a press statement Baloo admired 'the spirit in which Mr Gandhi has proclaimed his intention of sacrificing his life for the sake of the Depressed Classes'.[12]

Back in October 1931, during the Round Table Conference, Baloo had cabled the British Prime Minister opposing the proposal to have separate electorates. Now, B. R. Ambedkar was a Mahar, a member of the caste of village watchmen that enjoyed an uncomfortable relation with Baloo's Chamaar caste. Both communities were united by the discrimination they faced from high-born Hindus. Otherwise they retained their separate identities, and even competed for Government jobs. As a leader of the Chamaars, Baloo perhaps felt that Ambedkar's meteoric rise and militant rhetoric were a threat to his position and possibly to the welfare of his caste. And from what we know of his cricketing past, he was genuinely a meliorist, who hoped that in light of Gandhi's call the upper castes could be persuaded to treat the Depressed Classes more fairly. Ambedkar, on the other hand, was convinced that they would get a fair deal only outside the rubric of Hinduism.

Baloo's support to Gandhi's fast was thus consistent with his earlier stand. The fast began on 20 September, but Ambedkar was at first unyielding. He was slowly made to come around by his colleagues. With Gandhi's life under threat, Ambedkar was asked 'to leave his stubbornness and take into consideration that the other Untouchable leaders like Mr Baloo and Mr Rajah were with Mahatma Gandhi'. Baloo is said to have himself reminded Ambedkar that 'he was also a leader of the Untouchables and also had an equal right to express his views', which was that, at all costs, Gandhi's life had to be

saved.[13] Ambedkar yielded, and Baloo and Rajah were asked to negotiate on his behalf. They went to meet Gandhi in Yeravada jail, and
succeeded in arriving at a pact whereby Untouchables were alloted
more seats in exchange for allowing caste Hindus to vote for them.
On the 24th Ambedkar signed the 'Poona Pact', and two days later,
after it was ratified by the British Government, Gandhi accepted a
glass of orange juice from the great writer Rabindranath Tagore.[14]

There was no Quadrangular in 1932, just as there had been none
in 1931. With their leaders in jail, the members of the PJ Hindu
Gymkhana refused to participate. Without the Hindu cricketers there
could be no tournament. Its cancellation prompted a stinging rebuke
from the *Times of India*:

> it is evident that, while those in authority in the Hindu Gym-
> khana continue to mix politics and sport, the younger men will
> be deprived of the opportunity of playing the game against
> players of other communities. We cannot believe that it is the
> wish of the players themselves that the game of cricket should
> be influenced by political prejudice.[15]

With no games of their own, the Indian cricketers were keenly
following the progress of the English cricket team in Australia. They
knew the English captain's sporting ability from experience: in that
Test match of 1932, he had scored 79 and 85 not out against them.
But the reports from Australia that they read said rather more about
his character or, some would say, lack of it.

England's tour of Australia in 1932–3 is still the most controversial
in cricketing history. With a little help from his friends, the visiting
captain, D. R. Jardine, had fashioned a strategy named 'Bodyline',
which aimed at physically intimidating the Australian batsmen. He
chose four fast bowlers – Harold Larwood the best among them –
whom he instructed to bowl short, bouncing balls aimed at the body.
A bevy of close fielders surrounded the batsman on the leg side, to
snap up catches from bats offered to protect their bodies rather than
their wickets. Back then there were no helmets to protect the batsman,
nor elbow-guards and thigh-pads either. Nor were there restrictions

on how many bouncers could be bowled in an over. Bodyline was a strategy which was within the law as it was then defined, yet clearly outside the spirit of the game.

Born in Bombay of Scottish extraction, Jardine was a lean, introverted Oxonian who was determined to come back from Australia with the Ashes. Bodyline was aimed above all at Donald Bradman, who had scored a mammoth 974 runs in the last England–Australia series. It was spectacularly successful: Bradman's run tally was cut by half, and the other Australian batsmen also succumbed. But the tactics led to serious injuries and were widely condemned as being contrary to the spirit of the game. As one wag observed, Jardine won a series but nearly lost an Empire. He was then, and for many years afterwards, the most hated Englishman Down Under. He was at the wicket one hot day at Sydney, when he was surrounded by some flies. He swatted them with his bat, when a voice hailed him from the outer: 'Let them be, Jardine, they are your only friends in Australia.'

One wonders what the gentle Duleep would have made of Jardine's tactics. The other Indian in the side does not seem to have approved. At one stage the Nawab of Pataudi was asked by his captain to join an already crowded leg trap, a clear indication that more bouncers would be bowled. Pataudi pretended not to hear, whereupon Jardine witheringly remarked: 'I see His Highness is a conscientious objector.' Another fielder was sent in his place, and the Prince was dropped for the next match. As a captain, Jardine could be brutally hard on his own men. When an England player took to bed with tonsillitis and temperature, Jardine commanded him to bat, saying, 'What about those fellows who marched to Kandahar with fever on them?'[16]

Bodyline has been the subject of two quite outstanding works of cricket history. J. H. Fingleton's *Cricket Crisis*, published in 1946, is an account of a participant observer, written by a man whom Harold Larwood (Jardine's fastest bowler) called the bravest batsman he ever bowled to. Lawrence Le Quesne's *The Bodyline*, published in 1983 to mark the tour's fiftieth anniversary, is a work rich in historical depth and psychological insight.

Both writers focus on the personality of Jardine. Fingleton paints a portrait of an arrogant colonialist; cold, aloof, by his bearing and dress presuming a superiority to the descendants of convicts. Fingleton thoroughly disapproved of Bodyline, but had none the less to admire the man's character. Jardine, he wrote, was

> the most hated sportsman ever to visit this country, yet there was something indefinably magnificent and courageous in the resolute manner in which he stuck to his bodyline guns. They shouted, they raved, they stormed at Jardine in Australia and they cabled, but he remained calm.

Le Quesne's verdict was that 'the use of Bodyline in Australia, against Australia, implied an irresponsible degree of contempt for or indifference to public opinion and probable crowd reactions'. At the same time,

> it took a captain of exceptional strength of character and independence of mind to think through the logic of fast leg theory to this point and to shoulder the burden of obloquy involved in the use of it. It was his courage, and his unflinching readiness to accept the responsibility and to take the worst of the unpopularity that was going, that best explains the remarkable loyalty that Jardine commanded from his side . . .[17]

On this tour Jardine faced the wrath of the Australian crowd, the Australian press and the Australian cricket officials. Immediately on his return he penned his own account of the tour, *Quest for the Ashes*. The book claimed that 'leg-theory' (Jardine refused to use the term 'Bodyline') was nothing new, and had been used by Australian and English bowlers from the turn of the century. He combatively wrote that 'if a batsman of international class seriously objects to a short ball bumping', he 'would be well advised to consider the desirability of making way for rising talent which . . . can'.

The Australians, claimed Jardine, were 'extraordinarily sensitive to criticism'. They would give it but could not take it: 'unlike most Englishmen, the Australian, while impatient of criticism from without, is not given to criticizing either himself or his country. He reserves his criticisms for direction against other countries and their inhabitants.' He devoted a chapter to the crowd, dredging out from old newspapers accounts of how they had misbehaved over the years. According to Jardine, the Australian cricket lover, unlike his English counterpart, was prone to bouts of 'irrational hooliganism'. The England captain's view of the Bodyline controversy is summed up in this defiant quatrain:

> Australia's writers showed their claws,
> Her backers raged, her batsmen shook,
> Statesmen consulted – and the cause – ?
> Our bowling was too good to hook.[18]

SO MUCH FOR BODYLINE. Our theme here is D. R. Jardine's other and less remembered tour, which was as captain of an England team to India in the winter of 1933–4. Curiously, while Jardine's cricketers were travelling the sub-continent, another exhausting tour of India was being made by Mahatma Gandhi. Released from jail in April 1933, Gandhi had temporarily forsaken *swaraj* in favour of social reform. Ambedkar's challenge had shaken him badly, and he spent the following winter urging caste Hindus to join his campaign against Untouchability, and to allow low-caste children entry into schools previously closed to them. He had not, perhaps, chosen the most opportune time, for the urban Indian was to be greatly distracted by the entertainment offered by the visiting English cricketers. In their four months in the sub-continent Jardine's men would play thirty-four matches, spaced out among all the Provinces and the leading princely states. These included three official Test matches, the first to be played on Indian soil.

The MCC tourists arrived in Bombay on the morning of 12 October 1933. Their skipper was returning after twenty years to a city where both his father and grandfather had practised law. A microphone had been put up on deck, to enable Jardine to broadcast through All India Radio. The captions to his pictures carried the story of an unusual reception. 'Jardine found great difficulty in speaking on the microphone as the crowd surged round him and nearly swept the instrument away during his broadcast,' read one caption. 'Jardine poses for the photographer in company with his faithful servant who carried him when he was a baby in arms,' read another.

In his broadcast Jardine quoted Kipling's praise of Bombay and said he was delighted to count himself a citizen by birth of a great city. Later, in an interview with Associated Press, he remarked that he and his team 'represent the goodwill which the premier cricket club bears to all lovers of cricket throughout this great Indian Empire'. No one could be 'more jealous of their good name than myself, or more sensible of the honour done me by the Marylebone Cricket Club when they asked me to lead their team in the land of my birth'.[19]

This is exactly what the Viceroy and his men wanted to hear. Cricket might retrieve a shaky position, conveying to an undecided Indian public the merits of a continuing connection with the British. Jardine, for the moment, would play along, for after that acrimonious tour of Australia he needed to take the path of conciliation if he wished to retain his job.

The interviews concluded, the SS *Mooltan* carried on to Karachi for the first matches of the tour. In the Sind capital Jardine and C. S. Marriott, amateurs both, were the guests of the Commissioner, whereas the workaday professionals were billeted with English merchants. The cricketers played hard in the day and socialized vigorously afterwards. One evening they were the guests of the Karachi Parsi community, the programme featuring 'harmonium and singing and a graceful and rhythmical dance by sixteen beautifully attired Parsee ladies'.[20] On the morning of their departure they were presented with a civic address at a crowded Municipal Hall. Jardine sat in the centre of the dais, the Mayor of Karachi (a Parsi) on one side, the Vice-President of the Municipality (a Goan Christian) on the other. Printed in block letters on a silk scroll and presented to the English captain on a silver tray, the address stated:

> Mr Jardine, great though the fame you already have achieved and will achieve, as England's captain in other climes in years to come, we hope you will look back on your appointment to lead the first Test match team to the land of your birth as not the smallest of your honours. We feel, in fact, that the fathers of cricket have paid us a delicate compliment in sending their Test team under the command of one born within our shores.[21]

The winter of 1933–4 was a good time to be a loyalist of the Raj. The freedom movement, so intense and coordinated in 1930–2, was now disorganized and diffused. The Muslims and (more slowly) the Untouchables were abandoning the Congress, while the bulk of the Parsis and the Christians had stood apart from it anyway. Lord Willingdon looked like a man in charge, and his main adversary, Gandhi, had abandoned politics to work for the admission of Untouchables into Hindu temples. Into this welcoming vacuum stepped the cause of cricket. Indeed, even the now rudderless nationalists would express their racial animosities through it. When the selection committee for the home team was announced in early October, with all except one member being English, Maulana Shaukat Ali and L. R. Tairsee both shot off angry letters to the press, saying that it was a question of principle that 'the Indian team should be selected by Indians'.[22]

Jardine, of course, was to meet more Indian loyalists than Indian nationalists. He was 'visibly moved' by the Karachi address, and put together a graceful reply. The England captain, reported the *Times of India* man on the spot,

> said he believed that as a poet had said there were two worlds, one which they measure with rule and line and another which they measure with their hearts and imagination. In the beautiful address which he had received they had shown Karachi as K on

the map of India, and [for his team] the letter K stood for 'key'
in their hearts and imagination.[23]

From Karachi the tourists proceeded to Peshawar, where they
played a Northwest Frontier Provinces team and were entertained by
the Cheshire Regiment at the Khyber Pass. They then moved southwards, into the Punjab. Here they played the Governor's XI, at
Lahore, and also attended a party in their honour at the historic
Shalimar Gardens. Playing for the home side was C. K. Nayudu, on
loan to the Punjab from the state of Holkar to help boost the purse.
When he was appointed captain for the Test series, Nayudu sent
Jardine and his team, still on ship, a telegram which read: 'Wait till
you see me.' In fact the Englishmen saw him everywhere, for he
played as many as ten matches against them, appearing for local sides
which had no moral claim on him but wanted the material benefits
that his presence would generate. In this extended winter, Nayudu
played against the MCC for the Viceroy's XI at Delhi, for 'An Indian
XI' in Calcutta, for Vizianagaram's XI at Benares, for his own Central
India at Indore, for Central Provinces and Berar at Nagpur, for Moin-
ud-Dowlah's XI at Secunderabad – and in three Test matches besides.[24]
Jardine came to call his opponents 'C. K. Nayudu's roving circus'.
In fairness to the Indian, it should be said that he travelled second
class around the country while the MCC rested comfortably in first
class. And in the winter of 1933–4 Nayudu was pushing forty, too.

Nayudu was now in the employment of the Maharaja of Holkar.
This ruler had given the cricketer a splendid double-storeyed mansion,
a Dodge car and a well-paid post in the State Army.[25] His duties
were confined to the cricket field. As the Maharaja once said, 'I am
the ruler of Holkar, but C. K. is the King of Outdoor Games.' While
his bills were paid by Holkar, Nayudu in fact belonged to all of India.
After his innings against Gilligan's team he had become a national
hero, a *travelling* national hero. Every winter he would play in the
big show in Bombay, in the CP Quadrangular held in his home
town, Nagpur, for the Indians versus the Europeans in the annual
Madras Presidency Match, and for all kinds of pick-up teams in other

towns and cities. Wherever he went he was watched by an admiring crowd, all waiting, inevitably, for those sixers.

A decade ago, while researching an anecdotal history of Indian cricket, I heard again and again stories of spectacular hits by Nayudu. In Hyderabad I was told of a six he struck out of the Secunderabad Gymkhana into the Plaza Cinema. In Madras I was told of a straight drive out of Chepauk, which cleared the tall trees that ringed the ground to land in (in some versions, beyond) the canal outside. In my native Bangalore, stories of Nayudu sixers were not restricted to a single venue. At the RSI ground, he hit a young fast bowler into Bairds Barracks – a carry of 120 yards – and then told the victim, with perfect sincerity, 'Well bowled, son.' And when batting at the Central College, C. K. hit a six that landed in the compound of the Sagar Talkies, a strike that somehow symbolically united those great popular passions, cricket and the cinema.[26]

Had Nayudu been an Englishman he would have been an amateur. In his regal bearing and style of batsmanship he combined, shall we say, the best of Gilbert Jessop and Ted Dexter. But in India he was obliged to take a job, even if it meant mostly playing cricket. Still, with a father from Cambridge and a family steeped in the plays of Shakespeare, Nayudu was more of a *pukka saheb* than a flag-bearing nationalist. Yet his batsmanship became a vehicle for the articulation of suppressed national feeling. Millions of Indians thrust their own emotions and aspirations upon him. The strain, both physical and mental, must have been terrific. Yet he always bore it with dignity and poise.

Right-wing and left-wing, nationalist and loyalist, conservative and modernizer, all joined in this appreciation. Once, as Finance Minister of independent India, the austere and puritanical Morarji Desai refused to sanction foreign exchange for a touring team, asking: 'But where is another C. K. Nayudu to draw in the crowds to justify this expense?'[27] From the other side of the political spectrum, the Communist leader Hiren Mukherjee spoke of his first view of C. K., at Eden Gardens in 1927. Nayudu scored only 9, but, recalled Mukherjee, 'he had, in his short stay, made a glance to leg which gleamed for a fraction of a second and has been treasured in my memory ever since'.[28]

Better than these tributes from public figures is the story of the nameless boy who requested an autograph of Sarojini Naidu, President of the Indian National Congress, friend of Jinnah and Gandhi, a much-trumpeted poetess known as the 'Nightingale of India'. When a bystander asked the boy whether he knew who the lady was, he answered, 'Yes, of course. She is the wife of C. K. Nayudu.'[29] Then there was the lady fan who wrote to the cricketer when he was out shooting, saying, 'Now that you are in the jungles, you will have more time to read my letters.'[30]

It was in recognition of this status that the organizers of the MCC tour made certain that Nayudu would play against the visitors as often as he could. His first appearance, as we have noted, was for the Punjab Governor's XI at Lahore. On the day of the match a local paper wrote of Nayudu that 'he is our Bradman, our chief match winner, and not merely the gate attraction that people take him to be, though that too he incidentally is. On him depend all our chances of lowering the MCC colours.'[31]

At Lahore Nayudu hit his quota of sixes in scoring 116. Two young cricketers in the crowd later wrote of how his stroke-play signalled a broader political message:

> None will ever forget [Nayudu's] tremendous square hits when by just an easy flourish of his wrists the ball was flung from his bat sailing through the firmament – higher and higher it rose and the English fielders stood at the boundary lines first expecting a catch, then watching its course upward until it remained just a speck, becoming almost invisible, then cutting a curve [till] it fell over the far off trees across the road near the Montgomery Hall. Such a display I had never witnessed before in my life and the next day I had to play against Jardine's team at Amritsar. Nayudu had driven away all fear of the foreigner from my mind.[32]

Every sixer hit by 'C. K.' against the visitors' slow bowlers was as good as a nail in the coffin of the British Empire. I remember a shot he hit against James Langridge which sailed over the pavilion at the Lahore Gymkhana ground in what is now called Bagh-i-Jinnah. We madly cheered each shot past the boundary not only as a cricket performance but also as an assertion of our resolve to throw the British out of India.[33]

FROM LAHORE, Jardine's team moved on to the holy Sikh city of Amritsar, where they played a team captained by the Maharaja of Patiala. The leading nationalist paper of the Punjab had assured Jardine that he need not 'carry his Australian feelings to India which is not only hospitable but charitable'.[34] The loyalists, of course, came out in force. The town's Deputy Commissioner, A. MacFarquhar, ICS, issued a note to the press spelling out the programme in detail:

> The MCC arrives at Amritsar on November 8th, to play a three-day match. . . . On the afternoon of the 8th, His Highness the Maharaja of Patiala will open the Bhupinder Pavilion on the Alexandra Ground. A garden party given by leading citizens will follow, and that evening Sardar Santokh Singh, President of the Amritsar Municipality, will give a dinner. The following evening the Services Club will give a dinner, which will be followed by a free private cinema show at the Pearl Talkies arranged by Sardar Balwan Singh, proprietor. On November 10th, the Amritsar Club is holding a fancy dress dance.
>
> There will be a cricket lunch on the ground each day to teams. His Highness the Maharaja of Patiala will be the host on November 9th, C. Tirath Ram, Honorary Magistrate on the 10th, and Diwan Dilbagh Rai and Mr Madan Lal Ahuja on the 11th November. Khan Sahib Mian Hussam Din, Municipal Commissioner, will provide tea on the 9th, Mr Vidya Dhar Tandon on the 10th and Khan Bahadur Syed Budeh Shah on the 11th.
>
> Play will commence each day at 11 a.m. except on Saturday,

November 11th, when it will commence at 11.45 a.m. to allow
of an Armistice Service to be held beforehand.[35]

Foreign cricketers in India are more avidly sought than royalty,
everyone and his brother wanting a piece of them. The MCC team
of 1933–4 might very well have been the first to receive the full
treatment. The Deputy Commissioner of Amritsar, and of all the
other towns the cricketers visited, would have been besieged by
requests to entertain them. These requests, it appears, were processed
strictly with a view to social prestige and social diversity. By the
names posted by MacFarquhar we can discern a deliberate strategy,
allowing Hindu, Sikh and Muslim notables alike to patronize the
cricketers, and thus also cement their own links with Empire.

The integrative functions of sport were made manifest in a speech
made by the Maharaja of Patiala at the Services Club dinner. Speaking
as an 'old cricketer', he insisted that 'the commonwealth of sport
knows no distinction of caste or creed, community or race. It sub-
merges these unwelcome distinctions which cast their shadow on
human relationships in the single-minded devotion to play the game
in the spirit of the game.' Jardine, in his reply, added that 'cricket
which was the greatest of games was the greatest asset to the Empire'.[36]

From Amritsar the MCC travelled to Patiala, where they were
fêted afresh and also shown around the spectacular collection of
medals and jewels in the palace. The English cricketers worked off
the fat on the field and, afterwards, in a shoot in the private jungles
of the Maharaja of Patiala. The fast bowler Nobby Clark bagged a
cheetah, and some deer and partridge were also shot. In the last week
of November the tourists reached the Imperial capital, Delhi. Jardine
was to stay at the Viceregal Lodge, while the others were put up at
the Swiss Hotel, in the fashionable Civil Lines. The Maharaja of
Bikaner, the Imperial Delhi Gymkhana Club and the Roshanara Club
all hosted big parties. The veteran cricket writer E. H. D. Sewell
wondered how the MCC 'will be able to stand up and do their best
on the field of play . . . unless they are allowed to cut out some of
the festivities arranged in their honour'.[37] Sewell seems not to have

recognized the deeper meaning of the festivities, which was to dust off and advertise once more the old theory of the Empire of Cricket. Thus at the Roshanara Club ball, the President of the Legislative Assembly, Sir R. K. Shanmugham Chetty, suggested that the MCC visit 'had done more than all the sessions of the Round Table Conference. Cricket had always brought together prince and commoner on a common field, which was a good augury for the future . . .'[38]

One does not know about Prince and commoner, but even as Chetty spoke cricket was dividing Prince from Prince. In the capital the MCC were first to play a two-day match against Delhi and Districts. Jardine had invited the Maharaja of Patiala, lately his host, to play for the MCC, of which the Maharaja was a member. But the Viceroy was not pleased, for as far as he was concerned Patiala was in the doghouse. Just the previous summer he had been externed from the Raj's summer capital, Simla, allegedly for making a pass at an English girl. It was even rumoured that the object of Patiala's passion was the Willingdons' daughter. Disbarred from Simla, the Prince bought a nearby hill-top where he erected what remains the highest active cricket ground in the world.

In the Punjab, Patiala had entertained the English cricketers and taken them on *shikar*. Playing him for the MCC, as he was entitled to do under the club's rules, was Jardine's way of returning the favour. Willingdon felt that this would send a wrong message, especially in Delhi. When he suggested to Jardine that he should not include the Prince, the cricketer merely refilled his pipe. Later, Lady Willingdon took him for a walk in the Mughal Gardens and 'tried all her persuasive powers on him'. But Jardine would not yield.[39]

Patiala duly played against Delhi and Districts. The MCC's next match was against a Viceroy's XI, in which six resident Englishmen joined five Indians. For this match the Government of India shut down the Secretariat and Legislative Assembly. Many businesses also voluntarily downed shutters. These were, after all, the first big sporting events in the new capital of the Raj. New Delhi had taken eighteen years to build, but the first occupant of its first house had been a man sympathetic to Gandhi, Lord Irwin. His successor, however, would emphatically reassert the authority of the Raj. Lord Willingdon was a former Cambridge Cricket Blue, and well used to patronizing the game in India. While Governor of Bombay during the First World War he made it a point to watch the Quadrangular. Now, in a bigger job in a more important city, he went to the new Ferozeshah Kotla ground to watch play from a pavilion named after him.

Sitting not far from the Willingdons was the correspondent of the *Times of India*. The air was crisp and the sky cloudless. 'The ground this afternoon', wrote the journalist,

> was a memorable sight. In the Willingdon Pavilion, which over-looks it from the best vantage point, were the Viceroy and the Countess of Willingdon. His Excellency was full of bonhomie and evidently thoroughly enjoying the holiday and the cricket. Her Excellency was as vivacious as ever, and captured everybody's admiration by the radiating charm of her appearance in her beautiful dress of pale cyclamen, mauve flowered georgette and large picture hat of the same colours. Around them were several members of Council, a number of the ruling Princes and all New Delhi society, including a host of ladies, arrayed in some of their prettiest garden party frocks. The overflow from the pavilion was seated on rows and rows of chairs, arranged on the narrow terraces, which descend like broad steps below it to the level of the playing field.
>
> All around the ground was gathered one of the biggest crowds of the kind ever seen in India – even at one of the most exciting Presidency or Quadrangular matches in Bombay. On one's left they were tiered up twenty or thirty deep on a broad sloping embankment, mostly under cover of decorative awnings. To the right, where the spectators had to face the sun, there was a thinner array of people, their backs to a high fence, covered under a gorgeous riot of morning glory creeper, behind which again rose the fine old walls of Delhi city. Straight ahead over the heads of the players was another great throng, this time picturesquely set off by a background of tall dark trees, through

the tops of which shone glimpses of tall white city buildings and above them all the beautiful domes and minarets of the Jumma Masjid.

The whole scene was that of a great fête. Behind the crowded rows of onlookers refreshment caterers had large establishments for attending to people's wants throughout the day. Behind them again, on the open ground below the Feroz Shah Kotla, were parked in rows hundreds and hundreds of motor cars. Somewhere in the offing and always pleasantly within hearing a band played during most of the day. But the best music of all was the uproarious cheers of the crowds when a batsman played a fine stroke or a fielder made a good catch . . .

Tonight there is a great ball at the Imperial Delhi Gymkhana Club in honour of the visitors. Their Excellencies the Viceroy and the Countess of Willingdon are to be present, and there is certain to be a huge crowd on the floor.[40]

Delhi in November, the Viceroy and his lady in their proper place, and the Indians in *theirs*. Cricket was once more the means by which the permanence of British rule would be assured. But, unbeknownst to the chronicler, a chill had developed between the Willingdons and their chief guest. The Patiala episode had made Jardine determined to thrash the team wearing his host's colours. After the home side had been dismissed for 160, the MCC ran up a total in excess of 400. The Viceroy's XI had now to bat out a whole day to draw the match. Before play began an ICS man, Christie, got the pitch rolled for twenty minutes instead of the allotted ten, so that it would play easy. When Jardine found out he was livid. He said he would not lead his team on to the field unless Christie apologized. Another senior official told Jardine that 'if the Indian public ever got to know of such an attitude by an English captain British prestige would suffer'. Jardine was adamant, so finally the Viceroy himself instructed Christie to apologize, saying, 'My dear fellow, you are dealing with a tough proposition, the toughest that even the Australians had come up against . . .'[41] The match ended with Jardine's side winning by an innings.

When the MCC men left Delhi Lord Willingdon wrote with feeling to his sister:

> The cricketers have left us for elsewhere thank goodness. We had 15 of them staying here for 4 days! I don't like Jardine and don't wonder at the Australians hating him. He is a fine cricketer and very good captain, but he is the most self-opinionated man I've ever met, full of wind in his head, talks to all of us as if he and not we know much about India.[42]

WHILE THE MCC were travelling through northern India, Palwankar Baloo was planning a career move, from cricket to politics. In the last week of October he filed his nomination for a by-election to fill a seat in the Bombay Municipality. It was an open seat, and he chose to stand on the ticket of the Hindu Mahasabha. This, on the face of it, seems a strange choice. During the Communal Award's discussions in 1932 Baloo was befriended by the Mahasabha leader, Dr B. S. Moonje, and perhaps Moonje persuaded him to run on behalf of his party. Notably, the Congress did not put up a candidate of its own, and instructed its members to support Baloo. In an appeal for votes Baloo said he would 'ever strive for solidarity among the Hindus by advocating the necessity of Joint Electorates for the Hindus irrespective of caste and creed'. He was, he declared, against 'Separationists': 'I have always worked and have been working with a Nationalist point of view and I am working for the uplift of my Harijan brothers in a way which would not break them away from the great Hindu society.' Intriguingly, he had chosen that vehicle of social intermingling, the railway engine, as his electoral symbol.[43]

In England titled cricketers (such as Lord Harris) sometimes made a successful entry into politics. But Baloo's decision to stand for election seems to have been a 'world first' as far as the professional cricketer was concerned, anticipating, by many years, the move into politics of such men as Pakistan's Imran Khan and Guyana's Roy

Fredericks. It is thus surprising that, especially with the MCC tour on, Baloo chose not to mention his own achievements on the playing-field. On the day of the elections, the *Bombay Chronicle* announced that 'Baloo with Gandhiji's support gets good support from middle class Hindus'. From talking to voters its reporter got the sense that Baloo was 'ably supported by the middle class Hindus', whereas his main rival, Dr Homi F. Pavri, was 'well supported by Parsis, Muslims, Christians, Europeans and high class Hindus'. There was 'expected to be a rush of voters for Mr Baloo in the evening when office workers return home'.[44]

The day of the election Gandhi was in Nagpur, announcing the start of his All India tour 'to remove the curse of untouchability. Either untouchability must die, or I shall perish in attempting to remove it.' Statements like this evoked powerful reactions, pro and con: the reader, were he a caste Hindu, was just as likely to cast his vote against Baloo as for him. In the event, Baloo got 2,179 votes to Dr Pavri's 3,030. He would have done better had he traded on his cricketing past, but he seems to have underestimated the growing social appeal of the game or its relevance to politics.[45]

Jardine and his men, meanwhile, were slowly making their way to Bombay. From Delhi they travelled to Saurashtra, playing one match and spending the rest of the week in search of big game. Jardine went to Junagadh, the last redoubt of the Asiatic lion, and hired thirty beaters 'to induce a lion to sweep past his Machan on a tree in the recesses of the Gir Forest'. He sat in the Machan for three days before a lion came, but he successfully shot it and took the skin with him. His next stop was Killeshwar in Nawanagar State, once Ranji's own favourite forest. Beaters located a large panther, which grew aggressive when cornered and mauled two of them. Jardine fired some shots, and when the dust cleared they found an 8-foot-long panther lying stone dead. The shoot ended with a banquet at the Maconochie Club (so named for a former British Resident), where the England captain won a silver cup in the general knowledge competition.[46]

At last, in the second week of December, the cricketers reached the city of their captain's birth and the site of the first Test match. The papers seized the moment to print brief biographies of Jardine's forebears. His grandfather, William Jardine, went from a Law Professorship in Lahore to a seat on the bench at the Allahabad High Court. He died at thirty-two, of cholera, but two of his sons were to carry on his work in India. One, W. E. Jardine, joined the ICS, while the second, M. R. Jardine, scored 100 in the Varsity match before joining the Bombay Bar. Affectionately known as 'Snipe', M. R. was an examiner in English for the Bombay University, later Perry Professor of Jurisprudence and Professor of the Law College, and still later Advocate-General of the Presidency. In between these various appointments he played cricket against the Parsis and fathered Douglas. As one journalist colourfully wrote, the current England captain saw his first sunrise lying on his back in a house on Malabar Hill.[47]

Jardine's return to Bombay began with a strange experience. The day before the Test he accompanied his father's butler, Lalla Sebastian, to Sewrie cemetery. The butler, then in the employ of the Chief Justice, Sir John Beaumont, wished to lay wreaths on the graves of his relatives. After climbing the hill and going round the cemetery with his former *baba*, Sebastian complained of heartache. Jardine rushed him to the K. E. M. Hospital, where he was declared dead.[48]

Which student or participant of Bodyline would be prepared for Jardine taking time out to accompany his butler to a cemetery in between parties? India softened him; here, at any rate, he was not the cruel and heartless fellow of cricket lore. Nonetheless, we may be sure that when the Test match began his mind was focused absolutely on the cricket. For this first-ever Test on Indian soil a new double-decker stand was built to accommodate an extra 10,000 spectators. All Government offices in Bombay were closed for the first two days of the match, and the third day was a Sunday anyway. To help people get to the ground suburban trains ran on the weekday schedule.

On the morning of the match, the *Times of India* led off with a cartoon. The caption read: 'The Lion and the Tiger take the field –

and may the best side win'. A cricketer with a lion's mane was tossing with another with a tiger's head, while an interested kangaroo in white trousers looked on. This picture of an Empire brought together by sport was confirmed at the venue. On the roof of the Bombay Gymkhana flew three flags: the Union Jack in the middle, the red-and-yellow MCC flag on one side and the light-blue flag of British India on the other. This last had been designed, of course, by an Englishman. There was no question of the Bombay Gymkhana putting up in its place the saffron-and-green flag adopted as India's own by the Indian National Congress.

At the end of the match both sides and their supporters had reason to be pleased. England won, by a margin of nine wickets, but India had a new hero. This was the twenty-one-year-old Lala Amarnath, who hit a battling century on debut, putting on 186 in partnership with C. K. Nayudu, the runs coming in a single afternoon. Amarnath's hundred, the first ever by an Indian in Test cricket, took a mere 117 minutes, and included eighteen fours. When the players walked off the field at stumps, wrote the *Bombay Chronicle*, 'the police had to rush to the rescue of Amarnath, who was mobbed by the crowd on his way to the pavilion'. Once he had reached the safety of the pavilion, Amarnath was garlanded by the Mayor of Bombay and presented with expensive gifts by Hindu jewellers.[49]

A vivid if delayed account of the public reception of Amarnath's innings is contained in the premier newspaper of his home town, Lahore. 'At the close of play', remarked *The Tribune*,

> a section of the crowd seemed to go mad and would not be satisfied until Amarnath was presented before them. This was arranged to be done in front of the Hindu Gymkhana pavilion, and there was such a rush of spectators on all sides that many chairs and tables were literally broken to pieces.

Cups and presents were flowing in from his admirers, the paper reported. Their man, it said, had even been congratulated by the Maharajas of Kolhapur and Baroda.[50]

The following day's *Tribune* carried a remarkable excerpt

attributed to the Bombay correspondent of *The Statesman*. Since Amarnath's hundred, wrote this reporter in disgust, 'hero worship had been carried to ridiculous excess'. A reported sum of 20,000 rupees (the equivalent, perhaps, of a million rupees today) had already been collected for him. Moreover, the

> equivalent of the widow's mite was represented by a man who tried to press on the Lahore player what he confessed was his last six annas in the world. Amarnath has also been presented with a gold cup by a local goldsmith and I learn that in the heat of the excitement women were divesting themselves of their earnings and throwing them at their hero.... We may see Amarnath presented with a Taj Mahal yet.[51]

The hero returned to his native heath on 22 December, the tales of his epic innings and its still more epic aftermath preceding him. When the Frontier Mail arrived at Lahore, Amarnath was 'given a rousing reception by a large number of cricket fans and other sports enthusiasts who thronged the railway station'. The crowd clawed and pawed and garlanded him, but after they had dispersed, the *Tribune's* representative was able to place the *Statesman* report before Amarnath. The cricketer 'vehemently denied' he had received 20,000 rupees in gifts. By his accounting, he had been presented with 200 rupees by the Maharaja of Porbandar, with 50 rupees by the mother of his team-mate Vijay Merchant, and with 50 rupees by a gentleman of the PJ Hindu Gymkhana. Gifts in kind included a gold cup, a silver casket with a gold set within it, two watches, four English bats, a 'beautiful pair of hand gloves', medals, cups and 'various other things' collectively worth about 3,000 rupees. Some wealthy *seths* and Princes had promised to send other presents. As for 'the throwing of ear-rings and other ornaments' by women, apparently it 'was mere stunt, and according to Mr Amarnath, had been added to make the [*Statesman's*] statement look more picturesque'.[52]

A romantic reporter might have added a zero or two to the money he got, but there is no question that in Bombay, at the time, or in Lahore, later, Amarnath's debut hundred was met with an extraordinary display of popular emotion. 'I hope his head is screwed on firmly,' wrote E. H. D. Sewell in the *Times of India*, 'otherwise his cricket career will be a very short one. Already, his countrymen and women have done much to shorten it by overloading him with presents, little understanding that cricket is not built on such foundations.'[53]

IT WAS A NICE TOUCH that Lala Amarnath made his runs in partnership with C. K. Nayudu. It was a symbolic passing on of the baton. The venue was significant, too: the Bombay Gymkhana, that old centre of colonial cultural power. This was the place where the Hindus had played the MCC in December 1926, the place where the Hindus had defeated the Presidency in February 1906, the place that was the home of the polo players who once sought to push the native cricketers out of the Maidan. With only a little exaggeration, we may say that there ran a straight line from Shapoorjee Sorabjee through Palwankar Baloo and C. K. Nayudu on to Lala Amarnath.

Thus, suppressed behind the popular acclaim for Amarnath's hundred was a great deal of nationalist feeling. As with C. K. Nayudu's innings against Giligan's side, the public was responding as much to a cricketer's skill as to his (strictly temporary) humbling of the best the ruler could offer. Indeed, in a reception at their next stop the English cricketers got their first taste of the other and sometimes seditious India. This party was thrown on Christmas Eve and hosted by Calcutta's Mayor, S. K. Basu. In his speech the Mayor looked to a future rather different to that anticipated by Jardine's men and their admirers in the Secretariat or the *Times of India*. 'When the edifice of India's *swaraj* was built,' remarked Basu, 'historians will take note not only of the contributions made by the politicians but also of those made by sportsmen who would meet their British compeers on an equal ground in the cricket field . . .'[54]

Unfortunately, Jardine was not around to hear this. Between the Bombay and Calcutta Tests he was out shooting in the jungles once more. A lion was a decent enough trophy, but a tiger, the pride of the Indian forest, would be better still. He first visited the state of Datia, where he claimed a nilgai and a sambhur, but no tiger. He then crossed over the border into Gwalior, where he thought he would have better luck, since his uncle had once been Resident there. The Maharaja presented Jardine with a matchlock rifle with silver inlaid barrels, and set up a shoot 'in some of the likeliest looking tiger country imaginable'. He bagged a sambhur with 28-inch horns, but 'had not the luck to add a Gwalior tiger to his increasing list of Indian trophies'. His mood was spoilt further when his colleague, the leg-spinner C. S. Marriott, successfully shot a tiger.[55]

The Calcutta Test coincided with the holy month of Ramadan, and the host side had four Muslims. These included the fast bowler Mohammed Nissar, who could bowl only four overs in his first spell. An English journalist wrote sympathetically of Nissar's 'pardonable lifelessness. It was long ago proved true that an army marches on its stomach. If that's empty the army is liable to produce a flat effort.'[56] When India batted, Nobby Clark, allegedly on instructions from Jardine, bowled bouncers. Dilawar Hussain was hit on the head and taken off the field. The umpire, Frank Tarrant, told the England captain that he would have to stop Clark from bowling. 'If you do that I will stop you from umpiring,' answered Jardine.[57]

In the event Dilawar Hussain returned to the crease and scored a half-century. Like Nissar, Dilawar was of course a Muslim. Yet Ramadan did not affect his performance: was this because he was less pious, or because it is far easier to bat defensively than to bowl fast on an empty stomach? We shall never know. But in the second innings Dilawar again batted resolutely, scoring a second fifty – at the time a record for a wicket-keeper in Test cricket – and helping India draw the match. The last overs were played out in a breathless hush; 'the only noises were the cawing of crows and the squabblings of coolies over the remains of lunch'.[58]

After Calcutta the tourists retraced their steps northwards, to Banaras. At a ball in honour of the Governor of the United Provinces, Sir Malcolm Hailey, Jardine decided to misbehave again. As the band struck up the Military Secretary walked up to the captain and told him: 'You will be the first to dance with Lady Hailey.' Jardine responded with a casual 'Oh', and picked up a pretty young thing and took her to the floor. When accosted in the middle he flew into a rage and said: 'I have travelled round the globe but have never been ordered to dance with anybody. I would have danced with Lady Hailey of my own accord, but not if commanded to do so.'[59]

In Banaras the MCC were to play a match against the Maharajkumar of Vizianagaram's XI. 'Vizzy' looked like Billy Bunter and played cricket like Billy Bunter. But he threw his money at the sport and had a craving to lead India. For this match he had hired the best Indian cricketers: Amarnath, C. K. Nayudu, Mohammad Nissar and Dilawar Hussain. He had even brought over a Ceylonese bowler, Kelaart. With these men playing above their form and the Englishmen playing below theirs, Vizzy's team won by 14 runs. This was the only time Jardine's team was to be defeated on tour.

Afterwards, there was some speculation that Vizzy had induced the England captain to 'throw' the match. Others wondered whether the MCC had been deadened by drink or seduced by the fabled dancing girls of Banaras. A more likely explanation is that Vizzy had promised Jardine a tiger. Indeed, he missed the next match, against Central India, choosing to spend it in a shooting block in Mirzapur reserved for the Maharajkumar. Alas, he drew a blank once more, bagging a bear but not the great striped cat he so desperately wanted.[60]

By now Jardine's bonhomie was wearing thin. Two months in and out of Indian trains would tire anybody. The excessive acclaim for Amarnath would also have put him off somewhat. Above all, there was that failure in the forest. At a reception in Nagpur in mid-January, Jardine expressed his disgust with the men who would lead India. 'The raising of an eleven from among the various members of the Round Table Conference would not be a bad idea', he said. 'Whatever their cricketing abilities might be, they would not fail to draw a good gate. I am not sure what they would charge for such entertainments, but I am afraid they will question the umpire's decision.'[61]

From Nagpur the tourists moved leisurely down the Deccan, playing in Hyderabad and Mysore before arriving in Madras for the third Test. At Jardine's insistence, Frank Tarrant was replaced by another umpire at the last moment. Was this because of their spat over Clark's tactics in Calcutta? Or because Tarrant's favourite pupil, the Yuvraj of Patiala, had been chosen to play for India? Tarrant's nationality could scarcely have helped him either. The Australian told the Associated Press that Jardine was upset by some of his decisions in previous Tests. 'Where are the sportsmen of 1934', he asked, caustically, 'if the captain of the MCC cannot take l.b.w. decisions with good grace?'[62] The Indian nationalists took up his case. Tarrant's dismissal, remarked one paper, 'is symptomatic of the spirit in which Mr Jardine conducts his captaincy'. He 'seems to feel that he is an Imperial General on a conquering expedition'.[63]

Although three matches in Ceylon awaited them, the Madras Test was the MCC's last scheduled match in India. Jardine's fastest bowler, Nobby Clark, again bowled bumpers, hitting an Indian batsman on the head. The England side was superior in all aspects of the game, and won easily. But the home team conspicuously stayed away from a post-match dinner hosted by the all-white Madras Cricket Club. The sources, unfortunately, do not give us the reason. Was this out of solidarity with Tarrant – a great servant of Indian cricket and a mentor to many of its players – in protest against Jardine's admittedly brief resort to Bodyline, or a general disgust with the ways of the English in India?

After Madras the MCC proceeded to Ceylon but were persuaded to come back to Bombay to play one last match in aid of the Viceroy's Fund for the victims of a massive earthquake in Bihar. The match was played at the Bombay Gymkhana, whose Secretary, a Mr Prideaux, peevishly issued press passes only to reporters of the Associated Press and the *Times of India*. Twelve Indian journalists, representing English, Marathi and Gujarati papers, were told to buy tickets if they wanted to watch the game. In protest against the 'unasked for monopoly of the two [white] reporters', the Indian papers refused to cover the match at all.[64]

When the Charity Match was over and the tourists had boarded their last ship, the *Times of India* wrote that their visit had been 'an unqualified success', with the English players having 'laid the foundations of yet another great cricketing country within the British Commonwealth of Nations'.[65] However, the *Bombay Chronicle*, smarting under Mr Prideaux's insult, now recalled all the other ones. The tour, it claimed, had been marked by

> a series of inexcusable and egregious blunders and bunglings. The composition of the Selection Committee, with a majority of non-Indians, the appointment of umpires [no Indian was on the panel], the removal of Tarrant and the unfortunate episode in Madras – all these have brought into prominent relief the utter failure of the Board of Control for Cricket in India to maintain the self-respect of Indians . . .[66]

THE ADDRESS D. R. Jardine had received in Karachi was a kiss of death, for he was never to captain England again. In the summer of 1934 the Australians were touring, and the MCC sensibly did not want to risk the row his appointment would create. The Australians might have detested Jardine, but Indians have reason to remember him more kindly. Through a long, tedious tour Jardine behaved himself, for the most part. Although missing stalwarts like Hammond and Sutcliffe, his team was still better than any previous combination to play in India. The matches they played stoked enormous interest. One paper complained of being 'overwhelmed with correspondence and articles, from those who know, those who think they know and those who certainly do not know all about cricket'.[67]

On Douglas Jardine's death in 1958 his opposing number in that series, C. K. Nayudu, wrote an obituary for the Madras weekly, *Sport and Pastime*. Indians are not very good at remembering the dead, being too superficial or too submissive, but on this occasion Nayudu got his man exactly right. 'As an opponent', he recalled,

> I found Jardine a tough fighter, a shrewd tactician whose knowledge of the game was very sound and profound. With a height of 6' 2" he was a commanding figure on the field. He was a strict disciplinarian and would not tolerate any opposition, defiance or nonsense. He was aloof and unsentimental. He commanded loyalty rather than won it.[68]

The admiration was mutual. Jardine admired C. K.'s batsmanship, saying he was a right-handed equivalent of that legendary English cricketer, Frank Woolley: as he put it, 'both remain masters of execution of every shot the game has known'.[69] And he admired his leadership, his ability to keep together an Indian team torn apart by caste, religion and princely affiliation. After the Bombay Test of December 1933 Jardine thanked the 'able and charming captain of the Indian team – C. K. Nayudu'. These words formed part of a Christmas and New Year's greeting where the MCC captain also spoke of the 'unfailing kindness and the genuine welcome which it has been our fortunate experience to have received everywhere'.[70] The cricket he saw and (especially) the hospitality he received led Jardine to say, as he was leaving these shores, that 'in ten years India will be one of the top cricketing countries of the world'.[71]

The last weeks of the tour might not have been so pleasant for Jardine – or for his hosts – but it was clear that India touched him. Later in life he often went back, mentally at any rate, to the country of his birth. A colleague of his in the City recalled that the middle-aged Jardine had an abiding interest in Hindu philosophy, which went with an antipathy towards Christianity. 'Kindly and high-minded', intent only 'on ethical and religious problems', there was now the 'faintest trace of the aloof, decisive cricket captain'.[72]

After the events of Bodyline had passed into history, someone claimed to have discovered the origins of Jardine's hatred of Australians. Back in 1921, playing for Oxford University against the Australian touring side, Jardine had reached 96 not out when play was called off on the final day. There was, however, provision for an extra half-hour, to play which both captains had to agree. In this case, with a young lad on the verge of a century, the courtesy was to be expected. But the touring captain, Warwick Armstrong, refused, apparently because until this point no Englishman had scored a hundred against his side. The insult was swallowed then, but twelve years later Jardine extracted a full revenge. One wonders if his affection for India and Indians can be explained along similar lines. When growing up in Malabar Hill, his butler Lalla Sebastian might have spoiled him rotten. He might have even have bowled to him with a tennis ball.

10. Politics and Play

On 12th December 1933, two days before the start of the first Test played on Indian soil, the PJ Hindu Gymkhana gave a dinner in honour of the home captain. At this dinner C. K. Nayudu spoke of how 'he very much longed to see the famous Quadrangular matches played in Bombay until four years ago'.[1] As it happened, the spectators in the city were as nostalgic as the players. After the Test was over, one P. D. Dalal wrote to the newspapers to complain of the PJ Hindu Gymkhana's boycott of the tournament from 1930 to 1932. The Gymkhana, said Dalal, 'must admit its mistake; not only that but make amends by making Bombay once more the Mecca of [Indian] cricket. This can only be done by playing the Quadrangulars again – and splendidly too.'[2] In his retrospective on the MCC tour, the venerable Dr M. E. Pavri suggested that the poor performance of Bombay players against the tourists was because of the absence of the Quadrangular, which meant that they 'were unable to show their usual form'. 'For Bombay cricket', he wrote, 'the Quadrangular tournament is a necessity, its popularity beng firmly established among the cricket-going public.'[3]

While the Bombay Quadrangular was in abeyance the game was progressing in other parts of the country. The Sind Pentangular was not disrupted, for that province was largely exempt from the influence of the Congress. Cricket managers in other provinces were busy forming their own associations and affiliating them with the Board of Control for Cricket in India. The Princes recruited cricketers and organized matches. In the chiefdom of Hyderabad an enterprising nobleman named Moin-ud-dowlah had started a Gold Cup tournament in 1930, inviting teams from all over India, deliberately setting up his show as an alternative to the Bombay cricket carnival.[4]

The Cricket Board, meanwhile, was proposing an All India tournament of its own. More than a dozen associations were now registered with it: all that was wanted was a trophy to compete for. When representatives of these associations met at Simla in June 1934, the Maharaja of Patiala offered to donate £500 for a trophy named for K. S. Ranjitsinhji. A nephew of Ranji, representing western India, suggested the design: a Grecian urn 2 feet high, with a lid, the handle of which represented Father Time. The first edition of the Ranji Trophy would be played for in the winter of 1934–5.[5]

The start of a new All India competition spurred the Gymkhanas of Bombay to revive the Quadrangular. In the five years since the tournament was last held the political climate had dramatically changed. The Muslims, as we have noticed, stayed away from the salt *satyagraha* and its associated movements. In the summer of 1932 Hindus and Muslims battled with one another for weeks in the streets of Bombay. There were attacks on temples and mosques, cremation grounds and graveyards. According to police figures 217 citizens were killed and 2,713 injured in the violence. Between May and July, 600 rounds were fired by the police and the military to disperse rampaging mobs. Some said the trouble started when a Hindu shopkeeper refused to give alms to a Muslim boy during Muharram. The Commissioner of Police, however, insisted that the

> explanation is to be found in the relations between the two communities. The mutual feelings of suspicion and distrust are more bitter today than at any time in my 30 years' service. The fierce political struggle of the last few years has disclosed acute differences of opinion, and with the prospect of consti-tutional reform in the near future each community fears that the other will get too dominant a position. In particular the civil disobedience movement has served to estrange the two communities. The Muhammadans as a body have constantly refused to take any part in it, and as a result they have been

subjected to pressure in the form of boycott and intimidation. When relations are so strained any trifling incident may lead to bloody warfare.[6]

The policeman's diagnosis was echoed by Syed Abdullah Brelvi, editor of the *Bombay Chronicle*. He had become editor in 1924, in succession to two India-loving Englishmen, B. G. Horniman and Marmaduke Pickthall. Under its first editors, the *Chronicle* had fought the good fight on behalf of the Palwankar brothers. Now, under Brelvi, the newspaper was drawn into a more portentous debate about cricket and politics, with respect to the tainted 'communal' nature of the great Bombay tournament.

It was said of Brelvi that he 'was monogamous in his loyalties and it was always the Congress for him'.[7] His life's work was to forge a unity of interest between India's two great, sometimes friendly, sometimes warring communities, Hindus and Muslims. Brelvi learned Sanskrit, supported the establishment of a League against Mullaism, and asked Hindus to reject the communal interpretation of India's past. The British challenge, he wrote, made it more urgent than ever before to stand united. To pit Hindu against Muslim was only to serve the interests of the rulers. Even in his moments of despair his broad humanity and patriotism shone through. 'If a modern Diogenes were to hunt out for Indians with his lantern in these days', wrote Brelvi in May 1926,

> he would be sure to come across fervid Hindus, bigoted Muslims and fanatical souls deeply engrossed with the problem of tirelessly finding out how unjustly their own particular community was being treated, and he would have to ask in sorrow: 'Where are the Indians?'[8]

This particular Muslim had participated in the Civil Disobedience movement, spending twenty-two months in jail for the cause. When he was finally released towards the end of 1933, Brelvi resumed his duties with a full-page editorial on the future of the freedom movement. The most critical task facing the Congress, he said, is 'the adjustment of the Hindu–Muslim difference . . . Who, that has carefully studied the history of India during the last four years, can deny that, when all is said and done, the main reason why we have come to the present pass is our failure to settle these differences?' 'There is no other organization than the Congress', thought Brelvi, which could bring about an 'abiding settlement' of the Hindu–Muslim problem.[9]

As these words were being printed, two other Indian Muslims were discussing the same problem in London. They were Liaquat Ali Khan, a prominent leader of the Muslim League, and Muhammad Ali Jinnah, who in 1930 had retired from politics and started a law practice in London. Khan was persuading Jinnah to return to India, and take over the leadership of a reactivated League. In early 1934 the lawyer agreed to come back. He too would seek an abiding settlement of Hindu–Muslim differences, but only outside the auspices of the Indian National Congress.[10]

ONE OF S. A. BRELVI's fellow jail-birds during 1932–3 was a fiery socialist named J. C. Maitra. Originally from Bengal, but settled in Bombay, Maitra was a campaigning journalist who had long battled against European control of sport in the city. He started an Indian Football League in opposition to the white-dominated Western India Football Association. In 1929 Maitra began his own journal, *The Sportsman.* Its stated aims were to 'encourage physical culture in all its branches', to 'foster the true sporting spirit among its members', to 'educate the younger generation to its highest ideals', but also to 'eradicate the distinctions between caste, creed and colour from the field of sport'.[11] This high-minded credo was temporarily put on hold by the Civil Disobedience movement. When the call came Maitra closed his journal and courted arrest. In jail he struck up a friendship with S. A. Brelvi. After their release they became colleagues at the *Bombay Chronicle,* as editor and sports editor respectively. Under Maitra's direction the back pages of the newspaper would become more political than ever before.

In September 1934, a full three months before the Quadrangular began, it was reported that

> the early rush of work has already started. Minor committee meetings are everywhere being held; over-worked secretaries are pulling up their sleeves and swotting at the typewriter and desk; and battalions of prospective Quadrangular players are every evening training at the nets, watched by hundreds of enthusiastic cricket fans.[12]

We know the destination of at least two letters typed by those secretaries. One, sent by the Islam Gymkhana, was to the Nawab of Pataudi, who they hoped would lead their side after his successful 1934 season in England. The other, sent by the PJ Hindu Gymkhana, sought the same honour from the Yuvraj of Patiala.[13] Meanwhile, it was reported that the Europeans were 'searching the length and breadth of the land for players to assist them'.[14]

As Bombay geared itself up for a long-overdue carnival, the anniversary of the Cricket Club of India was being held in Delhi. The CCI was registered in November 1933 by those enterprising characters, Grant-Govan and D'Mello; its professed aims were to promote sports in general and cricket in particular throughout the country. Another aim, not so well hidden, was to shift Bombay from its old, established position as the centre of Indian cricket. Grant-Govan and D'Mello had incorporated the CCI in the capital, and naturally invited the Viceroy to the first anniversary dinner. Lord Willingdon, we might say, was a Lord Harris writ large. He would first put the dissenters in jail and then seek, through cricket, to bind the Indians to the Empire. At the CCI dinner the Viceroy said he had 'always believed that cricket was the one game which helped to bring people of all races and nationalities together'. Willingdon noted, with pleasure, the presence of so many ruling Princes in the gathering. He emphasized the 'need of team work which ultimately won the game'. The Viceroy's advice to young cricketers was 'whoever was captain, back him, support him, and follow him'.[15]

Was cricket being used here as a metaphor for politics? Was the

Viceroy commanding unswerving loyalty in his capacity as Captain of India? One does not know how seriously Willingdon took his own words. He must have known, from his years as Governor of Bombay, that cricket could as easily set race against race, nationality upon nationality. Indeed, his speech of sonorous clichés exactly coincided with a debate on race within the cricketing community of Bombay. That winter the great West Indies cricketer, Learie Constantine, was touring India as a guest of various Maharajas. When he played in the Moin-ud-Dowlah tournament in Hyderabad his presence 'brought an exceptionally large crowd' to the ground. The fans in Bombay saw him briefly, when he played a one-day friendly at the Islam Gymkhana ground.

Some people now started a campaign to have Constantine included in the European team for the Quadrangular. All it needed was for the rulers to rename their team the 'Christians'. That would put them on par with the other teams based on religion, allow them to choose Constantine – at the time the finest all-round cricketer in the world – and also avail of such gifted Indian Christian players as Vijay Hazare and G. Richards. The proposal was beautifully simple and to their advantage, yet the Bombay Gymkhana rejected it out of hand.[16] 'The "White Brahmins" of the Bombay Gymkhana', remarked J. C. Maitra in the *Chronicle*, 'are afraid of losing their caste by enlisting non-Europeans in the European ranks!'[17] In his memoirs Learie Constantine also commented feelingly on the racism of the Raj. On tour in Australia he had 'found apparently no colour bar whatever in cricket. In India it is rigid; but then, white opinion in India is always half a century behind the rest of the world.'[18]

The case of Constantine allowed J. C. Maitra to mount the first of many broadsides against the very idea of 'communal cricket'. What, he asked, 'have Hinduism, Islam, Zoroastrianism and "white" Christianity got to do with cricket, or for [that] matter, with any game'? The secular nationalism that Maitra promoted sought to replace affiliations of caste and religion in favour of class and nation. He found few takers in the Bombay of 1934, with its cricket-crazy public hungry for their first Quadrangular in five years. As Maitra himself wrote, 'if the sale of tickets at the various Gymkhanas is any indication of its popularity among the votaries of the game, communalism has won with all ten wickets in hand'.[19]

In the first match of the tournament the Muslims defeated the Parsis. From an early hour 'streams of people made their way towards the Esplanade Maidan and the stands filled up steadily. It was the old Quadrangular scenes all over again.'[20] In offices and factories work was impossible, as the attention of all Bombay was 'narrowed to that sunny green spot, where our heroes were making hearts beat pit-a-pat'. This year, for the first time, there was live radio commentary on the games. All India Radio had commissioned a young Parsi journalist, A. F. S. 'Bobby' Talyarkhan, who held forth for six hours each day. Talyarkhan brought to cricket broadcasting a 'rich, fruity voice and a fund of anecdotes'.[21] He was ambitious and opinionated, with a voice that was 'beer-soaked, cigarette-stained'. His self-control was superhuman, for he would speak without interruptions (except for lunch and tea). (The Bombay journalist Frank Moraes once remarked that 'Bobby's bladder is as strong as his blubber'.) His broadcasts, wrote one reviewer, were 'firm, full of life, filled with the scent of playing fields'.[22] Talyarkhan's efforts further expanded an already expansive catchment. The game was now being followed ball by ball throughout the city, ears tuned to radios in 'little bye-lanes of Bombay, by sea-side suburbs, in bungalows, by the soft shades of mango-groves'.[23]

When the Hindus played the Europeans, they had in their ranks two Sikhs, the Yuvraj of Patiala and Lall Singh. The rulers had not picked Constantine, but they included a visiting Australian named Warne, a leg-spinner who was no relation to and greatly inferior in skill to Shane of that ilk. The Europeans' defeat was the object of much gloating. The Hindus, remarked J. C. Maitra, 'by the admission of the Sikhs into their fold, have shown that they are after all not so rigid in their communalism, as the "White Christians" in India. The word "European" may mean a White Australian, but not a dark West or East Indian.'[24]

In the final the Hindus were led by the Yuvraj of Patiala. Since

Pataudi had declined to play, the Muslims were captained by Wazir Ali. Small and dapper, Wazir was once called (by D. R. Jardine, no less) 'the best dressed cricketer in Asia'. He pioneered the half-sleeved cricket shirt: high-collared, well-creased, but sawn off at the elbow for the Indian heat. He also sported a white cravat around his neck. Born in Jalandhar in September 1903, educated in Aligarh, and employed as a Major in the Bhopal State Army, Wazir set himself up as the Muslim answer to C. K. Nayudu. He might not have had Nayudu's power, but he had plenty of application, staying at the crease and accumulating runs through cuts and cover drives.

Before the final the Muslim captain had his side fitted out in cream trousers, flannel shirts and striped blazers. The match attracted a record crowd. Thousands were turned away, and all vantage-points outside the ground were taken. Inside, people crowded into the tents, with sofas giving way to chairs to allow more people to sit and watch. Outside, late-comers or paupers sat atop buses, trees, poles and apartment buildings. The attendance, wrote the *Times of India*, had dispelled all doubts of the continuing popularity of the Quadrangular. It was proof also 'of the urgent need for a large sized cricket ground in Bombay'. The match itself was a thriller, closely fought all the way until the Hindus collapsed suddenly in the second innings, leaving the Muslims victors by a margin of 91 runs.[25]

As ever, the winning side was treated to a round of parties by their co-religionists. At a dinner hosted by the Young Men's Muslim Association, the Association's President said that the victory was due to 'perfect cordiality and team spirit': it showed 'that Muslims did not lag behind any other community in the realm of sports'. The winners took just pride in their 'esprit d'corps', while the losers complained about their 'absence of team spirit'. Hindu fans were particularly upset at the choice of the Patiala Prince as captain, over such trusted veterans as C. K. Nayudu and D. B. Deodhar. On the last day of the match an anonymous pamphlet was circulated suggesting that the Hindu selection committee had gone back to their old ways. Once, incompetent Brahmins were appointed over great low-caste sportsmen like the Baloo brothers; now, inferior Princes were preferred to more able commoners.[26]

In his own retrospective, J. C. Maitra questioned the very rationale of the Quadrangular. 'We cannot think of anything except in terms of communities,' remarked Maitra caustically. 'It is, therefore, up to the sportsmen who are supposed to be less saturated with the communal virus, to free themselves from its corroding effects and set an example to the others . . .' In November 1934 the Ranji Trophy had begun: should not this inter-provincial tournament now become the focus of the cricket season? Cricketers should be asked to declare a preference, to 'strain every nerve to make [the Ranji Trophy] a success'.[27]

Ten days after the tournament ended Maitra announced his candidature for the Bombay Municipality. He was standing as a Congress Socialist, on the same ticket as such nationalist luminaries as (the Parsi) Minoo Masani and (the Muslim) Yusuf Meherally. His manifesto described his work in raising funds for famine relief, and in promoting tennis and football tournaments. 'In sports journalism', said Maitra, 'I have striven to infuse a sense of national self-respect and honour.' Until about 1930 it had been easy enough to define the 'nation': namely, all those resident in India except alien Englishmen. And it was Maitra's party, the Congress, that professed to be this nation's sole and fully representative voice. Now that claim, as the journalist well knew, was increasingly under challenge. The cricket field in Bombay would become a battleground for the resolution of what was now the dominant question of Indian politics: was India a nation, or merely an assemblage of different communities given an artificial unity by British rule?

BEFORE THE 1935 carnival began, J. C. Maitra suggested that it be replaced by a Zonal Quadrangular, with teams representing different parts of India — east, south, west and north — rather than religions. This would act as a 'national solidifier' by transcending communal differences, and be 'a thousand times more attractive and entertaining'

from a cricketing point of view. The current tournament, on the other hand, had an 'unmistakable tinge of communal partisanship', and had 'outlived its purpose'.[28]

The socialist, alas, was out of tune with popular consciousness. The correspondence columns in his own and other papers bespoke of a terrific interest in the Quadrangular. A fan who plaintively called himself 'Tree Climber' complained that the seats at the venue had been monopolized by the Gymkhanas, who erected ever larger tents for their well-endowed members, while club cricketers had to resort to wooden perches outside.[29] A clerk at a cotton mill brought a case in court against a member of the PJ Hindu Gymkhana, who had absconded with 100 rupees of his instead of buying him Quadrangular tickets with the money.[30] A 'K. K. P.' of Kalyan demanded that the Municipal Health Officer build temporary urinals at a short distance from the stands, as was enforced by law in theatres and cinemas.[31]

In 1935 the Hindus played the Muslims in the final once more. Each day, 'long before play commenced the tents were fully occupied and the supporters of the rival teams were keyed up to the highest pitch of excitement'. Elsewhere in the city, cricket lovers 'thronged hotels and other public places where [radio] receivers had been installed'.[32]

The Muslims beat the Hindus again, by 221 runs, despite two battling innings of 101 and 53 by C. K. Nayudu. The Muslim captain, Wazir Ali, and his brother Nazir Ali both scored hundreds and their fast bowler, Mubarak Ali, played and took wickets despite a telegraphed order from his college principal in Lahore to return to class. When the last Hindu wicket fell, 'the crowd broke loose and besieged the ground and the Muslims out for trophies snatched the stumps and bails and ran off to the Pavilion'. Mubarak and his mates had now to attend several celebratory dinners before they could return home or to college. One was hosted by the Young Men's Muslim Association; a second by the 'Memon merchants of Cutlery Bazar'. The management of the Globe Talkies arranged for silver cups to be given away by the venerable Maulana Shaukat Ali. The cricketers and other guests then settled down to watch a performance of the film *Rashida*, which 'was very much appreciated by those present'.[33]

Before the tournament began, the *Bombay Chronicle* printed a letter by one C. Aguiar, pleading for the conversion of the Quadrangular to a Pentangular. As it stood, talented Indian Christians could not play in the carnival 'just because they do not belong to any of the four communities'. Either the Europeans should combine with Anglo-Indians and native Christians, said Mr Aguiar, or there should be a fresh, fifth team called 'The Rest'.[34] After the tournament ended the paper printed a letter by a Parsi fan complaining about his team's performance. They might have won their match against the Hindus, said 'R. P. G.', had it not been for their abominable fielding. This was 'far below the standard of average school-boys. And no wonder. Out of eleven members of the team at least five were blessed with tons of superfluous flesh and these amiable gentlemen physically outweighed nearly the whole Hindu eleven'. Their shameful performance had coincided with the creation of a Gagrat Memorial Fund. Opening the fund, the Grand Old Man of Parsi cricket, Dr M. E. Pavri, observed 'that he had not seen that champion cricketer Gagrat drop a single catch during the period of twenty years that he had played with him'.[35]

The Christian would search for a place in the sun, the Parsi would lament the decline of the race. The *Bombay Chronicle* generously gave space to these sentiments, but its own editorial was cast in a stridently non-partisan light. The retention of the championship by the once unfancied Muslims, it said, showed that the tournament had served its purpose in popularizing the sport among them as among Hindus, Parsis and Europeans. It allowed that 'communal tournaments were, perhaps, necessary at a certain stage in the history of Indian cricket in order to stimulate interest in the game among all communities'. However, it was time

they are given a decent burial. The Inter-University and Ranji Trophy tournaments are now equally effective substitutes, if not more effective. It is not conducive to the growth of healthy nationalism, especially among the younger generation, that the delight in watching the batting of a Nayudu or a Wazir Ali or the pride in the bowling of a Nissar should be tainted with even a trace of communalism.[36]

IN THE WINTER OF 1935–6 a group of colonials toured India calling themselves 'His Highness the Maharaja of Patiala's Team of Australian Cricketers'. This was a team of young hopefuls and has-beens, the latter including some of the holiest names of inter-war cricket, such as the captain, Jack Ryder, and his vice-captain, Charlie Macartney. One chronicler tells us that this team had their fill of whisky on tour; I suspect they had their share of women too (they were, after all, playing under Patiala's colours). But they were an immensely popular side, not least because they fraternized as much with the natives as with their fellow whites. An exclusively European club in Karachi made Ryder's men 'honorary members', but withdrew the privilege when the Australians indicated that they would bring Indians as their guests.[37]

This side was to play four unofficial Tests. Before these began, there was a lively controversy as to who would be captain. Since the Maharaja of Patiala had spent £10,000 to get the Australians over, he expected that his son, the Yuvraj, would be asked to lead the home team. The supporters of C. K. Nayudu opposed this. As one Bombay eveninger commented, 'we are living in a democratic age and it is time the fetish of superior "social status" as a gratification for captaincy [was] buried forever'.[38] The reference, very clearly, was to the Palwankars' battle with the Brahmins over the captaincy of the Hindus. In the event, the Yuvraj was made captain for the first match, Nayudu for the second, and Wazir Ali for the third and fourth.

The big prize, however, was the captaincy of next summer's tour of England. Nayudu, Wazir and the younger Patiala were all contenders, but eventually the man appointed was the Maharajkumar of Vizianagaram. 'Vizzy' was greatly envious of the Maharaja of Patiala,

who was a better sportsman and had deeper pockets as well. To match
Patiala he also opened out his purse to cricket and cricketers. In
addition, he shamelessly flattered his social superiors, starting with
the Viceroy. He had even proposed that the Ranji Trophy be
renamed the Willingdon Trophy, adding that he would pay for a new
and bigger piece of jewellery. The proposal came too late, but it did
not hurt when the time came to choose the captain of the 1936 tour.
The Delhi businessman, Grant-Govan, still ran the Cricket Board.
Thus Vizzy was appointed captain, with Major Britten Jones, the
Viceroy's Military Secretary, as the team's manager.

Vizzy loved cricket but could scarcely play it. Britten Jones never
played and had little interest either. This deadly duo wrecked the
chances of a superbly gifted side. Vizzy insisted on playing all matches,
including the Tests, disregarding a petition by the senior players that
he follow the example of Porbandar in 1932 and step down in favour
of C. K. Nayudu. The team was badly led, and carried a passenger
in its captain. Such runs as Vizzy made were a consequence of charity
and corruption. Before one match he gifted a gold watch to the
opposing skipper. 'I gave him a full toss and a couple of long hops,'
recalled the recipient, 'but you can't go on bowling like that all day,
not in England.'[39]

Halfway through the tour Vizzy and Britten Jones sent back the
team's finest all-rounder, Lala Amarnath, for 'insubordination'. The
captain detested C. K. Nayudu: he could not drop him, but rewarded
one player, Baqa Jilani, with a Test cap because he had insulted
Nayudu in front of everybody else. When Vijay Merchant started
scoring centuries his jealous captain instructed his opening partner,
Syed Mushtaq Ali, to run him out.[40]

In his clumsy and self-serving way, Vizzy appears to have been
stoking divisions between Hindus and Muslims so as to maintain his
rule. Riven by discord, the Indians played well below their potential,
losing two out of three Tests. At the end of the tour the great English
cricketer Jack Hobbs remarked that 'with all the keenness and skill
I have noted, India will never rise to the status of a leading cricket

country until all political and religious rivalries are forgotten on the field'.[41]

In contrast to the cricketers' showing in England was the stunning performance of the Indian hockey team in the Berlin Olympics. This team of commoners was led by a commoner, the remarkable Jhansi sepoy named Dhyan Chand. In their first four matches they scored thirty goals, conceding none. Their opponents were Hungary, the United States, Japan and France. In the final against Germany they at last gave away a goal, but scored eight of their own. With the black American athlete Jesse Owens, the Indian hockey team were the stars of an Olympics meant by its promoter, Adolf Hitler, to display the prowess of the Aryan race.[42]

Dhyan's vice-captain was a Muslim, M. Jaffer. The team included Sikhs from the Punjab and Christians from Tamil Nadu. The manager and assistant manager were both Indians. When their boat reached Bombay the hockey players were given a 'right royal reception' by their supporters. From the docks they were taken to the Municipal Corporation Hall, where the Mayor, Jamnadas Mehta, had organized a meeting in their honour. The socialist Mehta said in his speech that 'the secret of the Indian hockey team's success was that it consisted of the best men of India. If it had been selected on communal representation and reservation of seats on the lines of the Government of India Act of 1935, it would have been doomed to failure (laughter).'[43]

There might have been harmony on the hockey fields of Berlin, but not in the streets of Bombay. Two weeks after the Mayor's welcome to Dhyan's team, riots erupted in the city. A temple in Byculla, within shouting distance of a mosque, began construction of a community hall. The Muslims protested, saying that the religious hymns to be sung there, amplified no doubt by microphones, would affect their prayers. The Hindus insisted on their right to sing and play music. Fifty Muslims squatted on the open space where the hall was to be built. Arbitration began as to when music could be played and when it should be stopped. Before it had gone very far violence broke out in Byculla, soon spreading to Mahomedally Road and

Girgaum. From 15 to 22 October there was a series of pitched battles in different parts of the city. Since the police could not stop the violence the military were called in. When peace was officially restored, on 24 October, the casualties numbered sixty-one dead and 467 seriously injured.[44]

Within weeks, the people who had suffered in the riots, and perhaps also some who had participated in them, were distracted by the forthcoming Quadrangular. The trial matches had begun, and thousands of cricket fans were at the Kennedy Sea Face to watch them. The *Bombay Chronicle*, with the very recent violence in mind, thought that 'the time has definitely arrived for the stoppage of this communal fight in sport which merely adds to the bitterness rather than promotes friendly feelings between the respective communities'. Unfortunately, 'however much one may be against the Communal aspect of the Quadrangular, one cannot but freely admit that Bombay is almost inseparably wedded to it. [The fans'] love for it is so great that they would not talk of anything else, nor would they part with it so easily.'[45]

Poor J. C. Maitra! His political self detested the Quadrangular for undermining the prospects of national unity. His professional self had necessarily to give it prominence. He wanted the tournament abolished, but his readers wanted to know the form of different players and the prospects of different teams, and to have detailed coverage of the matches themselves. For his own sake Maitra would polemicize in print against the Quadrangular, but for the sake of his readers he would also provide analyses, player portraits, scores, and post-mortems.

The Muslims had won in 1934 and 1935 and were desperate to complete a hat-trick. They again approached the Nawab of Pataudi to lead them, prompting criticism from J. C. Maitra. Why should the successful captain, Wazir Ali, be deposed, he asked. Could not the Prince behave like a 'true sportsman' and play under Wazir, as Duleep had played under Vithal for the Hindus in 1928?[46] In the event, Pataudi declined to play at all.

The PJ Hindu Gymkhana was determined to stop a Muslim hat-trick, and invited P. Vithal to serve on its selection committee. Shaking aside the claims of those two Princes, Vizzy and Patiala, he chose as captain his old friend and sometime rival, D. B. Deodhar. In the semi-finals the Hindus defeated the Muslims, aided by a magnificent century by the hero of the England tour, Vijay Merchant. A journalist seated in the stands described how 'the intervals are alive with conversation, tea, "sing garam", khara bor, cold drink, prophecies, wise saws, reminscences of old cricket days, of how to do it, and how not to do it'.[47]

As ever, there were also people watching from high points outside. Tragically, a branch of a loaded tree broke, and the men perched on it fell heavily to the ground. One spectator, Dhaku Ramji, later died of his injuries, the only known fatality in the history of the tournament.[48]

Deodhar hurt his finger in the first match, so another commoner, the Bombay batsman L. P. Jai, stepped in as captain. In the finals the Hindus comfortably beat the Europeans by 257 runs. The fifty-seven-year-old Frank Tarrant scored 78 in his side's first innings. Also playing for the losers was the feared exponent of Bodyline, Harold Larwood, who had just landed in Bombay at the invitation of the Maharaja of Patiala. There were anticipations that he would floor the Indian batsmen 'with the mighty swings of his arms with the greatest of ease'. But Larwood would much rather have been in Australia, bowling for G. O. Allen's visiting side. Made a scapegoat for following Jardine's instructions in 1932–3, the Nottinghamshire fast bowler was in India to make money coaching young men in the Punjab. His heart was clearly not in it; after bowling without reward in the Quadrangular he refused to carry on to Patiala, taking an early boat home instead.[49]

The victorious Hindu team were entertained to a dinner at their Gymkhana, the food and drinks paid for by the Merrymakers Club. In his speech L. P. Jai said 'they owed their success entirely to team-spirit and cooperation, and the whole team had played as one man. He was particularly glad to see that the silver cups they were presented with were all alike.'[50] This was a telling remark, for the Hindus had in the past been torn by differences of caste, sect and princely allegiance. Hindu fan and player alike believed that it was their rivals, the Muslims, who more readily played as a *qaum*, that is, as a single, cohesive and unified social community.

IN LATE COLONIAL INDIA sport and politics would always influence one another, but never more so than in 1937. In that year country-wide elections were held under the Government of India Act. True, the legislators and ministers so elected would have to report to the Governor of the Province, always an Englishman, and would have their policies executed by members of the Indian Civil Service, most of whom were whites. The outcome of the 1937 elections would not be *swaraj*, and the franchise itself was restricted to people of education and property. Even so, the 1937 elections were an advance, the Raj's first real move towards asking Indians to represent and rule themselves.

Opposing the Congress was M. A. Jinnah's Muslim League and a variety of parties representing provincial or sectional interests. One such was Dr B. R. Ambedkar's Scheduled Caste Federation. In 1935 Ambedkar had disavowed the Poona Pact and begun asking for separate electorates. He was now sure that Hindus could never atone in any meaningful way for Untouchability. In September and October 1935 there were horrific attacks on Untouchables in the Gujarat village of Kavitha. Ambedkar immediately announced that he and his followers would convert to another religion, for he saw no future for the lowest castes within Hinduism. Islam, Christianity and Sikhism were the alternatives he was considering.

Asked by a reporter of the Associated Press to comment on Ambedkar's decision, Palwankar Baloo said he regarded it 'as suicidal'. From his own experience of thirty years in public life, he would say that 'conditions had changed considerably and there was a real feeling of goodwill on the part of the majority of caste Hindus at the lot of the Harijans'. The discrimination he had himself faced was not now experienced by the Untouchables, at least in the cities. Baloo spoke of the 'new spirit created by the work of Gandhi', and 'appealed to the Harijans to wait patiently and give a chance to the reformers'. To Gandhi's name Baloo added those of Ranade, Gokhale, Tilak, Shraddananda and Chandavarkar, upper-caste Hindus who had likewise lobbied on behalf of their social inferiors. 'Mr Baloo hoped that Dr Ambedkar for whom he had great respect and reverence would follow the example of those great Indians and instead of feeling tired and disgusted because of the attitude of a handful of reactionary Hindus, would continue to toil for the uplift of his Harijan followers.' But were Ambedkar to insist on leaving the Hindu fold, then 'the Harijans in general and the Chamars in particular whom he claimed to represent would never agree to change their religion'.[51]

These words were spoken in October 1935. Within fifteen months Baloo's statement was being put to the sternest test. For the Congress had chosen the cricketer to contest against Ambedkar for a seat to the Bombay Legislative Assembly. This was a seat reserved for a Scheduled Caste candidate, in the E and F Wards of Bombay city. There were three seats to be contested in these wards: two open, one reserved. Each voter had to name three names.

In 1937 Baloo was living in the suburb of Khar where he had built a spacious house for his and his brothers' families. On the entrance was engraved a cricket shield with stumps and bats within it. From the recollections of his son and nephew two things stand out: the patriarch's insistence that studies must come before sport, and his devotion to the Congress. They had vivid memories of Baloo going for weekly meetings of the Bombay Corporation, wearing a long *khadi* coat in the manner of the province's Prime Minister, B. G. Kher.[52]

The contest between Baloo and Ambedkar was the final twist in a long, complex relationship. Once, the cricketer had been the young student's hero. Later, in the 1920s, after Ambedkar had returned from England, they would meet to discuss the fate and future of the Depressed Castes. When the lawyer began cultivating a mass constituency he would invoke his association with Baloo. When Ambedkar disagreed with Gandhi on separate electorates the cricketer helped bring about a compromise. The Poona Pact had broken down, and now Ambedkar sought to change his religion. Baloo, on the other hand, still put his faith in the well-intentioned Hindu. Thus, a quarter of a century after the young Ambedkar had presented the welcome address to Baloo following his epic 1911 tour of England, the two men came to fight an electoral battle in the city of Bombay.

In its press note the Congress said of Baloo that 'he is a famous cricketer. He is a staunch Nationalist and was of very great help in bringing about the Poona Pact. [He] stands against disruption of the Indian Nation for the sake of any community.' Baloo, said the party, was chosen 'against Dr B. R. Ambedkar backed up by all forces of reaction'.[53]

In a fuller statement, the Publicity Committee of the Bombay Provincial Congress Committee called the Baloo-Ambedkar contest a 'pitched battle of All India importance'. The doctor, in its view, stood 'against the Congress and therefore against the forces of freedom and progress and is supported by all reactionary and anti-national forces.... Every available strength has ... to be mobilized on the side of the Congress which is the Joint Front of the people against Imperialism. Every vote will be a deciding factor in the election contest in the constituency.'[54]

Ambedkar came from a family background steeped in disadvantage. No capitalists or Princes supported him either. Why then did the Congress regard him as 'reactionary and anti-national'? Principally because he had argued, on the basis of historical fact, that the British had given more opportunities to the Untouchables than had previous Hindu regimes. This conclusion allowed Ambedkar to cooperate with the rulers and accept assignments from them. His association with the British was made more suspect by his sharp opposition to Gandhi's position on caste. While the Mahatma respected Ambedkar and admired his courage, his disciples and devotees could not abide the challenge to his authority by a much younger man. They chose to attack him as dangerous and disrespectful; as, in a word, '*anti-national*'. Behind that abusive appellation lay the worry that his following might grow and grow, that more Untouchables would come to follow the Mahar lawyer than would follow the Congress and its Mahatma.[55]

Interestingly, the Bombay City Congress had selected S. A. Brelvi for a reserved Muslim seat and the talented young Mangalorian Joachim Alva for a reserved Christian seat. As with Baloo, the voters were being urged to put 'Country before Community'. But Brelvi and Alva both had continuously active political pasts, both were long-time Congressmen, and neither had to oppose a famous name. Baloo had only fitfully engaged in formal party politics, and he was now pitted against the most formidable of Untouchable leaders. The cricketing metaphor is inescapable: it would be the hardest match he would ever play.

The candidates for Bombay were all vetted by the Congress strongman, Sardar Vallabhbhai Patel. Almost twenty years later, a Bombay journalist was still puzzled by the candidate's selection: 'Baloo was a Harijan, but there were plenty of other aspirants. He was a popular cricketer, but unknown to politics. The selection caused much surprise because few had suspected that Sardar was a cricket lover.'[56]

It was not so much love of cricket as knowledge of politics that prompted Patel's decision. Baloo was chosen as a sporting hero who had once been a hero of his opponent as well. More to the point, he was a Chamaar, and Patel knew from the Census of India that these city wards had a fair contingent from that particular caste. The canny Sardar must also have hoped that the choice would pin Ambedkar down to his constituency, stopping him from making extensive speaking tours in support of his other candidates.

The Congress High Command sent out its stars to bat for Baloo. Consider the report of a packed election meeting held at Matunga on Saturday, 9 January 1937. The Congress candidate was introduced by Patel's own right-hand man, K. M. Munshi, shortly to become Home Minister in the Bombay Government. Baloo, said Munshi, 'had been a great cricketer in his younger days and had once scored [off] many an opponent. Hence let the opponents take heed that they had to face a first-class bowler'. 'A vote for Baloo', continued Munshi,

> is a vote for the Poona Pact. That seat for the 'E' and 'F' Ward should be fought for tooth and nail. It is a seat which is of an all-India importance. Dr B. R. Ambedkar, who went to the Round Table Conference, entered into the historical Poona Pact, and even before the ink was dry on the paper, he tried to secede from the Hindu faith. Every vote for Mr Baloo was a vote for the Poona Pact. If Baloo falls, the Poona Pact falls, and with it all of us fall.[57]

After Munshi came Baloo. The cricketer told the voters that

> he personally was not interested in contesting the elections. Though he had not taken [a] very prominent part in politics, he had always come forward to help and take part when necessity demanded. Otherwise, he preferred to remain in the background. The call of the Congress came. At the last moment he agreed to stand on behalf of the Congress, and he did not even know from what constituency he would be asked to contest the seat in the assembly.
>
> After the nominations were filed, he came to know that he was contesting the same seat as Dr B. R. Ambedkar was contesting. It was providential coincidence. As he said before he did not want to go to the Legislature, but what were they to do when seats were reserved for them in the House. They had to be occupied. He was sure the voters would cast their vote for him, the Congress candidate as against Ambedkar.[58]

Other reports suggest that Ambedkar had filed his nomination before Baloo. It is clear nonetheless that the cricketer was diffident and deeply unsure about challenging the rising star of the Scheduled Castes. Although they had recently had political disagreements they had once been friends. Baloo's son and nephew both told me that he was very reluctant to fight Ambedkar in the elections of 1937.[59] I suspect that in the end he might have been persuaded to do so by the longstanding President of the Hindu Gymkhana, L. R. Tairsee. Within the Gymkhana Tairsee had always fought for the rights of the Palwankar brothers. But as a loyal Congressman Tairsee was prone to view Ambedkar as something of an upstart. And as a devout and practising Hindu he was totally opposed to Ambedkar's decision to take his followers out of the fold.[60]

The Marathi-language Congress paper, *Navakal*, forcefully campaigned on Baloo's behalf. It reminded its readers of how, soon after signing the Poona Pact, Ambedkar had started speaking of conversion. It spoke of how Ambedkar 'had himself accepted Baloo's greatness many times'. The lawyer had often expressed his 'great respect and regard' for the cricketer. It offered, in illustration, the story of how Ambedkar was once felicitated by Baloo at a function organized by the Cobblers Union. This, in truth, actually showed the remarkable emergence of Ambedkar as an Untouchable leader. For once, as in 1911, Ambedkar had felicitated Baloo; now it was the other way around. The paper seems to have recognized this, for immediately after recounting the incident it asked its readers 'to vote for Baloo and not be hypnotized by Ambedkar's personality'.[61]

The nationalist press, characteristically, blanked out Ambedkar's own speeches. We do, however, have a report of an unauthorized intervention made by one of his supporters at a Congress meeting in Mazagaon. A Mr Kadam said here that while the Scheduled Castes would vote for the two other (upper-caste) Congress candidates in E and F wards, 'their third vote they would give to Dr Ambedkar because he is a Barrister and Mr P. Baloo, the Congress candidate, was not even a BA'.[62] The Congress strove to cancel this slur by invoking a barrister of their own, Jawaharlal Nehru. A week before the elections Nehru visited the city. The leading Bombay Congressman K. F. Nariman asked the voters to pay homage to him in the most practical manner, by placing all their votes in favour of the Congress candidates. In this cricket-mad city Nariman compared the most charismatic Congressman to the most charismatic of cricketers. 'Jawahar', he said, 'plays Bradman's cricket. It is clean and sporting.

Even were he to commit mistakes and throw away his wicket more than once he is sure to pass the score of the rest.'[63]

On polling day Vallabhbhai Patel appealed to the Bombay electorate to vote for 'the Congress Harijan candidate as a matter of duty'. It was reported that Ambedkar's supporters came to vote in trucks, the Congressmen in cars. But many would have walked to the booths or taken a train. In the end, Ambedkar got 13,245 votes, while Baloo received 11,225. It had been a close-run thing. Later, the *Bombay Chronicle* suggested that Baloo's defeat was due to a 'spoiler', the labour leader Joglekar who had stood as an independent and garnered 10,000 votes. If the Congress had prevailed upon Joglekar to resign, complained the paper, then 'Dr Ambedkar would have been positively swamped'.[64]

THE CONGRESS was the clear winner in the elections of 1937. In April, Congress Ministries assumed office in the provinces of Madras, Bihar, Orissa, Bombay, Central Provinces and the United Provinces. Its most serious loss was in Bengal, where the Krishak Party took power in coalition with the Muslim League. The Krishaks were a party of peasants, and also overwhelmingly Muslim. In Bengal, more than anywhere else, the Congress was in effect a party of the Hindus.[65]

This is a book principally about cricket in Bombay. But here it takes a small detour through football in Bengal, a sport likewise soaked in the sweat and grime of communal politics. And, also, in the summer of 1937, in its blood.

The first great football team of Calcutta was Mohun Bagan, which in 1911 made history by defeating the all-white East Yorkshire Regiment in the final of the prestigious IFA Shield. Its members and patrons were chiefly from the westernized sections of the Calcutta upper class. From the 1920s Mohun Bagan was strongly challenged by East Bengal, whose followers were from the other side of the Presidency, from the lush deltaic districts of what is now the sovereign state of Bangladesh.

A decade later the Mohammedan Sporting football club arrived to take on the two older giants. It represented the desires and aspirations of a religious grouping which, in Bengal at any rate, had always been economically and culturally subordinated to the Hindus.[66] Its footballing victories were invariably cast in religious terms. In a memoir of his Calcutta boyhood, the poet Samar Sen wrote of how 'Mohammedan Sporting's dramatic rise and amazing record betokened a primal urge for a place in the sun'.[67] The Mohammedans displayed 'a team combination, aggressiveness and killer instinct never seen before in Indian football'. For these eleven players wearing the club colours of black-and-white were 'not merely playing a game but fighting for the entire community's honour'.[68]

Mohammedan Sporting first won the Calcutta Football League Championship in 1934. It won again in 1935 and 1936, and in 1937 was unbeaten in its early matches. On Friday, 11 June it was defeated by East Bengal, the sole goal coming late in the second half. After the match the winning team had to be escorted off the field by police sergeants. The losing side's supporters went berserk. Chairs were thrown at rival fans. A youngster of thirteen who was cheering East Bengal was stabbed to death. There were other less serious knifings. Later, fights between Hindus and Muslims broke out in several parts of the Maidan. 'Stones, periscopes, umbrellas and sticks were the ammunition used.' Inside the enclosed area of the players tempers also ran high. One Mohammedan player beat up the Secretary of the East Bengal club. The players stayed under police escort until late into the night, returning home only after the constables had successfully dispersed the irate fans.[69]

All eleven players in the East Bengal side were Hindu, all eleven of their opponents that day, Muslim. The communal polarization was further heightened by the fact that the match was played on a Friday. Plenty of spectators, and perhaps a few Mohammedan Sporting players as well, would have gone to the mosque for *jumma* or communal prayers before proceeding to the Maidan. 'ALL FOR LOVE' was how the city's leading English daily titled its editorial on the match. In Ireland, said the paper,

Roman Catholics and Protestants hate each other violently for the love of God. In India communities hate one another violently for the love of the game. If a side and its supporters cannot take a beating without the savagery seen on Friday it were better that inter-community games were forbidden by some Criminal Law Amendment Act.[70]

A paper sympathetic to the Congress more straightforwardly called its editorial 'Communalism in Sport'. The incidents on Friday, it remarked, could not be dismissed as the 'handiwork of a few desperadoes'. For it was

> common knowledge that communal partisanship often finds a very disgraceful expression in language whenever a Moslem player comes to grief at the hands of a Hindu opponent. . . . [T]orrents of abuse that greet Hindu supporters when they venture to cheer players who have the misfortune not to be Mohammedans, have come to be an intolerable nuisance.

Such provocation could easily lead to violence, and for 'the police to stop misconduct when the crowd is very large is next to impossible'. The way out of this difficulty was to disbar sporting clubs that were communal in nature from being affiliated to the Indian Football League: 'Let there be at least one place where we can meet as comrades and where we can take defeat in a sportsmanlike spirit.'[71]

These editorials prompted a pained reply from the Secretary of the offending club. Minor things, wrote K. Noorudin, 'have been much exaggerated as a deliberate move by certain interested people to vilify Mohammedan Sporting Club, and its supporters'. He spoke of 'malicious and one-sided propaganda of a section of the press', and appealed to 'the members of the public, both Hindus and Muslims, Indians and Europeans to be cool and not to be inflamed by provocations', 'to cooperate with us in our efforts to promote the growth of Sport and Sportsman like spirit without any tinge of racialism and communalism'.[72] This last statement takes one's breath away. Was not the very *idea* of Mohammedan Sporting itself communal, as exclusive and divisive as the idea of an all-white Gymkhana?

In Bombay, J. C. Maitra was following the events in Calcutta with a worried fascination. He was a Bengali, and a football lover to boot. But how could the game be played if linesmen and referees were too scared to officiate in Mohammedan Sporting's games, as 'their lives may be worth a moment's purchase were the mob to get at them at the time of their heat'? The Indian Football League was thinking of disaffiliating the club: that would be punishing the players for the behaviour of their supporters and be read as an indictment of the entire Muslim community of Bengal. What were the lessons for the cricket field of Bombay? There had been no violence thus far, perhaps because the game's followers were from the 'educated class'. But here too 'the virus of communalism is spreading rapidly, [and] no one can foretell when it will reach the danger-point'. The solution, short and simple, was to abolish all communal clubs and communal tournaments. 'Otherwise, sport will become another front on which communal battles will be fought to the utter degradation of the nation and negation of sport itself.'[73]

Three months after the Calcutta affray Mohammedan Sporting came to play the Rovers Cup in Bombay. This football trophy had been the monopoly of British regimental teams since its inception forty-five years previously. In 1937, however, two Indian teams reached the final, Muhammedan Sporting and Bangalore Muslims. Despite its name, the Bangalore side also had Hindu and Christian footballers. The Calcutta team, however, included Muslims alone. The evening before the final, the Bangalore Muslims were given a 'Dinner Party in the South Indian style' by the South Indian Educational Society in Dadar, a body dominated by Hindus, indeed by Brahmins.[74]

The Bangalore Muslims won the Rovers Cup final by the narrowest possible margin, one goal to nil. Inevitably, it was interpreted as a victory of nationalism over communalism. The Congress workers of A ward threw a party for the footballers of Bangalore. The main speech was given by S. A. Brelvi of the *Bombay Chronicle*. Brelvi thought 'the most pleasing feature of their victory was that it was achieved by a team which consisted of Hindus and Muslims'. Moreover, this inter-denominational team of Indians had defeated the strongest European combinations. 'Indians were world champions in hockey and wrestling', concluded Brelvi, 'and it would not be long before they proved their superiority in football.' In his reply, the club's Secretary, Mr Esmail, remarked that

> though their team was known as Bangalore Muslims, they always took care to include their Hindu brethren in it. They had proved that just as through Hindu–Muslim cooperation they wanted to secure their country's freedom, so, through similar cooperation, they could vindicate their country's name in sports.[75]

THE QUADRANGULAR of 1937 was planned against this heady backdrop: the victory of the Bombay Congress in the 1937 elections, and the victory of a Hindu–Muslim side in the city's premier football tournament. This year, in fact, the cricket carnival would have both a new format and a new venue. At last, the organizers had agreed to the inclusion of a team named 'The Rest', to include Indian Christians, Buddhists and Jews. The newly named Pentangular would be played at a magnificent stadium built near Churchgate Station in south Bombay. This was being promoted by the Cricket Club of India, whose presidency had passed, in 1934, from R. E. Grant-Govan to the Maharaja of Patiala. The Maharaja had reason to dislike Delhi, so when the Bombay Government gifted the CCI a decent plot of land, he decided the stadium would be built in that city. It was to be named for the departing Governor, Lord Brabourne. Typically, the Maharaja made a big grant towards its construction. Gujarati and Parsi businessmen contributed generously as well.[76]

Two months before the Pentangular began, it was the target of a frontal attack by the Congress Chief Minister of Madras, C. Rajagopalachari. He was speaking at the second anniversary of the Madras

Cricket Association, a body whose President, Dr P. Subbaroyan, was also a member of Rajagopalachari's Cabinet. Subbaroyan, who was soon to take over as President of the Board of Control for Cricket in India, was a vigorous promoter of the Ranji Trophy and had an aversion to Bombay's prominence in the cricket world. His views resonated with those of his Chief Minister, in whose inclusive nationalism there was no place at all for communal groupings.

Rajagopalachari was one of Gandhi's closest associates and a towering figure in the Congress. Naturally, his statement was widely reported in the Bombay press. Just as naturally, the *Chronicle* supported him. As J. C. Maitra pointed out, had the Quadrangular been played on a non-communal basis, the claims of the Baloo brothers 'would have been recognized earlier and without any ado'.[77]

Maitra also reported that Rajagopalachari's remarks had 'sent some people in Bombay into hysterics'. One 'V. S. P.' wrote to say that the cricket carnival was actually an exhibition of inter-communal amity, showing that 'our cricketers may yet be able to achieve what our politicians and leaders have signally failed to bring about'.[78] A more weighty intervention came from L. R. Tairsee. Cricket, he claimed, had led 'to levelling of caste distinctions [among] the Hindus'. The Baloo brothers were 'treated as equals'; that was 'due to cricket and the problem of Untouchability was solved before those who talk about it now were born – I mean politically'. Tairsee went on to defend the format of the Quadrangular. 'To talk of non-communal cricket in Bombay is to talk about the man in the moon.' The PJ Hindu Gymkhana President argued that 'communal cricket has in no case led to trouble – as politics have. Is it seriously proposed to say good-bye to politics? Let Rajagopalachari answer.'[79]

The Cricket Club of India was claimed by its promoters to be 'cosmopolitan in conception and execution'. This, the first proper sports stadium in the sub-continent, was intended to help raise Indian cricket to international standards, to provide the facilities for its further growth. It would host Bombay's Ranji Trophy matches, but also the annual cricket carnival. There is little question which the public preferred to see. As one contributor to the new Stadium's souvenir ruefully remarked, 'it is a sad reflection on the vast army of cricket fans in this country that they would rather watch communal cricket than the best talent of different provinces in friendly rivalry'. Whatever its professed aims, the claims of commerce were to ensure that a cosmopolitan, national club would principally act as a showcase for cricket played on religious and racial lines.[80]

This year the communal tournament was shifted to the end of December, to allow for a tour by an English cricket team led by Lord Tennyson. On 7 December the Cricket Club of India was due to play against Tennyson's side, this the first-ever match at the Brabourne Stadium. Before play began the stadium was formally inaugurated by the Governor, Sir Roger Lumley. The Governor read out a message of congratulation from the mother of all cricket clubs, the MCC. The chief benefactor, the Maharaja of Patiala, then spoke. He quoted a Sanskrit saying to the effect that the cultivation of the body is the first essential of *dharma*. He suggested that the new stadium, built halfway between England and Australia, was ideally placed to host great international contests. And then he spoke movingly of the first, and greatest, princely cricketer: 'Who can come to this central home of cricket in India without remembering our great Ranji?' He hoped that the stands would be named the 'Ranji Memorial Stands', and promptly issued a cheque for 5,000 rupees towards this. Patiala appealed to his 'Brother Princes, to all Patrons of Sport, and to all Sportsmen, young and old, in India, to subscribe liberally towards this International Memorial to one who was so dear to us and who brought honour to India in the world of sport'.[81]

The news reports of the ceremony suggest that no Indian politicians were present, no Congress Prime Minister of Bombay nor any of his ministers. Who were the Indian cricketers there? Was Palwankar Baloo in the audience, listening to the Maharaja of Patiala? Would anybody remember him at a moment like this? But did he not mean as much to Bombay and Indian cricket as Prince Ranjitsinhji?

THE FIRST PENTANGULAR was scheduled to be the first tournament held at Bombay's lovely new stadium. In the event it was a damp squib. The PJ Hindu Gymkhana withdrew its side at the last moment as it was not allotted enough seats for its members. Originally, the Cricket Club of India allotted 2,000 seats apiece to the Hindus and the Bombay Gymkhana, and 1,250 each to the Islam and Parsi Gyms. Later this was changed to 2,000 for all. The Hindus were dissatisfied with parity, asking that their share be increased proportionately as there were more of them. L. R. Tairsee, who had lately denied that sport ever created bad blood among communities, issued a statement saying that 'the Hindu Gymkhana expects all Hindus to cooperate with them in their fight for a square and straight deal'. Behind such remarks was an arrogance borne out of the Congress's recent success in the elections. The *Chronicle* rightly commented that underlying the dispute was the 'obnoxious spirit of communalism'.[82]

With the Hindus not playing, interest in the tournament 'had the bottom knocked out of it'.[83] The Muslims won easily, but all the matches were poorly attended. The Bombay cricket fans were compensated somewhat when the PJ Hindu Gymkhana organized a festival match between teams captained by C. K. Nayudu and D. B. Deodhar respectively. In November Nayudu, now forty-two, had been dropped from the Indian side which played an unofficial Test against Lord Tennyson's team in Bombay. He was smarting under the insult – he had been called for practice before being told to go home – and so were his supporters, who believed his dropping was a product of 'capitalist and princely domination' of Indian cricket.[84] This Indian hero was loved most well in this cricket-mad city – the future Test cricketer K. M. Rangnekar wrote feelingly of what C. K. meant to Bombay schoolboys like himself:

> Even if Colonel Saheb got out without scoring a run, just to see him striding from the pavilion to the crease was worth our money. We were so bewitched by his gait, that small boys like myself, used to follow him after the match, when he walked

from the Brabourne Stadium to Marine Drive where he stayed. It looked as if a tall Eucalyptus tree was walking amongst shrubs.[85]

But this year Nayudu had been dropped from the Bombay 'Test' and, because of the PJ Hindu Gymkhana's fight with the CCI, he would not play in the Pentangular either. In response, L. R. Tairsee organized this contest between two pick-up elevens, in a happy marriage of profit and principle. For this compensatory match in Nayudu's honour his admirers turned up in their thousands at the Kennedy Sea Face, their presence made easier by the fact that the tie was played in Christmas week. The *Times of India*, no friend of the organizers, was constrained to admit that the match was played 'before the biggest crowd that has ever thronged the Hindu Gymkhana ground'.[86] There were more than 15,000 inside, 'a large number being members of the fair sex. Over and above the 15,000, who had paid for admittance, every point of vantage surrounding the Gymkhana ground had its quota of people, who had come late, and had failed to get admittance.'[87]

The two teams were strong, including the best of the Hindu cricketers and also talented Parsis and Christians. The match was deliberately timed to coincide with the Pentangular final. Mushtaq Ali captained the Muslims in the Brabourne Stadium, but once that match finished early came over to the PJ Hindu Gymkhana ground to assist the side of his mentor and Holkar captain.

The stars on show in this festival match included Vinoo Mankad, Vijay Hazare, D. D. Hindlekar, Shute Bannerjee and Jaoomal Naoomal, but most of the spectators had come to honour C. K. Nayudu. On this warm December day, cooled just a little by the sea breeze, Nayudu was

> the idol of the huge crowd. Whether 'C. K.' played a ball, sent down a delivery or did some fielding, everything was cheered. Going out after tea on Sunday, he was literally mobbed by youthful admirers, each wanting to touch their hero on the back. Evidently they forgot that the Major's broad shoulders carried a covering of human flesh and there was a limit to slaps of

appreciation. When stumps were drawn Nayudu had to run to the Club House to avoid being shouldered. The crowd was not to be outdone fully and they refused to disperse unless Nayudu came out. The Major had to appear three times on the Club House top deck before the thousands, who called for Nayudu, decided to tread their way back.[88]

Nayudu was 80 not out overnight. He resumed his innings on Monday morning, to scenes of 'enthusiasm perhaps never witnessed before on a cricket field'. Before play began,

> a number of flower sellers with a cute sense of trade demands paid for admittance and got to the crowded stands with loads of garlands. As Nayudu came in sight of his 100, these floral emblems of admiration were bought fast at fancy prices. A boundary gave 'C. K.' his century. This was the signal for general turmoil as almost simultaneously there was a rush from all sides towards India's cricket idol and he had to countenance practic-ally a smothering of flowers. The air was rent with bombs and crackers, and rounds of cheers continued for close on 10 minutes.[89]

Nayudu scored 120 in 175 minutes at the crease, hitting twenty fours, showing his critics 'that at forty-two he was better than India's best youngsters'. His innings was captured on camera by the Sagar Film Company. Their film of the match, with A. F. S. Talyarkhan's commentary, was then shown in cinema theatres across India. The advertisement for this film invited the 'thousands who had been turned away' from the festival match to see their hero, the 'King of Cricket', captured at the crease.

There were also other tributes. A local jeweller presented Nayudu with a gold medal and a silver cigarette case. Most remarkable of all was an advertisement for a Hindi film made by the celebrated director V. Shantaram. This film, *Duniya Na Mane*, featured a heroine who, like the great cricketer, had fought doggedly for her rights. Shantaram's posters bore in big type the headline 'NAYUDU WAS SURPRISED'. The text spoke of how 'Major Nayudu was surprised when he discovered at the last minute that he was dropped out of the Test team.' But 'how much more surprised – and shocked – should Nirmala be when she too discovered at the last minute that she was marrying the wrong man'.[90]

In the documentary made about Nayudu's innings, and more so perhaps in the advertisement used by V. Shantaram, were brought together modern India's two central obsessions: film and cricket. Nayudu was the first and (to my knowledge) also the last cricketer whose name and prestige were used to market a popular Hindi film. That, in its own way, is as great a compliment as any he ever received.

Nayudu's greatness was general and contextual – because of *when* he played – but also distinctively individual – because of *how* he played. His repertoire included plenty of strokes other than the lofted straight drive. Since, like me, the readers of this book will never have seen him bat, let me reproduce two assessments by contemporaries. The first is by the greatest of all cricket writers, Neville Cardus. Before we read on, let us remind ourselves that C. K. was already thirty-seven when Cardus first saw him at the wicket:

> Nayudu has stupidly been called the Bradman of India. He shows no resemblance to a great and flawless and rather steely master. Nayudu is lithe and wristy and volatile. Bradman is sturdy and concentrated: he never suggests that elusive and poetic quality which is best called sensibility. Nayudu is a very sensitive batsman: from each of his strokes you get the impression of a new-born energy, of a sudden improvisation of superb technique. Nayudu is not at all mechanical. Watching him from the ring, you get a delicious suggestion in his play of fallibility. Unlike Bradman his skill is his servant, not his master. The glorious uncertainty of cricket is not endangered by Nayudu.

Next, this description by an anonymous Indian critic:

> In many a pavilion and clubhouse in India, there hangs a photograph of a cricketer, standing erect with bat raised, who glares defiantly from under the peak of his cap as though daring the bowler to do his worst. It depicts C. K.'s outlook on the game.

Kankaiyya was a genius that brooked no opposition. There was no bowler to whom he would pay deference. . . . He would drive a half-volley and then next ball flick one off the middle stump to the fine-leg fence. When he cover-drove it was as though some one had wound him up with a key and suddenly released the spring. He would stand on his back foot, crash the ball past the bowler and then move across and back-cut between first and second slip, a stroke that can be described as being almost posthumous.[91]

The match organized by the PJ Hindu Gymkhana in December 1937 and its aftermath were perhaps the last full display of the extraordinary affection that C. K. Nayudu commanded among the citizens of Bombay, among Muslims and Hindus, workers and capitalists, men and women and, not least, children. No Indian before him, and very likely no Indian since, has so majestically played the part of the sportsman as folk hero.

The response to Nayudu would have been terrific anyway, but in this year of 1937 it was perhaps over-determined by the coming to power of Congress ministries. That, if in a limited sense, was the self-rule the party and its public had long struggled for. The sectarian opposition – Jinnah's Muslim League, Ambedkar's Scheduled Caste Federation and the like – had been taught a lesson in the polls. The Congress was sovereign, and its followers could look forward to the coming, under its leadership, of *purna swaraj, complete* independence. The latest round of tributes to Nayudu thus reflected not – as in the past – an aspirant nationalism, but a nationalism that was at least half realized.

Ironically, the political successes of 1937 also inspired a series of polemics against cricket. If the demise of alien rule was imminent, why not the extermination of an alien sport? In March 1937, one M. N. M. Badruddin wrote a long essay in the *Bombay Chronicle* titled 'India Must Give Up Cricket!' This, he said, was an aristocratic game, meant for the English nobility, for those who liked to 'attend ceremonial parades, rich dinners and to pass away their tiresome

hours in their club rooms and cricket fields'. A poor country like
India could not 'afford this leisure and pleasure – if it is a pleasure
at all'. Badruddin recognized that 'many do go crazy and spend all
their precious time munching away gram and monkey-nuts on a
cricket maidan'. But cricket's hold in India, he suggested, was part of
a subtle colonial ploy to tame the otherwise rebellious public. If the
loyalist Unionist Party, rather than the Congress, was in power in
the Punjab, this was because 'the Punjab is the most cricket minded
province in India'. Young students subscribed to the British-owned
paper, *The Statesman*, because it gave the best sports news: in consequence, 'most of them know too well where Bradman is today, but
would struggle to give a ready reply to a question where is Jawaharlal
today?' Cricket, in sum, was a 'rapidly advancing cancer' which must
be resisted and exterminated: it was 'in no way in keeping with our
poverty, our political condition or national outlook and as such is
highly detrimental to the complete realization of our cherished hopes,
ambitions, ideas and dreams'.[92]

Later in the year, the *Chronicle* printed another tirade on similar
lines. Cricket, wrote 'N. J.', is a 'game of the classes and has never
appealed to the masses'. In India it was 'associated with feudalism'
and 'has brought upon communalism'. It was promoted by 'princes
and plutocrats' to please their masters. It was a game 'more imported
than intrinsic'. Some, admittedly, saw it as a way of settling accounts
with the rulers, but there were other and better ways to 'realize and
respect our national worth'. After all, the French 'did not don the
pads to undo Waterloo, nor is it necessary for us to raise cricket to
the status of a national pastime to undo Plassey'.[93]

This was an Indian nationalist variant of an argument once
advanced by Leon Trotsky to C. L. R. James: that spectator sport
was a ruling-class conspiracy to keep the workers tame. Or, to introduce some necessary jargon, that cricket was a hegemonic device
which promoted false consciousness. Like James, we must sensibly
reject this.[94] Certainly the *Bombay Chronicle* treated these jeremiads
with a splendid unconcern. It printed them, but only before the
cricket season or after it was over. While the games were on the paper

covered them *in extenso*: Ranji Trophy matches, Quadrangular matches, tour matches and even club matches. It might, on principle, have been opposed to 'communal cricket', but it knew cricket itself to be an Indian game, answering to an interest that was as much of the masses as of the classes. Those who followed the doings of C. K. Nayudu, for example, were numbered in the tens of millions. If this indeed was false consciousness, it was on a truly spectacular scale.

11. The Mahatma Is Called

THE 1937 CARNIVAL FAILED because of the Hindus' withdrawal. They were keen to come back, however, and the Cricket Club of India were happy for them to return. The CCI agreed to give the PJ Hindu Gymkhana an extra 500 seats: fewer than they wanted, but more than any other community had. Thus the tournament of 1938 was the first real Pentangular. There was much anticipation, especially as C. K. Nayudu had been appointed captain of the Hindus.

The 1938 carnival was prefaced by an intriguing debate within the community of Bombay Parsis. One section felt the decline of their cricket very keenly. Once, the real contest to look forward to was Parsis versus Europeans or Parsis versus Hindus; now it was Hindus versus Muslims. One writer complained of how his community's cricket team had slipped from 'the first rate to the fifth. Oh for those glorious days when defeat was rarely known and when our young and old mingled and indulged in vociferous cheering and clapping . . .'[1] As it happened, in the summer of 1938 a great Parsi industrialist, Sir Nowroji Saklatwala, Chairman of Tatas, died, and one proposal to honour his memory involved a coaching scheme for young Parsi cricketers. It had been a decade since their lads had won anything, but the organizers hoped that this scheme would help bring back the palmy days of Parsi cricket.

The proposal met with a scathing response from the brilliant, maverick Parsi journalist, D. F. Karaka. He mocked the community's 'utter disregard of present-day conditions, this living in a dead past . . . this unnecessary racial pride, this over-emphasis on preserving our stock from mixed breeding'. The Parsis needed instead seriously to ponder their future: to ask how they would involve themselves in the building of a new India. Saklatwala loved sports, admittedly, but Karaka did not think that he 'should be remembered by a series of good cricket scores'. Rather, the money raised for the cricket coaching scheme should be used to set up a college 'away from the hub of Bombay', where young men both Parsi and non-Parsi, rich and poor, would be sent to acquire 'some intellectual equipment and backbone'.[2]

In the event, the Parsis lost the first match of the 1938 tournament to the Europeans. Appropriately, the Hindus met the Muslims in the final. But to the disgust of *their* fans, they lost by six wickets. As one observer rather dramatically put it, the 'hero-worshipping exultants of Bombay were dumb'. How could 'a team as great as the Hindus be rushed pell-mell to defeat by six wickets by a much weaker combination like the Muslims?'[3] The winning captain Wazir Ali provided the answer. Speaking to reporters at the Victoria Terminus while he waited to board the Peshawar–Lucknow Express, Wazir said he was 'proud of my boys who, I must say, were just like the members of the same family on and off the field'. He continued: 'Every player gave his loyal and whole-hearted support to me and we owe this victory chiefly to our splendid team work. It is therefore no wonder that our solidarity carried the day.'[4]

Solidarity and team-work were, it seems, just what the Hindus lacked. And they said so themselves. Before the final, 'one of the most prominent Hindu cricketers' had told J. C. Maitra that 'the Muslims always played as one man'. After it was over, it was suggested that several players did not cooperate with Nayudu on instructions from their employers. C. K. was on the staff of the Maharaja of Holkar, but his three key bowlers, who under-performed, were working for the Jam Saheb of Nawanagar. The PJ Hindu Gymkhana President went to the press, alleging a 'conspiracy against C. K.' orchestrated by those who paid the players' cheques. 'Princes have polluted politics', said L. R. Tairsee; 'Let them not pollute sports. They can patronize the stadium . . . but their interference in play will not be tolerated.'[5]

The events on the cricket field bore an uncanny resemblance to the world of Indian politics in 1937–8. In the year that the Congress had been in power their provincial governments were torn apart by faction fights. Right-wing Congressmen intrigued against left-wing Congressmen, and vice versa. Ministers were dissatisfied with their portfolios; mere legislators were upset at being left out of the ministries altogether. Meanwhile, Muhammad Ali Jinnah successfully persuaded his followers that the Congress Governments were 'anti-Muslim'. The Congress were accused of promoting spinning by women, vegetarianism, and the glorification of Hindu heroes in school textbooks. 'Islam in Danger' became the League's rallying call, as Muslims everywhere were urged to band together and fight for their rights. Old Khilafat leaders like Maulana Shaukat Ali joined the *mullahs* in touring the countryside to campaign against 'Congress Raj'.[6]

By the time of the next Pentangular that Raj was over. In the small hours of 1 September the Nazis invaded Poland, and two days later Britain declared war on Germany. The Viceroy, Lord Linlithgow, now unilaterally offered the support of the people and materials of India to the war effort. No Indian, high-born or low, was consulted beforehand. The Congress leaders were rightly outraged. Both Nehru and Gandhi, it must be noted, had spoken out against Hitler and the Nazis at a time when some leading British politicians admired them and others thought that, despite their vulgarity, they were still a welcome bulwark against Bolshevism. When war broke out the Congress offered full support if the British promised independence for India after it was over. This seemed reasonable: after all, the Allied Powers claimed they were fighting for democracy and freedom. Should that not include freedom for the coloured peoples too? In the last week of October, after Linlithgow had declined to commit himself, the Congress governments decided to hand in their papers.

The Quadrangular was played all through the First World War, and the Pentangular would not be disturbed by the Second. But this was the first carnival in decades in which L. R. Tairsee had no part. When he died on 30 August the newspapers recalled his founding of the Bombay Home Rule League, his service as a Municipal Councillor and his Presidency of the Indian Merchants' Chamber. As a social worker he had founded maternity homes in Nasik and Alibagh and campaigned for better facilities for railway passengers. The obituarists did not forget Tairsee's services to cricket. As the President of the PJ Hindu Gymkhana he visited it every day. Although he was not orthodox or communal, Tairsee 'felt keenly for the degeneracy of the Hindu race and helped all movements for raising the physical stamina and the moral level of the Hindu community'.[7]

As if in tribute to the man, this degeneracy was now arrested. C. K. Nayudu was the Hindus' captain once more, and this time his flock behaved themselves. In the first round they easily beat their old rivals, the Europeans. The captain's arrival at the wicket, commented a Muslim newspaper, 'caused a ripple to go round the stands and the crowd settled down to see some big hitting . . . Major Nayudu caused the crowd to go wild with excitement when he hit Wensley for two successive sixes . . .'[8]

In the semi-final the Hindus defeated their even older rivals, the Parsis. C. K. scored 47, and his younger brother C. S. hit a century. When they achieved the vital first-innings lead, there was an 'ear-splitting crescendo of applause from some 20,000 throats and some 40,000 hands all functioning as one ever-widening source of sound'.[9] After the match the Nayudus were the chief guests at a reception hosted by the South Indian Association in Matunga. Born in Nagpur, domiciled in Indore, they were nonetheless of southern stock, and their brethren would have them know this. On behalf of the Andhra Mahasabha Dr Swamy drew the audience's attention to the 'international reputation' of the Nayudu brothers. Another doctor, S. S. Krishna, chose to cast his praise in ecumenical terms. He paid 'tribute to the impartiality and broadmindedness of Major C. K. Naidu who had trained as his *chelas* Hazare, Bhaya and Mushtaq along with his brother C. S. Naidu . . .' The names listed were of a Christian, a Parsi and a Muslim, all of whom had played under C. K. in the Ranji Trophy.[10]

There was, wrote one reporter, 'a spirit of camaraderie' in the Hindu ranks 'which was absent during the last few years'.[11] In the final they met their new but now most feared opponents, the Muslims. Twelve thousand people showed up when play began on the first day, a Friday; but the crowd steadily swelled, reaching 30,000 by lunch. This must be read as evidence of absenteeism, with clerks and college students marking attendance before sneaking off to the cricket, perhaps taking their bosses and teachers with them. At the weekend the stadium was packed from 9 a.m. Some cricketers would complain of the steel-and-concrete of Brabourne, saying they preferred the colourful tents and circus-like atmosphere of the Gymkhana.[12] Some fans would complain of the greater visibility of the rich in the new venue. In the Bombay Gymkhana the whites sat in their pavilion under whirling fans, but otherwise the crowd mixed the masses with the classes. Here, the CCI had set aside a good part of the stands for its members, for the Indian rich who, as always, were exhibitionist. Thus 'cricket is no more the game it was. It is all silk-cushions and padded chairs – green spots and shandy-glare-glasses and velvet pads.'[13] But as stadiums went this was prettiness itself, with the grass immaculately kept and the glass panels cheering up the concrete. And it allowed twice as many people to watch the cricket.

The match was meant to last four days, but was over in three. There was 'a veritable riot of jubilation in the Hindu camp when victory was announced. Besides the usual rush of garlands, crackers were fired in abundance – a new feature of this year's Pentangular.'[14] Also a new feature was a reception in Poona, held only for four members of the winning side. These men – the two Nayudus, M. M. Jagdale and K. V. Bhandarkar – all played for Holkar, whose Maharaja was a Maratha by blood. Thus this tribute was offered to them by the ancient capital of the Marathas, organized by two of the city's colleges and its premier sporting Gymkhana. Seven thousand people turned up at the Poona Young Cricketers ground, where the four Holkar men were presented with wrist-watches and 'gave a display of their cricket art for about an hour'.[15]

The big party, of course, was held at the PJ Hindu Gymkhana in Bombay. In attendance were all eleven cricketers, the Chief Justice and leading Congressmen. After the speeches, presents from the

public were offered to the players: 'a fine dress' for one, 'a necktie
and pin' for another and 'various other gifts' for the rest. The 'singing
of "Bande Matram" by Miss Padmini Shete terminated the proceedings'.[16]

This last was the most significant for 'Bande Matram', a patriotic
hymn composed in the 1880s by Bankim Chandra Chatterjee, has a
strongly Hindu cast to it. Its singing under state auspices in secular
and independent India has been a matter of fierce dispute. Should
its singing at the PJ Hindu Gymkhana in 1939 have passed without
notice? Perhaps not. For, as J. C. Maitra mournfully remarked in his
report on the Hindu–Muslim final, 'there is not the least doubt that
the communal aspect of the Tournament has a greater attraction
for the public than mere class and colour of play'.[17]

IN THE THIRD WEEK OF March 1940 the annual meeeting of the
Indian National Congress was held in Ramgarh, in Bihar. Maulana
Abul Kalam Azad was elected President. With the understanding that
comes of years spent in the same prison cell, Jawaharlal Nehru wrote
of Azad that he was the very 'soul of dignity and self-respect and
restraint. There is not one atom of vulgarity in him.'[18] The Maulana
was a considerable scholar of Arabic and Persian, an author, a
journalist, a devout Muslim and a life-long Congressman. His
Presidential Address at Ramgarh has justly been called a 'piece of
magnificent eloquence'.[19] It was 'India's historic destiny', said Azad,
'that many human races and religions should flow to her, finding a
home in her hospitable soil'. Having come here 1,100 years ago,
'Islam has now as great a claim on the soil of India as Hinduism.'
These centuries of shared history 'have enriched India with our
common achievements. Our languages, our poetry, our literature,
our culture, our dress, our manners and customs, the innumerable
happenings of our daily life, everything bears the stamp of our
joint endeavour.' From this splendid syncretism of cultures only one
political solution was possible. 'These thousand years of our joint life

has moulded us into a common nationality. . . . No fantasy or artifical scheming to separate and divide can break this unity.'[20]

The Congress session ended on 20 March. Two days later the Muslim League met at Lahore and passed a resolution envisaging independent, Muslim-majority states in the north-east and north-west. If and when India became free, the League argued, these states would have direct relations with the Crown. The Muslims, it was now being claimed, were not a minority, but a distinct nation of their own. And future political developments must reflect this.[21] As the League's President put it, with characteristic sarcasm, he wanted no part of a united India in which 'brother Gandhi has three votes and I have only one'. Muhammad Ali Jinnah's view of 'the problem in India' was that it 'is not of an intercommunal but manifestly of an international character'. It was a 'dream that Hindus and Muslims can ever evolve a common nationality. . . . The Hindus and Muslims belong to two different religious philosophies, social customs, and literature. They neither intermarry, nor interdine together, and indeed they belong to two different civilizations which are based mainly on conflicting ideas and conceptions.' Divergent cultures must necessarily mean separate states. 'If the British Government are really in earnest and sincere to secure the peace and happiness of the people of this Subcontinent, the only course open to us all is to allow the major nations separate homelands, by dividing India into autonomous national States.'[22]

The Congress claimed that when the British finally went home they would leave behind a single, culturally cohesive nation. The Muslim League answered that within British India there were at least two nations-in-the-making; one Hindu, the other Muslim. The existence of the cricket Pentangular seemed to confirm this: and in the monsoon of 1940 the British in Bombay decided to promote a soccer Pentangular. The Hindus, Muslims and Europeans were three of the teams; The Rest was a fourth. Instead of the Parsis, who were not known for their partiality to football, there was a special slot alloted to the Goans, who were.

The announcement of another communal tournament provoked

a savage attack from the nationalist press. The *Bombay Chronicle* conveyed the regret of 'every nationally minded Indian'. Here 'we find a body of Englishmen doing something which is calculated to widen the gulf between the communities'. Perhaps the organizers felt that the tournament would be 'a great financial success . . . like the Cricket Pentangular. But where is the guarantee that the friendly rivalry of the initial stage would not develop into a grand feast of communal jealousy and bitterness of feeling in the near future?'[23]

The Soccer Pentangular was played in the second week of July, without any incidents. But violence soon reared its head on the fields of Bombay. On 22 July a first division football match was reported in the papers under this uninspiring headline: 'FIGHT AT COOPERAGE: BAD REFEREEING CHAFES CROWD: UMBRELLAS, SHOES AND FISTS IN THE FRAY'. Caltex, a largely European team, was playing South Kanara, a wholly Indian one. Caltex were two-nil up, but then Kanara equalized. Two minutes before time the European referee awarded a penalty to Caltex. According to the *Chronicle,* 'two players from the Caltex side were seen signalling the referee that he had given a wrong decision'. Before the spot kick was taken the crowd invaded the field and stopped play.[24]

In mid-August the prestigious Rovers Cup began. An early match inspired this headline: 'ANOTHER COOPERAGE BATTLE: CROWD ATTACKS POLICE'. This time Young Goans were up by a goal against the Welsh Regiment, but the English soldiers equalized late in the game. The Goans protested that it was off-side. The referee refused to change his decision, whereupon the fans rushed on to the turf, breaking the boundary fittings to get there. The constables who tried to stop them were beaten up.[25]

Following this affray the white-dominated Western India Football Association banned the Young Goans for three years. The anger of their fans now spilled over into the newspapers. One letter-writer, A. F. D'Souza, accused the English-owned press of spreading innuendoes and falsehoods: 'Much has been written by your Anglo-Indian morning and evening contemporaries – who represent the cult of showing Indians their place – regarding the hooliganism of the Goan crowd. But they had no eyes to see the Tommies rushing on to the field – and why were they rushing on to the field?'[26] F. C. Fernandes said the suspension of the Goans was 'devoid of the three great principles which an Englishman prizes so highly – fairplay, sportsmanship and justice. And seeing that the Young Goans were judged in their absence and not even given a fair deal, one asks in consternation, wasn't there one "Englishman" on the committee?'[27]

In the semi-finals of the Rovers Cup the Welch Regiment played Mohammedan Sporting, before a packed house. The Calcutta side won by the clear margin of three goals to nil. 'Mohammedan Bombay went mad with joy on Thursday,' reported the *Times of India*. 'There were scenes of great jubilation during the match, especially when the Mohammedans got their goals, and when play was over the crowds swarmed on the ground from all sides, and escorted their favourite players enthusiastically off the field.'[28] There were similar scenes after the finals, where Mohammedan Sporting beat Bangalore Muslims one-nil. The Calcutta team was all Muslim, whereas the Bangalorians had five Hindus, four Muslims and two Christians.[29] When the two sides had played each other in 1937, at a time when the Congress was riding high, the cosmopolitan team had come out on top. In 1940, when the Muslim League was mounting a strong political challenge, it was the communal side that won.

FOR THE SPORTING PUBLIC of Bombay the Rovers Cup, played at the end of the monsoon, was merely an appetizer for the great cricket *tamasha* hosted at the Brabourne Stadium in December. In 1940 both players and fans had to take account of grave developments off the field: notably, the intensification of the Congress–League battle and the intensification of the war in Europe. Some months before the tournament Syed Wazir Ali, the captain of the Muslims, appealed for Indians to stand by their rulers in this, their darkest hour. 'At this critical juncture in the history of the people who gave us cricket', he said, 'it is the sacred duty of the entire Indian sporting world, players and public alike, to render all possible support to Britain in the noble cause for which she is fighting the most ruthless and unsportsmanlike foe civilization has yet known'.[30]

The Congress had offered that support in September 1939; and in June 1940 the offer was renewed, but on condition that the British promised independence afterwards and put in place a 'National Government' in Delhi now. When the Viceroy said no once more, Gandhi was under pressure to mount direct action. He temporized, eventually authorizing 'individual *satyagraha*'. His ascetic disciple Vinoba Bhave was the first to invite arrest, on 17 October. Hundreds of others followed, including Jawaharlal Nehru. The easiest way to have yourself put in jail was to shout anti-war slogans outside a magistrate's office or police station.[31]

While the first lot of Congressmen were being put into prison, K. S. Duleepsinhji asked cricket fans to follow and support the Ranji Trophy. Inter-provincial competition, said this great nephew of a greater uncle, was the best way to develop Indian cricket. Duleep considered 'inter-communal cricket an unfavourable influence on the whole'.[32] Many fans in Bombay naturally disagreed. When it was announced that C. K. Nayudu would lead the Hindus, it was evident that 'pocket-money will be saved henceforward to carry many a youngster to the Brabourne Stadium to see the Major lead his men once more in the annual cricket battle'.[33]

The parents of these youngsters were divided. The Congress-minded thought the show should be stopped this year at least; the League-minded or simply non-political thought it could carry on as usual. In the last week of November Wazir Ali issued a statement from Bhopal, saying he 'fully believe[d] that the Pentangular is not in the least anti-national and will and must go on in the interests of Indian cricket'.[34] This brought a riposte from a Congress Muslim, Musaji J. Kapasi, MA, LLB. 'I do not very much know of the conception of nationalism of Mr Wazir Ali', he commented. 'These matches have ultimately poisonous effect on the public, specially students and collegians, who take the greatest interest in them'. It was 'accepted on all hands that Pentangular matches are anti-national and their immediate and ultimate effect is to foster communal feelings'.[35]

In early December the Bombay Pradesh Congress Committee (BPCC) decided to intervene. Their men were courting arrest daily while practice matches were being played on the Maidan. On the first day of the month, Purshottamdas Tricumdas of the BPCC recalled to the press how

> during the 1930 movement the public and gymkhanas continuously expressed their sympathy with the national struggle by refusing to stage this 'tamasha' . . . I do not want to interfere with the people's pleasure and I am not a 'killjoy'. But I want to sound a note of warning that if matches are played our opponents are certain to exploit the occasion to show that the public of this great city which gave such a splendid account of itself between 1930 and 1934 is today indifferent to the struggle which is far from such.[36]

Tricumdas's statement was printed on the 2nd. That day's papers also carried a statement issued by 'C. K. Nayudu and 21 others', asking that the tournament be stopped *for this year only.* The country, it said, was in turmoil, and Prime Ministers, ministers and legislators were all being clapped into jail. At this juncture, believed C. K. and his fellows,

> when all of us are thinking in terms of communal harmony and freedom for the country, it is but natural that many young men, some of them leading sportsmen, should feel that we should not indulge in the Pentangular cricket this year. How can we think of sports and play cricket when our trusted leaders are being thrust into prisons to rot behind bars?[37]

The following day the call was repeated and reinforced by K. M. Munshi, lately Home Minister in the Bombay Government. Munshi was a brilliant man but a narrow-minded one, and a certifiable killjoy. Appropriately, he was speaking at a 'party [sic] of the Prohibition

Guards'. He told his lemonade-sipping audience that to watch the cricket carnival now would send absolutely the wrong message.

> When India is denied the right to be a comrade of Britain in War, when 1,500 elected representatives of your country have decided to prefer to be locked up in British jails . . . I ask you, will you be able to enjoy the Pentangular? Will not the cricket carnival be exploited by those who are against your country by telling the world that whatever your elected representatives may do the people are so happy and reconciled to their unfortunate lot that they have time to go and enjoy cricket matches?[38]

Munshi rested on the extreme right wing of the Congress. From the left, the Bombay Students Union also called for a ban on the Pentangular. The matches would be used 'for imperialist purposes', said the Union: to stay away from them 'would be an effective popular vote against the present policies of the Government'. It was 'inopportune' to 'emphasize communal differences which the Pentangular matches inevitably tend to do'. This appeal was addressed to the general public: however they responded, it was a 'sacred duty' for all students not to attend. 'The Students' Enclosure must present a deserted appearance.'[39]

These statements were joined by a call from distant Madras. It came from Dr P. Subbaroyan, lately a minister in the Provincial Government, and the serving President of the Cricket Board. As he prepared to offer *satyagraha*, Subbaroyan said that 'the future of Indian cricket lies in the Inter-Provincial tournament being kept the chief events of India'. The Pentangular with its communal edge should be stopped, for 'with political Pakistan in the offing we do not want sport to be evolved in the same fashion'.[40]

These pleas were addressed, in the last instance, to the PJ Hindu Gymkhana for all other Gymkhanas were emphatically for the tournament's continuation. The Parsis liked the Pentangular because it placed them, a community numbering thousands, on par with groupings numbering hundreds of millions. For much the same reason the Europeans liked it too. The rulers were beholden to the idea of a

divided India anyway, as their encouragement of such replicas as the
Pentangular football tournament had recently shown. And by 1940
many Muslims had turned their back on a united India; they saw a
separate cricket team as a prelude to a separate nation.

It was the Hindus of Bombay who were caught in a bind. Placed
against their undoubted love of the Pentangular were the insistent
claims of Congress nationalism. With their leaders in jail, and given
the insolence with which the Viceroy had treated their offer of
conditional cooperation, could they turn up this year at the cricket?

A large number thought they could. A large number thought
they could not. Caught in the crossfire was the PJ Hindu Gymkhana.
Which way would they turn? They cautiously decided to approach
the court of last appeal, Mahatma Gandhi. On Thursday 5 December,
a three-member delegation of the Gymkhana caught the night train
to Gandhi's ashram in Wardha. They were the President, S. A. Shete,
the Vice-President, M. M. Amersey, and a member of the Managing
Committee, Jamnadas Pitambar. The trio had decided to consult
Gandhi on the propriety of holding the Pentangular and of the
Hindus participating in it 'at this crisis in the political history of
the country'.[41] It was suggested then, and also said afterwards, that the
delegation went to seek Gandhi's permission to carry on with business
as usual. For the Hindu Gymkhana had garnered enormous profit
and prestige from the annual *tamasha*, and saw no reason to give it
up, even at a time such as this.[42]

What answer did the Mahatma give them? As it was to be his
most direct, considered and consequential intervention in the world
of cricket, it can only be quoted in full:

> Numerous inquiries have been made as to my opinion on the
> proposed Pentangular Cricket Match in Bombay advertised to
> be played on the 14th. I have just been made aware of the
> movement to stop the match, I understand, as a mark of grief
> over the arrests and imprisonments of *satyagrahis*, more especially,
> the recent arrest of leaders. A deputation of three representatives
> of the Hindu Gymkhana have also just been consulting me as

to what their attitude should be. I must confess my ignorance of these matches and of the 'etiquette' governing them. My opinion must, therefore, be taken as of a layman knowing nothing of such sports and the special rules governing them.

But I must confess that my sympathies are wholly with those who would like to see these matches stopped. I express this opinion not merely as a *satyagrahi* desirous of getting public support in some way or the other for the movement. I must say at once that the present movement is wholly independent of such demonstrations of adventitious support. But I would discountenance such amusements at a time when the whole of the thinking world should be in mourning over a war that is threatening the stable life of Europe and its civilisation and which bids fair to ovewhelm Asia. I would rather that all those who are blessed with intelligence and opportunity devoted both to devising means of stopping what appears to be senseless slaughter. It is like an ill wind which blows nobody any good. And holding this view I would naturally welcome the movement for stopping the forthcoming match from the narrow standpoint I have mentioned above.

Incidentally, I would like the public of Bombay to revise their sporting code and erase from it communal matches. I can understand matches between Colleges and Institutions, but I have never understood the reason for having Hindu, Parsi, Muslim and other Communal Elevens. I should have thought that such unsportsmanslike divisions would be considered taboos in sporting language and sporting manners. Can we not have some field of life which would be untouched by communal spirit?

I should like, therefore, those who have anything to do with this movement to stop the match to broaden the issue and take the opportunity of considering it from the highest standpoint and decide once and for all upon banishing communal taints from the sporting world and also decide upon banishing these sports from our life whilst the bloodbath is going on.

I say this in fear and trembling and with apologies to Mr

Bernard Shaw and others who think that a nation's amusements must not be interrupted even while its flower of manhood is being done to death and is engaged in doing others to death and in destroying the noblest monuments of human effort.[43]

The Pentangular, Gandhi suggested, was wrong in 1940 because the world was in the middle of the most brutal war in human history. Despite that much-quoted jest – 'I think it would be a good idea' – the Mahatma's love for Western civilization was perfectly genuine. During the Battle of Britain this enemy of the British Empire had wept at the possibility of Westminster Abbey being burnt to the ground. Cricket at this time could not possibly be countenanced. But the Pentangular was also wrong, and not just in 1940, because it solidified communal differences. The Mahatma's credo was Hindu–Muslim unity: he had fought for it, and he was to die for it. Hindu–Muslim unity necessarily meant the unity of India. Did not the existence of a tournament on lines of community then undermine the idea of an inclusive nationalism? For if the Muslims were allowed a separate cricket team, what was to stop them demanding a separate nation?

The only note of insincerity in this deeply felt statement was the reference to himself as a 'layman'. In truth, many of Gandhi's people regarded him as an oracle, and he knew it. In the city of Bombay, with its large Gujarati population and reputation for political participation, his following was immense. Within a day or two of Gandhi expressing his opposition to the Pentangular this became clear. The nets put up at the PJ Hindu Gymkhana for their stars to practise in were lying empty. Fans were queueing up to demand refunds for tickets they did not want to use.

One group who had reason to welcome Gandhi's statement were those who patronized the Cricket Championship of India, otherwise known as the Ranji Trophy. This tournament was growing in popularity, but slowly. The Princes and Congress sympathizers who ran the various provincial teams naturally wished ill of the Pentangular. Their opposition was driven by self-interest, but it also had an element of principle. For the Ranji Trophy was leading to a genuine democra-tization of the game, geographically speaking, by creating new centres of cricket outside of Bombay. The island city had its own very strong Ranji team, of course, but so did northern India, Punjab, Maharashtra, Madras, Bengal, United Provinces, Holkar, Baroda and Nawanagar.

Among the individuals who welcomed Gandhi's statement were the *Chronicle* duo of Brelvi and Maitra, and the patriotic Parsi broad-caster A. F. S. Talyarkhan. Earlier in 1940 Talyarkhan had written an essay identifying the future of Indian cricket with the progress of the Ranji Trophy. 'I feel certain', he said, 'that the Cricket Championship of India will bring young cricketers much more to the fore than will the Pentangulars.' The 'great tragedy' of the Bombay carnival, he remarked, was 'that communities are afraid of losing, as if defeat meant the loss of cultural and religious worth!'[44] Now he said the day he heard of Gandhi's reservations was 'the happiest day of my life'. He had always been uncomfortable with a form of cricket which asked lovers of the game to 'pay to watch Nayudu as a Hindu, Wazir as a Muslim, Palia as a Parsee'. Sport should be a vehicle for national unity, not sectarian divisiveness. Talyarkhan hoped that with Gandhi's intervention the 'communal score-book' would be closed once and for all.[45]

A 'certain section of the Press [had] said that they would not give a line to the cricket tournament after Mahatma Gandhi's statement'.[46] But other sections of the press would. On 9 December, the *Times of India* attacked Gandhi for straying into the world of cricket. There were people, it said, who wanted to 'butcher' the Pentangular to make a political statement. Even 'Sevagram has been consulted', and

> Sevagram has spoken. We confess we cannot see the connection between *satyagraha* and cricket. As well [might] Mr Bradman advise Mr Gandhi to abandon *satyagraha* at this time because 'it isn't cricket'. Mr Gandhi, we feel, would resent this counsel, and our own local Bradmans may justifiably be aggrieved at Sevagram's intrusion. War is no time for extravagant revels, but

since when has a cricket tournament become an orgy of merry-making?[47]

Typically, in saying politics and sports didn't mix the *Times of India* made its own politics clear. The established order was right, *satyagraha* was wrong. Inviting the Governor to grace the Pentangular was not political, but Gandhi asking for it to be stopped was. The newspaper's reaction to the Mahatma's statement was a spiteful expression of its general distaste for the man. But, for once in these years, it caught the popular mood better than its rival the *Bombay Chronicle*. If not the local Bradmans, at least the local Bradmans' followers were livid at being denied a taste of their skills this December. It seems, wrote 'A Cricket Fan', that 'the patriotic consciousness of the sponsors of this withdrawal movement was in abeyance until now, when they have been suddenly awakened to their sense of duty by some mysterious revelation'.[48] 'A Cricket Lover' wrote that it was only 'Congress swashbuckling that insists there are no communal compartments in this country. No sane man will deny the fact, however unpleasant it may be, that there are, in India, not only communal compartments but also a thousand and one caste compartments.' The Bombay festival had raised the standard of Indian cricket and infused 'enthusiasm about this manly sport into the hearts of rich and poor alike'. And while politics may heighten social divisions, 'the cricket ground is one of the places which brings together members of different communities in bonds of friendship and the spirit of sport. Such meetings afford better and healthier opportunities for them to understand each other.'[49]

Some letter-writers were not so shy as to suppress their names. G. P. Prabhu insisted that despite Gandhi's call the Pentangular must go on, for arrangements had been made and tickets bought and sold. Besides, cricket in war-time was a necessary consolation: 'It is all the greater reason for not interrupting a Nation's sports and amusements which are calculated to have a salutary effect upon the minds of its people, which would otherwise be depressed with dire consequences.'[50] This, according to Gandhi, was Mr Bernard Shaw's line, and it was followed also by one Russa Mehta, who thought likewise that 'we sorely need relaxation in the present depressing days of the war'. Why listen to Mahatma Gandhi, a man 'who had never played cricket, according to his own admission'?[51]

Such letters were printed gleefully by the *Times of India,* and as a matter of duty by the *Bombay Sentinel,* an evening tabloid edited by the progressive Englishman (and sometime *Chronicle* editor) B. G. Horniman. But no anti-Gandhi, pro-Pentangular letters seem to have been carried in the *Bombay Chronicle* in December 1940. This must in part have been due to respect for the Mahatma, and in part because his statement provided authoritative support to the *Chronicle*'s own opposition to the idea of communal sport.

On 11 December the Secretary of a local cricket club wired Gandhi asking whether he wanted only Hindus to boycott the Pentangular. The answer was that 'all who hold my opinion must refrain whether few or many'.[52] This cable, we may be sure, was displayed at the Extraordinary General Body Meeting of the PJ Hindu Gymkhana held on that meaningful date, Friday the 13th. Also on display was a letter signed by 500 Hindu cricketers arguing that the tournament must go on. The Gymkhana, it said, could not withdraw its team at the last moment. That would cause 'heavy losses' to the dozens of Hindu clubs whose finances depended on their selling the tickets allotted to them for the Pentangular.[53]

The meeting was the stormiest ever held on the premises. A large crowd had gathered outside, which heckled the members one by one as they entered the clubhouse. Recognized leaders of the boycott campaign were subject to a 'veritable fusillade of hostile slogans'. 'Hindus must play' and 'Stop drinking and gambling and then interfere with sport', were the slogans reported in the next day's papers. Doubtless other less decorous slogans were also articulated. The meeting was held in the badminton hall inside and was closed to the press. But reports suggested that it was 'a most disorganized affair. Both camps, for and against, were determined to have their say at one and the same time. Shouting generally drowned every effort to speak out.' The office-bearers found it impossible to distribute the ballot papers on which members were required to cast their votes. In the end, the members were made to leave the room one by one, telling an official their views as they departed. After 'three hours of storm and deafening clamour', the result was announced: 280 votes in favour of the boycott, 243 against. This result 'doomed the Pentangular, though it was a victory for those who respected Mahatma Gandhi's dictum', not many of whom, it seems, were in the crowd waiting outside, for on hearing the result they rushed into the clubhouse, shouting recriminations and hurling chairs. They had eventually to be dispersed by a police force consisting of three officers and a number of constables.[54]

The result of the PJ Hindu Gymkhana meeting prompted an extraordinary outburst from one of Bombay's most respected and politically active citizens, K. F. Nariman. Nariman had been a stalwart of the Congress through the 1920s and 1930s. His own preference was for the constitutional route: although he participated in the odd *satyagraha*, his heart was never in it. Perhaps because of this he was not made Prime Minister of the Bombay Congress Government in 1937, a post he thought his by virtue of ability and experience. The decision to deny him the Prime Ministership had been taken by Vallabhbhai Patel. Now, three years later, Nariman took it out on Gandhi, Patel's own mentor. He could 'understand though not appreciate' why everyone in the Congress, from the President downwards, should seek guidance from the 'sage of Sevagram' on political matters, but 'it passes one's comprehension as to why old and experienced cricketers should make a pilgrimage to the most unsporting spot on earth, to consult the least sportive Saint, who has perhaps never handled "Satanic" instruments like a ball and bat nor even witnessed this "Game of Devils" '. Why object to this cricket tournament, asked Nariman, when communal labels were tolerated everywhere else? There were Hindu hotels and Muslim hotels, and separate drinking bowls marked Hindu and Muslim at every railway station. Even the Muslim League, 'admittedly the most aggressive communal political organization, is recognized as such by the Congress'.[55]

Nariman said 'it was an open secret that Mr K. M. Munshi was the author of this [boycott] campaign'. He added that if L. R. Tairsee was alive 'and at the helm, he would never have allowed his pet institution to be dragged into a political campaign'. Nariman's grudge against K. M. Munshi was of old standing. Munshi was a scheming Gujarati Hindu, who when the Bombay Congress chose its leader in 1937 had helped poison the mind of that other Gujarati Hindu, Patel, against Nariman (a Parsi). He may very well have been the orchestrator of the boycott: we know that two of the three main instigators within the PJ Hindu Gymkhana were Gujarati. And had L. R. Tairsee been President of the PJ Hindu Gymkhana the club might have had the wit not to approach Gandhi in the first place. But Tairsee was dead, and the Mahatma had been approached and had given his verdict.

With the withdrawal of the Hindus the Pentangular was now devoid of competitive interest. The fans saw this, and rushed to return their tickets. All India Radio sensed that if there would be few to watch there would be fewer to listen. It cancelled live broadcast of the cricket, provoking a protest from a very interested party, the All India Radio Merchants' Association. The Pentangular broadcasts, it claimed, were the 'most looked forward to radio events of the year, by every class, community and creed'. More to the point, its cancellation would 'greatly affect its [the Association's] business'.[56]

For a tantalizing moment it looked as if the merchants might not be affected after all. After the PJ Hindu Gymkhana meeting, a bunch of Hindu clubs tried to cobble together a 'rebel' team, by approaching players one by one and asking them to play. The plan fell through when the Bombay Pentangular Committee – composed of the five sponsoring Gymkhanas – decided it would not accept this team. The tournament was eventually played to very poor crowds, with the Muslims defeating The Rest in a 'colourless final'.[57]

After the Muslims had won, the *Bombay Chronicle* ran an editorial entitled 'Bury the Pentangular'. While the 'communal basis may have helped to stimulate the game in its early career', it remarked, the tournament should now give way to a 'more congenial form' such as a Zonal Quadrangular, that had been proposed by J. C. Maitra as a secular alternative to the communal show.[58] Two days later, its popular columnist 'Dim' (D. F. Karaka) proposed an

> Unusual obituary notice: Indian Cricket does not regret to announce the glad and expected death of the Bombay Pentangular and the Pentangular Committee begs to thank Mr A. F. S. Talyarkhan and others for their message of sympathy and condolence. May it never rise from the grave![59]

It was to rise again, and within the twelve-month.

12. Closing Time

BETWEEN 1934 AND 1940 the Muslims won the Bombay cricket tournament four times. On the other side of the country, in Calcutta, Mohammeden Sporting won the city's football championship every year between 1934 and 1938, and again in 1940. These successes greatly pleased the leader of the Muslim League. In the last week of January 1941, Muhammad Ali Jinnah told a gathering of Muslim students at the Cooperage that 'the discipline which sports teach must be harnessed for the benefit of the Muslim community as a whole'.[1]

These sentiments were bound to provoke the followers of Hindu cricket. Their Gymkhana was determined not to repeat the fiasco of 1940. The twin calls of competition and commerce meant that in 1941 they would again sponsor a team to the Pentangular. This was welcomed by cricket lovers in Bombay, but distressed Hindus elsewhere. In the weeks leading up to the tournament a number of princely patrons expressed their opposition to the Pentangular. First off the mark was the Maharajkumar of Vizianagaram, the President, Secretary, captain and patron of the United Provinces Cricket Association (UPCA). In early October the UPCA passed a resolution asking the Board of Control for Cricket in India to 'rid the country of the canker of communal cricket'. Any cricketer who played in the Pentangular should not, 'for the rest of his cricketing life, be eligible to play for his province or his own country'.[2]

At the end of October the Jam Saheb of Nawanagar said he would not allow cricketers on his staff to play in the Pentangular. His boycott was more weighty than Vizzy's because he had better players and he spoke with the authority of the House of Ranji.[3] A week later the Maharaja of Patiala announced that none of his players would be available for matches conducted anywhere on communal lines. Inter-communal cricket, said the Maharaja, was 'unsuited to conditions obtaining in the country'. It was 'beyond comprehension as to how sports could have anything to do with caste, creed, and colour'.[4]

It was quite comprehensible to Patiala in 1934, the year he led the Hindu team in the Quadrangular. The reasons for this new-found opposition to communal cricket were pragmatic. On the sporting side, the Princes now each had their Ranji Trophy teams to promote. On the political side, they had to make their peace with the future rulers of a free India. If Gandhi and the Congress, for whatever reason, opposed communal sport, the Indian Princes could scarcely support it. The Congress's stand weighed especially heavily on the Maharaja of Patiala, for if the Punjab was partitioned the Sikhs would be pushed into a corner, unless they garnered the support of other groups.

Commoners with their own provincial teams joined in. In Madras the President of the Board of Control for Cricket in India, Dr P. Subbaroyan, again insisted that the Pentangular should be given up and the Ranji Trophy made the only first-class tournament in India.[5] The Secretary of the Maharashtra Cricket Association, M. G. Bhave, even wrote to Mahatma Gandhi asking whether his views had changed. This was clever, because the PJ Hindu Gymkhana had stayed clear of the Mahatma this year. Gandhi's reply reveals a man of consistent views who nevertheless regarded cricketers and cricket administrators as pests:

> Dear Bhaveji,
>   Your letter. I retain the same opinion as before. I am utterly opposed to communalism in everything but much more so in sport.
>   You may make what use you like of this opinion. Please do not ask me to do anything more. I have no time.
>   Yours sincerely
>   M. K. Gandhi[6]

The captain of Maharashtra, D. B. Deodhar, also came out against the Pentangular. Anticipating the charge of inconsistency, he said he had participated in it only so long as there was no alternative. Now the Ranji Trophy was there to take the place of the Bombay carnival. It was non-communal, and would more effectively help develop the game in other parts of India.[7]

Another Quadrangular veteran, K. G. Pardeshi, offered a way to abolish communal cricket without threatening Bombay's pre-eminence (Pardeshi, we may recall, was one of the heroes of Vithal's match of 1923). The five Gymkhanas, he suggested, should each sponsor a mixed team, named for an eminent citizen. These would be Sir Ibrahim Rahimutullah's XI, captained by a Hindu; Sir Chunilal Mehta's XI, led by a Muslim; Sir Homi Mehta's XI, led by a European; Sir John Beaumont's XI, led by a Parsi; and His Excellency the Governor's XI, captained by an Indian Christian. Each team would have two members apiece from four communities, and three from the fifth. Such matches, Pardeshi thought, would 'eliminate all communal feeling' from the carnival and also provide more competitive cricket, as all teams would be of roughly even quality.[8]

This year, for the first time, even the *Times of India* opened its pages to anti-Pentangular polemic. True, the other side still got more prominence, but the paper did print contributions it might earlier have consigned to the dustbin. The *Times*'s imperious editor, Sir Stanley Reid, had retired and gone Home, and although his replacement was another Englishman the assistant editors were Indians. Among the contributions published in the newspaper a letter and an editorial-page article stand out. The letter was sent by Altaf Hussain, a nationalist Muslim who invoked the holy name of K. S. Ranjitsinhji. In the 1920s, while a student in London, Hussain had met Ranji in connection with the establishment of an Indian cricket gymkhana. The Jam Saheb declined to help them, saying it would be 'suicidal to start any racial or communal movement in England in the sporting sphere'. He advised the students to join such English clubs as would take them, patiently breaking down the walls of prejudice as he had himself once done. This would promote mutual understanding between Indians and Englishmen. Ranji was convinced that 'creating racial and communal islands would be the bane of India'. Thus, said Hussain triumphantly, the present Jam's opposition to the Pentangular was in keeping with the memory of his great predecessor, who had wished to keep 'sport free from the racial and communal virus'.[9]

The editorial-page article was written by the distinguished jurist Sir Chimanlal Setalvad. The communal cricket tournament, he thought, had a particularly pernicious influence on the young. It encouraged them to think of themselves as Hindus, Muslims, Parsis or Christians, 'when they should, in the real interests of the country, be led to think and act always as Indians first and everything else afterwards'. Famous sportsmen had supported the tournament on the grounds that it improved the standard of cricket in India. But, Setalvad remarked, the opinions of those bred in the Pentangular were not of much value. Sport had to give way to 'higher considerations of national solidarity and unity'. One had to listen not to cricketers but to those 'who can take a longer view about cricket and its relation to national character and interests'.[10]

But it was of course the *Bombay Chronicle* that was in the vanguard of the movement against the Pentangular. The *Chronicle*'s editor, Syed Abdullah Brelvi, was a Muslim intellectual who passionately believed in a united India. The *Chronicle* saw itself as a Congress in microcosm; it stood for the same kind of socially inclusive nationalism. As the historian Mukul Kesavan has written, the party of Gandhi and Nehru 'had to prove to the Raj that the variety of India could be gathered under the umbrella of a single movement'. There was thus a 'Noah's Ark quality to Congress nationalism, as it did its best to keep every species of Indian on board'.[11] Brelvi himself was a Maulana Azad-like figure, a Muslim editor of an influential nationalist journal, much as Azad was a Muslim President of a (mostly Hindu) Congress. His colleagues on the paper included a Parsi, Karaka, and a Bengali, Maitra, as well as several Christians.

Failed and flawed as it might have been, there was still a heroic quality about the *Chronicle*'s inclusiveness. Indeed, without my intending it, in this telling of Indian cricket's social history a now forgotten newspaper has emerged as one of its central figures. The *Chronicle* once strove, mightily and in the end successfully, for the just recognition of a family of low-caste cricketers. Now, in the 1940s, it was in the vanguard of a campaign to keep religion out of sport. This campaign acquired a special resonance because religion was deepening its presence everywhere else, and because the newspaper's own editor was a Muslim.

Men like Palwankar Baloo and C. K. Nayudu brought cricket to the attention of nationalism and nationalists. Syed Abdullah Brelvi, for his part, brought nationalism to cricket. The communal tournament was a standing insult to the idea of one India which he and his party had laboured for and gone to jail for. His editorials repeatedly attacked the tournament for 'insidiously keeping alive [the] undesirable communal spirit which it should be the endeavour of every patriotic Indian to eradicate from every field of public activity, especially sports'. With the help of the Bombay Students' Union, the *Chronicle* convened public meetings where the public was asked to boycott the tournament and send the ticket money to worthier causes, such as famine relief or the promotion of peace between Hindus and Muslims. The key speakers at these meetings were generally Brelvi and A. F. S. Talyarkhan, the journalist who made his name broadcasting live commentary on the Pentangular. On Sunday, 23 November 1941 Talyarkhan addressed the annual conference of the Students' Union, held at the Gowalia Tank Maidan in the centre of the city. He said that the affirmation of communal identity, on the cricket field and outside, violated the idea of a shared citizenship, that 'we are all Indians before we are anything else'. 'It was a truism', remarked Talyarkhan,

> that no individual was born with the belief that he could show enthusiasm in sport only when it was marked 'Hindu', 'Muslim', or 'Parsi'. It was only in later life that they had been led into these water-tight compartments. It was not a matter of politics. It was not taught in schools. Students did not learn it from their parents. The conception had come into their minds only by the

Pentangular which was being deliberately played on a communal basis.[12]

The following Sunday, students joined older people in a large public meeting at the Chowpatty beach. On this occasion the star turn was Brelvi's. The editor suggested that the original sin was to convert the Parsi–Presidency match into a Triangular, which led inexorably to the Quadrangular and Pentangular. Rather, as in Madras, there should have been an annual match between Europeans and Indians. 'As in many other fields of public activity', said the editor,

> we followed the line of least resistance in stimulating the love of cricket among various communities. We seek to spread education in our country by starting denominational institutions and universities. We encourage sport and club life in our country by establishing communal sports institutions and clubs. We cater to the physical needs of the people by establishing Muslim restaurants and Hindu restaurants and while on railway journeys cannot quench our thirst except through 'Hindu Pani' or 'Muslim Pani'. We cannot carry on the administration of our home towns or of the country except through communal electorates. How far this line of least resistance has gone will be apparent from the fact that in what was hitherto the only swimming bath for Indians in our city you cannot have a swim except with your coreligionists, there being different times for Parsis, Hindus, Muslims . . .[13]

If they supported the Pentangular, Brelvi asked of his audience, 'how can you oppose separate electorates, or even Pakistan?' Talyarkhan, speaking next, drew the public's attention to their relationship to the Mahatma: 'When the greatest living Indian has condemned communal sports, if we cannot keep away from the Pentangular for one fortnight, we are fit for nothing.'[14]

These meetings were coordinated by a body calling itself the Citizens' Anti-Pentangular Committee. The pro-Pentangular movement had no organization of its own. Its forces were dispersed, but as insistent. Through the month of November 1941 every statement condemning communal cricket met with an equal and opposite reaction. An early and influential intervention came from the Bombay Cricket Association (BCA). This sent a powerful team to the Ranji Trophy, but its 103 constituent clubs were, for good reason, more inclined towards the tournament played annually in their bailiwick. A meeting of the BCA held on 5 November regretted the pronouncement by Dr P. Subbaroyan, the Cricket Board's President, against the Pentangular, rejected the view that it caused communal ill-will, and pointed out that 'the Bombay public is overwhelmingly in favour of the tournament and it looks forward to this fixture as an annual festival in which all communities take part'. It hoped therefore that the carnival of 1941 would 'receive the continued and fullest support from cricketers and the general public as heretofore'.[15]

Days later, the former secretary of the Cricket Board and former 'Rest' captain A. S. D'Mello also went public with the view that there was 'nothing communal' about the Pentangular. The tournament 'had given India very thrilling and top-class cricket, played in a very healthy spirit of competition'.[16] Then a more substantial voice suggested that to stop the Pentangular would mean 'the funeral of Indian cricket'. This was C. K. Nayudu, who seems now to have regretted his own opposition in 1940, which had been prompted perhaps by a momentary swaying to the political winds. Now he would rather remember how this tournament had, for a full twenty-five years, allowed him to display his remarkable talents before an adoring public. C. K. believed that the Ranji Trophy and the Pentangular could prosper together. For him the Bombay carnival was simply 'the greatest tournament in the world', providing 'a fortnight of first-class cricket'.[17]

Lowly letter-writers came out on the side of the Pentangular as well. Residents of Bombay took civic pride in what the tournament had done for the sport in their city: 'And look what the result has been! The standard of cricket is miles ahead of any other centre in India!'[18] The indefatigable Russa Mehta, who had attacked Mahatma Gandhi the previous year, endorsed Nayudu's claim that there had been no single incident of communal disharmony in the tournament's history. The beautiful and spacious Brabourne Stadium was built for the carnival alone, and 'it would be nothing short of calamity to abandon this tournament simply to satisfy the ambition of a few Princes interested in transferring the inherent popularity of Bombay's Pentangular to the Ranji Trophy Tournament'. Ranjitsinhji had been quoted as being against communal cricket; now Mehta would invoke him as one of its supporters: 'Let not the present Jam Saheb forget that his predecessor, the great Ranji himself, was a keen spectator of the Quadrangular Tournament and never raised his voice against it.'[19]

In the event C. K. Nayudu did not play, for his boss the Maharaja of Holkar decided to join the rulers of Patiala and Nawanagar in their boycott. Vizianagaram's edict was however defied by P. E. Palia of the United Provinces: when appointed captain of the Parsis, he decided to put community over province. Also playing was C. K's brother C. S. Nayudu. His employer, the Maharaja of Baroda, had decided not to intervene. With the return of the Hindus it was 'once again a Pentangular in actual fact'.[20] The cricket was good, and the price of entry cheap: 5½ rupees for a ticket for the whole tournament, only 3½ rupees if bought in bulk.[21]

The match of the fortnight was the semi-final between the Hindus and the Muslims, a contest which, as ever, had 'a glamour all its own'.[22] The crowds packed into the ground, disregarding the picketing outside by the Bombay Students' Union. The protesters were displaying placards with Gandhi's views, but the fans ducked past them and went through the turnstiles. After three days of standing unsuccessfully outside the stadium the students got into an altercation with the police. The constables used their *lathis*, and three boys were injured and taken to hospital, one with a broken collar-bone.[23] Inside, the Bombay batsman Vijay Merchant was making his way unhurriedly to an unbeaten double century. He made another double hundred in the finals, helping the Hindus defeat the Parsis by ten wickets.

The *Bombay Chronicle* had devoted plenty of column inches to the protest movement. When it failed, and the tournament went off as planned, they were obliged to cover the matches as well. The most plaintive comment on the whole show was provided by its sports editor, J. C. Maitra. The 'protagonists of communal sport', he complained, 'have ranged themselves to make common cause against the Congress. They want the edict of Mahatma Gandhi to be thrown overboard and thereby make him the laughing-stock of the sporting world.'[24]

IN FEBRUARY 1942 Singapore fell to the Japanese. Rangoon followed in March. The British now belatedly decided to send the Labour politician Sir Stafford Cripps to bring round Indian public opinion. Cripps came promising Dominion status after the war, but the Indians wanted popular participation in government now. Ministries on the model of 1937–9 were suggested. Negotiations broke down on the question of the defence of India. The Congress wanted at least joint responsibility: an Indian Minister of Defence at the centre with a British Commander-in-Chief. Cripps and his backers could not accept anything but total British control.[25]

After the failure of the Cripps Mission Gandhi brooded through a long, hot summer, before calling for a nationwide *satyagraha*. In early August the All India Congress Committee met at the Gowalia Tank Maidan in central Bombay, otherwise the venue for meetings of the Citizens' Anti-Pentangular Committee. On the 8th the AICC passed a resolution demanding that the British 'Quit India'. The Government arrested all the major leaders, but the disturbances had begun and were soon to escalate. Neither the British nor the Congress were prepared for the scale and spread of the protests, or its intensity. In many districts students and socialists assumed the leadership, and they had no doctrinal commitment to non-violence. Railway lines were sabotaged, telegraph wires cut, offices burnt and shops looted. Police stations were torched and, in some cases, policemen set alight. In places as far apart as Balia in the United Provinces, Satara in the Deccan and Midnapore in Bengal, the officers of the Raj abandoned their posts and fled from the rebels, allowing them to declare their own independent *sarkar*.

Bombay was at the centre of it all. The Congress's Quit India resolution was passed in the city. The promoters of the resolution, men like Patel and Nehru, were arrested here. The street protests that ensued led to thirty-three deaths in four days of police firing. Factories and businesses were closed as merchants fled to their native Gujarat and workers returned to their villages. Young Bombay socialists, such as Usha Mehta and Achyut Patwardhan, achieved legendary status by running an underground radio station for months without being caught.[26]

There could be no Pentangular in 1942, but by the autumn of the following year calm had returned to the city. The tide had turned in favour of the Allies in Europe, and the counter-attack against the Japanese was taking shape. Law and Order was favourable to the staging of the cricket carnival. Four of the five Gymkhanas were, as ever, on Law and Order's side. How would the Hindus respond?

In the first week of October 1943 the *Bombay Chronicle* condemned communal gymkhanas as 'an unhealthy and dying institution'.[27] Within a month it had to report an unexpected revival. In the city at least, there seemed to be no opposition to the Pentangular. The Gymkhanas were busy with their preparations. It was reported that the Europeans were 'trying to get the services of the veteran [D. R.] Jardine', then a military staff officer in India.[28]

The Pentangulars were due to begin in the last week of November. Ten days before the first match, a great Parsi veteran passed away. In his column in the *Bombay Sentinel*, A. F. S. Talyarkhan invoked another veteran, still living. 'May I request P. Baloo to send us his appreciation of R. P. Meheromji's batting?' asked Talyarkhan. 'It would be most interesting to know what the best bowler of his day thought about the best batsman of that time.'[29]

It would also have been most interesting to know what Palwankar Baloo thought of the controversy about the Pentangular's continuance. Would his own past memories of success in cricket have won over his political orientation as a loyal Congressman? His PJ Hindu Gymkhana, meanwhile, had pre-empted protest by pledging a part of their profits to the Bengal Famine Relief Fund. The other Gymkhanas followed. The *Chronicle* commented sarcastically that these pledges were meant to 'help the communal tournament first and then the suffering people'.[30]

On the first day of the Pentangular 20,000 people came to the Brabourne Stadium. 'The picketing resorted to by some youngsters', wrote a reporter, 'did not seem to have much effect on those who were bent on seeing the contest.'[31]

All India Radio, in deference to the popular will, had resumed its broadcasts. Cricket fans could listen to A. F. S. Talyarkhan in the day; and, if they wished, read him in the *Bombay Sentinel* in the evening. Talyarkhan's broadcasts were restricted to the cricket, but his 'Take It From Me' column was overtly political, aiming to end the Pentangular and thus his own role in popularizing it through the radio. His preferred mode was sarcasm, conveying his views in the voice of a mythical *doppelgänger*, 'Steve'. Steve had told him that V. D. Savarkar, the leader of the reactionary Hindu Mahasabha, had requested The Rest's captain Vijay Hazare to 'revert to Hinduism'.[32] Steve added that if the Muslims lost to The Rest, Jinnah would expel the team's captain, S. M. Kadri, from the Muslim League.[33] The columnist referred to the Muslim team as 'Pakistan', the context indicating a total disapproval.

The argument for the ending of Empire, suggested Talyarkhan, was made weaker by the existence of these embarrassing divisions in the field of sport. 'With what face', he asked,

> can we Indians talk about racial discrimination and aloofness, when, particularly in Bombay, no sport is sport unless it is religion against religion, community against community? What right have we to worry about the European's behaviour towards us when we are as yet incapable of resisting the temptation to eat, drink, think, play, as exclusive entities, among ourselves, we who belong to the soil of the country, to whom the country belongs?[34]

Talyarkhan wished his readers to believe that 'through sport they can grow up as Indians, play as Indians, live as Indians, die as Indians'. This meant an active promotion of the Ranji Trophy, with its multi-religious and multi-racial teams. A week before the Pentangular began, he told his readers of how in that other tournament P. E. Palia captained a 'side of non-Parsis for the honour of UP', how 'Ebrahim, a Muslim, [was] batting in a great partnership [for Bombay] with Merchant, the Hindu', and how 'an Englishman [C. P. Johnstone] can captain an Indian side at Madras and still get the fullest support of ten-thousand khadi-clad Madrasis'.[35] But a week after the carnival began he had to concede that the Ranji Trophy ran a ragged second in the popularity stakes. A supporter of the Pentangular, crowing with success, came up to Talyarkhan outside the Cricket Club of India and asked: 'Why don't you bring your Mahatma Gandhi to see the crowds?'[36]

On the first day of the Pentangular's first match, played between the Parsis and the Muslims, picketers outside the gates of the Brabourne Stadium attempted to turn fans away from the ground. But, the *Times of India* gloated, 'the futility of their efforts was reflected in the crowd that greeted the Muslim team as they followed their captain, into the field'.[37] The Muslims won this match, easily. Next, a crowd of 40,000 watched the Hindus defeat the Europeans by an innings in the first semi-final. In the second semi-final The Rest upset the Muslims, chiefly through an immaculate double-century by Vijay Hazare. Hazare's 248 was also a tournament record, going past the 243 not out made by Vijay Merchant the previous year. In the finals the Hindus ran up the huge total of 581 for 5 declared, Merchant reclaiming his record with 250 not out. The Rest were dismissed for 133, and following on, made 387. Of these runs Vijay Hazare scored a staggering 309. While Europe was at war the two Vijays were providing 'cricket such as has seldom been witnessed in any part of the world'.[38]

The day after the final ended, the Catholic Gymkhana threw a reception in honour of The Rest. Their side had never done so well, and their captain had played the innings of his life. Among those who spoke were the President of the Catholic Gymkhana and Vijay

Merchant. The Hindu generously called his rival 'decidedly India's greatest batsman of the day'. Hazare was presented with a purse of 12,000 rupees, and then the dancing began. Three hundred couples took to the floor, swaying to music by Micky Corea's band, loaned free of charge by the Taj Hotel. Chic and his Music Makers and the band of Tony Newnes also played. The dancing 'continued with unabated enthusiasm until long after the milkman had passed, highlighted by two particularly attractive cabaret numbers'. Thus was celebrated the greatest sporting triumph of one of Bombay's most colourful communities. The singers were Catholic, the dancers were Catholic, above all, the batting hero Vijay Hazare was Catholic. As with the Parsis and the Hindus and the Muslims, cricket provided the perfect means to further the pride and solidarity of the community.[39]

In this year's press post-mortem two items stood out. 'The Pentangular is over', wrote 'Dim' (D. F. Karaka): 'We hope there will not be another Bengal famine next year to justify another Pentangular.'[40] The other and lengthier comment was offered by an editorial in the Muslim League's newspaper, *Dawn*. Their cricket team had not done as well as hoped, but the point was to give it another chance, to establish that the Pentangular itself was a necessary and politically legitimate exercise. It was not, as some suggested, 'a ghastly slur on Indian nationhood'. It must not be made the target of Hindu politicians 'incapable of distinguishing between a wicket-stump and a bat'. It was merely a sporting festival where 'the successful team of young cricketers receive congratulations and prizes without being infected with ideas of communal rivalry in politics'. The Pentangular, wrote Jinnah's paper,

> has really nothing to do with Hindu–Muslim differences that await settlement in political terms if Hindus and Muslims wish to be free; but the trumpery protest is foisted on the situation to divert attention from the main problem and let them feel the emotional satisfaction of being busy, doing good.

Politics may create opponents, suggested *Dawn*, but cricket only fostered a spirit of contented togetherness. Thus in this year's tournament,

> Hazare came out as champion batsman and all hailed him as the Bradman of India without any trace of grievance that Amir Elahi did not figure among the victors of the season. Hindus, Muslims, Europeans, Parsis, Anglo-Indians, Goans and the crowd of miscellaneous nondescripts who enhance the fun of the occasion had crowded into the Brabourne Stadium. They had their money's worth, but Hindu political pietists profess to think that such divisions, fostered no doubt by the 'third party', are a danger to communal unity and Indian culture. To think that regional cricket would be of intrinsic aid in healing the 'communal canker' is to indulge in a far-fetched and artificial notion. Not that we have a word to say about the development of the game in diverse fixtures, but even if cricket was played on a regional exhibition corresponding to Professor Coupland's redistribution of India according to his riverine scheme, we do not see how that would simplify our political difficulty. The habit of swallowing camels and then straining at gnats is part of the spirit of political exhibitionship which appeals to some of our Hindu friends as the acme of wisdom and progress. American teams play against British teams without 'widening the gulf' and at the World Olympics different countries enter their champions without prejudicing the ideals of the League of Nations.[41]

Indian Muslims, it was implied, were already a distinct nation, even if it would take a formal territorial separation (as with America and Britain) to make this an established political and sporting fact. The curious thing about the *Dawn* editorial was that it was most likely written by the editor, Pothan Joseph, himself not a Muslim but a Syrian Christian from Kerala. He was doing a job, and doing it supremely well.

THE RELATIONSHIP BETWEEN Gandhi and Jinnah, those two London-trained Gujarati lawyers, was marked by distrust and suspicion on both sides. There does, however, exist at least one photograph of the two smiling together, with a toothless Gandhi, in a loin-cloth, placing an avuncular arm over a suited-and-booted Jinnah. The photograph was taken on the verandah of Jinnah's Bombay house in September 1944, during a week-long meeting to bridge the gap between the Congress and the League.

The talks broke down, and bitterly too. Jinnah charged the Mahatma with 'inciting the Muslims against me', and of asking for the 'burial of Pakistan'.[42] Even as the politicians were talking, the PJ Hindu Gymkhana announced that it would donate its entire profits from the 1944 Pentangular to the Gujarat and Khandesh Flood Relief Funds. A Calcutta journalist offered this laconic verdict: 'Communal cricket is not desirable but if communal cricket can bring some relief to suffering humanity let communal cricket live and prosper.'[43]

The Pentangular was due to begin on 15 November. The Bombay Pradesh Congress Committee urged a boycott of the tournament, saying that 'communal cricket in these days of increased communal tension is definitely detrimental to the interests of the nation'.[44] On the day of the first match, however, the *Bombay Chronicle* noted that there were even some 'Congress-minded folks who seem to disagree with Mahatma Gandhi's dictum in regard to the communal basis of the competition. Truly speaking, they have been so much used to it during the last 40 years or so, that they are drawn to it as a drunkard is drawn to a pub.'[45]

In 1944 the number of drunkards was on the increase, the fare in the pub more richly varied. The Maharajas of Holkar and Baroda had agreed to release their players 'as a special case' in view of the profits being donated to flood relief.[46] The followers of The Rest looked to Vijay Hazare for an encore. The Parsis, so long in the doldrums, were building a new side around talented young batsmen like Rusi Modi and Rusi Cooper. The Europeans, generally weaker still, could this year call upon the resources of the cricketers serving in India during the war. The *Times of India* wrote expectantly that the side sponsored by the Bombay Gymkhana 'will be one of the most powerful – if not the most powerful – sides ever seen in the popular annual festival'. Ten county cricketers were to play, including two great England cricketers – Joe Hardstaff, Jr and Denis Compton. The Voice of the Establishment provided the likely European side, with their current rank and county affiliation: Battery Sergeant Major J. Hardstaff (England and Nottinghamshire), Company Sergeant Major D. Compton (England and Middlesex), Major P. A. Cranmer (Warwickshire), Major N. S. Hotchkin (Cambridge and Middlesex), Flying Officer R. Simpson (Nottinghamshire), etc., etc. This sonorous listing of ranks and names conveyed the hope that Imperial pride would be restored on the playing-fields of Bombay, as if to match the Allied victories on the battlefields of France and Germany.[47]

But this was not Europe, and the Europeans lost to the Parsis in the first round. The Parsis then lost to the Hindus, while the Muslims prevailed over The Rest in the other semi-final. In the India of 1944 this was almost pre-ordained: that the political quarrel would be rehearsed and replayed on the cricket field. For the final 'the Brabourne Stadium was packed to overflowing'.[48] Over the four days almost 200,000 people watched a match that 'for thrills and spectacular effect could not have been improved upon even if it had been actually stage-managed'.[49]

The Hindus batted first and were bowled out for 203. The portly leg-break bowler Amir Elahi, a crowd favourite, took five wickets. The Muslims replied with 221. The Hindu second innings was built around a careful unbeaten hundred by G. Kishenchand, a Sindi from that mostly Muslim city, Karachi. They ended with 315, setting the Muslims almost 300 to win. It was a tough target, and the pitch was the worse for wear. In particular, there was a hollow pit on the bowling crease. The Hindu captain, Vijay Merchant, asked permission for the pit to be filled. The Muslim captain, Merchant's friend and All India opening partner, Mushtaq Ali, consulted his team-mates. They asked him to refuse, on the grounds that the filling up of the pit would only help the Hindu bowlers. But Mushtaq overruled them.

The game had to be played in the 'true [sportsman's] spirit', he told his team-mates, adding: 'if we lost the match, we would not be sold as slaves or sent to the gallows'.[50]

The pit was filled, and the Muslims went in to bat for the second time. Wickets fell steadily at one end while the opening batsman, K. C. Ibrahim – a Muslim from the largely Hindu city, Bombay – kept going. He was supported by the young Lahore collegian, Abdul Hafeez, and by Gul Mahommed. The Muslims' captain and best batsman, Syed Mushtaq Ali, suffered a nasty blow and retired hurt, but returned to hit a quick-fire 36. In the end the Muslims won by the narrowest of margins, one wicket, the winning runs coming twenty minutes before the end, with Ibrahim remaining undefeated on 137.[51]

It was certainly the most thrilling cricketing contest ever hosted at the Brabourne Stadium. A reporter covering the match called it 'by far the most exciting finish ever seen in the Bombay Pentangular', unequalled for its 'concentrated interest and spectacular effect', a 'final that will be remembered for many, many years'.[52] As indeed it was. Forty years later, it was recalled in print by one of the participants, Abdul Hafeez Kardar. After the Muslims had defeated The Rest, Kardar and his team-mate Nazar Mohammad were asked by their Principal in Lahore to return to play an inter-college match. Nazar went back, but Kardar 'told the President of the Islam Gymkhana that I considered loyalty to the cause of Muslims in India far greater than loyalty to a college team'. Kardar went on to play for Oxford University, Warwickshire and India. After 1947, he became Pakistan's first captain and led them to their first victories in Test cricket. All through his career, he wrote, 'whenever things went against me as a captain, I took inspiration from this great [Hindu–Muslim] match. It inspired me to fight till the last ball was bowled. It taught me to go for rich "scalps" [sic] the strongest possible opposition.' These were the lessons for later life, but Kardar would also recall 'the warm receptions that followed our victory over the very strong Hindu XI in the Pentangular finals. The celebrations and congratulations lasted through Christmas and took us right into 1945's New Year bells.'[53]

In 1943 The Hindus had defeated The Rest easily, but Hazare's epic innings had lent the loss a peculiar glow. The victors could be generous, for the losers were a small, sweet and politically docile minority. The Pentangular final of 1944, contested between two large and increasingly hostile groupings, was a different kettle of fish altogether. For quality of play and dramatic shifts of interest this match was the equal of any in the history of Indian cricket. Like the Partition of India, it was a desperately close-run thing: and the Muslims won in the end.

IN THE WINTER OF 1944–5 C. K. Nayudu entered his fiftieth year. The Cricket Club of India decided on a celebration to honour him. This was scheduled to run from 26 February to 2 March 1945. As in 1937, an eleven captained by D. B. Deodhar would play an eleven led by Nayudu. Only the venue was different: the Brabourne Stadium instead of the PJ Hindu Gymkhana.

The week before the Golden Jubilee match Nayudu was in Madras with his Holkar side, to play in the semi-finals of the Ranji Trophy. C. K. had often batted before large crowds in this southern city. Moreover, Madras had a vast population of his fellow Andhras. These got together under the banner of the Andhra Vidyarthi Vignana Samithi to throw a lavish party for their hero, held at Woodlands Hotel in Royapettah. The local dignitary who welcomed him spoke of how 'the Andhras were proud of Colonel C. K. Nayudu, who had reached such eminence in cricket'. Nayudu, in his reply, thanked his compatriots for their affection but observed 'that cricket did not recognize any communal or racial distinctions but was international'.[54]

Now Nayudu had playing under him, for Holkar, cricketers from all parts of India and of varied religious backgrounds. (At this time the Holkar XI even had an Englishman, Denis Compton.) From a cricketing point of view, he thus suggested, he was much more than an 'Andhra'.

In the past, certainly, Nayudu's appeal had cut across boundaries of region and religion. His Golden Jubilee match now beckoned. But would Bombay, that catholic and cosmopolitan city, respond to him in 1945 as it had in 1926 and 1937 and all the years in between? Nayudu was older now and, on the field at any rate, had been eclipsed by younger stars like Merchant and Hazare and Mankad. The uncertainty about how Bombay would receive him is poignantly captured in the columns of that Indian nationalist and Nayudu-worshipper, A. F. S. Talyarkhan. The day before the Jubilee match, Talyarkhan passed on the rumours that the Brabourne Stadium would not be full. The students were preparing for their examinations, and there had been a surfeit of cricket anyway. Not three months had passed since the great match between the Hindus and the Muslims. Besides, the Jubilee match would be immediately followed by the Ranji Trophy final between Holkar and Bombay, also to be played at the Brabourne Stadium.

Talyarkhan sought to crush those rumours of poor atendance with this clarion call:

> Now is Bombay's time to show that all the mass hysteria which has invariably attended C. K.'s appearances on our maidans is put into some really concrete and appreciative form. Now let me see those stands filled. Now, when a man who has thrilled, entertained and enlightened us about the game of cricket, has reached the end of his sunny career, is the time for Bombay to demonstrate in unmistakable way its appreciation. Can Bombay fill a stadium for old C. K.?[55]

The answer, as revealed in the following day's Bombay *Sentinel*, was that it couldn't. The crowd was not more than 10,000, less than one-third of the stadium's capacity, this despite the quality of the teams, with Vijay Merchant, Vinoo Mankad, Vijay Hazare and Amir Elahi playing for Deodhar's XI and Mushtaq Ali, Rusi Modi, Denis Compton and C. R. Rangachari for C. K.'s. Talyarkhan now worried that

unless something unexpected pops up the rest of the three days, we are going to feel rather ashamed of ourselves . . . if students can't come because of their studies, let them set about making a big collection. . . . And it is also up to those sethias who used to pay up to fifty rupees a sofa to watch C. K. in his younger days to make their contribution right now. Wake up Bombay . . . [Or] does a C. K. Nayudu only get showered with gold bricks and presents when he is playing as a Hindu? Is [the Muslim League newspaper] *Dawn* right after all? Shall I prove right after all?[56]

Talyarkhan was, as usual, giving non-stop commentary on this match. Over the radio he also called for spectators to come, and on the second day more people did indeed turn up. The critic now hoped that 'C. K. will not go empty-handed from here', particularly if he himself scored 'that appropriate-for-the-occasion hundred', and if 100 of his younger admirers who could not come because of their studies each asked a rich man to contribute 100 rupees apiece.[57] In the event, Nayudu's own scores were 18 and 9, inadequate compensation (from the organizers' point of view) for hundreds scored by Merchant, Mankad, Hazare and Compton. The crowds were noticeably thin on the last two days, prompting this agitated post-match reflection by Talyarkhan:

> What are we in Bombay going to do about a thumping purse for C. K.? . . . There must be some token of gratitude from a city that has talked, thought and enjoyed C. K. Nayudu all these years. It is this that must trouble the conscience . . . [A] way must be found to make up for the empty coffers of the Golden Jubilee Match . . .[58]

After the match was over, a 'rousing reception' was given in honour of Nayudu. It was held at the Sunderabai Hall and hosted by the PJ Hindu Gymkhana. The President of the BCCI, Dr P. Subbaroyan, was in the chair. Vijay Merchant spoke of Nayudu's influence on the younger generation of Indian cricketers, Denis Compton recalled his impact on English crowds, and J. C. Maitra said it was the Colonel 'who had popularized cricket in the country'. He added, meaningfully, that C. K. was 'an indigenous cricketer who had his grounding in India and not abroad'.[59]

Nayudu, in his reply, graciously thanked the public of Bombay for 'their high sense of sportsmanship'. But this sense of sportsmanship, it has to be said, was not really reflected in the final purse. Thus Nayudu was given a gold bat by a local jeweller, and a cheque for 18,000 rupees, 10,000 of which had been contributed by the Cricket Club of India. Thus *Dawn* was at least half right; for the collection would have been greater, perhaps far greater, had the Nayudu benefit match instead been played between Hindus and Muslims. Defeated by the size of the purse, A. F. S. Talyarkhan sought consolation in its contents. 'It is a good thing for the future', he remarked, 'that a great cosmopolitan Club should shoulder the burden and not a communal body; for C. K. belongs to India and not to any one community'.[60]

Other events were held to commemorate Nayudu's Jubilee, held in Delhi, Indore and Calcutta, for example, the last organized by the Mohun Bagan football club. The cricketer issued a statement to the press, to be released all over India, thanking his friends and well-wishers. Here he recalled, for their benefit and his, a long career at the crease. He spoke of some of the famous cricketers he had played with or against, Parsis like Kanga and Warden, Muslims like Yusuf Beg, Europeans like Greig and Tarrant, and Hindus like Vithal, Shivram, Ganpat and Deodhar. Among the bowlers he singled out Palwankar Baloo for special mention. 'Baloo's deceptive flight and ability to vary his pace was magnificent and he could perhaps be ranked with the greatest left-arm spinners of the world.' But there was also a telling comparison between the fans who followed him in his younger days and those who came to the cricket now. The stadiums were now bigger, acknowledged Nayudu, 'but the crowds of the past followed the game with almost a religious fervour and a gusto all their own. A section of the crowd today may be more fashionable but the old crowd definitely enjoyed the game as much as the new.'[61]

This statement, gracefully worded though it is, cannot fully conceal the more elemental feelings that lie behind it. For the lukewarm response to Nayudu's Golden Jubilee match was illustrative of a more general feature of modern sport: the painful and at times tragic abandonment of the hero once he is past his prime.

●

IN THE LAST MONTHS OF 1945 a team of Australian Servicemen came touring. This side, led by Lindsay Hassett and including Keith Miller and other gifted cricketers, had played a series of 'Victory Tests' in England to celebrate the successful conclusion of the war. The Australians played three unofficial Tests and several lesser matches in India. They were fine cricketers and fine human beings, whose lack of racial or class prejudice made them more popular by far than any previous side of touring Englishmen.[62]

The Australians went home in November, and attention now turned to the carnival in Bombay. The *Bombay Chronicle* opposed it, as usual.[63] So did the Maharaja of Patiala, who pledged to donate a trophy for an annual zonal tournament to be held in Bombay as a replacement for the Pentangular. 'No sport can achieve front-rank international status', said the Maharaja, 'if it is directed into narrow communal grooves.'[64] Following his lead, the Princes collectively enforced a ban on their cricketers. Thus Hazare stayed in Baroda, Mushtaq Ali and C. S. Nayudu in Indore, and Amarnath in Patiala.

But, as the *Times of India* remarked, 'the Pentangulars will continue as long as the Gymkhanas find it profitable'.[65] When the tournament was played in January 1946, at least the best Bombay and Poona players were on display. In one semi-final the Hindus defeated the Europeans by an innings. In the other the Parsis beat the Muslims by four wickets.

While the Maharaja of Baroda had not permitted his players to participate this year, his lady was present at the Brabourne Stadium. Indeed, the Hindus played the final with bats presented to them by Maharani Chimanbhai Gaekwad. Apparently, she had wanted to make her gift in 1944, but due to the slowing of shipping lanes during the war the consignment arrived eighteen months late. The bats were in time, however, for the final of 1945–6. And so 'one of cricket's quartermasters, or should it be cricket's quartermistresses, issued to the Hindu team its new armour in readiness for the coming battle with the Parsis'.[66] With their new equipment the Hindus defeated the Parsis by a handsome margin of 310 runs.

The week after the Bombay *tamasha* the annual Lahore Triangular was to be played. But the participating teams – Hindus, Muslims and Sikhs – all had their attention diverted by the elections due in March. At the last moment the tournament was scrapped, 'in view of the rapidly worsening communal situation consequent upon the election fever that is daily growing'. When the elections were held the Muslim League did well in Punjab, a province it had long coveted but not previously made a mark in. In other states the League likewise won the majority of seats reserved for Muslims.[67]

Between March and June 1946 a three-member Cabinet Mission toured India, to negotiate terms for Independence. Jinnah insisted on the creation of Pakistan. The Congress just as stoutly opposed it. Meanwhile, the Viceroy proposed an Interim Government based on a Congress–League coalition headed by Jawaharlal Nehru. The Congress Ministers took the oath of office, but the League's nominees delayed joining them. His electoral successes had emboldened Jinnah to raise the stakes. All his life he had been a constitutionalist, prepared to argue out his case in legislatures, courts and the press. Now he called for a Direct Action Day, asking his followers to hold public meetings, marches and *hartals*. It was an open invitation to violence. On Jinnah's designated day of action, 16 August, riots broke out all over India. Worst hit was the city of Calcutta, where 4,000 people died in the rioting.[68]

Through the summer of 1946, while the communal temperature rose at home, an Indian cricket team was touring England. Its captain was the Nawab of Pataudi, and its members included Hindus, Muslims and Christians. It was outplayed in the Tests but acquitted itself creditably against the counties. Some of its cricketers showed themselves to be of world class. Vijay Merchant batted beautifully, scoring in excess of 2,000 runs on tour, and Vinoo Mankad completed

the all-rounder's double of 1,000 runs and 100 wickets. On the eve
of their departure for India the cricketers received two contrasting
messages of farewell. The socialist Sir Stafford Cripps, President of
the Board of Trade, looked forward to a free India. He expressed
confidence that the friendships the cricketers had made on tour 'will
help to bring about good relations between the two countries for
which we all hope and to which we look forward'. In his message,
Sir Pelham Warner, an ex-President of the MCC, looked back at the
ties that bound India to the Empire. He praised the cricketers for
their 'charming manners', then added: 'England has not forgotten –
nor is she likely to forget – the magnificent bravery of your soldiers
during the recent War'.[69]

Would there be a Pentangular in 1946? In the first week of
September the newly elected President of the Board of Control for
Cricket in India, A. S. D'Mello, gave a talk in Bombay on the
'unifying influence of cricket on our national life', on how the game
was 'bringing together the different communities on a healthy non-
controversial and recreative plane'.[70] This was a not-so-veiled defence
of the Pentangular and, indeed, this stalwart of The Rest was can-
vassing the Princes to send their players for the carnival. J. C. Maitra
chastised the Board President: 'The growing communal tension in
the country is none of his concern. He naively suggests that communal
rivalry in the field of sports is the best method to promote
communal harmony.'[71] But when the Board met in Baroda in the
last week of September, D'Mello was no longer the same man. His
views regarding the Pentangular tournament 'had undergone a sudden
change'. The 'gruesome Calcutta massacre was still fresh in his mind'.
He was now 'convinced that in the present temper of the country it
was the duty of the Board to consider very carefully the advisability
of holding the Pentangular Tournament this year or ever again in the
future'.[72] At its next meeting, two months later, the Board passed a
resolution stating 'it disapproved of communal cricket and if the
Cricket Club of India agreed not to stage any communal tournament
the Board would be pleased to authorize the CCI to run the Zonal

Tournament permanently on terms and conditions to be mutually agreed upon between the President and the CCI'.[73]

The pub was to be finally closed down. It had stayed open too long anyway. By the end of 1946 the creation of Pakistan was a certainty, and the carnival a source of embarrassment to all but its most die-hard supporters. That winter, instead of the Pentangular the Brabourne Stadium hosted a Zonal Quadrangular, this the culmination of a twelve-year campaign by J. C. Maitra to replace communal cricket with a non-denominational alternative. In the finals West Zone – with the Muslim Ibrahim playing alongside the Christian Hazare, the Parsi Modi, and the Hindus Mankad, Adhikari and Phadkar – played against North Zone, which was likewise ecumenical, its eleven including the Hindus Amarnath and Kishenchand and the Parsi Irani alongside half a dozen Muslim cricketers. The quality of cricket and cricketers was top class, but the crowd response was indifferent, with only a few thousand fans showing up to see the matches. Hartley, in the *Times of India*, had a ready interpretation for this: namely, that 'the suspension of a tournament which for something like fifty years provided Bombay's cricket festival is having a bad effect'. The absence of the Pentangular, he added, was 'killing interest in the game among players and spectators alike'. J. C. Maitra, in the *Chronicle*, resented the implication that Bombay 'has really no liking or love for cricket and only wants a display of communalism in the name of cricket'. Bombay's love for its favourite sport, he insisted, 'is far greater and more intense than that'. Why then were the crowds so poor? Because, said Maitra, 'of the current inflammable political situation'. There was a state of high tension between Hindus and Muslims; with the 'uncertainty of the future in every walk of life, the fans have no mind for a game which demands hours of attendance for days together'.[74] Until the end, these two Bombay newspapers would quarrel about what the game of cricket meant to the people of their city.

13. The Condemned Playground

IN HIS HISTORY OF BODYLINE, Lawrence Le Quesne writes that 'war, politics and sport have been the three great furnaces of mass popular emotion this century: in the past, religion was the greatest of all, but in the Christian world anyway its fires have cooled'.[1] In the India of the 1930s and 1940s, however, its fires were more brightly lit than ever. The heat from these fires scorched the streets, the classrooms, the markets, the courts, the factories and the playgrounds. It is this, indeed, that makes cricket in modern India so singular. In other times and other places politics has spilled over on to the sporting field. Here religion was added to the mix, devastatingly.

Consider this trifling incident. On a January evening in 1933 a group of Hindu boys were playing cricket in Northbrook Gardens in central Bombay. On the side of the field a group of Pathans had gathered, preparatory to breaking the fast of Ramadan. One Pathan was accidentally hit by a flying cricket ball. The offending batsman was promptly beaten up. A mill-hand watching the cricket, Hindu by the sound of his name – Swami Gurayya – intervened, and was thrashed in turn. Some Hindus gathered and began throwing stones. Reinforcements came from Kumbharawada, the potters' colony close by. The defenders of cricket now rushed the Pathans, shouting 'Maro, maro' ('Beat them up, beat them up'). The worshippers, outnumbered, drew their knives, stabbed a few advancing Hindus and themselves retreated to Grant Road. Meanwhile, the noise attracted the Muslim young men of the neighbourhood. In the ensuing mêleé a Hindu lorry driver was assaulted, cars stopped and passengers assaulted. By the time the police came and dispersed the mob three people had been killed and thirty injured.[2]

The Pathans have never been partial to cricket. Even now, international matches at their capital city, Peshawar, are played in half-empty stadiums, whereas anywhere else in the sub-continent the grounds would be filled to capacity, with thousands of latecomers turned away at the gate. The violence at Northbrook Gardens began as a simple clash between pleasure and prayer. A boy attempting to emulate C. K. Nayudu saw one of his sixers crash into the body of a famished but spiritually intense bystander. Would a cricket-loving Muslim have been more sympathetic, and simply handed over the ball with a few words of chastisement? We cannot say. What we do know is that a cricket-loving Hindu then got into the act, demanding an apology. When he was beaten up as well, cricketers and spectators regrouped as Hindus and Muslims – to deadly effect.

A MIX OF SPORT, religion and politics, with war in the backdrop: such was the annual cricket carnival in Bombay. Its existence was a bizarre paradox: a nakedly communal tournament that grew in and was nurtured by the most progressive and cosmopolitan city in modern India. One can now understand the depth of feeling of those who so bitterly opposed it. For the Indian nationalist, for the Brelvi or the Talyarkhan, the affirmation of communal identity on the cricket field violated the idea of a shared citizenship: that 'we are all Indians before we are anything else'. The Pentangular's existence mocked the inclusive nationalism, transcending the divisions of caste and religion, advocated by such men as Mahatma Gandhi and Jawaharlal Nehru. It was argued, first, that the tournament's antecedents lay in British divide-and-rule policy, and second, that its continuation lent strength to the illegitimate but dangerously fashionable demand for Pakistan.

That the rulers had deliberately promoted the organization of sport on communal lines was widely believed. An American journalist visiting India on the eve of Independence wrote that 'British divide-and-rule policy had reached even into the schools: in sports Hindu teams battled Muslim teams; with graduation the contest became a competition for jobs'.[3] Writing just after Independence, the celebrated Poona cricketer D. B. Deodhar claimed that

> the communal form, in topmost Indian cricket, came into exist-ence only because the Burra Sahibs in India, in the earlier days, had an undisguised superiority complex in all their dealings with the Indians. The British officers who came to India to protect the British Empire were encouraged by higher authorities to maintain very little contact with the 'Natives' as they sneeringly called the Indians. The British, therefore, opened their separate exclusive clubs in the three Presidency towns of Bombay, Cal-cutta and Madras, followed closely by establishment of [such] clubs in other cities such as Poona and Bangalore. The Parsees who picked up the game also picked up the separatist tendency of the British along with it. On the one hand, the British did not admit the Parsees to their 'sanctified fortresses'. The Parsees, therefore, had perforce to have separate clubs. But in those clubs they could have allowed other Indians. Unfortunately, this was not done. Consequently the Hindus also had to follow the same path. Muslims, last in the field, were compelled to follow suit.[4]

The racism of the colonial clubs was demonstrable. But this excerpt also suggests that Hindus were victims rather than willing accomplices in communal cricket. That, however, seems to be a retrospective reading, influenced perhaps by the composite nationalism promoted since the 1920s by Gandhi and his ilk. For if the British were exclusive, so was Hindu society, with its meticulous detailing of ritual boundaries between castes and sub-castes. Indeed, cricket clubs in late-nineteenth-century India often willingly organized themselves on the basis of caste. The rulers might have thought the Quadrangular format to be 'natural' to India, but they did not bring it into existence unaided. 'Communal cricket' was moulded as much by Hindu caste prejudice as by Parsi social snobbery, by Muslim cultural insularity and by British racial superiority.

Even if the origins of the Quadrangular did not lie wholly in British divide-and-rule, what about its continuance? Did not the tournament's growing popularity in the 1930s and 1940s feed directly into the movement for Pakistan? More specifically, did communal cricket foster and intensify communal hatreds? The players thought not. Two Sind sportsmen, one Hindu, the other English, asked those who thought that communal cricket 'breeds bad feeling' to 'come to Karachi and see the sporting rivalry and good fellowship which exists amongst both players and spectators', adding, 'they will go away with a greatly altered opinion'.[5] This was written in 1928, in something of a cricketing backwater; but a decade later the same claim was made by cricketers in the thick of things in Bombay, where (and when) the sporting as well as the political stakes were visibly higher. An earlier chapter quotes the Muslim cricket captain Syed Wazir Ali as arguing, in November 1940, that 'the tournament is not in the least anti-national and will and must go on in the interests of Indian cricket'.[6] The following year, when the fate of the Pentangular hung in the balance, the Hindu captain C. K. Nayudu claimed that the tournament had not encouraged 'any communal differences. It has fostered healthy rivalry and promoted communal unity. It has brought communities together and not divided them.' For C. K.'s fellow townsman Mushtaq Ali, the carnival had 'always promoted a very healthy spirit of rivalry and inculcated [a] sporting spirit among players and the public'. In his experience, 'ripples and roars of applause, from all the stands around, have greeted good performances without distinction, whether it was for [the Hindu] Nayudu's sixes, [the Muslim] Nissar's ball-taking fizzers or the [Parsi] Bhaya's smart pieces of fielding'.[7]

The cricketers' statements have the ring of sincerity, but was this really the case? Did sporting battles between Hindus and Muslims heighten appreciation of each other's skills and achivements, or did they instead serve as a prelude to more dangerous battles elsewhere? There is a long-running and still inconclusive debate on the subject.

One thinks, for example, of George Orwell's characterization of international sport as 'warfare minus the shooting'. In November 1938,
when the Pentangular controversy was beginning to hot up, another
British writer put it this way: 'Optimistic theorists', commented
Aldous Huxley,

> count upon sport as a bond between nations. In the present state
> of nationalistic feeling, it is only another cause of international
> misunderstanding. The battles waged on the football field and
> the race-track are merely preliminaries to, and even contributory
> causes of, more serious contests.[8]

Completing this picture of unanimity among British novelists is Alan
Sillitoe, who thinks that sport is 'a means of keeping the national spirit
alive during a time of so-called peace. It prepares the national spirit for
the eventuality of war.'[9]

Sportsmen themselves have tended to argue otherwise. In 1968,
when the International Olympic Committee was contemplating the
readmission of South Africa, black athletes in America threatened a
boycott of the Mexico Olympics. Jesse Owens opposed the boycott,
noting that 'we have been able to bridge the gap of [racial] understanding in athletics more than anywhere else'.[10] Owens very likely
had in mind his own experience in the Berlin Olympics thirty-two
years previously. In those Games, Owens beat the blond, blue-eyed
German, Luz Long, in the prestigious long jump. Hitler stormed
angrily out of the stadium, but Long himself ran over to the black
jumper to envelop him in a hug of congratulation.

The cricketers on opposing sides in the Bombay tournament
generally had a warm regard for one another. Palwankar Vithal wrote
in his memoirs that while the teams naturally played to win, there
was no occasion in which 'sadness was converted into anger or
joyfulness into arrogance. Once the game was over the players from
the contesting teams used to come together forgetting that they were
supposed to be rivals. Hindu cricketers and Muslim cricketers
were very friendly with each other.'[11]

After the Muslims had won the Quadrangular in 1935, Wazir Ali said 'he never played a match for winning but for the pleasure of playing a good game. The Hindu team played the match in a true sportsman's spirit and he was glad a spirit of true harmony and comradeship prevailed between the two teams.' On the first day of this match, Wazir, while fielding in close on the off side, was hit below the belt by a hard drive from Lall Singh. He fell prostrate to the ground, but was assisted off the field by the rival skipper, C. K. Nayudu, who had rushed from the pavilion to help him.[12] This incident confirmed a remark of a spectator that 'when a player gets hurt in the match, great affection is shown by the captain and fieldsmen of the other community in rendering first-aid'.[13] In the final match of the 1943–4 tournament Mushtaq Ali was badly injured while batting, and the doctor had said he could take no further part in the match. He was inclined to agree, but had his mind changed by Nayudu, who was not playing in this match but whose sympathies should have been on the side of the Hindus. When the Muslims faltered in their final chase, C. K. commanded Mushtaq to disregard his injury and bat, saying that 'the team must always come before the cricketer'. The 36 runs scored by Mushtaq helped take his side to victory.[14]

The cricketers, by and large, were bewildered by the criticisms of the Quadrangular and Pentangular. The tournament had brought them fun, fame and fortune as well as friendships, conducted between and across communities. They could not understand why some of their fellow Indians, cricket fans among them, wished to bury it. Long after the tournament had ended, it continued to be publicly mourned by its greatest participants. Writing in 1954, C. K. Nayudu insisted that 'one of the chief reasons of the rapid rise of Indian cricket was the great incentive of playing with and against cricketers of world repute that the Europeans in the Quadrangular invariably included in their teams'.[15] Writing in 1981, Vijay Hazare argued that 'although the Tournament was run on the communal lines we never experienced any religious hatred. Nor did the crowd show it.'[16] And in 1992, Syed Mushtaq Ali reminded a young journalist that 'sportsmen epitomize the finer values of humankind. Even while playing a

tournament like the Pentangulars . . . we never had any communal considerations.' He then retold the tale of how C. K. Nayudu
encouraged him to bat despite his injury in the final of 1944. His
conclusion was forceful and unambiguous: 'We cricketers personified
secularism.'[17]

Among these posthumous statements in defence of the tournament, perhaps the most evocative came from the pen of Vijay
Merchant. The 'communal feeling between the Hindus and the
Mohamadens', remarked the great opening batsman, 'is a product
of politics and not of sport. As a matter of fact, cricket and the
communal series brought them closer together than any other aspect
of life.' Merchant offered as an illustration the 1936 Quadrangular,
played against the backdrop of bloody clashes between Hindus and
Muslims in Bombay. In the cricketer's recollection the riots broke out
the day before the tournament began. Some officials of the PJ Hindu
Gymkhana now wanted to withdraw their team. The final decision
was to be taken by the President, L. R. Tairsee. On the morning of
their first match, a large crowd of Hindus had gathered at the Bombay
Gymkhana, awaiting their President. This is how Merchant remembered it:

> In all his majesty, tall, erect and dhoti-clad, Tairsee strode into
> the Bombay Gymkhana pavilion, went up to the captain of the
> Hindu team and said, 'The Hindus are playing in this tourna-
> ment, get ready. More than anything this tournament may help
> the riots to subside before the tournament is over.'

The Hindus played, and won. By the time the tournament ended,
ten days later, the riots were over:

> Never before in the history of riots in Bombay had a communal
> series of matches brought about an end to riots as quickly and
> effectively. This is an answer to those who maintain that
> communal matches were responsible for communal feeling in
> Bombay. Actually it was quite the opposite.[18]

This was written in 1974; thirteen years later, Merchant went back to the incident in an interview with a group of historians. He spoke again of the formidable Tairsee, clad in Gandhi cap, long coat and *dhoti*, and his command to his team to play on despite the riots raging outside. They did play on, and

> throughout those 10 days there was not one communal incident. In a crowd of 25,000 people who were not housed in a stadium but on planks and chairs and a shamiana which could be set on fire in a matter of minutes, not a single communal incident took place. That showed that although communal feeling generated by the British was there outside, on the sports field there had never been any such incident. I think [these matches] generated a feeling of fellowship better than any other gathering.[19]

This is a compelling story, and it is embarrassing to have to dispute it. However, the riots of 1936 actually took place in the month of October; a calm, albeit an uneasy calm, had returned to the city well before the cricket began. In the last week of October the troops were taken off the streets, the Home Member of the Bombay Government informing the District Commander 'that public confidence was now sufficiently restored to allow the troops to stand down and to discontinue demonstration patrols'.[20] Indeed, as the Quadrangular was being played in mid-December, a columnist remarked that 'the communal riots are now merely an ugly memory, and their last vestige, the Curfew Order, was removed early in the present week'.[21] Perhaps the Hindus, drawn to play the Muslims in the first match, were nervous that violence might recur, and perhaps Tairsee assured them that it would not. But the cricket did not *stop* the riots. The old cricketer's recollections were flawed by the romance with which he remembered the now long-dead tournament.

SURELY NO ONE DISPUTES that sport has always brought together *sportsmen* of otherwise hostile groups, whether black and white, Brahmin and low-caste, or Muslim and Hindu. But does it also bring

together the larger communities to which the sportsmen belong, or
does it rather reinforce ancient hatreds and rivalries? We may agree
with Mushtaq Ali that the cricketers themselves personified secularism, but what about their supporters? A former Governor of Sind
was convinced that 'communal matches bind communities together
and foster harmony on and off the field, not only in cricket but in
other games'.[22] After the tournament of 1943–4, the *Times of India*
described it as 'nothing more than clean, healthy rivalry between the
various communities'. It demanded that the 'hardy anti-Pentangular
joke be dropped once and for all and let us try to cement the good
feeling that has been created through the medium of Pentangular and
Quadrangular sport'.[23] The President of the Cricket Club of India,
Sir Homi Modi, said that

> the sporting public of Bombay has given a most convincing and
> resounding answer to [the] charge that the Pentangular breeds
> communalism and racial ill-feeling. Never in the whole history
> of cricket in this country have such enormous and enthusiastic
> crowds been seen. There has been an atmosphere of tenseness
> at many stages; to a certain extent, there has been partisanship,
> inevitable and legitimate in the circumstances. Not a head was
> broken, however, not a tooth knocked out. There was great
> good humour throughout the proceedings and keenness and
> enthusiasm which have to be seen to be believed. I say to
> the critics: For goodness' sake, stop this vendetta against the
> Pentangular and turn to the things that really matter in the
> creation of a better feeling amongst the various communities.[24]

These remarks were not completely disinterested. The British
considered communal divisions to be ordained by nature and
incapable of supersession. The Cricket Club of India, which hosted
the tournament, naturally wanted it to prosper. So did the individual
Gymkhanas. In 1954, with the memories of the tournament fast
fading, the PJ Hindu Gymkhana insisted that in all the years it had
been played, between three teams and then four and finally five,
'there had not been one incident which could even remotely give

grounds for such an apprehension [that it increased communal tension]. On the contrary, the tournaments were played in a very cordial spirit.'[25]

Cordial, yes, if one had only the players in mind, but the fans? In 1935 one journalist sitting in the stands noticed 'the unmistakable tinge of communal partisanship which is the bane of those tournaments'.[26] In 1941 another journalist suggested that the 'wild over-enthusiasm' that greeted C. K. Nayudu's innings against Gilligan's team and Amarnath's knock against Jardine's side ran 'along communal lines'. One explanation for the fervour and the acclaim was that the centuries were scored by Hindus in a city where cricket fans were taught to divide themselves on the basis of religion: thus, 'appreciation would not have been carried to the same pitch if the performances had taken place outside Bombay'.[27] The testimony of A. F. S. Talyarkhan tends to confirm this kind of reading. The letters he received from radio listeners ran along depressingly predictable lines. If he said something adverse about the Muslim wicket-keeper he would receive telegrams which asked: 'Why only Dilawar? Why don't you criticize [the Hindu wicket-keeper] Hindlekar?' And if he praised Wazir Ali's captaincy, someone would be sure to ask: 'What about our C. K.?'[28]

The partisanship was noticed by the reporters; out in the middle some cricketers noticed it too. D. B. Deodhar, writing about his going out to bat in the Hindu–Muslim semi-final of 1936, recalled that

> at such critical moments, the spectators [would] shout and upset the incoming batsman. On the Bombay Gymkhana, where the Quadrangular was played till then, the boundary was very short, and the batsman could hear the damaging and discouraging remarks hurled at him. I will never forget the hell of noise and the attempts of Wazir's team to disturb my concentration.[29]

Five years later, the Maharajkumar of Vizianagaram wrote that 'if one were to visit the stands during the Pentangulars at which the Hindus and Muslims face each other, one could see for oneself with what

vengeance each community wishes the other the worst and the language used is "Down with the Mussalmans" or "Down with the
Hindus" '.[30] Sir Chimanlal Setalvad, writing at about the same time,
pointed out that fans who garlanded a century-maker from their own
community ignored the achievements of the other side. 'Among the
illiterate masses', said Setalvad, 'sport on a communal basis is a
positive menace. Thousands of people of all communities look upon
victory or defeat as a gain or blow to communal prestige.'[31] Or, as a
letter-writer more subtly put it, 'the cricket Pentangular has undoubtedly shown that if it does not harm relations between player and
player, it undoubtedly embitters relations between the hasty-minded
and narrow-minded sections of each community.'[32]

Other people saw it very differently. Jeering at the other side, said
one fan, was absolutely harmless: 'it is mostly done to add a little fun
to the otherwise monotonous moments'.[33] In the wake of Mahatma
Gandhi's statement of December 1940, Russa Mehta dismissed talk
that the Pentangular intensified communal feeling, for 'Hindus and
Mohammedans may have broken their heads at weddings, funerals
or other religious processions and meetings, but in all these many
years I have never known rival cricket teams ever coming to blows'.[34]
In the same week, and in much the same vein, the distinguished
lawyer and politician K. F. Nariman spoke of how 'a Muslim pavilion
is patronized by Hindu spectators and Muslim visitors are equally
welcome in [the] Hindu pavilion'. It was a credit to both players and
spectators 'that even in tense and exciting moments when a mixed
crowd of all communities, of 30 to 40 thousand is almost on tenter-
hooks, there has never been a single incident recorded in any of the
fixtures played for the last so many years, though we have heard of
riots in football matches and even violence and murder in non-
communal games with mixed teams'.[35]

There were some Hindus and some Muslims who thought the
Pentangular intensified communal hatred, and other Hindus and
other Muslims who thought it did not. Supporters and opponents
were to be found amongst every community, perhaps within every
family. In 1943, when A. F. S. Talyarkhan was vigorously polemicizing

against the tournament in the columns of the *Bombay Sentinel,* the *Times of India* ran a long letter by another man with the same surname. Speaking of Vijay Hazare's great battle against the leg-spinner Amir Elahi, this Taleyarkhan said the spectators

> were ready to do credit to the skill of either because we looked at them as cricketers both, not as Amir Elahi of the Muslims, and Hazare of The Rest. And this crowd of 30,000 consisted of Hindus, Muslims, Parsis, Europeans, Anglo-Indians, Goans, indeed every community under the skies of India. I ask you now, is or is not the Pentangular, far from being a snag, a solution to communal unity in India?[36]

To be sure, the fans could be ecumenical in their appreciation. In 1941, when the anti-Pentangular movement was at its height, a biographer of the great C. K. Nayudu thus recalled a Hindu–Muslim match of 1935:

> I was sitting in the Bombay Medical Gymkhana Pavilion and by my side there was a Muslim spectator of course entertaining and expecting the victory for his side, which was exactly against my wish. Some time later Amir Ilahi got Naidu out and it was a shock to me, but I was more surprised to find that Mohemedan student murmuring to himself 'Bahut bura ho gaya' meaning thereby that this is a very sad incident. This goes to prove that all great players are welcomed by everybody, no matter what caste or creed.[37]

To this recollection is appended an afterthought: 'I hope Mr Talyar-khan will read this.'

WHETHER OR NOT A. F. S. Talyarkhan had read this he had certainly read Neville Cardus. He knew the Muslim student's support for C. K. Nayudu to be but a local variant of Cardus's boyhood prayer: 'Please God, let Victor Trumper make a hundred tomorrow: out of an Australian total of 127 all out.' The sporting fan's admiration for an opposing player can be effortlessly disassociated from the partisan support to his own side. During the Pentangular the admiration of cricketers was generous and catholic, yet the identification of teams strictly followed communal lines. As the Bombay columnist Rustom Vakeel wrote in 1936, 'somehow justice is done to the player, whoever he maybe, of whatever caste or creed or colour. The beauty of stroke or delivery is always appreciated.' But there was yet the 'serious drawback which mars the good effects of these unique carnivals', that is, 'their communal character'. For 'as long as there is emphasis on community in the tournament the man who says let the best side win is either uttering a fiction or is a Mahatma'.[38] It was not only in Bombay that the partisanship was naked. In towns hundreds of miles away, college students would divide up into Hindu groups and Muslim groups, each following the radio commentary from their distinctive points of view.[39]

It is hard to disagree with the considered judgement of A. F. S. Talyarkhan: 'the story of communal cricket in the raw' was that it 'provides a chance to flaunt the superiority of one community over another'.[40] I was born long after the Pentangular ended, but what I have read about it suggests that so far as the crowd was concerned, 'at bottom there [was] in everyone a certain relish in the animosity, a pleasure in the battle, and the sense that life in the towns would be uselessly dull without a passionate identification with an object': the object being a side of cricketers that, in some essential and elemental self, belonged to oneself.

The words just quoted actually come from an account of football in eastern India in the 1930s.[41] But they might as well have been written about the Bombay Pentangular. Admittedly, unlike in the Calcutta Maidan, here no heads were broken, no umpires assaulted or players beaten up. Cricket was not football. Its tempo was slower and its action drawn out over four full days. The outcome of each match was not dependent on a single mistake, as is often the case in the other more violence-prone game. The chairs broken inside the PJ Hindu Gymkhana clubhouse that December evening in 1940 was the most extreme manifestation of violence related to the Quadrangular or Pentangular. The three people killed in the riots that followed a flying cricket ball in January 1933 were the only fatalities in a hundred years of the game in Bombay. But, as A. F. S. Talyarkhan put it, 'it was not necessary to wait for bloodshed before they could say if a thing was right or wrong. They could decide that question on moral lines and not on physical lines. Were they going to wait for a bloody riot at the Brabourne Stadium before they gave up communal cricket?'[42]

The love of *their* cricketer could cheerfully co-exist with dislike of *their* community. This much was clear to most people who watched cricket in Bombay in the 1930s or 1940s. But was this always the case? Or was this paradox the consequence only of the Indian National Congress's intensifying dispute with the Muslim League? Writing in 1938, the Calcutta critic J. M. Ganguly distinguished between two phases of the Quadrangular, one happy and harmonious, the other tainted by the virus of communalism. When the tournament was conceived, wrote Ganguly,

> the sports atmosphere was clear and unclouded by communal and sectarian feelings. On the open green field and under the bright blue sky players forgot their communities and only thought of playing the game, while those who cheered them from the sides only applauded real merit and fine performance irrespective of the caste, creed or the community of players. Everybody revelled in the game, the victor and the vanquished, and the supporters of either. Victory in the Quadrangular was not taken as a communal victory, but merely as a result of better peformance by the winning side, and which did not leave behind any rancour or mean jealousy, but only fired the ambitions of others to do better next time. The Quadrangular tournament, thus, in those days did not harm, but rather engendered healthy rivalry and gave added keenness to the cricket.
>
> Those happy days are now gone, thanks to those self-seeking leaders who want to gain their ends by raking up communal fanaticism, and who would not rest on their oars after doing all

the mischief they could in the political sphere, but would go
out in search of new fields and pastures green. Even the sacred
field of sport they would not leave unmolested. That is why
things have become what they are on the cricket field today.
That is why Quadrangular cricket has degenerated into
communal cricket and communal rivalry.[43]

This was written with only Hindus and Muslims in mind. In truth,
there was no uncontaminated past when the result of a cricket match
was not interpreted in ethnic or religious terms. Rancour and jealousy,
triumph and exaltation had marked the competition from its origins.
Certainly, as the case of the Baloo brothers showed, cricket might
help erode social distinctions *within* the community. Yet in the way
competitive cricket was conceived and structured, it would necessarily
consolidate one community against another. On the cricket field and
elsewhere, Hindus found themselves opposed to Europeans on
grounds of race; to the Parsis on account of economics; and, most
consequentially, to the Muslims with regard to whether free India
would be one nation or two. Communal cricket thus always had
within it elements of communal conflict. No one understood this
better than Indian cricket's first historian, who was also Indian
cricket's first rebel, the instigator of the anti-polo petition of 1881.
To those who would believe that the crease was so narrow as to allow
white to become black or Untouchable become Brahmin, to those
who saw communal cricket as a Khilafat movement in perpetuity,
consolidating rather than working against harmony between Hindus
and Muslims, Shapoorjee Sorabjee offered this early warning: 'To
expect all political differences to disappear or all available self-interest
to be forgone upon the institution of cricket relations is to live in a
fool's paradise.'[44]

NATION

History's Residues

14. The Commonwealth of Cricket

IN THE SUMMER OF 1946, while the Nawab of Pataudi's team was touring England, the General Secretary of the All India Congress Committee launched a broadside against India's favourite sport. Is cricket 'really worth all this tom-toming and pomp'? wrote B. V. Keskar. Had it 'any place in future India, a place where it can be useful to the public and the younger generation'? The Congressman himself failed 'to see any future for it'. For cricket was a game 'purely English in culture and spirit', 'a part of the English countryside, with its peculiar climate and social customs' – 'like fox-hunting and fishing'. There it was a game of the gentry and nobility, and here 'it has always remained a game patronized mostly by the Maharajas, the rich and the snobs'. Its existence in India, thought Keskar, was 'but a sign of our utter slavery', our tendency to 'copy blindly the habits of English civlization, and ape the likes and the preferences of the English "gentleman" '.

Keskar allowed that cricket was a 'popular sport' in Bombay city, followed by the students and the middle classes. Elsewhere it was 'living almost exclusively on the patronage of the Princes, for whom it becomes an outlet from the boredom of having nothing else to do'. The game was unsuited to the Indian climate and to the democratic spirit of the soon-to-be free nation. Keskar was certain it would soon be supplanted by inexpensive and participatory sports like football and athletics. Cricket, he insisted, 'can only thrive in the atmosphere of English culture, English language and English rule. It will never be able to survive the shock of the disappearance of British rule from our country. With the fall of British power, it is bound to lose its place of honour and slowly grow out of date.'[1]

Keskar was an educated man, a foreign-trained PhD no less. Unusually for an Indian of his generation he had studied in France, not England, a fact that must help explain this particular aversion. He seems also to have regarded cricket as a sissy sport: his own hobbies, as listed in the Indian *Who's Who*, included 'hiking in mountains', while his 'special interest' was the 'youth movement'.

Keskar's polemic was complemented a few months later by an attack on cricket from another interested quarter: a player of a less charmed sport. This was Janaki Dass, the Secretary of the Indian Cycling Federation. In October 1946, Dass attended the World Championships at Zurich, where cyclists of other nations spoke to him of their abhorrence of cricket. These conversations were summarized in an article published in the *Bombay Chronicle* on his return. The delegates at Zurich, Dass reported, were amazed by the 'keen interest' which his nation of 'starving millions' showed in an expensive and time-consuming sport. The Irish delegate told Dass that 'cricket is infested with all the elements of Imperialism'. It was used by the British to carry on propaganda in their occupied territories, whose people 'are taught to look to London for any inspiration'. The French delegate remarked that the game of cricket 'implies the particular characteristic of the British, namely hero-worship which leads to slave-mentality – the greatest boon of the British to its so-called Empire'. The delegates were 'unanimous . . . that only aristocrats who do not know the value of time and money can indulge in this game'.

Thus chastised, Dass looked around the globe, and found ringing confirmation of the Zurich consensus. Cricket was 'entirely unknown' in freedom-loving America, socialist Russia, the whole of Europe, Japan, China and most of Africa. Why must Indians play it? Dass hoped that

> with the advent of the National Government in India, any black-
> spot stamped by British Imperialism on the face of India may
> be wiped off; and Games and Sports which build health and

character and which cost little, like Athletics, Wrestling, Swimming, Cycling and the most important of all, Hu-Tu-Tu, our national sport, should be encouraged to let one and all of India's teeming millions participate and thus contribute to the health and culture of the nation.[2]

●

BUT, AS EVERYBODY KNOWS, the black spot grew blacker, and spread alarmingly. India became an official Test-playing nation in 1932, and had played a total of seven Tests, all against England, when it became a free nation. Between 1947 and 1956 its international calendar was massively packed. In those years it made cricket tours to England, Australia, Pakistan and the West Indies, and received those countries in turn. In 1955–6 the New Zealand cricket team also toured India. In the first decade after independence the Indian cricket team played a staggering forty-two Test matches.

This number does not include the fifteen 'unofficial' Tests played against three visiting Commonwealth sides. This was a novel experiment, the sending of multi-national teams to promote and further the game in India. Never before had players of more than one country toured together. Indian crowds of the late 1940s and early 1950s were thus privileged to see 'at once the carefree cricket of the West Indian, the orthodoxy of the Englishman and the grimness of the Australian'. As an official brochure remarked, 'whatever might be the outcome of the matches, there is no doubt that the tour will result in fostering goodwill and cementing the friendly ties between India and the Commonwealth countries'.[3] A Bangalore weekly concurred: cricket, it said, 'is the invisible cord which binds together the Commonwealth countries'.[4]

The visiting cricketers were of high quality, and the matches fiercely contested. The three Commonwealth tours contributed enormously to the development of cricket in the regions, for they met provincial sides and played 'Tests' where these had never been played before. But the cricketers did not always see themselves as willow-wielding envoys. One tourist, the Englishman P. A. Gibb, left a revealing diary of the 1953–4 tour, published years later in the *Wisden Cricket Monthly.* The diary gave as much attention to social life as to cricket. The tourists were generally put up by expatriates; planters or timber merchants or editors who had stayed on after 1947. Like visiting sportsmen of all colours and times, they sought out unattached women for their evenings. Gibb, married and with children back home, showed rather more interest in an air hostess named Yvonne than in the games he played or the ancient monuments he was taken to see.[5]

One problem the visitors stoutly coped with was the scarcity of liquor. In deference to Mahatma Gandhi's memory, alcohol was not served at official receptions. Even the Deputy High Commissioner of the United Kingdom, staying in Jinnah's old house atop Malabar Hill in Bombay, served soft drinks out of respect for the Indians present. In Delhi the cricketers were given a reception by the Prime Minister. It 'was an experience to be in the same room as Mr Nehru', wrote Gibb, to be talking to the great man with other great men looking on from photographs on the wall. But there was no alcohol, for 'the Prime Minister is not supposed to drink. We were offered coffee and tea.'

Nehru and Gibb shared an *alma mater*, the University of Cambridge. They would have had a decent conversation, but lesser dignitaries subjected the cricketers to speeches steeped in sanctimonious humbug. Cricket, once the handmaiden of Empire, was now being squeezed into the service of the United Nations view of the world. A speaker at Nagpur spoke on Cricket and the Universal Declaration of Human Rights. If all ministers were cricketers, he thought, 'there would be little serious friction in the world'. In Mysore, the President of the Cricket Association told the Commonwealth team how their conduct 'promotes good friendship and understanding between peoples'.

Gibb's diary captured the manifest love for cricket and cricketers. Driving to Bombay airport, he passed the three Gymkhanas on the Kennedy Sea Face: 'even at eight in the morning the grounds were crowded with cricketers practising at the nets'. Wherever the Commonwealth cricketers played the stadiums were full, the spectators engaging the fielders in banter and throwing them oranges and bananas. In one match the attendance was below par, because of 'the absence of Frankie Worrell. The crowds will go miles to see him.' The fans wanted to see the great West Indian bat, score a hundred even, but only their side must win. On the last day of the Delhi 'Test', Gibb went home for lunch with five of his team's wickets still standing. He made paper planes for his host's little boys, and when he finally put on the wireless nine wickets were down. 'We rushed back to the ground and arrived just as all was over. Indian spectators pressed round us in vociferous jubilation, waving hands in triumph and blowing bugles in our faces. I was quite glad to get out of it.'

Here is an early intimation of all that went to make cricket in free India: the energy, the excitement, the noise and the nationalism.

BEFORE 1947 BOMBAY was very much the capital and centre of Indian cricket. With the end of the Pentangular the Ranji Trophy came into its own, and a process of decentring began. The knock-out format was replaced by zonal leagues, five or six teams in each zone playing one another before the top team qualified for the knock-out. The growth of local patriotism was also helped by the reorganization of states, done on a linguistic basis after 1956. The state's cricket team came to embody its cultural pride. But an attractive thing about the Ranji Trophy was that it never completely succumbed to the Government of India's States Reorganization Committee. As new states were formed they were granted their teams, but older teams were allowed to carry on despite the death of the political unit whose name they carried. Thus Baroda and Saurashtra played alongside Gujarat, Hyderabad alongside Andhra Pradesh, and Bombay alongside Maharashtra. There were also sides representing the Indian Railways and the Services.

Within each zone there were fierce rivalries. Tamil Nadu versus

Karnataka, Bombay versus Maharashtra, Delhi versus Services: these matches attracted crowds in excess of 20,000. Provincial feelings were intense, to be eventually transferred to the national side. The selection of the Indian team was preceded and followed by fierce debates about who should be included and who not. In deference to these feelings the national selection committee has one member from each of the five zones, this fellow in turn rotating between the different states.

A prime carrier of cricket news between and within states was All India Radio. When the MCC toured India in 1951–2 to play five Test matches, the Minister of Information and Broadcasting was that well-known opponent of cricket, B. V. Keskar. The editor who published Keskar's original piece of 1946 later recalled receiving 'thousands of letters' that sought to demonstrate 'the utter foolishness of his stand'. The ordinary fan considered the Congressman's article to be 'an act of vandalism against one of India's most honoured sports'.[6] Presumably some of these letters were shown to Keskar. Initially, the Minister had decided that he would not promote film melodies or cricket broadcasts. Classical music and discourses on development were how the masses would be uplifted instead. Eventually, Keskar was persuaded to start a separate channel for Hindi film music and to sanction live broadcasts for the Tests. Millions then bought radios to listen to one channel or the other. During the Test matches college students and office workers alike concealed transistors in their clothing. For others at work or on the move, the best place to get a quick update was the *paanwallah*, whose little radio spoke softly amid the tins and boxes of his trade. In time, live commentary was to be broadcast in the vernacular on Ranji Trophy matches as well.

B. V. Keskar's sanctioning of cricket broadcasts was a sensible politician's response to the dramatic spread of cricket in independent India. He could see that it was no longer – if it had ever been in the first place – a game merely patronized by the Maharaja or the snob. In the cities it was followed by all classes of people; and it was also evoking interest in the countryside. With that other pet hate of the Minister's, popular film, it was helping to knit India. The game of cricket uniquely fused local patriotism with nationalism, the process both conveyed and inspired by All India Radio. 'When Umrigar drives a ball to the boundary', wrote a Marathi writer in the 1960s,

> a Manmadkar dances around the house! When Manjrekar is run out at Kanpur, a Nagpurian experiences a pang and starts abusing his brother for being a *panothi*! When, at Calcutta Baig misses a catch, a Bombayite feels that his house has come down on his head. And when we lose a Test at Delhi, even the household servants feel that they have lost something – such is this cricket mania![7]

As the most influential of the non-aligned nations, India was visited by Cold Warriors of both sides. The greatest scientists and economists of the world came to help this nation on the move. Disenchanted with the materialism of their own culture, musicians like George Harrison and writers like Allen Ginsberg travelled to India to seek out gurus and seers. By far the most popular and welcomed foreigners, however, were the cricketers. Writing in 1971, an essayist in the *Illustrated Weekly of India* captured the extraordinary interest generated by a cricket tour. Since 'every educated Indian is an authority on cricket', in the weeks before the tour begins ' "Letters-to-the Editor" columns are flooded with advice and weighty comments. Sports scribes have a field-day and contribute lengthy articles, second only to editorials in their pomposity.' The discussions were not confined to the press alone. For cricket was 'also No. 1 topic in offices and factories, homes and restaurants. Those who have never seen Gavaskar bat, wax eloquently over his cover-drives, and damsels sigh at the mere mention of Vishwanath's name.' But 'hell really breaks loose' when the Indian team is announced. Cries of 'Nepotism' and 'Favouritism' fill the air, and processions and demonstrations are held demanding the inclusion of this player or the dropping of that one.

What 'puts a stop to this controversy is the arrival of the adversary'. The visiting team lands at Delhi's Palam Airport. 'Amidst popping flash bulbs, they are welcomed by a coterie of ministers, senior government officials and local bigwigs, and mobbed by hundreds of cricket fans.' The following day they are the guests of the Mayor, the day after that the guests of the Prime Minister or President. The touring team 'attends on the average 3.2 receptions per day. Socialites fall over each other to host them.' Outside, the police is putting to flight a mob of disenchanted cricket-lovers, who have queued up through the night for a ticket for the Test, to be told at the booking counter that the tickets have been sold out. The 'problem is purely arithmetical. Can a stadium of 50,000 capacity seat a little over 500,000 people? A facet of a developing economy is now revealed which would have astounded even Adam Smith. Tickets are offered and bought at 100% premium.'

During the Tests those who own a transistor listen to the commentary. The less fortunate 'sit glued to someone who in turn is sitting with his ears glued to you-know-what'. Half the Tests are drawn, and the home side loses the other half. The post-mortem begins, to continue until the next series begins. Meanwhile, the winning captain is giving his last press conference before returning home. He starts by 'lauding the enthusiasm of the people (actually he is rather frightened by it).' He refers to the friendly spirit in which the cricket has been played, 'and hopes, without so much as twitching a muscle, that the relations between the two countries will improve as a result of this series'. He then singles out two or three young Indian cricketers as being of unusual promise. He 'ends by saying that India will soon be a force to reckon with in international cricket. And before you can say "Perjury!" he boards the Boeing.'

The essay's introduction could as well have served as its conclusion: 'Every nation has a preoccupation. In China, it is Mao; in Latin America, it is Revolution; in India, it is cricket.'[8]

After watching Australia play England at The Oval in 1953, the Hungarian humorist George Mikes claimed that cricket 'was invented for a rich and leisurely nation and it now keeps the memory of richness and leisure alive'.[9] What would Mikes have made of the game's appeal among the poor in a poor country? For, as the Quadrangulars had long ago demonstrated, cricket in India was not a game of the elite alone. When the West Indies toured India in 1966–7, a correspondent described the rush at the ticket counters at the Brabourne Stadium as 'reminiscent of the storming of the Bastille'.[10] Fourteen years later, as India prepared to play England in a Test match in Bombay, a journalist wrote of the consequences for life in the city:

> The cobbler and the tailor leave awl and needle to see cricket; the doctor leaves the scalpel in the patient's skull and elopes with his nurse to watch the match; and the paunchy boss stares vapidly at the sales chart because he is helpless without his lissom secretary whose boy-friend has given her a ticket to cricket somewhat alliteratively. And, see, the schools are empty because the masters have gone to find out the score, and the offices are empty because . . . well, the offices are empty. . . . Cricket, Lata Mangeshkar and the transistor make India one nation.[11]

Like the Hindi film, cricket in India transcended the boundaries of class and region. With the help of two innovations, it was to reach further yet. The first was satellite television, which took the game from cities to small towns and villages across India. Cricket on television captured two social groups previously not infected by the bug: the housewives and the farmers. The second innovation was the coming of one-day cricket. India played its first one-day international in 1974, and played only 150 such matches in the next fifteen years. Between 1989 and 2000, however, it played almost 300. These matches, whether played in India or abroad, were all beamed live. For the big games the television audience was counted in the hundreds of millions. As one journalist remarked, 'soap operas had been replaced in terms of popularity and advertising power by the mega event of the century – one-day cricket. For the Indian viewer it has turned out to be the longest-running, uninterrupted saga of runs, overs, sixes, fours, wickets, victories and defeats.'[12]

The process was greatly aided by the hosting, by India and Pakistan, of the 1987 World Cup, the first time this tournament was played outside England. The allocation of the World Cup was a triumph of anti-colonialism. The President of the Indian Cricket Board, N. K. P. Salve, had been given two tickets for the 1983 final, to be played at Lord's. When his team unexpectedly qualified, Mr Salve asked the MCC for two more passes, for friends who had just flown out from India. The MCC refused, whereupon Mr Salve set about organizing the associate members of the International Cricket Council in a revolt that led eventually to the World Cup being shifted out of England.

This, at any rate, is the version given out in *The Story of the Reliance Cup*, a book released by Mr Salve just before that tournament began. The parallels with another rebuff are not hard to establish. Back in 1896, in the South African town of Pietermaritzburg, one Mr M. K. Gandhi was thrown out by an Englishman from a railway compartment for which he had (or so he thought) bought a legitimate ticket. The Mahatma's rebellion was slower in coming, for it was fifty-four years before he was successfully to throw the oppressor out of India. The moral for the white man? Never mess around with an Indian lawyer.[13]

In the 1987 tournament, twenty-seven matches were played in twenty-one venues, each match watched by capacity crowds and shown to people elsewhere by India's state-owned television company, Doordarshan. The teams were pursued by shrieking fans wherever they went. No previous event in Indian history – with the possible exception only of Independence and Partition – attracted a comparable number of column inches in the English and vernacular press. The excitement steadily built up through the early league matches, and reached a peak when India and Pakistan both reached the semi-finals. Alas, the dream final did not come to pass, for India lost to England, and Pakistan to Australia. Yet the contest between *those* two old enemies drew in more than 100,000 spectators to Eden Gardens, without question the largest crowd ever present at a cricket match.

Nine years later the sub-continent hosted the World Cup again. The frenzy this time was more fierce, for the catchment area of television had rapidly expanded. Four hundred million people watched the matches, perhaps four-fifths of these in South Asia. A journalist covering the show somewhat breathlessly captured the impact of it all:

In Calcutta *paras*, youngsters hurl themselves across the concrete earning sobriquets like Jonty-da. Employers peer at sheaves of leave forms and don't wonder why. At street corners, motorcycles are being bartered for tickets. Firecrackers, stored from Diwali, are sold at a premium. Exams are arriving, but Newton's Third Law of Motion must make way for an examination of Wasim Akram's strike rate. Fathers start pontificating about the 'good old days' of Test cricket, while mothers keep asking what a Chinaman is doing on the field. Cricket anyone? Make that everyone.[14]

In adroit recognition of this huge and captive audience, companies both Indian and foreign rushed in to advertise on television and on stadium billboards. A business weekly called the World Cup 'the biggest marketing extravaganza in India this decade'. Before the tournament began, Coca-Cola and Pepsi-Cola, American drinks breaking into this non-baseball market, bid for the rights to sponsor the Cup. When Coke won, and commissioned a stream of cricketing ads, its rival answered with commercials of its own, featuring famous cricketers parading about drinking Pepsi and saying, 'There's nothing official about this one.'[15]

With the spread of television and the growing integration of India into the world market, cricket has successfully consummated its marriage with consumer capitalism. The makers of chocolates and ice-creams and refrigerators and whisky all choose top cricketers to model for and market their products. One happy consequence of this has been a spectacular rise in cricketers' income. Once, men who had played cricket for India were paid a paltry 50 rupees per Test match. Some Test cricketers died destitute, and even a cricketer as acclaimed in his playing days as C. K. Nayudu had to struggle in his last years. Nayudu's younger daughters remained unmarried because he could not raise the money for their dowries. When he died, in 1967, he was subsisting on a meagre pension of 400 rupees per month, supplemented by the odd (and low-paying) coaching assignment.[16]

Now cricketers are paid about 100,000 rupees for every one-day match they play for India, and perhaps twice that for a Test match. Moreover, there are many more matches played each year. Apart from these on-field earnings there is the income that comes in from endorsements.

The best Indian cricketer now playing earns an estimated 4.5 million dollars a year.[17] In view of the fan following, there was always a unique glamour about playing cricket for the country. Now there is an added financial inducement, the possibility of earning a thousand times as much as the average Indian. Once, cricket could bring you fleeting fame; now, it can also bring you an enduring fortune. This has acted as a spur to individuals from what, in a cricketing sense, are less fashionable parts of India. In the past, Indian Test sides used to be dominated by players from the big towns and cities, from Madras, Calcutta, Bangalore, Puné, Chandigarh, Delhi and, above all, Bombay. But recent international stars have come from what an older generation would have considered wildly improbable locations: from places like Najafgarh in Haryana, Gadag in Karnataka, Srirampur in Maharashtra, and Cuttack in Orissa.[18]

Along with the cricketers, the organizers have also reaped monetary reward. The financial affairs of the Board of Control for Cricket in India are not open to public scrutiny, but one may safely say that it is in robust health. Informed sources tell me that in 1990, before the coming of satellite TV, the Board's earnings were about two crore rupees a year; now it is close to 300 crore rupees, or roughly 65 million dollars. Also flush with funds are the various provincial cricket bodies which host international matches. A less happy consequence of Indian cricket's new-found financial wealth is the growing entry into the sport of the much reviled political class. As I write, the cricket boards of Bihar and Mumbai are headed by former Chief Ministers; of Madhya Pradesh by a former Union Minister; and of Delhi by a current Union Minister. Two among recent Presidents of the Indian Cricket Board were Union Ministers.

The links between politicians and sport, admittedly, are not new. Thus a remarkable tribute to the continuing hold of cricket in post-colonial India came in the form of a pamphlet issued during the

Emergency of 1975–7, when democratic freedoms were in abeyance and Mrs Indira Gandhi and her son Sanjay ran the state without interference from parliament, the press or the judiciary. In October 1976 the Directorate of Advertising and Visual Publicity put out a brochure with the title *Jawaharlal Nehru: the Skipper of Modern India*. The cover carried a photograph of Nehru striding briskly out to bat, clad in spotless whites. Inside were photographs of Nehru playing other sports; badminton, billiards and croquet, sometimes with a young Mrs Gandhi looking on. There was another cricket photo, of Nehru sitting contemplatively on a chair, padded up, bat handle stuck under his chin. At first sight the text did not seem to fit the images, for it spoke of Nehru's political values, his concern for world peace, his concern for the poor and his love of liberty. But at some deeper subliminal level they were expected to match. The dictator was seeking legitimacy through the memory of her still-revered father, the words speaking of his values, the pictures of his chosen recreations. To the historian the idiom is strikingly familiar. It recalled Lord Willingdon, the Captain of a United and Loyal India. Mrs Gandhi could not dress herself up in whites, but she could use her father's photos instead. That she and her sycophants chose cricket to seek the people's loyalty was a perverted tribute to the game, but a tribute nonetheless.

What, one wonders, would the parson James Pycroft have made of the spread of cricket among Indians who were never meant to play it? Or the writer of that 1930 guide-book, which helpfully explained the elements of the English game to the visiting Indian student? Both men, perhaps fortunately for them, did not visit the sub-continent. Nor, it appears, has the philosopher Roger Scruton, who has recently written of how cricket exemplifies 'the reticent and understated character of the English ideal: white flannels too clean and pure to suggest physical exertion, long moments of silence and stillness, stifled murmurs of emotion should anything out of the ordinary occur and the occasional burst of subdued applause'.[19]

But other English cricketers and commentators have come, and have left their impressions. Indeed, one can fruitfully track the 'Indianization' of cricket through the writings of visiting English-

men. These have viewed the taking over of their game with a mixture
of horror and fascination. There is a veritable genre of travellers'
accounts that purport to be about cricket but which actually tell more
of the heat, the dirt, the diet – the last especially – of the trains that
run late and the telephones that don't work, the rats in the air-
conditioning and the leaks in the plumbing – as if to say: how can
one play *our sport* in conditions like this? The aspect of cricket that
is foregrounded is the umpiring – which, naturally, is sub-standard.[20]
The essay on Indian cricket most often reproduced in English
anthologies is Ian Peebles's 'Tragedy in Thunderpore', an account of
how an MCC fast bowler ran past the batsman at the other end and
into the pavilion to attend to the dysentery that, in these minds at
any rate, is inseparable from cricket in the sub-continent.

There are exceptions. Thus Scyld Berry ended his book of
the 1981–2 England tour with a thoughtful assessment of the progress
of the game in India. He praised the sportsmanship of the players,
noting that 'in this respect Indian cricketers have become more
English than the English'. He remarked upon India's strengths in spin
bowling and classical batsmanship – arts on the decline in England
– the size of the stadia, the quality of the cricket equipment, the
reach of the radio, the health of the sport's finances and the vastness
of the population. 'Cricket in India should soon become the most
popular sport in any country in the world,' he concluded. Although
'the game grew up thousands of miles away, India is destined to
become the capital of cricket'.[21]

It has, helped by factors Berry could not have anticipated: India's
unexpected victory in the 1983 World Cup, the massive spread of
television, and the sub-continent's own hosting of World Cups in
1987 and 1996. In the winter of 2000–1, an English county professional came to India to learn how to bowl-spin. (This itself was a
notable inversion: for once such a man would come here to teach,
not to be taught.) He was – the phrase is unavoidable – bowled over
by the importance accorded to a game that, in its native land, now
lagged way behind in the popularity stakes. 'Being a cricket fan in
India is like being a football fan in England,' he wrote a trifle

mournfully. 'You have the masses and the media on your side.' Indian cricket was 'the national game in a way that few other countries can claim an attachment to any sport and in India a star like Sachin Tendulkar is a bigger celebrity than David Beckham is in England'.[22]

James Pycroft once wrote of how English settlers and colonists always took their bats and balls with them. One sure sign of how *Indian* cricket has become is that when Indians settle overseas they always take their sport with them, particularly to the United States, where there now exist successful communities of Indians on the East and West Coasts, engineers and doctors by profession, and cricket players and cricket fans by avocation. A South African writer settled in the States has written of how he feeds his own nostalgia for the game he grew up with. He travels to Seattle and the Bronx to watch cricket matches between teams composed mostly of Indians, with the odd Pakistani and West Indian thrown in. One of the more succesful teams is Microsoft Cricket Club, its eleven composed of Indian software engineers who learned to play in Bombay or Bangalore. But this is no social cricket: there are several regional leagues run on a professional basis, and the matches are played hard, and to be won.[23]

On a recent trip to California, I myself saw a match in the Bay Area Cricket League, played on a lovely ground in Merrin County, a slice of green between the mountains and the sea. One team was composed wholly of Gujaratis; the other was more cosmopolitan, with Bengalis and Tamils playing under an expatriate Jamaican. I was also told of a cinema theatre in Freemont which shows live telecasts on a large screen of big matches played by India, the action met by bouts of cheering or angry remonstrance.

IT IS EASIER to document (and celebrate) the Indian love for cricket than to analyse or explain it. A follower of Professor Edward Said might dismiss it as a relic of colonialism. To quote one literary critic – speaking at a seminar at an American university that I attended – 'the continuing popularity of cricket in India demonstrates the hegemony of colonial ideals of masculinity on the unconscientized postcolonial consciousness'. Certainly, the Indian version of anti-colonialism has been softer than some others. The Americans, having got rid of the British, were determined to rid themselves of their games too. American football crowded out soccer from above, and baseball vanquished cricket from below. Indeed, baseball's promoters systematically defined it as 'anti-cricket': faster, tougher and more action-packed. Its American origins were stressed, and its palpable connections to the British game of rounders strenuously denied.[24]

By contrast, Indian intellectuals and politicians have cheerfully embraced the game of cricket despite its British origins and idiom. In 1966, when India played the West Indies in Calcutta, *The Times* of London marvelled at the playing of this English game between two coloured countries. For the 'wily anti-colonialist of the Sukarno type', it remarked, the India–West Indies Test would be seen as 'a most subtly corrupting trick of neo-colonialism'. In Calcutta that argument would find few takers. If cricket was so popular there, said the paper, 'all credit to the ordinary, workaday Indians that their anti-colonialism does no more than occasionally chip the nose from the statue of some long-departed viceroy'.[25]

The lead had come from the very top. Mahatma Gandhi was a 'lukewarm supporter of cricket',[26] but Jawaharlal Nehru enjoyed watching the game, and played it on occasion. This product of Harrow and Trinity would teach the sons of friends how to play the defensive stroke,[27] and would put in an amiable appearance, bat, pads and all, during the annual match between the Lower and Upper Houses of Parliament. Then there was Sarvepalli Radhakrishnan, who, in the 1930s, would sneak off from his post as Spalding Professor of Eastern Religions at Oxford to watch C. K. Nayudu bat at Lord's. Later, as Vice President and President of the Republic of India, Radhakrishnan inserted the names of Nayudu and Mushtaq Ali into the list of those receiving India's highest civilian awards. The Board of Control for Cricket in India sensibly invited the philosopher to preside over its Silver Jubilee celebration, held at Delhi in February 1954. Radhakrishnan remarked here that 'like the other symbols of

The Muslim team that won the Bombay Quadrangular Tournament in 1934. The balding man sitting in the middle of the second row is their captain, S. Wazir Ali, known as the 'best-dressed cricketer in India'. The celebrated fast bowler Mohammed Nissar is seated to the left of Wazir, and the charismatic opening batsman S. Mushtaq Ali is in the first row on the left.

It keeps you fit !

C. K. Nayudu recommending a brand of liver tonic, 1941. Nayudu was almost certainly the first Indian cricketer to appear in advertisements. His name and fame were used to market tea and other consumer products, and even a Hindi feature film.

TODAY I WANT
NO FAVOURS, BOWLER,
I AM ONE OF YOU....
· · · · · · · · · · · · · · ·
TOMORROW IS
ANOTHER DAY —
DEPENDENT ON
TODAY.

HARGREAVES

A cricketing Maharaja, as depicted by a British cartoonist. Indian princes, like English aristocrats, always preferred batting to bowling. Most, like the man caricatured here, were not very good at it; but there were exceptions, such as K. S. Ranjitsinhji.

Vijay Samuel Hazare, hero of the Rest in the Pentagular tournaments of the early 1940s, and captain of the first Indian team to win a test match (against England in February 1952). This photograph was taken in the mid-1990s, at the Polo Grounds, Baroda, venue of some of Hazare's finest innings.

Jawaharlal Nehru

the skipper of modern India

The cover of a brochure printed during the Indian Emergency of 1975–7, when democratic freedoms were in abeyance. The photo shows Mrs Indira Gandhi's father, Jawaharlal Nehru, going out to bat in the annual match between the Lower and Upper Houses of Parliament. The Indian love of cricket and the public admiration of the (always democratic) Nehru were being invoked to help promote loyalty to his non-cricket-playing and authoritarian daughter.

Cricket on a Calcutta street, c.1995. Note how the game forms part of the fabric of daily life, played while housewives go to market and men chat idly on the pavement.

Cricket at the Bombay Gymkhana, c.1998. The ground and pavilion, here hosting a humdrum club match, once hosted the great Triangular and Quadrangular tournaments. This, in other words, is where Palwankar Baloo took his wickets and C. K. Nayudu hit his sixes.

Slum dwellers in Mumbai watching a cricket match on television. Judged by the focused intensity with which the game is being followed, this could either be the final of an important limited-overs tournament or a match between India and Pakistan.

British civilization – the ballot box, the limited liability company and the revised version of the Bible – cricket has come to stay in India'.[28]

A Test match extends over five full days, with six hours of play each day. The extended leisureliness of the game is, of course, why the Americans would not take to it. During the high noon of the Victorian era, a team of English cricketers led by Dr W. G. Grace visited the United States. At the end of the tour one of Grace's men wrote of how cricket had to contend against

> the business habits of Americans. They will not give the time necessary for the game. They will snatch a few moments from the counter for baseball, and they would do the same for cricket; but the same two men may be in at the one game the whole time they can devote to leisure, and they are not charmed with monotony, even if it be High Art. Whereas, at the other game, they may see several sides out in the same time. We believe this to be the true social position of cricket in the States. Time is money here, and there is no denying that much of that valuable commodity is egregiously cut into ribbons at cricket. Americans might learn much, if they chose, from our noble game: if it inculcates one thing, it preaches and practises patience, it enforces self-control, it eliminates the irascible, it displays the excellence of discipline, it is more eloquent than Father Matthew on temperance and sobriety. With all respect for baseball and its disciples, we believe that it principally encourages the two leading failings of American character – ultra-rapidity, quicksilver-sosity, or whatever else of lightning proclivity you like to call it – and ardent speculation.[29]

Indians have plenty of time for High Art, and for much else besides. Five days or thirty hours: an unconscionably long time for an industrial and industrious American, but a bare wink of the eye to the Indian. Cricket fits in easily with the rhythms of what is still – in its essence – an agrarian culture, accustomed to thinking in cosmic or calendric rather than clock time. Indians have no difficulty aimlessly filling up the hours. Consider how they will stop to gaze at the scene of an accident: passengers leaning out of a bus window, the driver too; joined by cyclists, motor-cyclists, car owners and pedestrians: all looking, looking, looking. (An American would rush past without a glance or, were his Christian conscience to prompt him, at least get the injured on their way to hospital.)

The structure of the game also resonates well with the Indian ethos. For cricket is both slow and slow-moving, with the action spread out and interrupted instead of fast-paced and concentrated. A ball is bowled, then the bowler walks slowly back to the top of his run. At the end of six balls 'Over' is called. The fielders take their time to change positions. A wicket falls, and the departing batsman contemplatively walks back, and his replacement as leisurely walks in. After an hour's cricket there comes a four-minute drinks break. After two hours, play stops for lunch. This is a forty-minute interval. A twenty-minute break for tea comes at the end of the next session of play. At 5 p.m. stumps are finally drawn for the day. The players retire to their hotels, to stay there until play resumes the next morning.

'Give me a break,' says the American sarcastically. To watch cricket is to have a long, long break, interrupted by micro-seconds of action. With soccer or tennis the spectator has eyes only for the ball. The cricket fan, however, can appreciate individual idiosyncrasies of character: the manner of a bowler's frustration, for example, or the gestures of batsmen before and after a stroke, or which player congratulates his team-mate and which stays silent. The interrupted nature of play encourages the spectator to participate actively, through barracking and conversations with players on the boundary edge. In between balls and overs, and more so during the longer breaks, he can talk about the past and future of the game with his fellows.

All other games start and end in a single afternoon. Here, play is temporarily stopped in the evening, to resume sixteen hours later. The uncertainty is gripping, and at the end of five days there might not even be a conclusion, a 'draw' rather than a win for either side, an outcome that has a curious appeal for the Hindu, many of whose myths stress negotiation and compromise rather than unequivocal victory or defeat.

Cricket watching is a collective and participatory exercise, indulging the Indian taste for chatter and disputation, gossip and debate. The game has come to mean something quite different here from what it did, and often still does, in its original home. Very recently, the British House of Lords discussed the decline of sport in their elite public schools. One peer, Lord Putnam, quoted the lines spoken by Sir John Gielgud in *Chariots of Fire*, a film Putnam had directed: 'Our games are indispensable in helping to complete an education. They create character, they foster honesty and leadership, but most of all an unassailable sense of loyalty, comradeship and mutual responsibility.'[30]

One wonders what even the educated Indian cricket fan would make of this. For the gap between British precept and Indian practice is huge. This was recognized as early as 1870 by the Bombay correspondent of the *Pioneer* newspaper. 'The comparative silence with which Englishmen go through exercises', he remarked, 'contrasts curiously with the nasal vociferation of the Parsees, who so continuously do cry over their cricket.'[31] In this respect the Hindu and the Muslim have been comfortably the equals of the Parsi. In the winter of 1937–8, a team of English cricketers toured India. They included Norman Yardley, a student of St Peter's, York and the University of Cambridge, and a future cricket captain of his country. After four months of playing in front of packed stadiums Yardley wrote with feeling of 'the complete and utter inability of Indians to do anything without the most deafening yelling and excitement'. The Indian crowds were 'keen and amazingly knowledgeable, but rather too apt to shout or even barrack after every ball'.[32]

The cricket watchers that Yardley knew clapped politely after every boundary hit or wicket taken: if they spoke any words at all these were 'Well played, sir', muttered inaudibly into the pipe or into the beard. The English football fan might be noisy and ill-mannered; the English cricket fan, never. Non-industrial (and non-Western) peoples view the game very differently. In the summer of 1963 Frank Worrell led the West Indies cricket team on a triumphant march through the grounds of England. The cricketers were followed everywhere by a horde of excited fans. In the middle of the crowd, silent and observant, sat the novelist V. S. Naipaul. Lord's Cricket Ground during an England–West Indies Test match, he remarked,

> is almost unrecognizable. The free seats are packed with West Indian workmen. For them cricket is a drama. Every ball holds danger. Their participation is intense and vocal. Hall will be cheered throughout his long run. Applause will never be polite. It will hold a groan of anguish or it will be an eruption of joy. When a West Indian batsman gets his century cushions and mackintoshes will be thrown into the air; men will spontaneously dance. Such a crowd is bound to have some effect on a game; and it was interesting at Lord's to see how the West Indian spectators had begun to infect the English who, it is said, are phlegmatic. It was in this West Indian atmosphere that I grew to appreciate cricket in Trinidad. Its absence in England, and a corresponding dullness of play, lessened my interest; and it lessens even now, when I go to Edgbaston and hear no shouts from the glum, mackintoshed Midlanders, and feel that the players are too separate from the crowd and their activities on the field strictly private.[33]

Naipaul wrote this for an Indian magazine, and of course there were many people of Indian origin who watched cricket with him in Trinidad. For the Indian, as for the West Indian, sport is theatre, a sphere of fun rather than a school for life.

INDIANS HAVE MORE TIME; Indians like doing things together; Hindus don't really mind a 'draw'; Hindus are culturally syncretic and choose to absorb foreign imports rather than reject them: these are the lines on which we might begin to explain the extraordinary Indian love for cricket. To these cultural factors we must now add a strictly instrumental one: the motive of national pride. While India was a colony, cricket was a means of settling accounts with the rulers. A Hindu victory over the Europeans invariably brought forth editorials on how sporting equality must be followed by political equality. After Independence the new nation has come to identify cricketing prowess with patriotic virtue. No other sport can play this role. In cricket alone does India compete on something like equal terms in the international arena. True, the Indian cricket *team* has never been top dog: that honour has alternated for the last forty years between Australia and the West Indies. But India has regularly produced cricketers of world class, individuals who have held world records and been ranked at the top of this or that list. Less regularly, but with more spectacular consequences, the Indian cricket team occasionally achieves a series or championship victory against sides ranked higher than itself.[34]

One such win came in December 1959, when India defeated Australia in a Test match in Kanpur. Its architect was a previously obscure Gujarati off-spinner called Jasu Patel. Watching the match was the Maharajkumar of Vizianagaram, who had adroitly made his peace with republican India by returning his knighthood to the Queen. Vizzy now hailed Patel as 'another from the region of Gujarat who humbled the pride of a foreign power without a weapon. If the Mahatma did it with his spinning wheel, Jasu did it with his off-spin.'[35] When, five years later, India beat Australia once more, Vizzy drew attention to the fact that the Test more or less coincided with the great Dusshera Festival, which celebrates the victory of the good King Rama over the evil genius Ravana. 'Shabash India!' crowed Vizzy. 'It was a real Vijaya Dashami, a day which will be remembered for victory.'[36]

What may read to some as hysteric hyperbole was actually a sentiment fairly widely shared. Vizzy, opportunistic as ever, had captured the popular mood. Intriguingly, the Indian captain against Australia was another Prince, but an altogether better cricketer than Vizianagaram. This was the Nawab of Pataudi, the son of the man who had played for England under Jardine in 1932–3 and had later led India on its tour of England in 1946. Like his father, the younger Pataudi was a batsman of skill and courage. While in his first year at

Oxford he had lost the use of his right eye. Those who saw him before his accident predicted he would be the next Bradman. Even with one eye he was close to world class.

Pataudi became captain of India in 1962, aged only twenty-two. With his regal background and his cricketing genius went his marriage to the celebrated film star Sharmilla Tagore. Altogether, he was the most charismatic Indian cricketer since C. K. Nayudu. In 1967–8 he led India to its first series win overseas, in New Zealand. He now seemed set to lead Indian cricket well into the 1970s. But in the winter of 1969–70 he suffered a serious loss of form. Then, in August 1970, his title was taken away from him when the Prime Minister, Mrs Indira Gandhi, abolished the privy purses and other entitlements of the Princes. The 'Nawab of Pataudi' had become 'M. A. K. Pataudi'. The hardest blow was to follow, for in January 1971 he was replaced as cricket captain of India by the Bombay batsman Ajit Wadekar.

Pataudi's response to this twin demotion was dramatic. He chose to stand for the 1971 Parliamentary Elections, in the Gurgaon constituency. He would fight on the ticket of the Vishal Haryana Party, and against Mrs Gandhi's Congress. No sooner had he announced his candidature than the old cricketer Lala Amarnath said he would oppose him. The Lala was standing as an independent. But within days he had withdrawn in favour of the Congress candidate, saying:

> I was always anxious that the Nawab who represented a system which was retrograde to the progressive policies of our Prime Minister should be opposed even if it was a wrong match on a difficult pitch. I am sure that the Gurgaon electorate would not be carried away by glamour but act dispassionately by voting for the Congress which alone can deliver the goods.

In his own speeches Pataudi assured the electors that he was 'one of them'; that he owned only 25 acres of land; that in his state 'Hindus and Muslims have always lived as brothers'. Sharmilla Tagore also addressed select gatherings on his behalf. Yet he was trounced in the polls by the Congress candidate, getting only 22,979 votes (out of 398,638 cast). He even lost his deposit. The newspaper headlines were predictable: 'Pataudi bowled middle stump'.[37] There was, in fact, a countrywide wave in favour of the Congress. Mrs Gandhi's populist policies – the nationalization of banks had acccompanied the derecognition of Princes – and her electoral slogan of 'Garibi Hatao' ('Abolish Poverty') helped her gain a comfortable two-thirds majority.

While the elections were on, the Indian cricket team was in the Caribbean. Here they comprehensively upturned the form-book, defeating a strong West Indies side led by the incomparable Gary Sobers. The cricketers returned to 'a fantastic homecoming'. More than 10,000 fans thronged to Bombay's Santa Cruz airport to see, touch and garland them. From the airport the heroes were whisked away to the Brabourne Stadium, which they entered on an obligatory red carpet. Speeches were made by the Mayor of Bombay, a senior minister in the Maharashtra Government, and the Presidents of the Board of Control for Cricket in India and the Cricket Club of India. The crackers, screams and camera flashes at Brabourne were compared by one reporter to the thunder, lightning and rain of the Bombay monsoon. This time, those who wrote paeans to the cricket victory recalled not Gandhi but Churchill. Never, remarked the veteran journalist Raju Bharatan, 'was so much owed by so many to so few'.[38]

Later in the year Pakistan and India were both due to tour England. The Pakistani cricketers arrived first. For an early reception in Mayfair they had to enter the hall under police escort. A crowd of more than 1,000 Bengalis had gathered to jeer and taunt them with cries of 'Go back, murderers', 'Pakistani bastards' and 'Boycott the butchers'. These were references to the ongoing suppression of the Bangladeshi freedom movement, which had led to many killings at the hands of the Pakistan army and an exodus of several million refugees into India. Indeed, everywhere they went the Pakistani cricketers – themselves, of course, innocent of any crime – were met by angry protesters. At Worcester a placard at their match read: 'Pakistanis play cricket in England – their fathers commit genocide in Bangladesh'. One poster showed a cricketer with a rifle; another showed a cricketer beating a woman and child with a bat.

The previous year, a popular movement had successfully brought about the abandonment of a tour of England by a side of white South African cricketers. The East Bengalis wanted an encore, and had enlisted thirty Labour MPs in support. The British press was divided on partisan lines. The *Daily Telegraph* felt that 'encroachments on sports by politicians who wish to control it or use it for ideological ends must be repugnant to the British people'. The *Daily Mirror*, on the other hand, thought the protests by Bengali students were justified, for 'only the ignorant, the insensitive or the intransigent can expect them not to resent the presence of representatives of a Power which is oppressing their kinsmen'. The Lord Mayor of Birmingham asked the Pakistani cricketers to sign a bat for auction, the proceeds to go to cholera-striken Bengali refugees in India. When they refused, they were chastised by the former England captain and current Bishop of Woolwich, David Sheppard, for not putting 'simple humanity in front of political expediency'.[39]

The Pakistans lost the Test series by one match to nil, and the Indians stepped in. One of their more publicized acts was to sign a bat and auction it for £10,000, the proceeds sent directly to the refugees from East Bengal. Meanwhile, on the field, they won the only match of three to end in a result, played at the Oval. This was their first victory in England in forty years of trying, and the home side was very good indeed, fresh from defeating a strong Australian side Down Under. The *National Herald* of Lucknow, a paper founded by Jawaharlal Nehru, suggested that the victory had something to do with his daughter's progressive politics. Previous Indian teams had better individual players, it said, but this 'one is a team of commoners, without a prince with a privy purse . . . Wadekar's team have taught India lessons in courage and discipline and adventure, how to fight battles and how to win them.'[40]

In fairness to the Nawab, he had been among the first to send Wadekar and his men a congratulatory telegram. (And he was, in time, to play under the captaincy of the commoner. However, the

National Herald editorial was representative of a general and widespread exultation. A leading cricket magazine asked its readers to 'Roll out the Red Carpet: from Santa Cruz to the CCI'.[41] They did, but the flight back to Bombay was diverted at the last moment to New Delhi, to allow the players first to meet Prime Minister Indira Gandhi. Mrs Gandhi was known to keep Chief Ministers waiting for months for an appointment, but she knew the worth of a well-circulated photograph of herself with victorious cricketers.

At New Delhi's Palam Airport, the cricketers were greeted with a huge Air India hoarding. This depicted the airline's mascot, the Maharaja, in an exaggerated bow of deference, saying: 'Welcome cricket heroes, I bow(l) to thee.' They proceeded to the Prime Minister's house where Mrs Gandhi, dressed in a printed sari, was photographed with the captain, Wadekar, then with England's chief destroyer, Bhagwat Chandrasekhar, then with the manager, Colonel H. R. Adhikari, and finally with the entire team.[42]

After the audience with Mrs Gandhi the cricketers continued on to Bombay. When they finally reached Indian cricket's capital city, a crowd of 150,000 lined the long road from Santa Cruz airport to City Hall. The *Hindustan Times* wrote of how

> The entire city was dressed up for the occasion with buntings; welcome arches and what not as if to honour a visiting high dignitary. Indeed, for those countless fans who could not watch the historic triumph at the Oval, the return of the players seemed to be the next best thing. They mustered in strength at every vantage-point and expressed their joy in a variety of ways – through colourfully brought out posters, by bursting crackers and blowing trumpets and by showering the players with rose petal and gulal [powdered colours]. Wadekar and his gallant warriors deserved all these and even more.[43]

Old Bombay hands said this was a greater reception than that accorded to the Pope or the Queen. *The Illustrated Weekly of India*, a magazine then at the height of its popularity, ran a nine-page cover story entitled 'Indian Cricket's Big Breakthrough', adorned with action photographs and boxes containing tributes to India's victory offered by such foreign cricketing icons as Sir Donald Bradman and Keith Miller. Miller put it well: 'India, once looked upon as in the Little League of Cricket, are in the Big League. And strong contenders for the best team in the world.'[44]

In the ensuing correspondence two letters stood out. M. V. Nagarajan of Madras wrote of how on the day of the Oval win he referred to the Number Code of the Post and Telegraphs Department, to find that there were twenty-seven different kinds of greetings – Happy Diwali, Merry Christmas, Heartfelt Congratulations on the Birth of a Baby Boy, Deepest Condolences on Your Recent Loss, etc., etc. – but 'none suitable for greeting winners in sports'![45] Sharper still was a letter written by Sudhir S. Trivedi of Ahmedabad. When India defeated the West Indies, he pointed out,

> there was no great exhibition of jubilation and appreciation. But all India went hysterical over our Test victory in England, associating it with national glory. I attribute this national hysteria to our feeling of inferiority when confronting England. It is deplorable that though 24 years have passed since India became free, we as a people have yet to overcome this sense of inferiority complex.[46]

This put the jubilation in context somewhat, and the cricketers themselves were brought down to earth by Lala Amarnath. The veteran observed that the Indian team would have lost the other two Tests had rain not saved them. As the Lala sardonically put it: 'Hitler, whose armies were thwarted at the gates of Moscow, called the Weather God a Jew or a Russian. Illingworth [the England captain] must now be identifying the Rain God as of Indian origin'.[47]

A further twelve years were to pass before India won anything of substance on the cricket field. But this was the big prize, the World Cup itself. The tournament was played in England, and the fancied teams included the hosts, Pakistan and the West Indies. India started as 50 to 1 outsiders, and even the captain, the superb all-rounder Kapil Dev, thought only that his men were 'capable of a surprise or two'. But they played above themselves to reach the semi-finals. In this round they beat England. Now they would play the West Indies, who had won the trophy in 1975 and 1979, and were generally regarded as unbeatable in the one-day game.

For the final at Lord's the rival supporters 'had turned the ground into a carnival with the cymbals and bongos of the West Indian supporters in disharmonious rhythm with the dholaks and temple bells of the Indian supporters'. The latter fell silent when Kapil Dev's side were shot out for the low score of 183. But a few West Indian wickets fell early, panic set in the lower-middle order, and finally they fell 43 runs short.

Back home, the rising news weekly *India Today* ran a cover story entitled 'Miracle at Lord's'. This was, it said, 'Indian cricket's finest hour'. The magazine garnered sound-bites from the respected British critic John Woodcock – who called Kapil Dev the 'Severiano Balles-teros of cricket, a man capable of heroics' – from the captain's mother – 'his success is the result of hard work' – and from his sister – 'I just knew his devotion to the game would bring glory in the end.' It then added a magisterial comment of its own:

> For too long has Indian cricket been hamstrung by personal rivalries, inner tensions, regional loyalties and above all, the crippling call of commercialism. One man, in the short space of time as captain, counsellor and friend, has altered all that – mainly by personal example.[48]

As it happened, Indira Gandhi was now Prime Minister once more. She sent an early telegram to the cricketers, which said, *inter alia*, that 'My slogan is India can do it. Thank you for living up to it.'[49] (This slogan, with the cricketers' photographs, was then displayed on state-owned petrol stations all over India.)

The patriotic spirit had caught the players. When they landed at Bombay airport to a crowd shouting 'Kapil Dev Zindabad', the captain immediately corrected them by saying 'Bharat Zindabad'. After a reception in Bombay, the players went home for a few days, and reassembled in Delhi to meet the Prime Minister. For her reception to the players, held on the lawns of Hyderabad House, Mrs Gandhi was dressed in cricket colours: a dotted white sari with a matching white blouse. The Prime Minister spoke to each player, held the Cup herself, posed for photographs and made a short speech where she told the players: 'Shabash, keep the flag flying.' What she said next was more notable: to quote a press report, 'the Prime Minister however expressed surprise that the English press was underplaying the achievement of the Indian team. She said the entire nation had been thrilled at the victory.'[50]

THE ASSOCIATION of cricket with patriotism was made easier by the internal diversity of the winning teams of 1971 and 1983. The players came from all parts of India, and from different religious backgrounds. The 1971 side had Hindus and Muslims as well as a Parsi and a Sikh; the 1983 team had no Parsi, but the other three faiths were represented, and there was a Christian as well.

The *annus mirabilis* of Indian cricket also happened to be the *annus mirabilis* of Mrs Indira Gandhi. The cricket victories of 1971 took place in between two personal political victories for her: in the elections of January, and on the battlefield in December. Indeed, after that winter's war against Pakistan – which India won, comprehensively – the cricketers were commandeered for national service. They were asked to play a round of matches to raise money for the Bangladesh Fund. At these games, played all over India, lesser politicians sought also to reflect some of the glory on to themselves. The cricketers, wrote one critic in disgust, 'became part of a multipurpose circus that went round and round the country – a bandwagon to climb for leaders from all shades of public life'.[51]

The nationalism of Mrs Gandhi was a curious mixture of paranoia and triumphalism. Even at the time of her greatest victories she spoke darkly of the 'enemies of the nation'. In 1971 these were the Princes, the capitalists and the Western world. The United States had openly supported Pakistan and even sent the Seventh Fleet into the Indian Ocean. In this context cricket and cricketers would be used to help Indira, and India, keep those ever-threatening forces at bay.

When the Indian team won the World Cup in 1983, Mrs Gandhi was not as firmly in control as in 1971. Her party was riven by inner tensions, her nation riven by regional loyalties – or disloyalties – in particular the rebellions then active in Assam and the Punjab. And the external enemies were also present: note the brooding reference in her speech to the apparent hostility of the British press to Indian cricketers. To suggest that Indira Gandhi saw herself as the Kapil Dev of politics may not be entirely far-fetched. She was the counsellor to and captain of the nation, helping it to overcome regional loyalties and personal ambitions and stand united and tall against other nations.

It is instructive to compare the cricket victories of 1971 and 1983 with an earlier triumph. In January 1952, India won its first-ever Test match – against England, at home. Now India had been free for less than five years, a republic for less than two. Surely this sporting victory against the erstwhile rulers should have been seen as a triumph of the anti-colonial spirit? It was not. The Prime Minister sent the players a congratulatory telegram, but did not host a reception for them. The press, that generally reliable barometer of public opinion, was noticeably muted in its appreciation. There were no parallels drawn with patriotic struggles, no attempt to harness sport to higher causes. Editorials merely suggested that the win 'provides an important stimulus for the game in this country'.[52]

The India of 1952 was not the India of 1971; Jawaharlal Nehru was not Indira Gandhi. Then, the nationalist spirit poured into the making of the concrete that built dams and the steel that made factories. The new nation's energies were channelled into social and economic development. There was a countrywide consensus on the policies of the Congress Party – which was then in power at the centre and in all the states – as well as an overwhelming respect for its leader. Nehru's control over his party and his nation was more or less complete; it did not need external aids such as cricket victories. In any case, in Nehru's vision sport occupied a subsidiary place.

He wished 'India to do it' in other spheres: in uplifting its people from poverty, in promoting Hindu–Muslim harmony, in mediating between the superpowers to prevent the Cold War from becoming hot.

Sporting nationalism has always been most intense where there is a general feeling of insecurity or inferiority. Back in the nineteenth century, victories at cricket reassured Australians that people of convict stock could best the British at their own game. As one journalist wrote in 1898, after a successful Ashes campaign, 'this ruthless rout of English cricket will do – and has done – more to enhance the cause of Australian nationalism than could ever be achieved by miles of erudite essays and impassioned appeals'.[53] Later, in the 1930s, the spectacular achievements of Donald Bradman were viewed by young patriots as an effective answer to the cultural arrogance of England: 'No Australian had written *Paradise Lost*, but Bradman had made 100 before lunch at Lord's.'[54]

Move outside of cricket, and consider the skilful use of sport by the Cuban dictator Fidel Castro. In the 1970s, the Olympic victories of the runner Alberto Juanterena and the boxer Teofilo Stevenson were viewed by Fidel, and by many of his countrymen, as a defiant thumbs-up to the Big Bully up north. Now, with the economy on the brink and dissidence rising, the Cuban Communists still seek to put sport in the service of patriotic pride.[55] Meanwhile, the sole Arab soccer team in the Israeli first division subsumes the hopes, frustrations and vengeful feelings of the million Muslim citizens of this Jewish state.[56] And when Iran defeated the United States, the Great Satan, in the 2000 soccer World Cup, the streets of Teheran were flooded with joyous celebrators. Watching them were expatriates in the United States who had fled Khomeini. Now 'in some magical way, Iranians in the two countries seemed unified again – unified in a way that transcended government or politics'.[57]

The social historian Hans Medick once told me how for Germans of his generation their country's victory in the World Cup final of 1954 marked its honourable re-entry into the world of respectable nations. That win, by three goals to two in a desperately close-fought match against Hungary, wiped out the stain of Hitler, the Holocaust and military defeat. In his memoir of the century, Günter Grass recalls that epic match through a young German listening to the radio in Munich. When the last whistle blew, the youngster exults: 'We're the world champions, we've shown the world what we're worth, we're back, losers no more, we can sing "über alles in der Welt" under our umbrellas in the Bern Stadium and around the radio in my Munich room.'[58]

The Germans are losers no more, inside the sporting arena or outside it. Should the cricket craze in India be compared with the Brazilian love for soccer, then? In that country soccer has become the vehicle for the unfulfilled aspirations of everyday life. The game of football provides a 'breathing space between a horrific immediate past and an anxiously uncertain future'.[59] Brazil still grapples with an unequal society and an imperfect democracy, but at least they win the World Cup, world sport's greatest prize, once in every two or three attempts. In India, however, the expression of sporting nationalism is accentuated both by the continuing poverty of its peoples and the very widely dispersed nature of its on-field triumphs. Between 1986 and 1999 India did not lose a single Test series at home, playing in a climate and general environment suitable to its players and on pitches doctored for its spin bowlers. In the same period it only won one Test match overseas, in Sri Lanka. It has won one World Cup out of seven played thus far. It is thirty years since it won a Test series in West Indies, and it has still never won one in Australia. But hope lingers, kept alive by memories of other victories: in the West Indies and England in 1971, the World Cup in 1983, the World Championship of Cricket in 1985.

Meanwhile, the integration of the world through television and the liberalization of India's own economy have made comparisons with other countries more obvious and less palatable. India will never be a Tiger to match the other Asian Tigers. India ranks at about 150 in the World Development Report, just below Namibia and just above Haiti. It is the cricketers, and they alone, who are asked to redeem these failures.

Especially in the last decade, cricket nationalism has become more intense and ferocious. One sign is the increasing hostility to cricketers from other countries. In the past, the Indian cricket fan was inclusive in his sympathies; he would worship the West Indian Frankie Worrell and the Englishman Tony Greig alongside Vinoo Mankad and Gundappa Viswanath. This characteristic seemed to confirm the remark of the anthropologist Verrier Elwin that whereas Christians believe more in God, Hindus believe in more Gods. But it appears that Hinduism has become semiticized. Chauvinism has triumphed over generosity. Our side must win, at any cost. Stone-throwing, arson and other acts of vandalism have become increasingly common, especially when India is on the verge of defeat.

Such hyper-nationalism places a massive burden on our cricketers. The greatest batsman in the game today is an Indian, Sachin Tendulkar; the problem is that his team-mates are not a quarter as gifted. If he fails with the bat in a crucial match, India must lose. If he scores a hundred, India might just win. The burdens that Tendulkar carries have been conveyed with a chilling eloquence by the poet and critic C. P. Surendran:

> Batsmen walk out into the middle alone. Not Tendulkar. Every time Tendulkar walks to the crease, a whole nation, tatters and all, marches with him to the battle arena. A pauper people pleading for relief, remission from the lifelong anxiety of being Indian, by joining in spirit their visored saviour.
>
> Wednesday or Friday, Tendulkar lifts his gleaming bat, points it like a sword towards the TV cameras after his customary hundred, and a million hands go up in blessing; and in begging, pleading silently for redemption from the oppressive reality of their existence; seeking a moment's liberation from their India-bondage through the exhilarating grace of one accidental bat. One billion hard-pressed Indians. Just one hero. . . .

The poor Indian lifts his hands to Sachin Tendulkar in supplication: give us respite, a sense of liberation; lift us up from the dark pit of our lives to well-lit places of the imagination with your skill-wrought perfections. Give us an idea of what a light thing life ought to be. Take our blessings; but give us a break. Please win. Win for us losers.[60]

This was written in April 1998 while Tendulkar was enjoying an astonishing run against Australia. He had scored two Test centuries against the Australians in India, and two one-day centuries against them in Sharjah. India won both the Test series and the one-day competition. Eighteen months later, when Tendulkar led an Indian side on a tour of Australia, many fans fancifully looked forward to an encore. But on their own wickets and in front of their own crowds the Australians were an altogether different proposition. After India were humiliated, losing all three Test matches by large margins, a friend sent me some jokes circulated on e-mail by disenchanted fans. A selection is offered below:

Q. What's the Indian version of a hat-trick?
A. Three runs in three balls.

Q. Why don't Indian fielders need pre-tour travel injections?
A. Because they never catch anything.

Q. What's the Indian version of LBW?
A. Lost, Beaten, Walloped.

Q. What do you call an Indian with 100 runs against his name?
A. A bowler.

Q. What do Indian batsmen and drug addicts have in common?
A. Both spend most of their time wondering when their next shot will be.

Q. Who spent the most time on the crease of anyone in the Indian touring party?
A. The lady who ironed the cricket whites.

Q. Why are Indian cricketers cleverer than Houdini?
A. Because they can get out without trying.

These jokes were manufactured by Indians working in the Gulf and the United States, super-patriotic as expatriates tend to be, but sufficiently urbane and cosmopolitan to leaven despair with mockery. Back home, the response tends to the vicious. Newspapers call into question the fitness, probity and patriotism of the defeated cricketers. Fans burn their effigies on the streets and sometimes throw stones at their homes. Win or lose, it is hard work playing cricket for India nowadays. I suppose the ever-increasing pay packet compensates.

In seeking the emotional allegiance of Indians, cricket has entered into an amiable competition with the Hindi film. In 2001 these two passions came together with spectacular effect in the form of *Lagaan*, a Bollywood film that placed the game at its heart. Set in the nineteenth century, the film's plot centred around a cricket match played as a wager between a bunch of unlettered peasants and a group of British military men. If the Indians won, the colonial land tax would be forgone; if they lost, the tax would be doubled. This somewhat implausible plot was redeemed by superb acting and cine-matography, and by well-integrated song and dance routines. In the end the white man lost (naturally) and the tax was waived. The film was a runaway success, commercially as well as critically. It has, however, been criticized by scholars of post-colonial studies, who have begun swarming around it like hyenas around a carcass, sniffing its shots and dialogues for traces of misogyny and collaboration.

In the last months of the year *Lagaan* was nominated as the official Indian entry for the Oscars. At about the same time, the former England cricket captain Mike Denness levied a set of heavy penalties on Indian cricketers. This was done in his capacity as the match referee in a series played between India and South Africa. One of the cricketers he punished was the peerless Sachin Tendulkar, for allegedly tampering with the ball. Denness's action led to an extraordinary outburst of protest. The Indian Cricket Board threatened a split in world cricket if his sentences were not reversed. In parliament, poli-ticians of the ruling coalition as well as the opposition described the act as an insult to national honour. On the streets, effigies of Denness were burnt, and placards proclaiming Tendulkar's innocence carried.

This particular controversy underlined both cricket's unique place in Indian culture and Sachin Tendulkar's status as the only flawless Indian. Our industrialists are known not to pay taxes and our film stars are famous for sleeping around. Our politicians have exhausted every expletive in the book. But, till Denness came into the picture, Tendulkar's behaviour was exemplary; he had never talked back to an umpire, or sledged the opposition, all this while scoring more centuries in international cricket than any other batsman. Besides, he was known to be devoted to his wife. The referee's verdict sought to challenge all this. Denness was judged to be especially motivated as he should have known that Sachin is a notorious nail chewer: what would he tamper the ball with?

LET ME NOW OFFER, very briefly, the autobiography of a cricket-crazy Indian. The first cricket stories I heard were of my father's heroes, men like C. Ramaswami, a ferocious left-handed hitter who played for the Indians versus the Europeans in the Madras Presidency Match, and Lala Amarnath, whom my father saw bat, bowl and keep wickets in a match at the Brabourne Stadium. One was a local hero, the other emphatically a national one.

The first foreigners I have memories of were the MCC touring side of 1963–4. It was this tour that placed my first cricket book in my hands. It was issued by Esso, the oil multi-national, and it contained details of the touring party and their likely Indian opponents, picture on one side, thumbnail sketch on the other. In those pre-Murdochian days it represented a giant step in the march of sports sponsorship. You could collect the publication at the nearest petrol pump. We read here of 'Micky Stewart, the stalwart Surrey opener', and of his counterpart 'M. L. Jaisimha, the dasher from the Banjara Hills'. The photos were of a piece, the players all clad in double-knit sweaters, white ringed with dark blue, no question of disfiguring logos and adverts, let alone pink pyjama suits.

These, then, were the first foreign names that I learned to enunciate: Binks, Bolus, Stewart, Smith, Larter, Parks and Barrington.

There was no television, so we knew not how these English cricketers looked or acted in the field; the names and portraits were all we had to indicate how they might bowl or bat. An older friend – nine to my six – gave me an early lesson in the creative indigenization of the foreign game. He would play on the name of the visiting off-spinner, J. B. Mortimore, sometimes calling him J. B. Mangaram – after a local confectioner – or, when we were playing, J. B. 'Fat Peacock', a translation into English of 'Moti-More'. The acculturation would be suitably dramatized: coming in to bowl with a tennis ball, my friend would sway unsteadily as he ran, like an over-fed peacock.

When I was eight, and started reading the sports pages more seriously, I decided I had to choose a Ranji Trophy team to support. (It was about this time that I began reading A. A. Thomson and Neville Cardus, one a Yorkshire partisan, the other a Lancashire one: they both taught me that one must first find a club or province before one found a country.) The state I lived in, Uttar Pradesh, was out of the question: it was the weakest team in the weakest zone. Two options presented themselves: Tamil Nadu, the land of my forefathers, and Karnataka (then Mysore), where both my grandfathers had settled. I chose Karnataka, most likely because four of its players had been chosen to represent India against the West Indies in the series then being played.

The state was now taken care of. Country had been chosen for me by birth. The first Test matches I have distinct aural memories of were played between India and Australia in the winter of 1969–70. I could not bunk classes, for my mother taught in the same school and we left home by the same bus. But after school I would catch an hour of play on our Philips radio. And of course I read the reports and scores in the following day, especially the reports and scores of India's victory at New Delhi. That win was made more sweet because the visiting captain, Bill Lawry, had announced beforehand that his side would win the match in four days, and he would go fishing in the Jumna on the fifth.

Delhi was a six-hour bus ride from the town we lived in. When the next bunch of foreigners came along, in 1972–3, I persuaded my father to let me go to watch them. An uncle bought me a ticket and an aunt offered to put me up. By now my reading had picked up enormously. I wanted, of course, to see India win, but I also wanted to meet the great wicket-keeper Alan Knott, of Kent and England. Cardus and Thomson had told me of the long line of Kentish stumpers: Evans and Ames, and Hubble and Huish before them. I had decided that when Knott answered the telephone I would greet him as the worthy successor to them all.

With some enterprise I located the cricketers' hotel, where the receptionist allowed me to dial Knott's room. When he picked up the phone I forgot my lines: 'Mr Knott, I want to meet you,' I said, lamely. To his 'Why?' I answered: 'Because it is important'. '*Everybody* says it is important,' said the wicket-keeper, and quietly put down the phone.

The following day I saw Knott, from a distance of 70 yards, as he came out with the England side on the first day of the Test. I had never been in such a noisy crowd before, and I cannot say I did not enjoy it. The cricket was gripping, too. This was the match in which that magical slow left-arm bowler Bishan Bedi got his hundredth Test wicket, the achievement greeted by a huge banner displayed by his fans in the East Stand: SPIN HUNDRED MORE. This was the match in which that blond giant Tony Greig first demonstrated his kinship with the Indian crowds, falling dead to the ground when a cracker burst in the stands.

I did not meet Knott, and my side did not win either. England won by six wickets, the match finishing just after lunch on the fifth day. After it was over I walked back to my aunt's house. Later I would make sense of all that I had seen and learnt, but what mattered at the time was that India had lost. It was a long walk, through the heart of New Delhi, and the streets were deserted (it was Christmas Day, and the shops and offices were closed). I mournfully noted the streets, named for the Indian nationalists – Tilak, Kasturba Gandhi, Motilal Nehru, Maulana Azad. At least they had won *their* battle, I thought.

The following morning's newspaper did not mention the Test

match on the front page. For while India was losing in Delhi a great Indian was dying in Madras. He was Chakravarti Rajagopalachari, writer, lawyer, philosopher and patriot, the man who succeeded Lord Mountbatten as Governor-General, the man Gandhi called 'the keeper of my conscience'. His death was reason enough to relegate the Test to the inside pages, surely a unique occurrence in the history of Indian cricket and Indian journalism.

Exactly a year later I was on holiday in Bangalore. At the newly built Chinnaswamy Stadium I watched Karnataka defeat Delhi in the quarter-finals of the Ranji Trophy. I stayed on for the next match, against Bombay, who had been champions for fifteen years on the trot. They would have won this year too, except that at a key stage of this match their captain and leading batsman, Ajit Wadekar, slipped and was run out. (Long afterwards I met Wadekar, and reminded him of this. 'New shoes,' he answered, by way of explanation.) Karnataka went on to win the semi-final and to defeat Rajasthan in the final. They have since won six more championships. And I have watched better and bigger matches. But for pure joy nothing will ever compare to having seen, *at the ground*, my Karnataka become the first team in fifteen years to defeat Bombay.

In the summer of 1974 I joined St Stephen's College in Delhi, principally to play for its cricket team. Early on I won 500 rupees in a quiz competition and invested it in a short-wave radio. When I was not playing cricket I was watching cricket, and when I was not doing either I was listening to cricket. When a Test match came to Delhi, about once in two years, I joined the scramble for tickets. Like kerosene and sugar and motor-cars, these were scarce in the command economy. One could queue up all night and still be told at the counter that there were no tickets left. It was best to spread one's bets widely, to tap friends whose fathers were Joint Secretaries to the Government of India and uncles who knew cricketers who might have a spare pass. The days before the Test brought forth a desperate uncertainty: would I enter legally on the morning of the match?

This is not the place to write of the cricket *per se*, of the hundreds hit in front of me at the Ferozeshah Kotla by Vivian Richards and

G. R. Viswanath and the wickets taken by Prasanna and Chandrase-khar.[61] One off-field recollection, however, is pertinent to the theme of this book. India were playing the West Indies, at Port of Spain, and chasing 400 runs in the last innings. The year was 1976, the month April: smack in the middle of Indira Gandhi's Emergency. The last day's play, running from 8 p.m. to 3 a.m. Indian time, was followed in the college quadrangle by a group huddled around my transistor. Against the odds, India won, scoring 406 for 4, a record winning total in 100 years of Test cricket. At the end the Hindi commentator on All Indi(r)a Radio, Ravi Chaturvedi, offered the victory to the matriarch. 'Yeh Indira Gandhi ka desh hai,' he yelled ('This is the land of Indira Gandhi'). 'Ye bis sutri karikram ka desh hai,' he shouted next ('This is the land of the twenty-point pro-gramme', launched by the Prime Minister to discipline and improve India).

I HAVE SPOKEN thus far of the people who were watching cricket in independent India. But who has been playing the game, and who pays for them? The Ranji Trophy has supplanted the Pentangular, and corporations have supplanted the Princes. These were the game's new patrons, firms such as Tatas and Mafatlals and ACC, who ran their own cricket teams and paid their players a salary not to attend office. The public sector also generously stepped in to help the game. In the 1950s and 1960s, both Indian Railways and the State Bank of India employed large numbers of Ranji Trophy and Test cricketers. Other state-owned firms to have cricketers on their rolls include the Oil and Natural Gas Commission, the Steel Authority of India, Indian Airlines and the Syndicate Bank.

The first great cricketers of Indian origin were Ranji and Baloo, a Prince and an Untouchable, but their successors have come over-whelmingly from the middle classes. In the late 1970s, the Australian scholar Richard Cashman investigated the social background of the 143 men who had been capped for India up to the time of his research. Only seven, he found, were born in a village, each moving to a town shortly thereafter. Seventy were born in a provincial or national capital. Another forty-nine hailed from district and divisional towns. The level of education was surprisingly high: as many as eighty-one were graduates, and forty-nine others had high school certificates. The reason for this was not necessarily love of learning. Many cricketers stayed in the classroom merely to play in the inter-school competition, the Cooch Behar Trophy, or in the Rohinton Baria inter-university championship. Both tournaments were highly competitive, a good performance aiding one's elevation to the Ranji Trophy team and, with luck, to the Test side itself.

In a fascinating appendix Cashman provided the father's occupation, a handy guide to the exact social status of India's top cricketers. Many were sons of lawyers, bank officers and minor bureaucrats. Others had been born to police inspectors, store-keepers, and school-teachers. The father of one was the *peshkar*, or accountant, of the rich and famous Tirupathi temple in southern India. The father of another was identified as 'personal assistant to ex-Deputy Finance Minister'. Moving up the social scale, three Test cricketers were sons of industrialists; seven, sons of Rajas or Maharajas.[62]

Bombay was one place where one could observe the democratization of cricket at work. The first step was to open out the communal Gymkhanas. A. A. Jasdenwala of the Islam Gymkhana led the way, admitting 300 non-Muslim members in 1949.[63] Ironically as the Gymkhanas became non-denominational, new centres came into being. The action was moving northwards, to the suburbs of Dadar, Matunga and Shivaji Park, the heartland of the city's Marathi-speaking middle class. In the first half of the century, wrote A. F. S. Talyarkhan, it was in the Maidan and the three Gymkhanas on the Kennedy Sea Face that talent was 'nurtured and fully flowered. Outside, in other parts of the town, the game was a mere recreational pursuit with every nerve strained to reach the magic green which is within a mile's radius of Flora Fountain.' By the 1950s, however, 'the cricket of Bombay may be said to embrace every inch of land between Borivli and Colaba, played by all communities, and all sections of the public'.[64]

One casualty of the decade of the fifties was the *Bombay Chronicle*. Syed Abdullah Brelvi had died in 1949, and the paper limped on for a few years more, the last issue coming out in 1956. India was free, even the *Times of India* had passed into Indian hands, and there no longer seemed any need for a paper founded on anti-colonial sentiment. Still, it was a loss, not least to the cricket world. What would the *Chronicle* have made of the changes in how the game was played in its city?

The cricketers produced by Dadar Union and Shivaji Park Gymkhana have included Vijay Manjrekar, Subhas Gupte, Sunil Gavaskar and Dilip Vengsarkar. Their fathers were, respectively, an insurance manager, a railway engineer, a marketing executive and a scientific officer. Their achievements kindled Marathi pride and spurred a thorough-going reorganization of Bombay cricket. For years the Bombay Cricket Association (BCA) had to have its matches hosted by the Cricket Club of India (CCI), a body run by upper-class Parsis and Gujaratis. In the late 1960s the BCA asked the CCI to allot it more seats for Tests hosted at the Brabourne Stadium. The CCI, then headed by the great Vijay Merchant, refused. In response the BCA's President, S. K. Wankhede, used his position as a minister in the Congress-run State Government to obtain a piece of land to build a new cricket stadium. At the ceremony where the foundation stone was laid, Vijay Merchant whispered to a friend: 'That is how far they will get. No stadium will come up here.' He grievously underestimated the force of Marathi pride, its ability to raise money from an emerging Marathi-speaking bourgeoisie and through soft loans from its very own Government of Maharashtra. The Wankhede Stadium was commissioned in January 1975, making the Brabourne Stadium into a modern monument, of interest only to cricket historians.[65]

The leading Marathi-speaking cricketers of independent India have been middle-class but high-caste. There has been the rare proletarian, such as the factory worker's son Vasant Ranjane, and Eknath Solkar, whose father was the groundsman at the PJ Hindu Gymkhana.

One player is rumoured to have been a Dalit, but apart from him all Test cricketers from Bombay and its neighbourhood have been of upper- or middle-caste origin. Why is this so? How was it that the great family of Chamaar cricketers did not inspire others to follow?

Before we answer that question we must record the deaths of the two pre-eminent Palwankars. When Baloo died in July 1955 the giants of the cricket world paid homage to him. Vizzy referred to the bowler as 'the all-time great player of the country'.[66] In a moving essay, A. F. S. Talyarkhan offered his own boyhood memories of watching Baloo bowl:

> The gloss is off the ball and the skipper throws it to a flannel-clad player, a quiet, unassuming sort of chap, looking the least deadly of all on the field. But a ripple of cheering would burst forth because that was the signal for things to happen. One can see Baloo even now, that short, easy run, that very facile delivery as the left arm came over, always the unbuttoned cuff of his flannel shirt dangling at the wrist, always the batsman dangling in his mind where to play the ball and when. . . .
>
> I can see him jogging in to bowl, behind his arm the picture that was a packed Bombay Gymkhana, the grass ever so green.
>
> I can see that dangling shirt cuff, that blue cap, the follow-through and that little thrust of the head, as if the brain had also followed through, in between the pads and the bat, to lift the leg-side bail.

His cricket was exemplary, and so was his character. 'P. Baloo is dead', said Talyarkhan,

> but we who have memory remember his work, his personality and his presence.
>
> These cricketers, chaps, were the truly great Indians, giants who learned the game without coaches and trainers and camps, who had a look at the Britisher and did likewise, only better.

Don't forget that an Indian bowler went to England in those mighty days of 1911 and took one hundred wickets.

And in those so-called pioneering days, India had produced cricketers who were gentlemen, who took no part in politics of the game, whose sole business it was to give of their best . . .[67]

Vijay Merchant, speaking at the Santa Cruz crematorium, suggested that 'it would be a long time before India could produce another great bowler like Baloo'. Baloo 'belonged to a generation of cricketers who played the game in the golden age when the ball was hit as it was meant to be hit and the bowlers treated the ball as a weapon of attack'. In that age, said Merchant, 'bowlers did not waste their efforts by bowling negatively'.[68]

Both Merchant and Talyarkhan spoke of Baloo as an early nationalist hero and a gentleman of the golden age, who embodied the true spirit of the game. Neither, notably, mentioned his caste, because in the India of the 1950s it was not the polite thing to do. Another report was a little less coy. Baloo, wrote the anonymous obituarist in *Indian* Cricket,

> was born poor and he was a Harijan. But, fortunately, Baloo was spotted by [J. G.] Greig and proclaimed to the world as a bowler of great possibilities. That itself would not have been enough had not the Hindus accepted him into their fold and made him play with them. In the beginning of the century, a Harijan boy mixing with caste Hindus was a thing unheard of. It was almost a miracle, and yet it was proof of the catholicism of caste Hindus.[69]

The tone of self-congratulation is marked, and to be deplored. Here the struggles and the protests were forgotten, and the caste Hindus made to look so very good. Thus is history written by the winners. Just as later versions portrayed Lord Harris as the 'builder of Indian cricket', so the caste Hindus now became the generous-spirited patrons who accepted and encouraged Baloo.

Some others must have seen it differently. For the newspaper

reports of Baloo's death also mention that 'a few Harijan members of
Parliament and of the Bombay Assembly' were in the big crowd that
gathered at the crematorium to pay their last respects. These politicians understood that the achievements of Baloo and the dignity
with which he carried himself had a general meaning for all Indians,
but a special charge for those, like themselves, who had the ill-luck
to be born on the wrong side of the tracks.

P. Vithal died in November 1971. The *Times of India* recalled
how 'in Vithal's heyday the Princes ruled the game, but Vithal was
equal to them when it came to anything on the field'. It reported
that he was a fixture at the PJ Hindu Gymkhana 'till the other day',
reminiscing of matches and players of his own era. 'His immaculate
approach and attire', commented the paper, 'were a reproach to the
slovenly players of our time.' This time, in a private remembrance,
Vijay Merchant made reference to his caste. After Vithal's playing
days were over, Merchant had employed him in the textile mill his
family owned. This was characteristic. Where he could, Merchant
would find jobs for talented cricketers from poor families; or, if they
died early, raise money for their families. (Among those he helped
in this way were the Test cricketers Amar Singh, S. G. Shinde and
D. D. Hindlekar.)

When, after Vithal's death, his son wrote to thank him, Merchant
graciously wrote back that 'all that we did for your good father, the
late Mr P. Vithal, was out of tremendous respect for him, both as a
cricketer and as a man. Very few of his generation, with the handicap
that he suffered from, would have risen to such heights but for great
determination and outstanding talent.'[70]

Another handsome tribute was offered by D. B. Deodhar. Now,
Deodhar and Vithal had found themselves on opposite sides in 1920,
when the Brahmin was appointed captain and the Harijan went on
strike. But the breach was quickly healed, with Deodhar playing
under Vithal from 1923 to 1926, and being selected by Vithal as
captain of the Hindus in 1936. In their old age, the two men were
brought together once more by the Poona broadcaster Bal J. Pandit.
In 1960 Pandit began an annual P. Vithal Coaching Class for young

cricketers. Vithal came down from Bombay to inaugurate it, playing some ritual balls bowled to him by Deodhar.[71] They stayed in touch until Vithal's death in 1971. A decade later, on his own ninetieth birthday, Deodhar movingly remembered his old friend and colleague:

> The special feature of P. Vithal's batting was his cover-drives, and strokes to square and long leg. He was an aggressive player, who used his feet to drive. He always scored speedily. . . . Because of his aggressive game the Quadrangular matches were thrilling and spectacular. As a leader he was friendly with all the players and never lost his temper. If he would have been born some fifty years later, all the modern amenities and facilities would have been available to him, and he would have acquired even more distinction.[72]

True enough. Is it only the partisan in me that prompts the comment that Baloo and Vithal were, as sportsmen and social symbols, as remarkable as Jackie Robinson? And yet how different has been their fate. There are statues of Robinson in Los Angeles, in Daytona Beach and in Montreal. There is a Jackie Robinson Parkway that links the boroughs of New York. And new biographies of Robinson are published every other year.

On the fiftieth anniversary of Robinson's first match in the major leagues, President Bill Clinton led a commemoration at the Shea Stadium in New York. 'We look at this as both a celebration, a ceremony and an opportunity,' remarked one of the organizers. They hoped 'to educate people about the man, as to what he was, what he accomplished and what he meant to our game and to our nation'. Mr Clinton, who insisted on attending despite recent knee surgery, thought it 'hard to believe that it was fifty years ago that a twenty-eight-year-old rookie changed the face of baseball and the face of America forever. Jackie Robinson scored the go-ahead run that day; we've all been trying to catch up ever since.' 'If Jackie Robinson were here today,' the President continued, 'he would say we have done a lot of good in the last fifty years, but we could do a lot better.'[73]

The ceremony was beamed live to a large television audience. In the days preceding it the newspapers were chock-full of exhortative pieces about the links, potential and desirable, between sports, civil rights and the American Dream. Once, Jackie Robinson was a hero to blacks; now, he is a hero to all Americans. He has been dead many years, but, as Jules Tygel notes, Robinson is now 'even more of a national icon, more firmly embedded in American culture than ever before'.[74]

The Palwankars, by contrast, are unknown to the Dalit politicians of today, unknown even to cricket historians. The birth centenaries of Baloo and Vithal both passed by unnoticed. Is this because they played before India became an official Test-playing nation? Or because Baloo fell out with the acknowledged giant of the Dalit renaissance, Dr B. R. Ambedkar? Or should we simply pin the blame on that always available scapegoat, the lack of interest in history among Indians?

Some stories told me by Vithal's son poignantly represent how later generations have treated the Palwankars. Sometime in the 1950s the campaigning editor P. K. Atre resolved to write a biography of the brothers. He took Vithal's sheaf of cuttings for this, but the album perished in a conflagration that engulfed the building where Atre's paper was printed and published. Likewise, the bat with which Vithal scored his remarkable hundred in the 1923 Quadrangular final was for many years displayed, with a silver plaque embossed on it, in the pavilion of the PJ Hindu Gymkhana, but in the 1970s this building too was destroyed in a fire. These two fires seem to symbolize how the story of the Palwankars has been lost to history.

Admittedly, the fate of Vithal and Baloo is not unexceptional. For there is nothing so transient as an Indian sporting hero. After C. K. Nayudu died, the Bombay Cricket Association organized a match in his memory. The players were India's best, but the takings at the gate were ridiculously low: 35,000 rupees in all, 10,000 rupees net of expenses. The *Free Press Journal* headline said it all: 'Memories Don't Click Turnstiles'. The city of Bombay had been 'privileged to have seen some of C. K.'s greatest innings', said the paper, 'but what has the local fan, the most diehard in the country, given in return . . .?

Nothing at all.' A. F. S. Talyarkhan thought this to be a product of a general amnesia: 'in a country where names like Patel and Nehru are almost forgotten today, it is probable that the name of a C. K. Nayudu means nothing'. He added: 'I pray the spirit of the great cricketer was not hovering over the empty Brabourne Stadium last week.'[75]

Still, we must ponder the apparent failure of the Palwankars to serve as role models, to encourage other low-caste cricketers to play the game at the highest level. This, again, is in distinct contrast to America, where the achievements of Jackie Robinson, Jesse Owens and Joe Louis have prompted a whole host of successful imitators. For the black boy in the inner city, and increasingly for the black girl as well, sport has become a spectacular vehicle of social mobility, so spectacular indeed that shortly before his death Arthur Ashe – himself a model to many younger tennis players – was constrained to offer this caution: 'The worry of black kids wanting to escape poverty or intolerance through sport is counter-productive. They need to aspire to be mechanics, doctors, lawyers too, because you cannot have equality just in the sporting world.'[76]

In India, the professions identified by Arthur Ashe have attracted Dalit children of determination and talent. These have preferred to be lawyers, doctors, bureaucrats or professors rather than sportsmen. As head of a large household, Baloo himself commanded his sons and nephews to 'Study, study, study'. Of his nine sons (by two marriages), two became professional cricketers, but among the others one was a lawyer, a second an architect, a third a personnel manager, a fourth a public relations officer. One of Baloo's granddaughters has an MA in German, while a grandson took a PhD in International Relations from the University of Geneva. Vithal's sons worked in clerical jobs, but one grandson is an architect based in Italy, another an engineer trained at the prestigious Indian Institute of Technology. There has been a tremendous social mobility in the second and third generation, made possible, of course, by the cricketing successes of the first.[77]

Notably, the sons of Baloo who became professional cricketers learned the game on the sly. One, Y. B. Palwankar, was a left-handed batsman and a marvellous fieldsman, who came very close to playing for India. He was a reserve for the Hindus in the last Pentangular. He appeared for Bombay in a Ranji Trophy final, scoring a strokeful 75 as his side won. He also captained Combined Universities against the West Indians. He scored a fifty, but his father was not watching; it was C. K. Nayudu who went over to Baloo's home to tell him his son had batted well. Afterwards, Y. B. Palwankar played as a professional in the Lancashire Leagues. When he finally retired, he wrote a poem entitled 'My Beloved Cricket'. The poem is, on the whole, undistinguished, but one verse does nicely capture the collective biography of the cricketing family Palwankar:

> Dost thou not humble the famed
> And bring the humble fame
> By thine own predilection?
> The leveller of all distinction.[78]

15. Sibling Rivalry

A SELECT CRICKET LIST features a dozen players who have represented more than one country in Test matches. Most of these dual-nationals played in the nineteenth century, and were white. There are the professionals, such as J. J. Ferris and Albert Trott, who represented Australia before becoming county cricketers in England and playing for the country of their adoption. There are the colonial adventurers, such as Frank Hearne and Frank Mitchell, who lived alternately in England and South Africa, playing for both. And there are the modern opportunists, such as Kepler Wessels, who migrated to Australia when South Africa was debarred from Test cricket but returned to the Veld in time to captain the first post-apartheid Test team, and John Traicos, who played for South Africa just before it was banned and for his native Zimbabwe after it was granted Test status.

The three Indians on this list all became Pakistanis after 1947. Two came to this country on Pakistan's first overseas cricket tour, in October–December 1952. These were Amir Elahi, the portly googly bowler, once a favourite with the Pentangular crowds, and the captain, Abdul Hafeez Kardar. Kardar was a cricketer-scholar, a man of personality and intelligence who almost single-handedly made Pakistan a Test-playing nation. Born into an upper-middle-class home in Lahore, Kardar played for the Muslims in the Pentangular, and then for All India in England in 1946. After Partition he took a degree in Philosophy, Politics and Economics at Oxford, also earning a cricket Blue. As a literary-minded journalist once wrote, 'if Plato were to be imagined as a cricketer, a wild fancy, he would perhaps comport himself much like this late scholar of Oxford'. When Kardar walked to the top of his bowling run, remarked this writer, he 'appears to be cogitating problems of foreknowledge, will and fate'.[1]

Kardar had a deep commitment to the idea of Pakistan, and a robust pride in the Muslim contribution to the sub-continent's history. He could also turn a decent phrase: every word in the books that appeared under his name was written by himself. Like that other Oxonian, Douglas Jardine, he commanded the absolute loyalty of his players. But Kardar was a nationalist in a way that the Scot was not. Jardine wished to win for himself and, at one remove, for his team. The Pakistani had a more elevated view of his responsibilities. Cricket was for him a means of consolidating the unity and identity of his new and vulnerable nation. From his sporting career one could have foretold that he would become a senior state official and a minister in the government of Pakistan's most powerful province, the Punjab.[2]

In October 1952 India and Pakistan had been neighbours for five years. Their quarrels had begun early. In 1947–8 they fought their first war over Kashmir. That state was claimed by Pakistan by virtue of its majority Muslim population, but its Hindu Maharaja had acceded to India. Especially in the Punjab, the violence before and after Partition had been horrific. The state was divided with each portion ethnically cleansed. In East Punjab, Muslims were killed or had fled, with Hindus and Sikhs meeting the same fate on the other side of the border. The minorities that remained – Muslims in northern India and Hindus in Sind and East Bengal – felt insecure. The nationalists in either country were suspicious of the other. Hindu chauvinists could not easily forgive the Muslim League for breaking up the motherland. Pakistanis were nervous of India's size and its greater economic and military strength.

For all this, there was much that united the two countries. Their respective national languages, Hindi and Urdu, had an extensive common vocabulary and were mutually comprehensible. The people on both sides wore the same clothes, ate the same kind of food, and sang the same songs. And Indians and Pakistanis alike were devoted to the game of cricket.

❁

THE PAKISTAN TEAM to tour India was announced on 20 September 1952. In a report on its last page, the *Dawn* newspaper, once Jinnah's own, wished the team success. It hoped 'they will do their best and leave a good impression wherever they play. They are ambassadors of goodwill and as such great are their responsibilities.' These sentiments were somewhat contradicted by the paper's front page. 'BHARAT AUGMENTS HER ARMY IN OCUPIED KASHMIR', read one headline. 'EUROPEAN PEOPLE FAVOUR PAKISTAN IN KASHMIR CASE', read another.[3]

On the day the cricketers left for India, the Government-owned *Pakistan Times* reminded them that the game was not the only thing. 'Pakistan expects her cricketers', it gravely announced, 'to play the game as it should be played, in a spirit of friendly competition, without rancour and without ill-will . . . We hope . . . that on the cricket field will be forged new friendly ties that will help to bring two estranged neighbours closer together.'[4]

This message was echoed from the Indian side when the tourists played their first match, against North Zone at Amritsar. They had crossed over by road, the captain travelling in a car with the Pakistani Deputy High Commissioner while his team followed by bus. At a reception for the visitors the Chairman of the Amritsar Municipality spoke of 'the sense of fairplay and sportsmanship that transcended all barriers and helped to strengthen friendship between countries'. Indeed, the 'extension of the spirit of comradeship on the ground to other fields as well would immensely help solve many outstanding issues between the two countries'.[5] Kardar, in his reply, said his team had brought with them 'a message of peace, commerce and honest friendship from their people'.[6] In a touching gesture, a Sikh youngster presented the Pakistan captain with a copy of the Holy Quran, left behind in Amritsar by a Muslim family.[7]

Cricket might bring India and Pakistan together, but politics kept them apart. The day the tourists arrived in Delhi, the Muslim League announced, in Karachi, the launching of an 'all-out struggle for the liberation of Occupied Kashmir'. As ever, *Dawn* carried the report on its front page. On the back page it reported the visits of Kardar's men to the *samadhi* of Mahatma Gandhi and the tomb of the medieval saint Nizamuddin Auliya: two spokesmen for communal harmony, one Hindu, the other Muslim.[8] Later, the Pakistan captain had a pleasant reunion with the old Lahore cricketer H. D. Khanna. Khanna had been forced to abandon his native city. It was, remarked Kardar feelingly, 'a great relief to find him well-established in his advertising business'.[9]

There were cricketers in India who had fled Pakistan, and cricketers playing now for Pakistan who were refugees from India. In Kardar's team were the Mohammed brothers, Wazir and Hanif, who came originally from the state of Junagadh, in Saurashtra. It was by the light of street lamps in Junagadh that they learned to play cricket. After Partition they moved with their family to Karachi. Wazir was a good bat, Hanif even better. He was barely seventeen years old, a schoolboy who stood 5 feet 3 inches in his socks. His team-mates affectionately called him 'Dilip', after the Bombay film star Dilip Kumar. But he was becoming a hero to many Indians as well. At Amritsar Hanif had scored a century in each innings, the youngest cricketer to accomplish this feat.[10]

Delhi was the venue of the first Test. The match was inaugurated by the President of India, Rajendra Prasad, a taciturn Bihari who back in 1944 had written a polemic against the idea of Pakistan. In his diary, Prasad noted that the visitors included as many as four schoolboys. He remarked upon Hanif's two centuries at Amritsar, wondered how many runs he would get in Delhi, and marvelled at his keeping wickets in addition to being a main batsman. Prasad was sufficiently keen on the visiting cricketers to invite them over to his palace for tea.[11] Joining him in admiration was the Prime Minister, Jawaharlal Nehru. He was introduced to the Pakistani players and 'had a word of praise and encouragement for the schoolboy cricketer Hanif'.[12]

The interest in the first Test was enormous. The Ferozeshah Kotla is, by Indian standards, a small ground: it accommodates no more than 25,000 spectators. For the others Delhi Telephones had dedicated four lines; these were the 'most popular and tapped phones' in Delhi.[13] Hanif scored a half-century, but the home side won by an innings. Notably, several of the opponents had played together before Partition: Hazare and Amir Elahi for Baroda; the two opposing captains, Kardar and Lala Amarnath, in Lahore.

The teams moved on to Lucknow for the second Test. Back in Pakistan, Kashmir Day was being observed, with 'popular demonstrations all over' pledging the 'liberation of Kashmir' and condemning the United Nations for 'inaction'.[14] On the field, the cricketers were crafting a historic Test win. It had taken India twenty years to win a Test match, but Pakistan had done so in its very first series. Before the match the history-minded Kardar took a walk around Lucknow's monuments, the Imambara and the Residency. The city, as he well knew, had once been the capital of a famous and flourishing Muslim kingdom. After his side had won by an innings, he went out

> for a last look at the Monkey Bridge and the cricket ground lying beyond it, where Pakistan had gained her first Test victory in her inaugural Test matches. The empty stands which envelop the ground and the resting place of Sarojini Naidu, the great Indian social worker, could not hide the slow-moving waters of the Gomti river, on whose banks Pakistan's cricketers had managed to lower India's colours within six months of our Cricket Board's recognition by the Imperial Cricket Conference.[15]

The Lucknow Test attracted a great deal of attention in Pakistan. All India Radio's commentaries were listened to in places big and small, 'be it in the house of the minister or in the paan shop'. Blackboards were put up outside offices and shops, where the scores were updated every over. For four days, wrote one Karachi journalist, 'everything was forgotten. No one talked about the political condition in the country, no one discussed about East–West Cold War. Not even the Hollywood pictures were talked about. No, there was just one thing to talk about – the Lucknow Test . . .' The Pakistani cricketers had chosen the venue for their first win well: 'that historic city of Lucknow, which for hundreds of years has been a cradle of [Muslim] civilisation and culture'.[16]

From Lucknow the tourists took a train across the heart of India, to Nagpur, where they were to play a Central Zone side led by the fifty-seven-year-old C. K. Nayudu. The 'monotony of thirty-six hours' in the train, remembered Kardar, was 'broken by the hearty welcome we were accorded by the Indian cricket fans at almost all our halts. These fans would knock at our doors in the middle of the night requesting us for autographs, asking for Hanif, his age, wanting to get as near as possible to see Fazal Mahmood and Nazar Mohammed, the heroes of the Lucknow Test match.'[17]

However, there were a few Indians who did not want the Pakistanis in Nagpur. The city was a hotbed of Hindi revivalism, the headquarters of the chauvinist Rashtriya Swayamsevak Sangh and a centre also of the Hindu Mahasabha, a political party still committed to the idea of Akhand Bharat, or United India, whose Government would scrupulously follow the Hindu scriptures. The Mahasabha's President, Dr N. B. Khare, lived in Nagpur, and thought he would use the cricketers' visit to help revive his fading political career. He announced that his party would picket outside the ground, demanding that the Pakistani cricketers 'go home'. His decision, he said in a press statement, was sparked by the treatment of Hindus in East Pakistan, which had led to thousands seeking refuge in India. 'It is evident', remarked Dr Khare,

> that Pakistan is intent upon ousting her unwanted population by the method of intimidation which includes outrages on womanhood. It is deplorable that at this identical period India has invited [the] Pakistan cricket team here. This action of

India may be regarded by some as replete with a noble sporting spirit. But I regard this action as an ignoble one devoid of any sense of honour and self-respect and an index of the depth of our moral and national degradation. My meaning will be clear if I recall to memory the action by the British a few years ago when a woman named Miss Ellis was kidnapped by the transborder Pathans.[18]

This last reference suggests that Dr Khare wanted the Indian Government to send its troops into Pakistan rather than allow their sportsmen in. Other patriots viewed Kardar's men very differently. A public reception was organized in honour of the cricketers, hosted by the Governor, Dr Pattabhi Sitaramayya, a veteran Congressman who had also written the official history of his party. The Governor spoke in emotional terms of the common culture and heritage of the two peoples. 'We are glad to see our old brothers in our own country,' he remarked. The presumed separation or separateness of India and Pakistan was 'an artificial feeling, nurtured by certain quarters, which must be completely wiped out'. Dr Sitaramayya could not himself understand this feeling, 'because no new physical barriers such as rivers or mountains had been created between India and Pakistan'.[19]

On the morning of the match the Hindu Mahasabha President was arrested under the Preventive Detention Act and taken to Nagpur Central Jail. ('Khare "bowled out",' crowed *Dawn*, justifiably.[20]) Any effect that Khare's protest might have had was neutralized by a stirring letter printed in the city's leading English-language paper, *Hitavada*. It was sent by M. D. Tumpaliwar, Secretary of the Nagpur Pradesh Congress Committee, and it read:

Sir – 'Boycott of Pak team' is the slogan visible on the roads of Nagpur since the last two or three days. This propaganda is popped up definitely by blind fanaticism. It is a systematic attempt to exploit and misguide the religious feelings of the people. When necessary, we shall not prove short of fighting with Pakistan on the battlefield. But it is certainly detrimental to the interest of the nation to disturb peaceful civic life evoking hatred of Pakistan day in and day out and cause deviation from reconstruction work.

Today's world is marching towards unity. Schemes of World Government are being deliberated upon. Political enmity existing between one country and the other should not be allowed to dabble in other fields.

I am confident people will not be misled by such communal propaganda asking for boycott of Pak team. Sportive spirit should alone be allowed to prevail in the field of sports.[21]

On their way to the match the Pakistanis did see a group of Mahasabhaites shouting offensive slogans: 'Death to Pakistan' and 'Pakistan team go back home'. But there was no trouble at the ground itself: on the contrary, every stroke in the Pakistani innings of 356 was applauded vigorously. As Kardar wrote, the departure was in marked contrast to their arrival: 'When we left the ground that evening to the cheering of hundreds of people I felt the inner urge of humanity for peace and cooperation.'[22]

The show moved on to Bombay, where the third Test was to be played. A number of elite Pakistanis descended on the city: Army men, civil servants and businessmen, taking the boat down the coast from Karachi as they were wont to do in pre-Partition days. The Bombay crowd cheered the visiting cricketers, especially Hanif and their old friend from the Pentangular, Amir Elahi. Kardar had dinner with his own old friend from those days, the Parsi batsman Rusi Modi.

From Bombay the visitors moved down the Deccan to the city of Hyderabad, until a few years previously the capital of the Mughal vassal state of the Nizams. The Pakistan captain, characteristically, would search for history's residues. The team played their match at the Fateh Maidan where, recalled Kardar, 'Aurangzeb Alamgir, the last of the great Moghuls, had encamped while his forces were fighting at Golcunda. To the North of the Maidan are the hills where the announcement of the Moghul victory was made by beating the drums.' Afterwards the captain visited the Salar Jung Museum to view its collection of arms and paintings, its wine-cup of the Emperor Jehangir, its sword of Tipu Sultan, the three rooms it had reserved for clocks and the two rooms it had kept for china. 'This is civilization,' he exclaimed,

> This is culture! And to perpetuate this, it seems, we must have a leisurely class, with the gift of taste and the resources to patronize and sponsor arts and artists. As we came out of the Museum into the world of mechanics and economists, we talked for hours about the Museum. It is certainly a wonder of the world![23]

Abdul Hafeez Kardar was perhaps the greatest cricketer-ideologue born outside the West. In his view Muslim rule had brought civilization to backward India. In Hyderabad and Lucknow he sought out sources of Pakistan's glorious past (no temples or churches were on his itinerary). In the battle field of Aurangzeb or the artefacts of Jehangir he saw confirmation of his country's role as the contemporary carrier of Muslim civilization in the sub-continent. Kardar took cricket far more seriously than did other cricketers. Good conduct and good performance were a means to an end, namely, the dignity of the Islamic Republic of Pakistan.

The Pakistanis had lost in Bombay, and hoped to level the rubber in Madras. They were well placed in this fourth Test, but then the rain came. An expectant crowd waited, and clapped and cheered whenever the groundsmen and the umpires walked out for an inspection. Eventually the match was called off. The rains had come after a prolonged drought, and were much welcomed by farmers. At a reception for the cricketers the Chief Minister of Madras, C. Rajagopalachari, mischievously remarked 'that if such fixtures could bring rain, he would like to organize them every year'. The Pakistani captain, understandably disappointed, replied that 'he was happy that the rains came, because this was required for a larger and much greater cause, but he regretted that the organizers of the match had been deprived of funds, which would have been used for the coaching of young cricketers'. He was too polite to add that the rain had also deprived his team of the chance of a win.[24]

The last Test was to be played in Calcutta, capital of undivided Bengal, and now home to thousands of refugees from across the border. Two weeks before the match the local unit of the Hindu Mahasabha began distributing handbills asking the public to boycott it. They praised their President, Dr N. B. Khare, for 'the noble sentiment and courage of conviction with which he tried to dissuade the Hindu-minded citizens of Nagpur from attending the match there'. Khare's Bengali followers would picket the Calcutta Test, but unlike their President, they took care not to offend the cricketers themselves. They realized

> that although sports have ordinarily nothing to do with politics and they have nothing to say against the conduct of the Pakistani players individually taken, they resolved that they would completely disassociate themselves from the said match as a mark of protest against the barbarous and squeeze-out policy of the Pakistan Government and as a mark of respect for the honour of the women of the minority Hindus of East Pakistan.[25]

The Mahasabha had as little success in Calcutta as in Nagpur. When the Pakistani team flew into Dum Dum, 'an unexpectedly big crowd drawn mostly from the student community thronged the airport'. The enthusiasm of the fans 'proved that the interest for the game was no less than football', otherwise the city's favourite sport.[26]

The evening before the Test began the Mohammedan Sporting Club hosted a reception for the visitors. The club had lost some of its clientele when the country was divided, but it still had plenty of patrons, the Muslims who had voted with their feet to stay in India. Welcoming the Pakistan team, the President, G. A. Dossani, hoped that 'the day is not far off when through sports the relations between the two parts of the great country, once called India, will be as friendly and united in one voice as we find now during your welcome visit to our Dominion'. Like Sitaramayya in Nagpur, Dossani looked nostalgically back to the days of an undivided India. In his reply, Kardar quietly insisted on the irrevocability of Pakistan, saying that 'through sports *separate* countries came close. He wished that India should pay a return visit to Pakistan before long to perform the [same] mission.'[27]

On the first day of the match a dozen Hindu Mahasabha volunteers assembled at the entrance to Eden Gardens, shouting 'Pakistan players go back' and 'Do not forget Pakistan is anti-India'. They were met with a splendid indifference. 'When the demonstration was going on', commented a reporter on the spot, 'thousands of spectators entered the field without taking any notice of it.'[28] The stadium was packed to capacity on all five days, the fans watching an absorbing Test which ended in a draw, with India having the upper hand. The hosts had won the series by two Tests to one, a result that pleased India, naturally, but also pleased Pakistan, much the smaller country and a novice in international cricket.

During the Calcutta Test Vinoo Mankad achieved the quickest double century in Test history. The *Amrita Bazar Patrika* brought out an eight-page supplement to honour him, printing articles from such worthies as C. B. Fry, A. E. R. Gilligan, John Arlott, Trevor Bailey and Alec Bedser. There was also a warm appreciation from a team-mate turned adversary. Kardar singled out Mankad's shrewdness as a bowler: 'Once he was my colleague and I have seen him deceiving them all – Compton, Hutton and many others who have made names in cricket. Now I am playing against him, and my opinion has not changed.'[29]

The Indian cricketers were old friends, yet Kardar was generous in his praise for Indian fans as well. At the conclusion of the Madras Test he told a Pakistani newspaper that 'generally the Indian crowds had been sporting and had watched cricket from the point of view of cricket'.[30] In Calcutta a local journalist extracted a more emphatic endorsement still. Kardar had spoken to him mostly of cricketing matters, of his admiration for Amarnath's captaincy, his memories of scoring 37 and 86 not out at Eden Gardens against the Australian Services back in 1945 and his opinion of the younger Indian players.

Then a leading question was asked, and an unguarded answer given. Kardar, reported the journalist, said 'he had not travelled much but wherever he had gone, he could say, there had been no communal feelings'. The whole report was carried under the headline: 'COMMUNAL FEELING NOWHERE IN INDIA: KARDAR'S IMPRESSIONS OF CRICKET TOUR'.[31]

This somewhat misleading headline was prompted perhaps by a spirit of one-upmanship, the sense that India was a secular, pluralist country whereas Pakistan was a theocratic state. There was much to be said for the contrast. The Indian team in the Tests had included a Christian and two Muslims. The Pakistani cricketers had no one representing their own minorities. The crowds everywhere had treated Indian politics' lunatic fringe, the Hindu Mahasabha, with the contempt it deserved. On and off the field the conduct of Indians confirmed that they had effectively separated religion from public life. Now, due to the promptings of a clever journalist, the captain of Pakistan had further confirmed the distance between his country and ours.

In his memoirs, written more than thirty years afterwards, Kardar took care to reject any such interpretation. During this Indian tour, he recalled, he had a conversation with Maulana Abul Kalam Azad at a reception hosted by the High Commissioner of Pakistan. Azad was then the Minister of Education in the Government of India: representing, as he had always done, the ideal of a 'composite culture' based on the unity of interests and aspirations between Hindus and Muslims. The conversation is not recorded in the newspapers of the time or – more notably – in the account of the tour that Kardar wrote immediately afterwards. But in 1987 Kardar claimed that when he met Azad

> he cheekily asked about the future of Muslims in India. [Azad] replied that Congress was committed to safeguard the minorities and since Muslims were a very large and important minority their interests were well protected. To his surprise, which received no response, I said to him, 'I believe that the

political future of Muslims in India lies in joining hands with progressive parties like the Socialist Party because Congress with its bigoted Hindu leadership will never protect their interests.' This observation came true when the Muslims supported the Communist Party in Kerala and thereby defeated the ruling Congress Party.[32]

Although in the odd provincial election they might have voted otherwise, through the 1950s and 1960s the Muslims of India were reckoned to be an assured 'vote bank' for the Congress. The conversation between Kardar and Azad, real or imagined, was not however about facts but about perceptions. For if one accepted that the Congress could effectively represent the Muslims there would have been no need for Pakistan in the first place.

IN 1952 THE WOUNDS OF Partition were still raw. The status of Kashmir and the position of Hindus in East Bengal were guaranteed to excite indignation. The talk of a 'shared culture' by Congressmen offended Pakistani patriots seeking to carve out a clear, separate niche in the world of nation-states. Gradually, however, the relations between the two neighbours assumed a measure of stability. Endless meetings of the United Nations Security Council failed to break the deadlock in Kashmir. India remained in control of the southern part of the state, Pakistan in control of the northern part. Each nation claimed the section of Kashmir, but no longer with the same intensity. Other preoccupations supervened. Pakistan was building an entente with the United States. India was leading the Non-Aligned Movement. Both countries were mobilizing resources rapidly to industrialize and remove poverty.

In January 1955 an Indian cricket team began a three-month tour of Pakistan. They played five Tests, the first in Dhaka in East Pakistan, the others in the western half of the country. A. H. Kardar was the home captain, and also a selector. To these duties was added that of a newspaper columnist. While the Indians were in his country, *Dawn* published a column by Kardar each Sunday, every word his own. Welcoming the visitors, the Pakistan captain asked his readers

> to believe me that all rumours concerning the hostility of spec-
> tators during our 1952 Indian tour are mischievous. There is
> not the slightest truth in the reports that the Indian spectators
> 'flashed mirrors at our batsmen', etc. In fact, we were welcomed
> wherever we played and if there was the general expectancy on
> the part of the spectators that the home side should win, it is
> understandable.

The Pakistani players, as much as the fans, were asked to behave with decorum. 'May the better side win', said Kardar, 'and the second best take its defeat with grace.'[33]

After playing a dreary draw in Dhaka the Indians took the long flight to West Pakistan. At Karachi airport thousands of fans awaited them. Some, at least, had come to welcome not the players but their manager, the legendary Lala Amarnath. The Indians dumped their bags in the hotel and fulfilled their diplomatic duties by visiting the mausoleum of Pakistan's founder, Muhammad Ali Jinnah.

It was Jinnah's politics that had led to an ethnic cleansing of the Punjab in 1947. In Karachi and Sind, however, there remained a fair sprinkling of Hindus, active in trade and commerce, but still not entirely secure in this professedly Islamic Republic. A Karachi Hindu wrote to *Dawn* putting the best possible interpretation on the cricket visit:

> Sir – the Indian Cricket Team is in our midst and each player
> is an ambassador of the country he comes from. I find a changed
> feeling for the better between India and Pakistan now which is
> indeed very good and will be helpful for both the countries.
> I think it is our duty to do our best to create the maximum
> amount of goodwill and friendship among the Indian players.
> This point is bound to have an echo in India.
>
> Yours, etc.
> P. R. F. Khilnani[34]

The cricketers moved on to Bahwalpur, the venue of the second Test. The Indians were billeted in one small house, four and five players to a room. When their captain, Vinoo Mankad, was asked what his eleven for the match would be, he answered: 'Let us first find a place to sit and select the team.'[35]

The better guest-houses in Bahwalpur were reserved for the entourage of the Prime Minister, Muhammad Ali. He was here in more than one 'official' capacity, for he also served as the President of the Board of Control for Cricket in Pakistan. Another VIP was A. F. S. Talyarkhan, invited by Radio Pakistan to commentate on the Test. The match in Bahwalpur was dominated by Hanif Mohammed's first Test century, an innings which invited gifts of money and carpets and much else besides.

In the last week of January the Governor-General of Pakistan visited India. He was received at Palam airport by Jawaharlal Nehru, and whisked off to the annual Republic Day parade. Here he sat next to the Indian President, Rajendra Prasad, while Prasad took the salute at the marchpast, with Hurricane fighter jets of the Indian Air Force thundering overhead. On his return to Karachi the Governor-General spoke of being treated with 'the greatest hospitality and consideration' in India. There was, he said, now a 'better hope than ever' of the settlement of disputes with Bharat.[36]

Meanwhile, the cricket show moved on to Lahore. The Muslims who lived here saw it as *their* city, the home of exquisite tombs and mosques built by the Mughal Emperors Jehangir and Aurangzeb. But the Sikhs were proprietorial about Lahore, too, for it was once the capital of a kingdom ruled by their man, Ranjit Singh. Before 1947, the Hindus were also present in bulk, dominating the city's markets and schools. Through the nineteenth century Lahore was the main centre of the great movement of Hindu social reform, the Arya Samaj.

After 1947 a vibrant, polyglot city became monocultural. Half a dozen Hindu families were all that remained. The rest had converted to Islam or simply fled. The only Sikhs now in Lahore were the guardians of Ranjit Singh's mausoleum, which lies in a *gurdwara* just outside the ramparts of the Fort. This was now an exclusively Muslim city, but the hosting of a Test match against India allowed it to recapture – if fleetingly – its more appealing past.

One man who had greatly looked forward to the Lahore Test was the writer Saadat Hasan Manto, whose stories about Partition have been widely and justly anthologized. Himself a former citizen of Bombay, Manto was listening to Talyarkhan's commentaries on the Bahwalpur Test, when he had a sudden seizure and died. He had told his friends, in what was almost his last conversation, that he wanted to see the Test match at Lahore.[37]

There are many reasons to regret Manto's death. One is that we shall never know what this prophet of inter-communal amity might have written about the 10,000 Indians who came across the border for the Test. For this match the usual visa restrictions had been waived. The Wagah check-post, usually so impenetrable from either side, was left open for the buses and trains which carried the visitors. Since Lahore was so close to the border, the Indian fans came every day from Amritsar. They returned home by nightfall; even so, this was certainly 'the biggest mass migration across the frontier since Partition'.[38]

The influx of Indians was reported by the Associated Press of Pakistan under the heading 'Friends Cried'. This was the scene outside the ground on the morning of the match:

> Ladies, Sikhs, Hindus and the local population waited patiently and decently for their turn in the serpentine queue lines running two to three furlongs in length sometimes even more.
>
> The city itself was in a gay holiday mood. The early morning bustle was reminscent of the Shalimar Mela, excepting that the composition of the crowd was of a higher order.
>
> Visitors from India, including a large number of ladies, sauntered undaunted on the roads and in the streets of Lahore, reminding one of the pre-Partition days and speaking eloquently of the state of orderliness that now prevails in the Punjab.
>
> Sikhs were particularly conspicuous and were the centre of attraction wherever they went. They were recipients of unsoli-

cited greetings and unexpected welcome. Some of them even cried when they embraced their old friends in the city.[39]

The reference to the crowd being of a 'higher' order is intriguing. Higher in what sense? Socially, economically or ethically? It seems that the Indian tourists stoked a warm nostalgia for the days of the undivided Punjab. *Tongawallahs* in Lahore gave free rides to the visitors; hotels offered free lunches and teas. Some money must have changed hands, for a sharp rise in the black-market rate of the Pakistani rupee was reported. Normally pegged at 100 for 70 Indian rupees, the rate during the Test was the reverse: 70 Pakistani for 100 Indian. Still, the camaraderie was altogether genuine. A journalist from Madras remarked that 'great fraternization among the Pakistanis and the Indians was witnessed everywhere during the Test match days'.[40]

The interested reporters followed the Indians back to the border. The visitors took tangerines and rock salt – items scarce in their own country – home with them, but said that 'by far the most precious thing we are carrying is the goodwill of [the people of] Pakistan'. Spot interviews by a Lahore journalist revealed a distinct 'change in their mental outlook'. A young Sikh of a West Punjab family told the reporter: 'I was a fool to imagine all these years that Pakistan is unsafe for non-Muslims. I have been here four days now and wherever I went I have nothing but goodwill and friendship.' A white-haired Hindu who lived in Lahore before Partition said that he felt 'as if I have returned to my old home. Lahore has not changed much. Nobody here asks whether you are a Hindu or a Muslim, or Indian or a Pakistani . . . It is so different from what many fanatics in East Punjab want us to imagine.'[41]

These remarks recall the interview given by A. H. Kardar to a Calcutta journalist before he left India at the end of the 1952 tour. He had then certified that minorities were safe in India; now Indians were returning the compliment, saying pleasing things about Pakistan to a Pakistani reporter. The cricketers confirmed this. On the eve of his departure from Lahore, Lala Amarnath suggested that this particular Test match had 'done a great deal to cement goodwill between the two great countries'. The Indian players, said their manager, had come to the city 'not only for the cricket, but also to renew old friendships'. Amarnath was particularly glad that the President of the Indian Board, the irrepressible Maharajkumar of Vizianagaram, had come for the match along with the Board's Secretary. They could see at first hand 'how sporting the spectators of my home town were'.[42] Vizzy, the captain who had sent Amarnath back home from England in 1936, now agreed with him. He wrote in a newspaper article that during the Lahore Test 'the highest in the Pakistan Government never thought of Kashmir, the evacuee property, the canal waters, the United Nations or the Security Council. It was clean good sport and nothing else.'[43]

No sporting event in living memory had evoked as much interest as this third Test. The ladies of Lahore had their hair waved and permed beforehand, and wore their 'choicest and fanciest dresses' to the match. Indeed, the entire city was 'crazy about cricket all these four days. Work in all offices – commercial and government – was slack. Almost the whole of Lahore – minus [those] who were lucky to go to the stadium – listened to the radio from 10 a.m. to 5 p.m. every day, while boys played cricket on the fields, in courtyards and in gardens – all in a gay holiday mood.'[44]

The Pakistan Governor-General had been warmly received in Delhi, and 10,000 ordinary Indians were made to feel at home in Lahore. However, in the last weeks of the cricket tour the goodwill on the field was set against the revival, off it, of the Kashmir dispute. The Pakistan Prime Minister, speaking in London, said that 'it must be a matter of the utmost concern to the conscience of the free world that after seven long years the four million inhabitants of Kashmir should still [be] denied the right of self-determination'. A Cabinet Minister, addressing a refugee settlement in West Punjab, insisted that 'the state of Jammu and Kashmir was destined ultimately to accede to Pakistan'.[45]

After Lahore the cricketers played their fourth successive draw, in Peshawar. The final Test was to be played in Karachi, in a wonderful new stadium built outside the city, on a patch of levelled ground surrounded by hills. This stadium, evidently Karachi and Pakistan's answer to Bombay's Brabourne, had cost 15 million rupees. It was built at breakneck speed, four months from start to finish, with 5,000 workers working round the clock in eight-hour shifts. To mark its inauguration, *Dawn* issued a ten-page cricket supplement, with contributions by the stadium's chief engineer sitting alongside essays on the game itself. Cricket, one contributor wrote, had become the national game of Pakistan: 'A Kardar and a Fazal now means to an average Pakistani more than a Clark Gable or Ashok Kumar.' The new premises were named the National Stadium, and in keeping with the spirit of the occasion a long essay was written on 'Aligarh University and Muslim Contribution to Cricket'. This traced the history of Muslim teams from the late nineteenth century, showing how 'cricket in the sub-continent owes a lot to Muslim initiative and enterprise and in particular to the glorious contributions of Aligarh'. Whether through ignorance or oversight – or worse – the author forgot to say that the first promoter of cricket in Aligarh was a Hindu, Pandit Rama Shankar Misra.[46]

For the Test itself the Stadium was packed, 50,000 people inside the ground and another 5,000 to 10,000 on the promontories overlooking it. *Dawn* counted 3,000 cars and 4,000 bicycles parked outside. Cricket in both India and Pakistan was an all-class game, but some classes were evidently more equal than others. One viewer complained that a few select stands had all the facilities: *shamianas* and carpets and flower-pots and bottled drinks on ice. The cheaper galleries had none of these, no protection even from the overhead sun. 'It is really a disgraceful attitude on the part of the authorities concerned', wrote A. F. Shaikh, 'that the poor man who will be forgoing a week's ration or the pleasure of replacing his torn shirt, in order to witness this Test match, should receive such nonchalant treatment.'[47]

In the end, rich and poor alike had reason to be disgusted with the cricket. The Karachi Test was also drawn. Abdul Kardar was determined not to lose at home. Vinoo Mankad was loath to take risks in his first series as captain. The bowlers of both sides bowled to stop runs rather than to take wickets. As an Indian critic wrote, 'the defensive approach to the game by both Mankad and Kardar ruined all prospects of reaching a decision, while whatever the justification, it took the life out of each match and reduced the whole series to a mockery'.[48]

Vinoo Mankad's views are unrecorded. But Kardar, in his column, admitted that the crowd were the 'real heroes' of the tour, displaying 'remarkable patience watching dull, lifeless cricket'. To sum up the series this Oxford scholar quoted the works of another. 'Mr [Arnold] Toynbee characterizes history as a challenge and response,' remarked Kardar. 'When the history of the present series is written it will go down as the series without a counter-challenge to the challenge of negative tactics.'[49]

Others were less gloomy, reading a cheering message into the fact that cricket was played at all. At a reception after the final Test, the Mayor of Karachi suggested that while the series featured five draws, the matches 'were a success for humanity'. Vizzy, speaking for the Indian Board, thought that 'where politicians had failed, we [cricketers] succeeded by coming nearer to each other'. He now grandly proposed that the two countries play each other every alternate year, on the England–Australia model. Those countries competed for the Ashes, so Vizzy suggested that India and Pakistan should play for an urn containing the soil of both countries.

It was a suggestion typical of Vizzy, derivative and witless at the same time. In what proportion, one wonders, would he have the soil of either nation? A pound of soil for India and a pound for Pakistan? Or in proportion to their populations? A more creative proposal came from a letter-writer, Syed Khan Bahadur of Rawalpindi. He said that India and Pakistan should play for a 'Gandhi–Jinnah Trophy', for a big shield bearing silver replicas of Mahatma Gandhi and the Quaid-e-Azam side by side. These would be based on 'photographs of corresponding postures of the two great statesmen', the money for the trophy's casting being contributed equally by the two Governments or, better still, from subscriptions canvassed from the general public.[50]

This was a splendidly well-intentioned idea. It is an appealing thought: Gandhi in his loin-cloth next to Jinnah in his suit and tie and fez, adorning a cricket trophy. It was generous of a Pakistani to place the names alphabetically, rather than demand, as a chauvinist would, that it be called the 'Jinnah–Gandhi Trophy'. But perhaps it is just as well that the proposal did not leave the pages of the newspaper. To place those two disputatious lawyers side by side, even in after-life, would have been a certain recipe for conflict.

FIVE YEARS LATER the Pakistanis came to India for a five-Test series. Both Boards of Control issued commemorative souvenirs. These, in some suggestive respects, were a study in contrast. The Pakistani souvenir had their national symbol – a red star – in a much larger font size than its Indian counterpart (the Asoka lions). The preliminary pages printed the Pakistani National Anthem in Urdu and English and displayed one full-page photograph of the 'Father of the Nation', M. A. Jinnah, and another of the President of Pakistan, Field Marshal Ayub Khan. There was also an exhortative preface by Ayub, who, as it happened, also served as the President of the Board of Control for Cricket in Pakistan.

The Indian souvenir, on the other hand, had both symbols set in the same size. There was no National Anthem printed, nor a photo of Gandhi. At this time the Pakistan elite had more reason to associate sport with nationalism. This might have been because Ayub's dictatorship did not enjoy quite the legitimacy within or outside his country that Jawaharlal Nehru's Government did. Interestingly, while the Pakistani publication advertised the strengths of the nation, the always money-minded Indian Board had a commercial for the British airline, BOAC emblazoned on its souvenir's cover.[51]

To welcome the Pakistani cricketers to India a then non-political, cricket-mad cartoonist named Bal Thackeray published a pamphlet featuring sketches of the players with a few lines about them underneath. Hanif Mohammed had his hair combed back in a quiff, and he was playing a hook shot. The choice of stroke was a product of the cartoonist's fancy: the forward defensive would have been more appropriate. The text described Hanif as the 'Little Master', 'the biggest stumbling-block to India in the coming series'. For 'one so young', commented Thackeray, 'he has rare restraint, for, like a veteran he digs himself in and masters the situation'.[52] Two years before coming to India Hanif had batted for 970 minutes to save a Test in the West Indies, the longest innings ever played in first-class cricket. Luckily Lord Harris, he who claimed that Asians would never equal Englishmen in the matter of patience, had long since been lost to the world of cricket.

The first match of the tour was against West Zone at Poona. Hanif Mohammed scored 100, and the organizers collected 80,000 rupees in gate money, half the proceeds going to the Poona Police Welfare Fund. A local Urdu poet composed a couplet in honour of Hanif, saying the batsman was endowed with the strength of the Prophet's son-in-law, Hazrat Ali, and would shine as brilliantly as the sun. The following week, in Baroda, the batsman was at the centre of a bizarre incident. A fan asked to shake hands with Hanif, and cut his fingers with a sharp ring. The Pakistani papers condemned this 'treacherous handshake' by a 'communal-minded pervert', but unfortunately gave no further details.[53] Now, Baroda is a city in Gujarat founded by Maratha adventurers, followers of the great seventeenth-century warrior-chieftain Shivaji. Shivaji had once killed an emissary of the Mughals, Afzal Khan, with a concealed pair of iron claws, literally hugging the unsuspecting Khan to death. Did this cricket fan take a perverted inspiration from the story of the Maratha hero? Did he hope thus to put the most dangerous batsman on the other side out of the Test matches?

Hanif's mother rushed down from Karachi to be with her son. Luckily the injury was not serious, and he recovered in time for the first Test, played in Bombay. During this match Hanif's wife gave birth to their first child and he naturally scored a century, his innings watched by an appreciative crowd of 40,000. As in 1952, Hanif was once more the Pakistani cricketer most Indians wanted to see play. It was reported that fans were paying 500 rupees on the black market for a 50-rupee ticket to watch him bat. *Dawn* printed a letter from a Rajinder Kumar of Nagpur, suggesting that the 'small cut on the tip of [Hanif's] finger could scarcely have been premeditated'. In any case, the Pakistani public must not judge 'the Indian sporting public by the foolish acts of single individuals'. Mr Kumar noted 'that Hanif is the darling of the [Indian] crowds, that every member of the Pakistan team is a hero to millions of cricket fans in India', 'mobbed and idolized everywhere', with crowds gathering to cheer them at intermediate stations on their railway route. This, said the Nagpur man, was 'a reflection of the general goodwill that prevails in India towards Pakistan, of which the best proof was the fact that although we lost the Olympic hockey title this year we were glad it was you who took it from us'.[54]

This might have been the majority sentiment. However, the cut on Hanif's finger was not the only foolish act of single individuals. A. F. S. Talyarkhan reported that the Indian batsman Abbas Ali Baig, a Muslim, was receiving poisonous letters suggesting that he was deliberately throwing away his wicket to the Pakistani bowlers. Talyarkan suggested that 'unless we can bury once and for all the idea that the Pakistan–India sporting contests are as between Muslims and Hindus only we had better put an end to rubbing against each other'.[55]

In the political background, both the note of inter-national harmony and the note of inter-communal discord could be heard. While the cricket matches were on, the Foreign Ministers of the two countries were meeting in Delhi, and their Information Ministers in Rawalpindi. The latter pair issued a statement calling upon the press to create 'a positive psychological atmosphere among the peoples of the two countries'.[56] Meanwhile, the papers carried reports of a speech made in Quetta by Field Marshal Ayub Khan, to the effect that relations between India and Pakistan could not be improved so long as the Kashmir question remained unresolved. How would this be done? Ayub himself was coy, but the President of Pakistan-held Kashmir claimed that 'the day was not far when the five divisions of the Indian Army would be repulsed from the valley and the whole state of Jammu and Kashmir liberated'.[57]

Before the Tests began the Pakistan captain, Fazal Mahmood, told a Bombay weekly that 'India is not a foreign country to me'. Fazal Mahmood spoke of the influence on his early cricket career of the former Indian captain, Vijay Merchant, and complained that 'national prestige and other such things are today being unnecessarily involved with cricket'.[58]

A shared culture and a shared history implied that sport should be kept free from politics. Once the two sides took the field, however, national prestige took precedence over attractive cricket. All five Tests were drawn. So were the nine lesser matches played by the Pakistanis in India. Everywhere tickets had been sold out in advance, but at the conclusion of the series the reaction of cricket fans was 'Thank the Lord, it's all over'. With both sides playing for a draw from the very first ball, this 'was the utter denial and negation of any sport, let alone cricket'. An Indian scribe obliged to watch it all commented that this was the 'most discouraging and disheartening' series ever played in the country.[59] Strikingly, the India–Pakistan contest – or no-contest – coincided with the most exciting series of matches in Test history, played Down Under that same winter between Frank Worrell's West Indians and Richie Benaud's Australian side.

IN JANUARY 1961, while the cricket was on, Abdul Kardar was visiting India to attend the Second Commonwealth Conference. Jawaharlal Nehru inaugurated the meeting. In his memoirs Kardar complained that the Indian Prime Minister 'spoke on the history of the Indian civilization but wherever he dwelt on the Muslim period he never used the word Muslim but of "Central Asian influences" '. The cricketer-turned-diplomat asked the leader of the Pakistani delegation to rebut Nehru, to highlight in his own speech the fact that in the city where they were meeting – Delhi – Muslims had contributed most fully 'to its architecture and cultural life'.[60] Kardar wanted to correct a 'blatant twisting of history', but it is a safe bet that in his speech Nehru did not use the word 'Hindu' either. The religious idiom was rigorously excluded from his public speeches. In any case, he had made the safety of the Indian Muslims central to his politics. Indeed, Nehru was often accused by Hindu chauvinists of being a 'Muslim appeaser', a charge superficially made plausible by his own love of Mughlai food, his Muslim mode of dress – the *achkan* – and his wide circle of Muslim friends.

Kardar's comments betray a certain paranoia, this widely shared by the ruling elite of Pakistan, who believed that Indians never really accepted their status as a sovereign nation. India was the Big Brother who patronized them, and who refused to give up Kashmir. By 1961 the military was firmly in control of Pakistan. In 1965 Ayub Khan launched an attack on Indian positions in Kashmir, provoking a twenty-one-day war on land and in the air. Six years later the two countries were at war once more. The lead this time was taken by India, in aiding the movement of secession among the Bengalis of East Pakistan. The war of 1971 led to the creation of an independent Bangladesh, in a serious blow to the 'two-nation' theory by which Pakistan was formed in the first place.

The bitter and costly wars of 1965 and 1971 put an end to cricketing ties between India and Pakistan. Notably, cricketers from the two countries played happily together in the English County Championship, and for Rest of the World teams in Australia and England. In December 1976 Ajit Wadekar became the first Indian cricketer to visit Pakistan in twenty years. A. H. Kardar, then President of his country's Cricket Board, had invited him to captain a World XI in a set of festival matches marking twenty-five years of Pakistan's Republic. On the flight to Karachi the Indian purred when he read the newspaper headline: 'AJIT WADEKAR TO ARRIVE TODAY TO CAPTAIN WORLD XI'. His mood was spoilt by the Immigration Officer at Karachi airport, who would not accept Kardar's letter of invitation as a substitute for a valid visa.

It took Wadekar five hours to get past passport control, but all other doors were open to him. Liquor was sent to his hotel room in

defiance of an Islamic ban. Refugees nostalgic for Bombay plied him
with kababs and tandoori chicken and demanded stories of film stars
in return. Wadekar was 'amazed to see people come and talk to me
with affection'. The 'people of Pakistan showed an eagerness to meet
us, talk to us and so restore friendly relations'. Among the friendliest
was the batsman Zaheer Abbas, who took the Indian visitor around
the sights of Lahore. Wadekar was moved by Abbas's acount of how
Sunil Gavaskar and he shared a room in Australia, playing for The
Rest of the World, while war raged between their respective countries.
'They shared the tension while consoling each other.' A broader
conclusion followed: 'A game of cricket can bring close together two
characters of different nature, culture and religion.'[61]

In the last quarter of 1978 an Indian Test side visited Pakistan.
New Governments were in place in New Delhi and Islamabad,
each eager to forget the poison of the past. The captain of India
was Bishan Bedi, a bluff, outgoing Sikh, a superb ambassador for
his country who had played for the same English county, Northamp-
tonshire, as his Pakistani counterpart Mushtaq Mohammad. Accompanying the cricketers was Lala Amarnath, invited by Pakistan
Television to be on its panel of commentators. The Lala was a popular
hero in Lahore, where he had once lived and played some of his
finest cricket. An earlier chapter has related his triumphant return to
the city after his century on Test debut in Bombay in December
1933. After Partition, Amarnath came back to Lahore as manager of
the first Indian touring side to Pakistan. The manager of the present
side, however, was Maharaja Fatehsinghrao Gaekwad of Baroda,
art collector, *shikari*-turned-conservationist, part-time cricketer and
member of the international jet set. When the visitors disembarked
at Lahore airport, they found a bus and a Mercedes waiting for
them. The cricketers trooped off towards the bus, and Fatehsinghrao,
naturally, advanced towards the Mercedes. As he reached the car he
was intercepted by the chauffeur, a liveried Pathan 6 feet 6 inches
in height. 'Tum udhar jao' ('You go *there*'), said the Pathan to the
Maharaja, pointing a finger at the bus, 'ye siraf Lala Saheb ke liye
hai' ('this car is meant exclusively for the Lala Saheb').[62]

As this anecdote suggests, at the time sport seemed to soar safely clear of the polluted stream of politics. Six months before the Indian cricketers went to Pakistan a Pakistani hockey team had come to India. The 'Test' at Bombay attracted a crowd of 45,000. In the gathering was Khushwant Singh, editor of *The Illustrated Weekly of India*, an erstwhile resident of Lahore and the author of a fine novel about Partition, *Train to Pakistan*. The scene at the beginning of the match, suggested Khushwant, seemed to underline the ideological divide between the two countries:

> The Pakistanis huddle together as rugger players in a scrum and say a short prayer for victory. With Allah on their side what fear have they of a team which has only one Muslim, one Sikh, five Christians, four Hindus and one of them even with a tintinnabulary name: Dung Dung!

By the end of the match, which Pakistan won by two goals to one, the writer was thinking more of what brought the neighbours together: 'Sports encounters seldom generate goodwill', remarked Khushwant. They are

> naively believed to do so between contending nations. But this one certainly did. The mammoth crowd gave the Pakistanis a great heart-warming ovation. This was largely due to the fact that no one really believed that this patchy Indian side with only two Olympic players and minus many of its best players had much of a chance against a team consisting of nine Olympians who knew each other like the backs of their hands. So why get your blood-pressure up and not take it in a spirit of bhai-bhaism? In any case the better team won.[63]

Bishan Bedi's cricket side of 1978 did have all the best Indian players. Pakistan won the series easily, but India won the return exchange at home two years later. Through the late 1970s and 1980s the cricket teams of the two countries played one another regularly. Pakistan had now slowly surged ahead of India in this particular game. Their victories were not, however, met with national exultation. Nor did

the defeated Indians take failure on the field as a national humilia-
tion. Perhaps they consoled themselves that their country surpassed
Pakistan in other spheres. It had better scientists, better writers, a
more vigorous film industry, and was a democracy besides. Win or
lose, sporting exchanges in the late 1970s could be understood in a
spirit of brotherliness, bhai-bhaism.

16. Kashmir Comes to the Pennines

I HAVE VISITED Pakistan twice, Karachi in February 1989 and Islamabad and Lahore in August 1995. The first time, Karachi was all warmth and cuddles: one had only to say that one had come from Hindustan for empty tables to appear in crowded restaurants and book prices to be slashed in half. The next visit, in Lahore especially, was clouded with suspicion and reserve, sometimes breaking out into hostility. When I invited a hotel executive to visit India, he answered that he wouldn't, for that was a land where they beat up Muslims. I asked a taxi driver whether the cricketer–politician Imran Khan would do well in the forthcoming elections. No, he answered savagely, how can we trust someone who has married the daughter of a Jew? Then, looking at my clothes, he asked if I would vote for him. When I said I was not eligible, being from India, he said he had a picture of the actor Sanjay Dutt up in his home. Dutt had recently been put in a Bombay prison after an unlicensed AK 47 rifle was found on him. The Lahore cabman, however, was convinced that Dutt was jailed only because his mother, the celebrated Indian actress Nargis, was a Muslim.

In between my two visits to Pakistan the insurgency in Kashmir began. The proximate cause was the Government of India, which had put in place a pliant and corrupt regime in Srinagar. But local discontent was also vigorously stoked by men from across the border. Pakistan was briefly experimenting with democracy, and its two leading politicians, Nawaz Sharif and Benazir Bhutto, were each accusing the other of not adequately supporting *jehad* in Kashmir. Joining the struggle in the Valley were thousands of Afghani and

Central Asian *mujahideen*, who had been thrown out of work by the death of the Soviet Empire.

While Muslims were persecuting Hindus in Kashmir – 250,000 Pandits fled the Valley in the early 1990s – the situation was exactly the reverse in other parts of India. From 1989 a movement to demolish a mosque allegedly built on a Ram temple in Ayodhya gathered pace. A wave of religious riots broke out in northern India, with Muslims being the main victims. The Ayodhya campaign was led by the Bharatiya Janata Party and its associates, the so-called Sangh Parivar, a band of narrow-minded chauvinists whose intolerance was in sharp contrast to the inclusive nationalism once promoted by men such as Jawaharlal Nehru and Maulana Azad.

With the violence in Kashmir and around Ayodhya, political relations between India and Pakistan deteriorated dramatically. There were daily exchanges of fire on the border, especially around a worthless glacier at 16,000 feet claimed by both nations. These developments affected cricket relations. There could be no tours of one nation by the other. But they could meet in third countries. Through the 1980s and 1990s India and Pakistan regularly played each other in the tiny Middle Eastern state of Sharjah, where an enterprising sheikh had financed a cricket stadium. These matches were attended by flag-waving expatriates in the Gulf and telecast to a large captive audience in the sub-continent. Pakistan usually won. This was because they had a better team, but some Indians gave a communal colour to it. The finals in Sharjah were played on a Friday and were interrupted for two hours in mid-afternoon for prayer. The insecure Hindu thought this was done specifically to 'charge up' the Pakistani cricketers. It was also claimed that the organizers in Sharjah chose umpires biased against India.

The Sharjah tournament became a favourite destination of the Indian super-rich: industrialists, film stars, models, politicians and mafia dons. The matches were skilfully marketed and were watched by more people (on television) than any other contest apart from the World Cup. There was very heavy betting, especially when India played Pakistan. Rumours were circulated of certain players being in the pay of bookmakers. In a pioneering investigation published in February 1995, the journalist Krishna Prasad sought to enter the shadowy world of the Indian bookie. He took his readers into the office of a Mr X, whose nine telephones linked him to punters in towns across the sub-continent. Betting on cricket was illegal but, said Mr X, wagers were placed on every ball in a one-day match. There were bets on when a wicket would fall, on when sixes would be hit, on which overs would be the most expensive, on highest and lowest individual scores, on who would take wickets and who wouldn't, and on which side would win the match.

The sums being won and lost by individual punters ran into millions of rupees. The scale of operations had, willy-nilly, drawn active cricketers into it. Some Indian and Pakistani players were said to be directly involved. As Mr X meaningfully remarked,

> It is not a joke the number of times India and Pakistan have lost from a totally winning position. Australia does not lose like this. New Zealand does not lose like this. The West Indies does not lose like this. It is so regular and systematic only with Indians and Pakistanis. Have you seen any other teams where for one batsman the ball does not come up enough for strokemaking and where, from the next, there is a rain of sixes?[1]

IN EARLY 1992 India and Pakistan played each other in Australia during the World Cup. India won the match, but Pakistan went on to win the tournament. I recall a conversation I had afterwards at the Delhi School of Economics, once known as a bastion of Indian liberalism. The students thought that Pakistan's victory was a conse- quence of theirs being an Islamic state. A basis in one religion gives a nation strength to win and compete, they argued. The young economists believed the Ayodhya movement, if successful, would result in a strong state run for and by Hindus, this in turn leading to satisfactory results on the cricket field.

Other Indians welcomed the Pakistan victory in the 1992 World Cup. A Delhi chauffeur told me, 'Akhir, Cup Asia main hi raha' ('At least the trophy came to Asia'). The record-breaking Bombay batsman Sunil Gavaskar was invited to attend the celebrations in Lahore and Karachi. He was asked not to go by Bal Thackeray, the sometime cartoonist whose Shiv Sena party was rapidly gaining influence in Bombay. Thackeray thought Pakistan and its people should be boycotted for sending arms and terrorists into Kashmir. Gavaskar, to his credit, went anyway.

In December 1992, the mosque in Ayodhya was demolished by a mob of Hindu fanatics. Perhaps no event has more deeply divided independent India. Many, like the present writer, thought it an act of sheer vandalism. But some others interpreted it as a delayed but emphatic assertion of Hindu pride. The demolition provoked further riots, especially in Bombay, where Mr Thackeray's Shiv Sena targeted vulnerable Muslims, burning houses and stabbing individuals. Muslim militants responded by planting bombs in banks and the stock exchange.

After Ayodhya the relations between India and Pakistan deteriorated further. The politicians on either side traded abuse. However, the cricket administrators came together, with Sri Lanka's help, to bid successfully for the 1996 World Cup. The possibilities of huge revenues from television persuaded the politicians to sanction the tournament. The draw ensured that India and Pakistan were placed in separate groups, each country playing all its matches at home. What if the two countries qualified to play against one another in the knock-out? The administrators, contemplating the takings, would not ask the question.

Sri Lanka, the third host, was also scheduled to play its early matches at home. Two teams, Australia and the West Indies, preferred to concede their match rather than visit the troubled island, citing reasons of 'security' (bombs planted by the secessionist Tamil Tigers were known to explode at random in Colombo). The Sri Lankans saw this as a slur on their hospitality. To show that the island was safe for cricket they arranged a substitute Goodwill Match, with a combined India–Pakistan side playing the home side. An Indian, Mohammad Azharuddin, would be the captain, and a Pakistani, Intikhab Alam, the manager.

The Goodwill Match was a spectacular success. The grateful Sri Lankans welcomed the players with cheering banners: 'WE SALUTE YOUR MAGNIFICENT GESTURE OF SOLIDARITY'; 'SRI LANKA WEL-COMES THE GOLDEN SONS OF INDIA AND PAKISTAN'; 'THANKS, INDIA AND PAKISTAN, FOR COMING TO SRI LANKA TO KEEP SOUTH ASIAN DIGNITY'. The Indian and Pakistani cricketers, friends as sportsmen always are, 'were poised and completely at ease with one another'. But observers read a sheaf of meanings into the match. It was a 'matter of speculation', remarked one journalist, whether this would translate into a 'stronger [South Asian] regional identity'. But 'as of now, India-Pakistan-Sri Lanka cannot be more unified. Ask any spectator at the Premadasa Stadium.' The match was indeed 'a rare moment of unqualified unity when all other political differences seemed sidelined – even at the level of governments'.[2] The Indian High Commissioner was quoted as saying, 'It was a wonderful and spontaneous gesture of solidarity by the cricketers.'[3]

A gesture of goodwill, but by *the cricketers*. No one at the time recognized the significance of this last caveat. The tournament went on, with the three hosts doing well enough to qualify for the quarter-finals in which, as luck had it, India and Pakistan were drawn to meet.

The moment of destiny had arrived. From Bombay Bal Thackeray called for a boycott of the match. Luckily the match was to be played in Bangalore, my home town, a cosmopolitan city with a good record of maintaining communal harmony. The police made a few preventive arrests of Thackeray's followers and announced that there would be no trouble at the venue.

All Bangalore wanted to be at the Chinnaswamy Stadium. The ticket I had lobbied for came through only on the evening before the match. On the day, I took my seat half an hour early. When I arrived, Imran Khan and Sunil Gavaskar were talking as they walked around the ground, the Pathan in *salwar kameez*, the Maharashtrian in regulation shirt and pants. The last time they had met at this spot was during a Test match ten years previously, when Sunil scored 96 and Imran led his team to a 16-run victory. The two men were friends, and on this day fellow television commentators as well.

It was a cracking good match. Were this a 'cricket' cricket book I might write more of the superlative stroke-play of both sides. India batted first and made a handsome 287 in their allotted 50 overs, with a composed 90 from their Sikh opening batsman, Navjyot Singh Sidhu, and an explosive 40-odd at the death from Ajay Jadeja. Pakistan answered with a dazzling opening partnership from Saeed Anwar and Ameer Sohail, left-handers both. For an hour and a half they played every shot in the book – hooks, cuts, drives, pulls, all met with a complete and deafening silence. It appeared I was the only man in the stadium applauding their strokes. This was a real shock to me, for I had twenty years' experience of this crowd and this stadium. In that time my compatriots had always been willing to cheer good cricket from the other side. Behind their sullenness lay two kinds of chauvinism, for the bowlers being hit around were all from Bangalore.

Anwar and Sohail got out and the Indians steadily chipped away at the rest. The veteran Javed Miandad, in his last tournament, was still in, batting with the tail while the rate required steadily mounted. I was sure that India would win. Once more, I sensed that I was alone. The people around me – I was sitting in the pavilion – remembered Miandad's last-ball six against India at Sharjah, which had won his side the match. When that shot was played, back in 1986, I was living in Connecticut. Everyone around me had seen the shot on television or heard it on the radio; I had only read about it when the Indian papers arrived in my university two weeks later. And where I now saw the man, ageing, they saw the myth, who would hit the last ball of this match also for six. But the poor fellow was hard pressed to reach the boundary along the ground. He was playing from memory, protecting his wicket without getting the runs. Nine an over were required when Miandad was run out by a direct hit. When he walked off the ground I stood up to applaud him. 'Why are you clapping?' asked an obnoxious fellow from a row behind. 'You should clap him too', I answered, recklessly. 'He is a truly great player, and this is the last time any of us will see him bat.' 'Thank God I shall never see the bastard again,' came the reply. How did I ever think that an uncertain internationalism would be equal to a single-minded patriotism?

After the match I walked home with an English journalist who was staying with me. The stadium lay at one end of Mahatma Gandhi Road, Bangalore's busiest; my house lay at the other end. It was only 10.30 p.m., but the bars and restaurants were closed. I learned later that they had downed shutters in the late afternoon, when Anwar and Sohail were blazing away. Certainly if India had lost, plenty of windows would have been broken in Bangalore, and perhaps a few (Muslim) heads too. India won, so instead there was an impromptu celebration in the streets. A bunch of louts assembled at a traffic intersection: dancing and shouting, they stopped every passing car and would not let them pass until the occupants joined them in singing, 'Bolo Bharat Mata ki Jai!'

Glory to Mother India. How about Father Pakistan? Cricket fans across that country smashed television sets. One college student, Jaffar Khan, fired a burst of bullets into his TV screen and then turned the Kalashnikov on himself. A heart attack that struck a fifty-five-year-old man produced the second fatality of the cricket match. When the cricketers returned home, a bunch of disenchanted fans had gathered at Lahore airport with abusive banners and baskets of rotten eggs. The plane was diverted to Karachi to save the players from their wrath. After they landed, the captain, Wasim Akram, received death threats. One fan filed a petition against Pakistan's 'disappointing' performance. The judge, accepting the petition, observed that 'corruption had destroyed the game of cricket in Pakistan'. A senior cleric, Maulana Naqshabandi, helpfully explained what the corruption was. 'Any nation which made a woman its ruler never prospered,' he remarked. So long as Benazir Bhutto was Prime Minister of Pakistan it could never win at cricket. According to Maulana Naqshabandi, the cricket débâcle was the consequence of Pakistan's 'obscene' imitation of Indian culture, with its habit of propelling women into public life.[4]

The Indian cricketers, meanwhile, proceeded to Calcutta to play against Sri Lanka in the semi-finals. The expectations of the fans had been inflated further by the win over Pakistan. But Sri Lanka had played superbly thus far. Their left-handed all-rounder Sanath Jayasurya was the player of the tournament. On the day of the semi-final, a Calcutta newspaper carried this extraordinary headline: 'BATTLELINES DRAWN, CITY BAYS FOR BLOOD'. 'If there is one villain in Calcutta today,' said the report underneath, 'it is Sanath Jayasurya.'[5] An earlier generation of Bengalis might have warmed to Jayasurya's batsmanship, but the present lot wanted to finish him off before his side played India. As it happened, Jayasurya failed, but the other – and scarcely less gifted – Sri Lankans got their side to 251. India had a chance if Sachin Tendulkar scored a hundred, but he was dismissed after scoring a mere 65. Defeat at the hands of lowly Sri Lanka, a country that until 1974 played an annual match against Tamil Nadu, an Indian province! The prospect prompted a barrage of bottle-throwing and chair-breaking that made the continuation of play impossible. Sri Lanka were awarded a match they would have won easily and legitimately had the crowd not intervened.

Cricket is not, or at least is supposed not to be, football. This was the first match in six World Cups to be disturbed by spectator violence. India were playing, India were the hosts, and it was Indian 'cricket lovers' who did it. It was later claimed that a 'small minority of boorish louts have sullied Calcutta's reputation as a wonderful sporting venue'. Bengalis who had thought of themselves as the epitome of civility and graciousness were horrified at the knock-out blow to their reputation. Others suggested that the violence was in keeping with their culture. Calcutta, commented one critic, 'has traditionally been an explosive and volatile city given to irrational emotionalism'. The Bengali mindset 'was imbued with a gory love of militarism and violence'.[6]

In truth, the culprit was not Bengali culture but a generalized Indian nationalism. Behind the crowd trouble at Calcutta lay the pricking of a massive balloon filled with unreal expectations. Before the World Cup, the Indian fans were made to believe that their hopes and desires would propel the home team to victory. Thus the National Institute of Design had made a 30-foot-high bat wishing the Indian cricketers 'Best of Luck'. Sponsored by Coca-Cola and weighing a tonne, this was mounted on a truck and taken to all major cities. Sunil Gavaskar was asked to sign first on the bat, his mark followed by a million lesser signatures. The promoters of this Disneyesque fantasy suggested that the bat 'embodies the hopes and aspirations of the entire nation'.[7]

The trouble at Calcutta would have been avoided if Pakistan had won the quarter-final. That is, the trouble would have manifested itself in or outside the Chinnaswamy Stadium instead of at Eden Gardens. Would we then be mourning cosmopolitan Bangalore's sudden loss of civility? Let us name the animal for what it is: an ugly and destructive nationalism, accentuated further by high-tension one-day matches played under high-wire lights. Under the floodlights the players become gladiators, the spectators thirsty Romans. With corporate sponsorship and block booking the genuine cricket lover has in any case been displaced by the overworked, overpaid, half-drunk and hyper-nationalist yuppie, like the guy in Bangalore who was glad to have seen the back of Javed Miandad. This fellow does not understand the game and comes only to see his side win. He is quick to praise and quicker to blame – a temperament to match the sport, for the limited over game punishes players heavily; no second innings for the batsman, no second spell for the bowler. One honest mistake can swing the game, leading to abuse, innuendo and violence.

The historian Rudrangshu Mukherjee, who has followed Calcutta cricket for four decades, wrote after the 1996 World Cup débâcle that 'it has become the assumption of people who go to Eden Gardens nowadays that the Indian team should always win'. This ridiculously unrealistic assumption was carefully stoked by the men who market the game. Thus

cricketers are no longer mere players. The world of media and advertisement has magnified their images and turned them into idols. As a result nobody is willing to believe that a captain can genuinely misread a wicket; that a batsman can be out of touch and therefore play a rank bad shot; that the best of fielders can drop the easiest of catches; that a bowler can have a bad day; and that a team – as was indeed the case on Wednesday at Eden Gardens – can be thoroughly outplayed by the opposing side. A cricketer is no longer judged by his performance but by the money he earns, what product he advertises, who sponsors his bat and even at times who he sleeps with. All this in the eyes of a credulous and prurient public gives to cricketers an extrahuman halo which is supposed to make them immune to failure and error.[8]

Indian liberals mourned the fiasco at Eden Gardens, but some Pakistanis positively exulted in it. A senior Lahore journalist wrote of how,

Thanks to the international television coverage, billions of people the world over saw with their own eyes the true character of the human species called Hindus . . . This is a blessing in disguise. India is not only known as a sporting country but made much of in the West as the largest democracy on earth. And morally too it is put on a high plane and for his non-violence creed Gandhi was almost regarded as Jesus Christ. This myth has now been exploded. The Indians have been seen for what they are. As for us in Pakistan, we have known them all along.[9]

The last matches of the 1996 World Cup conclusively demolished the spirit of goodwill which presaged it. What was now left of the demonstration of regional unity at the Premadasa Stadium? Indians had turned on Sri Lankans, Pakistanis had turned on themselves. Only the little islanders came out with any credit. They won the tournament, defeating the insolent Australians in the final. This came about despite the fact that *both* the Prime Minister and the President of Sri Lanka were women.

BY 1996 IT SEEMED CLEAR that cricket matches between India and Pakistan stoked rather than subdued nationalist passions. This might have worried the peacemongers, but it was greatly to the liking of commercial sponsors. After the World Cup an Indian firm decided to pay for an annual series of five one-day matches between the two countries, to be played in a little cricket ground maintained by the Toronto Skating and Curling Club. At the venue would be a few thousand enthusiastic expatriates. Back in the sub-continent, 500 million or more would watch the matches on television.

The Toronto event was advertised under the splendidly unironic name of 'The Friendship Series'. The first year's matches passed off without a hitch. However, the 1997 series was marred by an ugly incident. An Indian spectator singled out the fine but overweight Pakistani batsman, Inzamam-ul-Haq, for special attention. Haq, fielding on the boundary, was subject to sarcastic commentary on his weight. He was repeatedly called *aloo*, or potato. The cricketer later claimed that the fan was 'abusing my family, my religion, my country'. A well-behaved spectator confirmed that the offender was 'hurling religious abuse, all the time, at Haq'. An angered Haq called for a bat from the Pakistani twelfth man and jumped into the crowd in pursuit of his tormentor. Had the security men not intervened the spectator would have been severely thrashed.[10]

One newspaper, I recall, carried a front-page photo of Inzamam being escorted off the field, under the caption: 'NOT QUITE CRICKET, NOT QUITE KASHMIR'. After Toronto the Indians were due to visit Pakistan to play two one-day matches. When they landed in Karachi, Hanif Mohammed warmly welcomed them as the first Indian cricketers to visit the place in almost a decade. 'The more the exchanges' of cricket teams, said the great little batsman, 'the less emotional people will get. I would even go to the extent of saying that one day our two countries should unite again'.[11]

Hanif was speaking as a Mohajir, as a member of the community of refugees that helped build Pakistan but have been marginalized since by the dominant Punjabis. But one Indian journal likewise insisted that 'cricket is not war', that the tour was a 'triumph of amity', that despite terrorism in Kashmir cricket was 'a tool of diplomacy [which] had led ordinary Indians and Pakistanis to see and appreciate each other's cricketers as gifted human beings rather than cold, ruthless figures from an alien land'.[12] The amnesia was spectacular. The clash in Toronto had taken place only a month previously. Indeed, the Pakistani police were worried that one of their own might wish to revenge Haq by attacking Sachin Tendulkar. Snipers lined the street and occupied every rooftop between the airport and the players' hotel. Security for the Indian cricketers was on a par with that offered to visiting Heads of State.

The match in Karachi was disrupted by stone-throwing and shouting, the Indian players naturally being the target. Play was possible only when the match referee, a Sri Lankan, threatened that the hosts would have to forfeit the match unless the spectators were brought to order. India won at Karachi, but fortunately the hosts had won the previous match at Lahore. A draw at home was not much to the liking of the Pakistani fans, but defeat would have been far worse.

In the summer of 1998 India conducted a series of nuclear tests. Pakistan quickly followed. In both countries a small minority opposed the tests, while the majority celebrated them as an affirmation of national strength. The rest of the world watched with concern. Would Kashmir become a flashpoint for a nuclear war?

In early 1999 the Pakistan cricket team was scheduled to visit India to play three Test matches. The first two Tests would form a 'mini-series' of their own, whereas the last would kick off an Asian Test Championship in which Sri Lanka was the third participating team. In the first week of November, three months before the Pakistanis were due to come, Bal Thackeray announced that he would lead a movement to stop them. 'The Pakistani team should not be allowed to set foot on Indian soil', he said. 'As staunch Hindus you must not see their faces and boycott them,' he told his supporters. Thackeray attacked the Indian Cricket Board's President, Rajsingh Dungarpur, for saying that if the Shiv Sena would disrupt matches in Bombay, other venues were available. If Dungarpur had 'a modicum of national pride', thundered Thackeray, his Board 'would have banned matches with Pakistan on their own. Pakistani terrorists are killing our people in Kashmir. Women and young children are mercilessly slaughtered every day.'[13]

Thackeray's protest bears a remarkable resemblance to Dr N. B. Khare's opposition to the 1952 tour. Both men evoked 'hatred of Pakistan day in and day out'. Both men protested against a visit by a cricket team to direct attention to themselves and their ideology. Both men claimed to stand for a purer and less compromised nationalism based on Hindu pride.

History, said Karl Marx, happens twice, first as tragedy, then as farce. In India, where all things are turned upside down, farce preceded tragedy by fifty years. Would that Thackeray had been as much lacking in influence as Khare! The Hindu Mahasabha in 1952 was a minor party with no political clout. But in half a century Hindu chauvinism had moved from the political fringe to the political centre. The Shiv Sena in 1998 was the ruling party in the big state of Maharashtra. It was also a coalition partner in the Central Government in New Delhi. Thackeray commanded the absolute loyalty of thousands of goons who could bring life in Bombay to a halt. Hence the Cricket Board dared not risk a match in that city. But would Pakistan play elsewhere? For that Thackeray had to be overruled by the rulers in Delhi, who would have to risk withdrawal of support by the Shiv Sena in the Lok Sabha.

Ironically, Thackeray's opposition to the Pakistan tour was first expressed at a cricket tournament for boys sponsored by the Shiv Sena's *Saamna* newspaper. The rowdy ruler of Bombay has a deep passion for the game. He grew up in Dadar and often watched cricket at the Shivaji Park Gymkhana and, when he had an extra rupee, at the Brabourne Stadium. One of his clearest boyhood memories was of listening to A. F. S. Talyarkhan's cricket commentaries on the radio.[14] He had, we will recall, once made a living drawing caricatures of cricketers. After he entered politics his public pronouncements were steeped in cricket imagery. He commented on the dreadful Bombay riots of 1992–3 that while his side played five-day cricket,

the Muslims played one-day cricket (this a reference to the coordinated bombs set off in a single day in January 1993 to avenge the
pogrom of December 1992).[15] His followers controlled the Mumbai
Cricket Association. The most loyal among them, Manohar Joshi,
was at this time Chief Minister of Maharashtra as well as Vice-
President of the Board of Control for Cricket in India.

Thackeray has his own version of the so-called 'Tebbit Test',
named after the Conservative politician who demanded that West
Indian and Asian immigrants support England when they played
against any other country – including (or especially) the country
of the immigrants' origin. Thackeray's test was directed at the 100
million Indian Muslims. 'It is the duty of Muslims to prove they are
not Pakistanis', he has said. 'I want them with tears in their eyes
every time India loses to Pakistan.'[16]

Alas for Thackeray and the poor Indian Muslims – India lost to
Pakistan all too often. By the end of 1998 Pakistan had won forty-
one one-day matches against India and lost only twenty-five. Fear of
defeat was a key, if unspoken, reason behind Thackeray's opposition
to the cricket tour. He would cloak that opposition in super-patriotic
language, but behind it all was the acute defensiveness of the chauvin-
istic cricket fan.

In late December the Prime Minister of India said the tour
would go on. He assured the Pakistani players full protection. The
Communist Party of India (Marxist), the party in power in West
Bengal, remarked that if Bombay was too scared to host a Test they
would 'welcome the Pakistani cricket team to play in Calcutta'. We
'will organize the match in a big way', said the State's Home Minister.
'We will see who dares to create disturbances here.' He agreed that
the Pakistan Government was 'anti-Indian'. Its Intelligence Service, the
notorious ISI, was 'interfering in Kashmir and abetting fundamentalist
forces in India'. But, added the West Bengal Minister, 'We should
never equate the Pakistan Government with its people who are our
friends.'[17]

In this political debate between left and right, a lowly letter-writer
had perhaps the most sensible things to say. He was D. B. Malgi, a

retired police officer and club cricketer, who was old enough to recall the Pentangular. The 'British had brought cricket to India to create communal disharmony between Hindus and Muslims', argued Malgi. Now matches between two hostile neighbours posed a threat to the secular fabric of India. The matches would become a 'prestige issue', an outlet for 'fanatic cricket lovers in both countries [to] exhibit communal feelings against each other'. The Muslims in India were 'castigated as anti-nationals' for allegedly favouring Pakistan. This castigation was not restricted to cricket lovers but extended to 'the entire community, which is doubly wrong, considering that Muslims have made an equal contribution to the cause of our Independence'.[18]

The Indian Government had assured the Pakistani cricketers of 'fool-proof security'. But it was not only the Pakistanis who were nervous of the reaction of the Indian fans. The Indian cricketers had reason to fear them too. An indiscreet Cricket Board official had told a reporter that the senior players especially had reservations about playing at home against Pakistan. 'There would be too much tension,' they had told their Cricket Board. As the official put it, 'the players felt that losing to New Zealand and Zimbabwe would be tolerated by the public but not a defeat by Pakistan'.[19]

These reservations were overruled by the Board. The tour went on as planned. On 6 January, days before the Pakistani cricketers arrived, Shiv Sena goons dug up the pitch at Delhi's Ferozeshah Kotla ground, venue of the second Test. They also threatened they would release live snakes in the crowd when the match was played.[20] This was followed by an attack on the Cricket Board office in Bombay. Shiv Sena men vandalized hard-won and exquisitely crafted trophies, broke windows, threw files and attacked and injured an official. Sadly, only one of Bombay's forty living Test cricketers was willing publicly to condemn the violence.

The first Test was played in Madras, a city where the Shiv Sena has no presence at all. It was one of the most thrilling Test matches ever played. India lost by 12 runs, despite a brave, battling hundred by Sachin Tendulkar. At the end the winning team did a lap of honour in front of a cheering crowd. The Pakistani captain, Wasim Akram, was deeply touched, but the Madrasi's exemplary conduct should not have come as a complete surprise. For as Richard Cashman wrote years ago, 'a cricket crowd was a microcosm of the society around it and the general discipline of the Madras crowd was a reflection of the greater social and political stability of the city and the homogeneity of its population as compared with other major cities'. This city in southern India had no ancient memories of Mughal rule or modern memories of Pakistan. It had no history of refugee settlements or communal violence. Cashman quotes the veteran cricket writer Dicky Rutnagur, for whom the crowd at Chepauk 'epitomizes the character of the city in which it stands – clean, cultured and genteel'.[21]

The show moved on to that city of post-Partition refugees, Delhi. As in Bangalore in 1996, the police had taken potential mischief-makers into custody. Thousands of security men were at the ground. They were not made to exercise their weapons, for India won. In the Pakistani second innings Anil Kumble took all ten wickets, only the second time this had been done in Test cricket.

With one Test win apiece the result of the series matched the result of the 1965 Indo-Pak War: *dead* even. But there was a third Test to be played, in Calcutta, to begin the Asian Test Championship. Here India started brilliantly, reducing Pakistan to 26 for 6 on the first morning. But the visitors fought back, and after three and half days of absorbing cricket the match was evenly poised. India's fourth innings target was short of 300, within reach especially if Tendulkar batted well. But two wickets fell quickly, and then Tendulkar was run out in a freakish way. He had reached his crease, but to avoid an advancing fielder he ducked and temporarily left his ground, and a throw from the deep hit the wickets.

When Tendulkar was given out, bottles rocketed on to the field. Some fans, cellphones handy, rang home to find out what slow-motion television had shown of the dismissal. The answers they received encouraged them to shout 'Throw some more', 'Stop play', and 'No Sachin, no cricket'. Play was impossible, with fielders under threat from bottles and other missiles. The organizers flashed a message on the scoreboard: 'Please maintain the tradition of Eden Gardens'. This spurred more violence. A college student's reaction was, 'We aren't pansies and this is not Chennai. No cheers for a Pakistani victory lap. We have come to see India win or else we won't let them play.'[22]

Tea was taken early, and after the crowd had quietened play resumed. One reporter thought the 'crowd's stream of passion had perhaps run dry'. But they tanked up overnight. The following morning there were 100,000 people at Eden Gardens hoping India would win against the odds. Their hopes rested on Saurav Ganguly, the gifted left-hander who was also a native of Calcutta. But Ganguly was dismissed early, and the rubbish came back on the field: bottles, stones and worse. This had been anticipated, and the police reacted briskly. Play was stopped for an hour as the paying spectators were, to the last man, firmly escorted out of the stadium. Pakistan took the last wickets to an empty house. This expulsion of the crowd was a first in the history of cricket. As the journalist Sharda Ugra put it, at the biggest ground in the world 'India's biggest spectator sport has thrown the spectators out'. Only the players, the journalists and the ground staff remained. It was, wrote Ugra, 'like the Bolshoi performing the final scenes of Swan Lake watched only by the guys waiting to lock up'.[23]

Once again, the Bengali *bhadralok* professed to be shocked. The Home Minister's reactions are unrecorded. Clearly, he had not been at Eden Gardens for some time, otherwise he would not have assured the Pakistanis of hospitality and support. The Calcutta cricket crowd had changed almost beyond recognition. It was no longer made up of people who recognized good cricket wherever and by whomever it was played. A scribe in the stands described the fellows around him thus: 'the cellphone-toting yuppie, the sunscreen lotion-smeared Raybanned girls, the paan masala-chewing, rotund businessman'. Only 'one stereotype [was] missing in that steamy cauldron, among the screaming, flag-waving, foot-stomping multitude: Calcutta's characteristic cricket-lover, that well-informed, well-read person to whose ears there is no music sweeter than leather hitting willow'.[24]

●

IN MARCH 1999 the Indian Prime Minister took a bus to Lahore. Atal Behari Vajpayee is a poet among politicians, a liberal among fanatics who is sometimes called 'the right man in the wrong party'. As Foreign Minister of India in 1977–9 he worked for better relations with our neighbours. Twenty years later he went off to Pakistan at the invitation of its Prime Minister, Nawaz Sharif. Their meeting took place less than twelve months after the nuclear tests, amidst hope that it would inaugurate a new relationship based on confidence and trust.

Cynics said Vajpayee looked only towards his place in history, while Nawaz Sharif wanted better relations only to further the profits of his family's sugar business. Anyway, what was grandly called the Lahore Process was sabotaged by the Pakistan Army. As the snows melted on the high Himalayan peaks, it sent *mujahideen* to establish positions on them. The Indian Army was told of the infiltrators by a shepherd. When they finally woke up, the *mujahideen* were well ensconced on a dozen look-out points in the district of Kargil, in Kashmir. The Pakistan Army was keeping them supplied with food and arms. The infiltrators overlooked National Highway Number 1, running between Leh and Srinagar, and a route of absolutely critical importance. The Indian Army now began to try to shift them.

I was in England when the Kargil conflict broke out. I had actually planned to come in March, to look at some Gandhi-related collections in the British Library. But the trip had first to be cleared by a battery of clerks in Delhi reading the Foreign Exchange Control Act. When I got my pounds and reached London it was the middle of May. I had reason to thank the *babus* after all, for I had reached England just in time for the World Cup. Some friendly journalists arranged for a press pass, and I was able to squeeze in a few matches between visits to the archives.

The first was at Edgbaston, played between India and England. Next to me on the train to Birmingham sat a father and son, both wearing England shirts. The father was scrutinizing *Wisden*. His son asked him whether he agreed Sachin Tendulkar would be the man of the match.

At the ground England supporters were comfortably outnumbered, perhaps by five to one. Outnumbered, and outshouted too. The Midlanders wore England shirts rather than mackintoshes; otherwise, they were as glum as when V. S. Naipaul sat among them in 1963. The Indians were, if anything, even louder than the West Indians would have been (although perhaps less musical). Most of them were British citizens, emphatically failing the Tebbit Test while England fought to stay in the Cup. The noise level was terrific. I remember especially the reception that Rahul Dravid, the scorer of two centuries in the tournament already, received when he came out to bat. If one closed one's eyes it might have been Dravid's home ground (and mine), Chinnaswamy Stadium in Bangalore. Among the slogans on display that day one stood out. It was aimed at the Pakistani umpire who was officiating. 'Galli galli main shor hai, Javed Akhtar chor hai' ('The cry goes up from street to street / This man Javed Akhtar is a cheat'), shouted the chorus.

India scraped together 231, not a big score, but made more distant by the wickets lost early by England. The hosts were 80 for 3, with the match perfectly poised, when the rain came pelting down. Play was abandoned, but there were no taxis to get us to the station. With other spectators we sought refuge in a pub. Here, at last, the white faces were more numerous than the brown. As if to answer the hours of being outshouted, a bunch in England shirts started to chant: 'Cashmere belongs to Pack-is-tan.'

The following day, and in my absence, India won, the turning-point being the dismissal of Graham Thorpe. All the papers were agreed that Thorpe was batting beautifully, and that he was adjudged lbw by Javed Akhtar although the ball was clearly missing the stumps. Many times in the past had England been undone by a Pakistani umpire, but never before to benefit India while a mini-war was going on in Kashmir.

England were out, and India had qualified for the Super Six stage. They were to play Australia first, at the Oval. My conscience only allowed me to attend the second session. I left the British Library in time to catch the Indian answer to Australia's 282. I was sitting in the Media Overspill Box, far from the real press box, but in the middle of the crowd. The story of the Indian reply is best told through the witticisms of a bilingual Indo-Cockney who sat in the next row. When Sachin Tendulkar played the first over carefully, he said: 'He's only warming up.' When Tendulkar was dismissed and two other batsmen quickly followed, the comments came in profusion: 'Indian T Shirts half price now', 'Bring back Kapil Dev', 'Indian team for Stansted airport tonight' and finally, in Hindi, 'Cargo plane mein bhez do' ('Send them home in a cargo plane'). At 17 for 4 the wit asked: 'At least make the lowest score – 20 all out'. The match was now dead, but Jadeja and Robin Singh put together a face-saving partnership. They gradually got the score up to 50, then 100. The barracker encouraged them: 'Keep it up, India; we are used to milking the system, *slowly*.' Like all good comics he saved the best for the last. When it started drizzling in late afternoon he announced that Australia had been saved by the rain.

I STILL WONDER if the Indo-Cockney was present at India's next match. It was to be against Pakistan, no laughing matter. I myself had a press pass, but when I rang to make hotel bookings in Manchester I was told the cheapest room was £120 a night. Tickets for the Old Trafford match, bought weeks in advance, were being sold at five times the face value by Lancastrians who could not care less whether India or Pakistan won. The hoteliers, alerted to the horde of sub-continentals who were to descend on their city, had jacked up their rates too.

My ticket was free, but I would not pay £120 for a hotel room.

Luckily I remembered that Manchester was a centre of social anthro-pology. A friend at the London School of Economics rang a colleague in Manchester who had spent years in Banaras and published books on caste and religion. She was quite happy to talk shop with a fellow 'Indianist'. I was delighted to find a room for the night. It was, as the economists say, a 'Pareto Super-Optimum', a non-market trans-action that made both parties better off.

I had never been to Manchester before, but knew the city through the works of Neville Cardus. This son of a prostitute educated himself in the public library and at the Old Trafford cricket ground. Vijay Hazare, who played here in 1946 and 1952, wrote that the ground 'shines in the company of Jupiter Pluvius'.[25] Two Test matches had been rained off without a ball being bowled. But Cardus insisted that 'it does not always rain in Old Trafford'. His memories of the place were of its 'beneficent sunshine', the warmth burning up his face as he watched England play Australia or, better still, Lancashire play Yorkshire.[26]

Lancashire versus Yorkshire: two counties divided by the Pennines and by cricket, their ancient military rivalry converted into a modern sporting one. Cardus watched Roses matches from 1900 to 1939, a time when they were well attended and well contested (afterwards the crowds fell away, as did Lancashire cricket). He wrote about the matches with wry humour, deftly sketching the main characters and putting his words in their mouths. He wanted Lancashire to win, of course, but his most evocative portraits were of the opponents. There was the bandy-legged medium-pace bowler who came to life when the Lord heaped together some Yorkshire clay, blew into it and said: 'Emmott Robinson, go on and bowl from the pavilion end for Yorkshire.' There was Roy Kilner, the little left-hander who said of the Roses match that 'We all meet on the first morning, say "How do you do" and nowt else for three days, except "How's that" '.[27] 'No writer of novels', suggested Cardus, 'could make a picture of Yorkshire life half as full of meaning as the one drawn every year in matches between Lancashire and Yorkshire.'[28]

I had read Cardus, but as an English-speaking, cricket-mad boy in post-colonial India I had read the other side too. There was the Yorkshire writer who claimed that 'no clash of arms when Greek met Greek could have yielded more doughty accomplishment and daring than we expected and usually witnessed when White Rose and Red Rose met on the cricket-field.'[29] A. A. Thomson, a Scotsman domiciled in Harrogate, had even written a whole book on the Roses match, seen in popular stereotype as 'a war of attrition conducted by two grim sides of hard-bitten professionals, dourly defending their wickets, wives and children, in that order'. Thomson sought to humanize this stereotype, to write of the players and the sometimes attractive cricket they played, and of the spectators who invested these matches with meaning and wit. He marked the distance between the cricket and the original Wars of the Roses: now the 'warfare is inter-Pennine without being internecine'.[30]

On the train north I recalled my boyhood reading. The Manchester that Cardus wrote of was made by the drive and disinterestedness of a bourgeoisie determined to match the aristocrats of London. This was the city of the Hallé Concerts and the *Guardian* newspaper. It struck me that Cardus had never acknowledged the city's India connection, the fact that it was in the textile trade that the magnates had made their money. In the taxi from the station to my host's house, I passed Manchester University and a shaded park with statues of local notables. Then, suddenly, we drove through a slice of South Asia, the locality of Rusholm, with its National Halal Centre, its Shoba Jewellery Shop, its stalls selling videos of Hindi films and spices, its restaurants advertising *tandoori* chicken. What, I thought, would Neville Cardus have made of this?

At dinner that night my host told me of her ongoing research into diasporic Hinduism. The Indians settled in the North of England were doctors and businessmen: moderately well-to-do, and comfortable speaking English. Nostalgic for their homeland, they wanted their children to learn Sanskrit, and themselves supported the Hindu revivalist Bharatiya Janata Party. Yet they were eager to separate themselves, in English eyes, from the working-class Muslims who had come to Lancashire from Pakistan. These people had acquired a bad name in the wake of the Rushdie affair, and the expatriate Hindus further demonized them. Western Islamophobia thus entered into a relationship of mutual interest with the chauvinism of the non-resident Hindu.

I HAD COME TO this English sporting centre as part of a huge army of invading foreigners. The police, and more so the public perhaps, were terribly nervous. It was a curious inversion of a familiar flash-point. Generally, it was other countries who feared the coming of English football fans. Sometimes these fellows made trouble at home too. Cricket lovers, on the other hand, abided by the law: there had not been a single serious incident in the history of the sport. In England, that is. In the sub-continent a dozen Test matches had been interrupted or abandoned due to rioting and arson.[31] South Asians were volatile people, living in volatile times. Cricket contests between India and Pakistan were always steeped in nationalist passion. This was the World Cup, with a war in the background. Manchester was accustomed to scenes of violence produced by a football match. Would it now witness the first cricket riot in England?

In an editorial on the eve of the match, *The Times* cloaked its anxiety in bravado. 'Even when bullets are in the air across Kashmir', it said, 'the balls can keep flying at Old Trafford.' If 'diplomacy is war by other means', it added, 'then cricket should be crisis management by another, more attractive, method'. The British state was not so sanguine. There were policemen on horses, policemen on foot, policemen in plain-clothes, policemen disguised as ground stewards in green jackets. As the *Daily Express* remarked, 'No cricket match in this country has ever witnessed such tight control but then, no cricket match in this country has ever attracted so much tension as this.'[32]

On the big day I harassed my kindly host into making me an early breakfast. I reached Old Trafford at 10 a.m., an hour before play. Outside the ground I was accosted by an Englishman selling Indian flags. Now, what would Cardus have made of *that*? Or of so much else this day at his well-loved ground? Had Old Trafford ever had so many spectators inside? Had a *cricket* crowd in the city of Manchester ever made as much noise? Had there ever been a tinier proportion of free-born Englishmen among them? Had two teams ever played a cricket match while their armies fought a battle on an 18,000-foot hilltop a million miles away?

I had never watched Lancashire play Yorkshire, but I had seen India play Pakistan many times. One contest produced cutting humour and good literature, the other fed into nationalist hysteria. Cardus had attended his first Roses match in or about the year 1900. In 1949, he had written of his love of Old Trafford: 'the ghost of a happy small boy walks there, to this day'.[33] To imagine what the boy would have made of this battle in 1999 beggared belief. The ground where he spent his happiest days would now witness a game played by two warring countries in front of an utterly non-Lancastrian audience. And it would have almost as many security men as spectators.

By the time I entered the ground it was full, and loud. Above the drums and whistles one could faintly make out the cries: 'Pakistan Zindabad! India Zindabad!' Of the spectators at Old Trafford 90 per cent were Asian. Half of these had come over from the sub-continent for the Cup, the other half were resident in England. Ten thousand people were failing the Tebbit Test yet again. I couldn't care less about that, but I was anxious for the one man who was being put to the Thackeray Test: Mohammad Azharuddin, captain of India.

Through the 1990s, as relations between India and Pakistan sank lower and lower, a Muslim was skipper of the Indian cricket team. This was one of history's cruel jokes. Azharuddin was a lower-middle-class boy from Hyderabad, who had made a dramatic entry into Test cricket by making three hundreds in his first three matches. He was a wristy stylist who caressed the ball rather than hit it, a throwback to the age of Ranji and Duleep. He also fielded like an angel. He smiled and made friends readily, and was popular with team-mate, opponent and fan alike.[34]

Then, in 1990, Azhar was appointed captain of India. He had a young and untried team, and was not much of a tactical thinker himself. His side still won at home, on pitches amenable to the Indian style of bowling, but rarely abroad, and still more rarely against Pakistan. In other times this might not have mattered, but it was while Azhar was captain that the communal climate was turning particularly ugly. I can remember watching, on television, a limited-overs international played in South Africa on 8 December 1992. The Babri Masjid had been demolished two days previously. Azhar was a practising Muslim, and must have feared for the fate of his family in Hyderabad, a town notorious for its religious riots. On that day I saw him drop two easy catches. It was the fag-end of a tiring tour, and Indian cricketers were as yet unused to playing under floodlights. But the thought struck me that it might very well have been his state of mind which made Azhar miss the catches.

At least that match was not against Pakistan. Had it been, the mutterings would have begun: Azhar does not do his best against the Muslim nation. One failure against the old enemy and all Azhar's centuries and catches would be forgotten. Once, when Azhar scored a hundred and India won, Bal Thackeray announced that he was a 'Nationalist Muslim'. While campaigning for votes before the 1998 General Elections Lal Krishna Advani, the leader of the Ayodhya campaign, told an audience of Muslim youths that they should follow the example of Azhar and A. R. Rahman. The cricketer had been batting well, and Rahman had just composed a new version of the patriotic hymn, 'Vande Matram'.[35]

These compliments were poisonous in the extreme. They carried the insinuation that other Indian Muslims were not patriotic. And what if Azhar was bowled first ball for a duck? Did he then forfeit his status as a 'Nationalist Muslim'? As the popular mind became more communalized, one heard remarks against Azhar at bus stops and in drawing-rooms. Meanwhile, the Indian captain had abandoned his wife and two sons and taken up with a posh, English-speaking model from Bombay. The media were awash with stories about Azhar's extravagant lifestyle. He was no longer the honest lower-class boy made good, but a man placed above his station.

These stories were fuelled by a certain envy, written by journalists who resented the money made by cricketers possibly less intelligent and certainly less academically qualified than themselves. But Azhar had changed. The spontaneous openness of his personality had been replaced by arrogance. The successful captain had become a still more successful businessman. He flashed watches with diamonds embedded in them. He drove a Mercedes car given by an admirer. Stories were now afloat that these gifts were actually payments for work done, that Azhar was deeply involved with the world of bookmakers.

In the history of Indian cricket there have been many better cricketers than Mohammed Azharuddin. But perhaps only two who, in a symbolic and social sense, have been as significant. There was Palwankar Baloo, whose career mirrored the tortuous struggle against that most pernicious of human institutions, Untouchability. There was C. K. Nayudu, who despite himself came to embody the hopes of a nation-in-the-making. Now there was Azhar, who came to carry in his person and his career the fears of a nation in uncertain middle age.

The 'Hindu–Muslim problem' has dogged India for close to a century. There have been periods, as in the 1920s or the 1950s and 1960s, when social tolerance and political foresight have allowed the problem not to get out of hand. There have been other times when the mischief of politicians and the insecurities of citizens have made the relations between religions the fundamental fact of Indian life. Such were the 1940s, when the vigorous movement to end the Bombay Pentangular arose. And such were the 1990s, when a Muslim was cricket captain of a communally polarized India.

Once, India was celebrated as a haven of religious harmony in comparison with the fanatical state on the other side of the border. When, in the mid-1970s, an Indian hockey team visited Pakistan, its captain, Aslam Sher Khan, was asked by Pakistanis to defect wherever he went. Since their team lacked a sure full-back like himself, he was told, 'Why don't you come over here? Our team will be complete and you will be representing six crores of Muslims.' (A crore is ten million.) Aslam's answer was that he was happy enough to represent sixty crore Indians. He would then remind his interrogators that two Muslims had been Presidents of the Indian Republic.[36] A decade later the British writer Geoffrey Moorhouse came across a gifted Christian cricketer playing in Quetta. Moorhouse asked why he didn't move to cricketing centres like Lahore or Karachi, to better his chances of playing for Pakistan. The boy's reply was revealing: 'all the best jobs in the country, he said, went to Muslims and no Christian had a hope of getting anywhere in cricket – "not like India, where Roger Binny has made the Test team". He was a boy who had a talent, and he was sadly reconciling himself to a fact of life that would prevent him from exploiting it properly in his native land.'[37]

In a political beauty contest between India and Pakistan India would still win hands down. We are a democracy, they a military dictatorship. They a theocratic state, we a secular republic. Or are we? That is what our Constitution says, but the gap between theory and practice is growing. Especially when the Bharatiya Janata Party is in power, India can sometimes look like a mirror-image of Pakistan. There is an increasing hostility towards the minority communities, especially the Muslims.

For the Hindu chauvinists of the 1990s, three Muslims were stereotypical. There was the mafioso Dawood Ibrahim, who lived in exile in Karachi while orchestrating murders and bomb blasts in his native Bombay. Dawood was, unambiguously, the 'bad Muslim'. There was the scientist A. P. J. Abdul Kalam, who made rockets and missiles aimed at Pakistan and was well versed in Tamil literature and Hindu philosophy besides. Kalam was, just as unambiguously, the 'good Muslim'. And there was Mohammad Azharuddin, who could sometimes be good, as when he scored a century or his team won, and at other times bad, as when he failed with the bat or his team lost, especially if they lost to Pakistan.[38] The cricketer himself knew of this popular ambivalence, and justly resented it. 'I don't deny that people look upon me as a Muslim,' he told his biographer.

> But whenever I have gone out to bat, or to field, I have done so as an Indian and so it shouldn't matter what religion I follow.

I always thought such feelings never entered the game. . . . But I guess I will have to learn to live with it. But that can never prevent me from giving a hundred per cent for India every time I walk out.[39]

KARGIL IS FAR AWAY from Hyderabad, and further away from Old Trafford. But Azhar knew that this match was absolutely the sternest test of his life. Already, when India had lost an early match in the tournament to unfancied Zimbabwe, effigies of the captain had been garlanded with shoes and burnt back home. Mock funeral processions were carried out, and posters printed proclaiming 'Azhar hatao, desh bachao' ('Get rid of Azhar and save the nation').[40] India had still managed to scrape through to the Super Six stage of the tournament. They now *had* to win, against a Pakistan team who were in top form. The contest between bat and ball coincided with the battle back home with tanks and howitzers. This day at least, millions of otherwise fair-minded Indians were joining Thackeray in asking Azhar that deeply unfair question: which side was he really on?

As I have said, at this match in Old Trafford the players and spectators and mood were all Asian. The English thoughtfully supplied the weather. It was a grey and windy day, cold on the field and colder where I sat. The Media Overspill Box was on the top tier of the old pavilion, open on three sides. It was overcast all through, but the rain held off. The sun appeared once, in mid-afternoon, to reveal a magical view of the Pennines, running low on the horizon.

Azhar won the toss and chose to bat, no doubt remembering that in the 1992 and 1996 World Cups wins against Pakistan, India had batted first. Sachin Tendulkar came out to the wicket with Sadagopan Ramesh. Sachin had played a season of county cricket in Yorkshire, but this was probably the coldest day of young Ramesh's life (he comes from Madras). Ramesh played a few crisp shots before being bowled, retreating to the warmth of the dressing-room. Sachin was hitting his trademark straight drives. He had got to 46 when he lost his head and skied a catch to long-off. India's hopes for a decent total now rested on the in-form Dravid and the hopelessly out-of-form Azhar. Four years previously, Azhar had insisted on Dravid's elevation to international cricket. Now the younger man was paying back the debt. He was batting beautifully, his leg glides standing out. His captain was beaten three or four times an over. After every over Dravid would talk to Azhar, a helpfully encouraging arm around his shoulder. It was a splendid exhibition of team spirit. Gradually Azhar's feet started moving. The ball began to find the middle of his bat. Both men scored half-centuries as India ended with 227 for 6.

It was not a huge total, but the conditions favoured the fielding side. As in 1996, the three main bowlers were all from Bangalore: Srinath, Prasad and Kumble. All bowled well, Prasad especially. The dangerous Shahid Afridi went early, and so did Ijaz, caught beautifully at second slip by Azhar. The talented left-hander Saeed Anwar was batting with composure. Inzamam-ul-Haq was with him, but handicapped by a split hand. Anwar played two lovely drives in succession. Then he flashed at a ball seaming away, and the edge went fast and low between the wicket-keeper and first slip. Azhar dived away to his right and made the catch. This was probably the match's turning-point. Although the lower order fought hard, Pakistan ended 47 runs short of victory.

As the last wicket fell a British journalist next to me started phoning his report. 'Mohammed Azharuddin doused off the effigies of himself that had been burning from Bombay to Calcutta and kept India alive in the World Cup,' he began. This first sentence was a treat, but I could not get the rest for, seeing my eyes on him, the fellow moved off with his cellphone. I turned to look at the crowd assembled in front of the pavilion. Suddenly, there seemed more Indian flags (all day they had been outnumbered two to one). The biggest flag, held high by five men, identified its holders as being from 'BHUJ-KUTCH', an arid, dusty and cricket-deprived part of India adjacent to the Saurashtra of Ranji and Gandhi. The end of the match had stunned the Pakistanis. Their flags had been put away, but after ten minutes one reappeared. Its bearers began, bravely and patriotically, to shout 'Pakistan Zindabad'.

On the shuttle back to the train station I was accompanied by two Pakistanis and an Indian. The Pakistanis were young, and six feet tall, meat-eaters from the Punjab. The Indian was a tiny, middle-aged Gujarati from Leicester, weaned on goat's milk. This day he had drunk mugs of beer, and his side had won. Swaying from side to side, he taunted the Pakistanis. They reacted with commendable restraint. Otherwise, too, there was far less trouble than had been anticipated. One flag had been burnt, and only three people arrested.

The British police were relieved, but the British press was somewhat disappointed. A football-style bust-up on the ground, preferably to be followed by Hindu–Muslim riots on the streets: that was what the tabloids were in search of. The *Sun's* headline read: 'INDIAN HOPE TRICK: AZZA WINS BUT IT'S MUCH URDU ABOUT NOTHING'. The *Guardian*, a paper of quality, printed a telling photograph shot by Fayaz Kabli in Kashmir. An Indian soldier had a rifle in one hand, a transistor radio in the other. His expression was grim, his eyes crinkled up in fierce and worried concentration. The London edition of *The Asian Age* spoke in its front-page lead story of how 'REBORN INDIA KILL PAK: REAL MEN OF MATCH CROWD'. Other stories on the same page reported the death of six Pakistani soldiers in Kargil and the deployment in the conflict of the crack trainees of the Kashmir High Altitude Warfare School.[41]

The dailies at least had something to write about. After the match, I travelled back to London with the correspondents of our two leading English-language weeklies, *India Today* and *Outlook*. I thought I would analyse the day with them, discuss Dravid's batsmanship and Azhar's catches and the fighting spirit of the Pakistanis. But the cricket meant nothing to these cricket writers, and they were totally dissatisfied with the result. If India had lost, and India's captain had made a duck, they would have had the perfect cover story: 'AZHAR GOES OUT IN DISGRACE'.

The Old Trafford match was the subject of an essay in, of all places, the *Times Literary Supplement*. In his 'Bywords' column, the poet P. J. Kavanagh celebrated the 'un-English clamour' of a crowd which had 'triumphantly failed the Tebbit Test'. He contrasted the joyousness of the spectators with the grimness of the stewards on duty. 'Such frank release of national feeling', wrote Kavanagh, 'could do more for racial relations than any sullen pretence. There should be Test matches staged in England between India and Pakistan.'[42]

This was the comment of a well-meaning innocent. The low level of violence that day was, I suspect, only because of the fear of British justice, of having one's passport or residency permit cancelled by a spell in the locker. Kavanagh did not reckon either with the consequences for, or rather in, the sub-continent. What would have happened if an Azhar-led India had lost?

In the event, India did not qualify for the tournament's next stage, while the rivals went all the way to the final. The result of the final was conveyed in the vulgar headline of an Indian paper: 'AUSTRALIA TURN COCKY PAKISTAN INTO IMPOTENT JOKE'.[43] Unlike in 1992, no Indian wanted Pakistan to win once his own team was out. In some towns, processions were arranged to 'celebrate' Pakistan's defeat. One such, in the Calcutta suburb of Budge-Budge, developed into a minor riot after the celebrators threw stones at shops owned by Muslims. The police came, but retreated in the face of a hail of home-made bombs. Order was eventually restored by the Army. Three people died in the violence.[44]

Had Pakistan defeated Australia and won the Cup their followers would have forgiven the loss to India. Now, to be the second best team in the world was not enough. When the players reached Lahore airport, a crowd of 5,000 angry fans awaited them. Two hundred commandos could not stop the shower of rotten eggs. Under armed escort the cricketers reached their homes, but would not leave them for weeks. As on the border's other side, there was a sickening fickle-mindedness to the love of cricket. A man in Karachi beat up his brother for having named his son, before the tournament began, after the Pakistani captain. A sixty-two-year-old grandmother in Lahore accused the Pakistan team of taking bribes. She took off her bangles and offered them to the cricketers, saying, 'They are not men, they played like women.' Fans like these, and young boys, still make it their life's ambition to play cricket for their country.[45]

THE HISTORY OF cricket relations between India and Pakistan almost exactly mirrors the history of cricket relations between Hindus and Muslims in British India. Test matches between the two countries in the period 1952 to 1989 were as civilized as Quadrangular matches between the two communities from 1912 to 1929. There was an element of nationalist competition, admittedly, but this was within bounds and did not get cast in religious terms. Writing before the 1952 Bombay Test, a local journalist told his readers: 'India and Pakistan clash today. Now, don't get excited, it's only at the Brabourne Stadium. . . . Anyway, here's hoping the better team wins. The fight won't get to UNO you know . . .'[46]

Likewise, in the 1950s or 1960s, there was no question of a Thackeray Test for Indian Muslims. In two fields especially, cricket and film, their contributions were quite out of proportion to their share in the country's population. In 1994, at a scholarly seminar in southern India, the Kannada writer U. R. Anantha Murty complained that having grown up in a conservative Hindu milieu, he found it difficult to cast credible Muslim characters in his stories. I answered that I had no such trouble in writing my tales. For the history of cricket in independent India is studded with the deeds of Muslims: the incandescent stroke-play of Syed Mushtaq Ali; the skilful off-breaks of Ghulam Ahmed; the all-round genius of Salim Durrani; the sturdy workmanship of Syed Abid Ali; the superb wicket-keeping of Syed Kirmani; above all, the dazzle at the crease and in the out-field of Mansur Ali Khan Pataudi, one of India's longest-serving captains, and without question its most charismatic.

My riposte to Anantha Murty rang hollow even as I offered it. In or about 1990, with the trouble in Kashmir and Ayodhya, the politics of cricket entered a new phase. This last decade in South Asia has recalled the last decade of British India. Indo–Pak matches have been subject to the same over-determined scrutiny as the Hindu–Muslim matches in Bombay between 1937 and 1946. On this game of bat and ball have been superimposed notions of communal and national loyalty, honour and pride. Destructive in any case, these sentiments were made more deadly by the accident of a Muslim being cricket captain of India. Back in the 1960s, no one would have cared to question the patriotism of the Muslim captain of India (the Nawab of Pataudi), but in the 1990s they were questioning it all the time.

In a striking but futile flashback to those Pentangular days, the cricketers of the two countries are on terms of warm friendship. Fifty thousand Bangalorians wanted Javed Miandad roasted in March 1996. Two months later, the Indian team was on tour in England and Miandad was helping them at the nets, putting his own vast experience of English conditions at the service of his sub-continental brethren. The Indian and Pakistani players watch the same films, listen to the same music, eat the same food and speak the same language (nearly). The Pakistan cricket team's German physiotherapist, Dan Kiesel, taught by the newspapers to expect venomous hatred, was amazed at how friendly his wards were with the Indian opposition. 'I haven't seen the Pakistan team mix as well with any other team,' he remarked.[47] When all the participating sides were given a reception at Buckingham Palace during the 1999 World Cup, the Pakistani debutants hovered around Sachin Tendulkar, too shy to talk to him, but keen to soak in the aura of the greatest batsman in the world.[48]

Tragically, the gap between the cricketers and their publics is immense. In January 1998 India played Pakistan in the final of the Asia Cup. The match, played at the Bangabandhu Stadium in Dhaka, was a script-writer's dream: 600 runs scored in a day, individual centuries by those stylish left-handers Saeed Anwar and Saurav Ganguly, both sides in the game until the last over. The report in a respectable Indian newspaper began this way:

DHAKA: Thousands of Bangladeshis were hailing India again after a gap of 26 years since India helped them in their war of liberation in 1971. The reason: a second-last ball win over Pakistan . . .

The bare facts of the match were recorded and then the reporter noted that

> The Dhaka stadium, the scene of India's mind-boggling triumph . . . was barely two km away from the Suhrawardy Udyan where Pakistan's Gen Niazi signed the treaty of surrender and handed it over to Gen Jagjit Singh Arora.

Now the man who hit the winning runs, Hrishikesh Kanitkar, was singled out:

> . . . even as Saqlain threatened to wrest another match from India, they found their man of the hour, a 23-year-old from the land of the Peshwas, who displayed true grit befitting his lineage.[49]

I suppose one can explain away some of the fervour. Perhaps the correspondent had never previously reported an Indian cricket victory over Pakistan. But the reference to the war of 1971 was completely gratuitous: what did it have to do with the match being played? In truth, the Dhaka crowd was behind the Indians only because the best batsman on display was their fellow Bengali, Ganguly. And why the reference to the Peshwas? Was it because the reporter was himself a Maharashtrian Hindu, like Hrishikesh Kanitkar, but also like Bal Thackeray? And was he aware that the medieval rulers of Poona are remembered for their patronage of music and literature, but also for their hostility to low castes and Muslims?

Better-educated Indians have also seen cricket matches with Pakistan in military terms. In April 1999 an influential diplomat and former Ambassador to Islamabad wrote an article praising recent missile tests by India, tests that had come in the wake of two bad cricket defeats at the hands of Pakistan. 'What matters', said Shankar Bajpai,

> is that we should have enough strength for Pakistan to know

that it will not be able to fool around with us. . . . Only a strong Indian strike capability can ensure that Pakistan accepts detente as the only visible consequence of our both going nuclear. As in cricket, Pakistan is purposeful, relentless and always assertive, while we are careless, slack and hesitant.[50]

Not surprisingly, the military men of India and Pakistan themselves take cricket very seriously indeed. A writer trekking in the Kargil area in the autumn of 1998 asked a *jawan* he met about exchanges of fire across the line of control. 'The worst is when our countries are playing cricket,' answered the soldier. 'If they win, we can expect a few gun-shots in celebration, maybe an artillery round or two. If we win, they pound us for hours.'[51] After war broke out the following summer, the great all-rounder Kapil Dev went to the border to boost morale. The *jawans* he met asked him to tell the Indian cricketers playing in the World Cup that they might lose to anyone else but, please, not to Pakistan.

Within India, a loss to Pakistan at cricket is sometimes harder to bear than a loss on the battlefield. It is, as I have suggested, this fear of losing that prompted the boycott movement of Bal Thackeray in the winter of 1998–9. Men like Thackeray worry about the consequences for Hindu pride if our cricketers are thrashed by theirs. Indeed, after the 1999 World Cup, the Government announced that it would no longer allow India to play Pakistan in 'bilateral' cricket matches. They could play in multi-national tournaments, such as the World Cup, but there would be no more cricket visits across the border. Strangely, the Government has permitted Pakistani football and table-tennis teams to play in India. Queried on this contradiction, the External Affairs Minister answered that cricket matches between India and Pakistan were 'less cricket and more gladiatorial contests'. The Sports Minister insisted that 'cricket has come into the category of an extraordinary game. It has begun representing the sentiments of the people. We see cricket not as just a game, but as a symbol of the nation's sentiments.'[52] There is an unsaid sub-text here: we can afford to lose to them at football or table tennis, but not at cricket.[53]

❧

How deep has been the contamination of cricket by politics in India. And how old too. Cricketers once struggled for space on the Maidan, once struggled for recognition on the basis of skill rather than birth. Later, the deepening communal divide willy-nilly made the cricket field a theatre of party politics.

The history of this English game in the Indian sub-continent can be told through the cricketers. One can write of the artistry of the batsmen, whether stroke-makers like Sachin Tendulkar or technicians like Hanif Mohammed. One can speak of the distinctiveness of the bowlers, of the contributions by Indians to the art of spin and by Pakistanis to the art of swing and seam. One must not forget, either, the essential decency and civility of these cricketers, their readiness to make friends with the opposition and the complete absence in their vocabulary of the words of abuse that come so easily to cricketers of other countries.

The supporters have ennobled and enriched cricket as well. Their cheerful spontaneity and music and wit have made a sometimes dour game come alive. Cricket has been successfully indigenized, made part of the fabric of everyday life and language. Add to this the weight of numbers, the hundreds of millions of South Asians who have come to watch and pay for the sport. In a globalized and competitive world, this game, more subtle and varied than any other, would not have survived anywhere without their support.

This book has told the history of Indian cricket in other ways: through the master categories of race, caste, religion and nation. Of these the last two have been the most dangerous. Previously they worked separately, now they increasingly work together. They have produced a destructive passion unparalleled in the history of sport. Thus David Hopps, writing in Neville Cardus's old paper, has said that compared to an India–Pakistan cricket match a clash between

Rangers and Celtic – two Glasgow soccer teams divided by history and religion – was like 'a WI coffee morning'.[54] I had first thought it appropriate to end with this remark, an Englishman's description of what others have made of his game. But I have chosen instead a comment from Sri Lanka, a country which produces as good cricketers and as fanatical cricket followers as its more powerful neighbours. The Colombo journal *Pravada* has expressed its shock at the coverage of India–Pakistan matches in the Indian and Pakistani press, at 'the crudely militaristic metaphors and imagery used so freely to describe what happens on the playground.' The fans follow the reporters, calling for a revision of George Orwell's famous epithet. Sport 'is no longer war minus the shooting. It is war minus the nuclear missiles.'[55]

Epilogue

Who are the Indians who dislike cricket? There are the economists, who compute its negative impact on Gross National Product, who worry about the impact of absenteeism from factory and kitchen whenever a match is being shown live on television. There is the Anglophobe nationalist, deeply suspicious of anything not first thought of in the Indo-Gangetic Plain. *Dhoti*, yes, he says, but trousers, no. Sanskrit, yes, English, no. Tandoori chicken, yes, Kentucky Fried, no. The indigenist who shuns MTV and Miss World contests would like cricket banned as well. During the 1992 World Cup, M. M. Vyas of Jaisalmer wrote angrily to the newspapers: 'How long shall we Indians go on spending money lavishly, wasting precious time for the maintenance of this monument of slavery called cricket?'[1]

One ideologue who detested the game of cricket was M. S. Golwalkar. Golwalkar served for decades as *sarsanghchalak* or head of the Rashtriya Swayamsevak Sangh (RSS), which is roughly to the Bharatiya Janata Party what the SS was to the Nazis. He was the mentor of thousands of RSS workers, many of whom have since gone on to occupy important positions in public life. His pupils include India's current Prime Minister, Atal Behari Vajpayee, and its Home Minister, Lal Krishna Advani. In his speeches Golwalkar would come back, time and again, to the need to expunge this foreign game from the soil of India. Speaking in the 1950s, the RSS chief insisted that

the costly game of cricket, which has not only become a fashion in our country but something over which we are spending crores

434

of rupees, only proves that the English are still dominating our mind and intellect. The cricket match that Pandit Nehru and other MPs played some years back was the very depth of this Anglicism. Why could they not play Kabaddi, our national game, which has been acclaimed by several countries as a great game?[2]

In their opposition to cricket the indigenists are joined by those who play other sports. Cricket, it is said, promotes unfitness while stifling its competitors. 'Are we and our children condemned to stand and stare at cricket and do nothing else?' asked one writer:

Are our children going to be denied for ever the joys of running and jumping and the exultation of sheer *lila*? Do we want them to grow up into weaklings and with all their bodily facilities impaired and possibly atrophied because they can only be spectators of a game and not players of anything?[3]

Chief among these neglected sports is field hockey. Between 1928 and 1960, India was undefeated in Olympic competition. The greatest hockey players in history have been the Sikhs of the Punjab; one village in Jalandhar district, Sansarpur, has alone produced eighteen internationals. In the early 1980s the love for hockey mingled with the movement for a separate Sikh state, prompting an extraordinary letter to the editor of Punjab's leading English-language newspaper, *The Tribune*. The grammar and language are as in the original:

Dear Editor,

Sat Sri Akal. It is learnt that Radio and TV stations of Jalandhar are going to broadcast/telecast running commentary on series of cricket matches to be played between India and Pak. What a matter of great sorrow is it? Our national game is hockey. What treatment our hockey is receiving from AIR and Doordarshan. No commentary of a number of international hockey tournaments was broadcast/telecast. If they cannot telecast a one and a half hour long hockey match how did they telecast 4–5 day play of cricket, a time consuming game.

It is confirmed from the long observation that hockey, the national game of India, the game mixed in the blood of Punjabis, is greatly ignored. . . . So I have formally informed by AIR and Doordarshan that their bid to telecast a running commentary on Jalandhar should be strongly dealt with. We have informed them that the commentators should come to stadium with their heads on their palms.

In case the running commentary will be telecast/broadcast, we will blow off the commentator box with HE-36 bombs to be fired with the 2' mortar guns. The smoke bombs will also serve our purpose. Hence it is wise for the AIR and Doordarshan officials not to come to stadium for sake of their lives. They should have to think of hockey, football, athletics etc, in which India is lacking behind due to wrong policies of AIR and Doordarshan.

Here is a request for you. You being the Editor of a leading newspaper must write about this case so that people may also know what a kind of bad decisions are being taken by our media services, which result in downing of our national game.

I hope no commentary on Jalandhar Test.

Servant of the 'Panth'.[4]

The emotions expressed here might be extreme, but Indian hockey players certainly have reason to complain. They have the skill and commitment, but lack the facilities. Were fans and, following them, sponsors, to show greater interest, they might yet make our hockey team once more the best in the world. A former Indian hockey captain probably spoke for all his men when he said he 'hated' cricket,

not only for the man-hours it wastes but for its narrow objective. It is a lousy game in which everybody on the field aspires and makes efforts to get one poor man out. . . . This cricketing trait has imprinted itself on the national mosaic and signs of it are visible in every profession . . .[5]

Other kinds of sportsmen, killjoy economists, cultural nationalists: these groups have consistently opposed cricket. Very recently, however, many diehard cricket lovers have turned their back on the game. The provocation is 'Hansiegate', the betting scandal in which the former South African captain, Hansie Cronje, admitted to taking money from Indian bookmakers introduced to him by Indian cricketers. Meanwhile, one former Test cricketer, Manoj Prabhakar, claimed that the great all-rounder Kapil Dev offered him 25 lakh rupees to 'throw' a match. The charge was denied, but in the face of strong public criticism Kapil Dev resigned as national cricket coach. Four cricketers were dropped from the Indian team because of their ties with bookies. They included that gifted and tormented character, Mohammad Azharuddin. Hindu reactionaries had cast suspicion on his patriotism; it turned out that it was his probity that was in question. Since 1995 at least, he had been passing on privileged information to bookmakers. In some, admittedly minor matches, he had under-performed at their behest. Azhar's involvement came as a serious shock to those like myself who had delighted in his exquisite batsmanship, and who wished to believe the best about him only because men like Bal Thackeray believed the worst.

The nexus between players and bookmakers was first exposed by two young journalists, Aniruddha Bahal and Krishna Prasad.[6] The Delhi police took up the case, secretly recording Cronje's conversations on tour. Records of other cricketers' mobile phones revealed their own intimacy with malevolent bookies. At first, the revelations made the Indian fans turn savagely on their heroes. Opinion polls and cover stories confirmed that 'cricket is no longer a gentleman's game', that cricketers have had their head turned by all the attention, that they are as corrupt as the politicians, that 'it is high time other sports like kabaddi, basketball, hockey, football, and volleyball are encouraged'.[7]

Where the press led the market followed. Commercials with cricketers and cricket themes were dropped from television. The state passed its own verdict, with the Gujarat Government dropping a chapter on Kapil Dev from its Class X English textbook.[8] The senior Uttar Pradesh politician Mulayam Singh Yadav, a former all-in wrestler and confirmed Anglophobe, demanded in the Lok Sabha that cricket should be banned in India. Yadav told a journalist that he had 'scant respect for cricket. Look at all the scandals. Besides, I believe that this game is meant for servile countries that have always been ruled by the Western world.'[9]

Several years ago, the historian Sunil Khilnani suggested that like other globalizing countries, India was ripe for a thoroughgoing Americanization. The United States, he argued, had replaced Britain as the locus of cultural inspiration. Michael Jackson had recently sung to huge acclaim in Bombay, and Bill Gates dolls were selling in the streets of Calcutta. Khilnani quoted John Strachey, writing in the 1950s, that 'to know a no-ball from a googly and a point of order from a supplementary question is genuinely to have something in common'. He then added this caveat: 'But in a generation or two from now, Indians may be more familiar with the difference between a curve ball and a slider.'[10]

I thought then, and think now, that the obituary was premature. For cricket has made the necessary concessions to industrial time, as with the advent of one-day cricket, and the shift to floodlit matches so that people no longer need sacrifice work for play. In any case cricket is a more subtle game than baseball. It has a far wider range of possible outcomes for each ball, and thus a wider range of possible social responses. It is also more ceremonial. In all ways is it suited to the Indian ethos. Indians might come to drink Coke instead of tender coconut water, come to prefer Levis jeans to the sari, but they shall *never* abandon cricket for baseball.

Indeed, the serving US ambassador to New Delhi has himself acknowledged that in this particular respect Indian culture will remain impervious to American influence. In a speech to the Confederation of Indian Industry he remarked that his boss, President George W. Bush, 'has developed his foreign policy in much the same way as a captain of a cricket team approaches an international Test match'. The President, he continued, 'is not interested in limited overs. Instead, he has fielded a skilled and deeply experienced team that is ready for more than One-Day matches.'[11] The imagery is striking: where one would expect the arrogant American to expect the rest of the world to warm to baseball metaphors, this canny diplomat spoke the language of a game he himself does not understand but which his audience wholeheartedly and perhaps excessively loves.

Even the match-fixing scandal will not affect the craze for cricket in the long run. The patriotic fan has nowhere else to go. For the Sydney Olympics, this nation of a billion people sent a contingent of 200 competitors which collectively won one bronze medal. The hockey team finished seventh out of twelve competing teams. Months after the match-fixing scandal broke the fans had started coming back, encouraged by the fine performance of the Indian cricket team in a one-day championship in Kenya. Their return was welcomed by that pulse of the people, Pepsi-Cola, which soon aired commercials featuring the young, fresh and uncontaminated Indian batsman who had done especially well in Nairobi.

Writing in 1959, the respected Madras critic N. S. Ramaswami pointed out that all through Indian cricket's history 'opposition to it has never died; there has always been the parrot cry that it is too costly, that it is "foreign", that it consumes too much time'. But, Ramaswami continued, 'it will be nothing less than to mutilate the Indian spirit if cricket were to be banished from the land'.[12] That will never happen. One certain sign is that men like Vajpayee and Advani, who follow Guru Golwalkar's precepts in most other respects, have completely disregarded this particular prejudice. Were India to win an important match soon, almost the first photographs of the winning team will show them in the company of the BJP Prime Minister.

To illustrate cricket's extraordinary hold over India and Indians, let me offer a last anecdote, from a Test match played against Pakistan in Bombay in the first week of December 1960. The visitors batted first, and Hanif Mohammad opened the batting. On the second morning of the match, while some 40,000 crowded into the Brabourne Stadium, a smaller but no less intense crowd gathered in an Irani restaurant outside. That eatery had been chosen by the socialist leader, Dr Ram Manohar Lohia, for a press conference. Now, Lohia's pet hates were Jawaharlal Nehru, the English language and the game of cricket, generally in that order. To a group of acolytes and left-wing journalists Lohia thundered on about how the game of cricket symbolized our continuing colonialism, and how the last Englishman to rule India was complicit in this. Throw out Nehru, he said, and we can all happily start playing *kabaddi*.

The scribes departed, to file their stories. But after they had gone Lohia walked across to the nearest *paanwallah*, asked for a *paan*, and while chewing it continued: 'Kya Hanif out ho gaya kya?' The answer came back no, Hanif is still batting. He was out only at sundown, *run out*, for 160.[13]

In this cricket-mad land, even the most active of cricket-baiters always succumb to its charms in the end.

Acknowledgements

I am a social historian by profession, a cricket writer by inclination. For a long time I refused to mix business with pleasure, writing scholarly tomes burdened with footnotes during the week and fan's essays lightened with myth and anecdote over the weekend. This was a separation of work and leisure that I was proud of: the mark, I thought, of a thoroughly modern man.

I had always intended my two worlds to be kept in separate compartments. When, ten years ago, I began working on a book on the Bombay carnival, it was to deal with cricket and cricket alone. I hoped to document the styles and achievements of those players who had laid the game's foundations before India was granted official Test status in 1932. Mine was a work of celebration and rehabilitation, focusing on sport and sportsmen, with politics and society emphatic-ally left out.

Then one Monday, back at work, I got a call from a journalist asking what I thought of a recent attack on Mahatma Gandhi by a contemporary leader of the Untouchables. To answer the question I had to go back to the Poona Pact, the majestically flawed agreement of September 1932 between Gandhi and B. R. Ambedkar whose resonances stalk Indian politics to this day. Spurred on by the journalist, I read the accounts of the pact by historians. I learned that two men on the Untouchable side had helped negotiate a compro-mise: M. C. Rajah and Palwankar Baloo. Now, Rajah was a name well known to Indian historians; a leader of the depressed castes of the Madras Presidency, he had a record of social work and activism that stretched even further back than Ambedkar's. But Baloo? The scholars I was reading did not bother to identify him, apparently because they could not. But I knew, from my weekend reading, that Baloo was a famous cricketer who had made his name bowling the Hindus to victory over the Parsis and the Europeans. To me it was his *political* self that was a revelation. Baloo accompanying the greatest of Untouchable leaders to sign a pact with Gandhi was, I thought, akin to Jesse Owens or Joe Louis advising Dr Martin Luther King during his negotiations with Lyndon Johnson.

This discovery, that cricket and politics were united in the career of P. Baloo, led swiftly to the blurring of the boundaries between my two selves. To make a forgotten man known once more excited the historian's vanity. I was encouraged to explore what Palwankar Baloo had meant to a previous generation of sports fans and low-caste leaders.

But as the project proceeded I began to have doubts. Should I not call a stop to this blurring of genres, this potentially dangerous mixture of profession and passion? I thought I should write an essay on cricket and colonialism and then return to the *status quo ante*: history for business, cricket for fun. But two friendly readers of the essay put paid to these plans. The first, Ajaz Ashraf, sent me a Marathi pamphlet about Baloo that compelled me to ask for more. The second, Hans Medick, insisted that there was room here for a whole book: it would, said this acclaimed micro-historian, 'be a history of India from the edge'.

I continued to prevaricate. But then provocation was joined to encouragement. I happened to read a new edition of a book on Bombay, cricket's capital city, the home of countless Test cricketers who have collectively scored in excess of 50,000 Test runs. In her acknowledgements, the author thanked 'Vijay Merchant of the Hindoosthan Mills': a curious identification, for the person in question is better known as the founder of the Bombay School of Batsmanship. In her introduction, the author noted with gratification that in the decade since the book was first published 'little boys have relinquished the habit of playing cricket on traffic islands'. Later, in the main text, she spoke of how, crossing the Bombay Maidan, 'you need fear nothing but sunstroke, a cricket ball on the head, the sight of men relieving themselves in the peaceful air and, at certain seasons, a white bull'.

A sneer, a poor joke, and a mention of a great cricketer without identifying him: such were the sum and substance of the references to cricket in a book billed as '*the* biography of Bombay'. Could I, in the face of this appalling neglect, still keep my two spheres so separate? Should not one historian's blindness be made another historian's opportunity? Luckily, I was then a Fellow of the Nehru Memorial Museum and Library at Teen Murti House in New Delhi. I had been granted a Fellowship to work on environmental history; but a wink and a nod from the Library's legendary Director, Ravinder Kumar, allowed me to interpret my assignment more broadly. Change in research topic was justified by the appositeness of method, by the fact that I was spending my days amidst a collection of old newspapers housed in what was once the official residence of that cricket-loving historian, Jawaharlal Nehru.

My greatest debt, then, is to the librarians of Teen Murti House, in particular to Mr Sartaj Abidi and Mrs Indubala Sharma, the successive keepers of the newspaper collection, and in whose cheerful company I spent hundreds of hours. Also at Teen Murti, Mr Rajesh Chopra of the main library provided continuous assistance over a ten-year period. Two other repositories proved of crucial importance: the Anandji Dossa Collection at the Cricket Club of India, Mumbai, and the K. V. Gopalaratnam Collection at the Sports Authority of India in New Delhi. I am grateful to the eponymous donors of these collections, and to the librarians of the CCI and the SAI, Mrs Lewis and Mrs Poonam, for their generous assistance. For their support I would also like to thank the staffs of the National Library, the Oriental and India Office Collections of the British Library, the British Library Newspaper Collections, the library of St Stephen's College, the Maharashtra State Archives, the Green Library at Stanford University, the Mudd Library at Yale University, the library of the University of Washington, the library of the University of Oslo, the Bodleian Library, and the library of the Karnataka State Cricket Association.

I must, however, note with regret the non-cooperation of the Curator of the MCC, who chose not to answer letters seeking an appointment to examine the records under his keeping. This closure was more than compensated by the open access to their collections granted by other librarians and by sellers of second-hand books: by the pavement stalls of Delhi and Calcutta, by J. W. Mackenzie in Surrey and Roger Page in Melbourne, by the proprietor of 'Extra Cover' on Boundary Road in London, by Prabhu Book Service in Gurgaon, by Marine Sports and the New and Secondhand Bookshop in Mumbai, and, above all, by K. K. S. Murthy of the Select Book-shop, Bangalore.

Among the many friends and colleagues who provided help and encouragement I must especially mention Rukun Advani, Chandu Borde, Mary Searle Chatterjee, Marcus Couto, Keshav Desiraju, Raj Singh Dungarpur, Gopal and Tara Gandhi, Richard Hill, Niranjan Joshi, Sanjay Joshi, Munni Kabir, Sunil Khilnani, Prashant Kidambi, G. Krishnamurthy, David Lelyveld, Lucy Luck, Amrit Mathur, Suresh Menon, Richard Milner, Sujit Mukherjee, the late D. R. Nagaraj, James Nye, Mahesh Rangarajan, Mario Rodrigues, the late T. G. Vaidyanathan, Tunku Varadarajan, Rajendra Vora, A. D. Vyas and Eleanor Zelliot. Extended interviews were graciously granted by K. V. Palwankar, Y. B. Palwankar and Bal J. Pandit: these proved indispensable in reconstructing the story of the Baloo brothers. The veteran Bombay cricketer Vasant Raiji provided both moral and material support. Ayaz Memon and Chidananda Rajghatta arranged for a pass for the 1999 World Cup. My aunt Sumati Bagchee passed on a precious portrait of C. K. Nayudu. And I am honoured to have been able to use the work of my photographer friends, Sanjeev Saith and T. S. Satyan.

The book has benefited enormously from the comments on an earlier draft of David Gilmour, Mukul Kesavan, Rudrangshu Mukh-erjee, K. Sivaramakrishnan and Siddharth Varadarajan. For their vital research assistance I thank Sharad Mehendaley, Sharmilla Phatak, Rita Sridhar and Mugdha Yeolekar. My esteemed colleague, the ecologist Madhav Gadgil, took time off from his hectic schedule to provide vital information about the history and culture of his native Maharashtra. A very large debt is owed to Mukul Kesavan: since we first met in 1975, we have had innumerable and – for me, at any rate – educative discussions about cricket, history and cricket history.

The advice and critical insight of my agent, Gill Coleridge, have been indispensable in the making of this book. My editors at Picador, Mary Mount and Rebecca Senior, have been a delight to work with. A special word of thanks for my publisher, Peter Straus, who allowed his original commission to be further postponed so that I could publish another book on cricket. Peter's indulgence has been exceeded only by the indulgence of my wife, Sujata, and my children, Keshava and Iravati. To invert a famous declaration by P. G. Wodehouse, without their support this book would have taken twice the time.

Notes

Preface

1. The phrase is used in Charles Tennyson, 'They Taught the World to Play', *Victorian Studies*, vol. 2, no. 3 (March 1959).
2. James Pycroft, *The Cricket Field* (1851), in John Arlott, ed., *From Hambledon to Lord's: The Classics of Cricket* (London: Christopher Johnson, 1948), p. 62.
3. Pycroft, *The Cricket Field*, p. 63.
4. Quoted in André Bernard, 'Commonplace Book: Sports and Games', *The American Scholar*, vol. 69, no. 4 (Autumn 2000).

1. The Homesick Colonial and the Imitative Native

1. Nirad Chaudhuri, *A Passage to England* (London: Macmillan and Co., 1959), p. 16.
2. George Otto Trevelyan, *The Life and Letters of Lord Macaulay* (enlarged and complete edn: London, Longman, Green and Co., 1908), pp. 321–3, etc.
3. Churchill, *My Early Life: A Roving Commission* (1930: reprint Odhams Press, London, 1947), chapter 9, 'Education in Bangalore'. On 14 April 1897 Churchill wrote thus to his mother from Bangalore: 'Poked away in a garrison town which resembles a 3rd rate watering place, out of season and without the sea, with lots of routine work and a hot and trying sun – without society or good sport – half my friends on leave and the other half ill – my life here would be intolerable were it not for the consolations of literature.' See Randolph S. Churchill, *Winston Churchill: Volume I: Youth, 1874–1900* (London: Heinemann, 1966), pp. 298–9.
4. Quoted in Anthony de Mello, *Portrait of Indian Sport* (London: P. R. Macmillan and Co., 1959), p. 120.

5. James Pycroft, *The Cricket Field* (1851), in John Arlott, ed., *From Hambledon to Lord's: The Classics of Cricket* (London: Christopher Johnson, 1948), p. 63.

6. Extract from the *Madras Courier*, 23 February 1792, in H. T. Waghorn, compiler, *The Dawn of Cricket* (London: R. Tomsett and Co., 1906), p. 5.

7. Berry Sarbhadikary, ed., *Presenting Indian Cricket* (Calcutta: A. Mukherjee, 1946), p. 9; Sarbhadikary, *My World of Cricket* (Calcutta: Cricket Library, 1964), pp. 308–9. The second cricket club outside England, based at Haverford in Pennsylvania, began more than forty years later, in 1834. The Melbourne Cricket Club, Australia's first, was founded as late as 1838. See H. J. Moorhouse, 'The Calcutta Cricket Club', in *Cricket Association of Bengal: Silver Jubilee Souvenir* (Calcutta: CAB, 1956).

8. See S. Mutthiah, *The Spirit of Cricket: the MCC Story* (Chennai: EastWest Books, 1998), pp. 18–19.

9. Clipping of original newspaper in Willoughby Collection, Mss. Eur. F. 293/267, Oriental and India Office Collections, British Library, London.

10. The mention of the three southern counties is also noteworthy, for all had honourable cricketing histories. Cricket was played in Sussex as early as 1610, and in Kent by 1622. Hampshire was the home of the legendary Hambledon Cricket Club. Cf. Rowland Bowen, *Cricket: Its Origins and Development Throughout the World* (London: Eyre and Spottiswoode, 1970).

11. Denis Kincaid, *British Social Life in India, 1608–1937* (London: George Routledge and Sons, 1938), pp. 244, 281–2.

12. Some clubs, in fact, did not admit Indians until the 1960s.

13. W. O. Horne, quoted in Mutthiah, *The Spirit of Cricket*, pp. 24–5.

14. 'Doz', *Ragtime in Simla*, quoted in Queeny Pradhan, *Empire in the Hills: A Study of Simla, Darjeeling, Ootacamund and Mount Abu (late 19th and early 20th century)*, unpublished PhD dissertation, Centre for Historical Studies, Jawaharlal Nehru University, New Delhi, 2001, p. 211.

15. Cf. Henry Yule and Arthur Coke Burnell, *Hobson-Jobson: Being a Glossary of Anglo-Indian Colloquial Words and Phrases and of Kindred Terms; Etymological, Historical, Geographical and Discursive* (London: John Murray, 1886), pp. 310–11.

16. Contemporary account quoted in Scyld Berry, *Cricket Wallah: With England in India, 1981–2* (London: Hodder and Stoughton, 1982), p. 126.

17. Captain Philip Trevor, *The Lighter Side of Cricket* (London: Methuen and Co., 1901), pp. 266, 270–2.

18. E. H. D. Sewell, *An Outdoor Wallah* (London: Stanley Paul, 1945), pp. 43–4. Sewell was writing of the 1890s.

19. A. G. Bagot, *Sport and Travel in India and Central America* (London: Macmillan and Co., 1897), pp. 72–81.

20. Bernard Owen, 'My Days of Enjoyment at Ballygunje', in *A Century Later* (Calcutta Ballygunje Cricket Club, 1964), pp. 73f.

21. 'Some Incidents', ibid., p. 85.

22. Eckehard Kulke, *The Parsees in India: A Minority as Agent of Social Change* (New Delhi: Vikas Publishing House, 1978).

23. See Amalendu Guha, 'Parsi Seths as Entrepreneurs, 1750–1850', *Economic and Political Weekly*, 29 August 1970; idem, 'Comprador Role of Parsi Seths, 1750–1850', ibid., 28 November 1970.

24. Kulke, *The Parsees in India*, p. 36.

25. J. R. B. Jeejebhoy, 'Introduction', in H. D. Darukhanawala, *Parsi Lustre on Indian Soil, Volume I* (Bombay: G. Claridge and Co. Ltd, 1939), pp. 33–4.

26. As described by J. M. Framji Patel in his *Stray Thoughts on Indian Cricket* (Bombay: The Times of India Press, 1905), p. 2.

27. See Sharada Dwivedi and Rahul Mehrotra, *Bombay: the Cities Within* (Bombay: Eminence Designs, 1995), chapter 1.

28. 'The Maidan Described as a Popular Recreation Ground', chapter 7 of D. E. Wacha's *Shells from the Sands of Bombay: Being My Recollections and Reminiscences, 1860–1875* (Bombay: The Indian Newspaper Co., 1920).

29. Shapoorjee Sorabjee, *A Chronicle of Cricket Among Parsees and The Struggle: Polo versus Cricket* (Bombay: published by the author, 1897), p. 8.

30. Framji Patel, *Stray Thoughts on Indian Cricket*, p. 8.

31. Manekji Kavasji Patel, *History of Parsee Cricket* (Bombay: J. N. Petit Parsi Orphanage Captain Printing Press, 1892), pp. 10–11.

32. Shapoorjee, *A Chronicle of Cricket*, p. 18.

33. There were 16 annas to the rupee, and twelve pice to an anna.

34. N. S. Ramaswami, *From Porbandar to Wadekar* (New Delhi: Abhinav Publications, 1975), pp. 4–5.

35. Framji Patel, *Stray Thoughts on Indian Cricket*, p. 10.

36. Shapoorjee, *A Chronicle of Cricket*, pp. 15–16.

2. Searching for Space

1. F. S. Ashley-Cooper, 'Some Notes on Early Cricket Abroad', *The Cricketer* (Winter Annual, 1922–3).

2. Anon, 'Hindu Cricket', *Indian Social Reformer*, 18 February 1906.

3. Pherozeshah Mehta, quoted in H. D. Darukhanawala, *Parsis and Sport* (Bombay: published by the author, 1934), p. 61.

4. F. S. Ashley-Cooper, 'Some Notes on Cricket in India', *The Cricketer* (Spring Annual, 1927).

5. This paragraph draws on advertisements for cricket goods carried in the *Bombay Gazette*. But cf. also Richard Cashman, *Patrons, Players and the Crowd: The Phenomenon of Indian Cricket* (New Delhi: Orient Longman, 1980), pp. 2–3.

6. Vasant Raiji, *India's Hambledon Men* (Bombay: Tyeby Press, 1986), pp. 76–9.

7. Ibid., p. 78.

8. Manekji Kavasji Patel, *History of Parsee Cricket* (Bombay: J. N. Petit Parsi Orphanage Captain Printing Press, 1892), pp. 20–22.

9. Quoted in Shapoorjee Sorabjee, *A Chronicle of Cricket Among Parsees and The Struggle: European Polo versus Native Cricket* (Bombay: published by the author, 1897), p. 32.

10. Quoted in H. D. Darukhanawala, *Parsis and Sports*, pp. 60–61.

11. With the exception of a paragraph on the subject in Mihir Bose's *A History of Indian Cricket* (London: Andre Deutsch, 1990), p. 22.

12. Unless otherwise stated, this account is based on Shapoorjee Sorabjee, *A Chronicle of Cricket*, pp. 68–124.

13. Notably, colonial gymkhanas allowed other sports on their premises only 'so far as not to interfere with cricket'. Cf. Henry Yule and Arthur Coke Burnell, *Hobson-Jobson: Being a Glossary of Anglo-Indian Colloquial Words and Phrases and of Kindred Terms; Etymological, Historical, Geographical and Discursive* (London: John Murray, 1886), p. 311.

14. *Jam-e Jamshed*, 10 July 1879, clipping in File No. 806, vol. 50, Judicial Department Records for 1879, Maharashtra State Archives, Mumbai.

15. Public Works Department (hereafter PWD) Resolution No. 139E, 620 of 1882, 13 April 1882, in Compilation 2, Vol. 3300, Military Department Records for 1878–82, Maharashtra State Archives, Mumbai.

16. Letter from Cecil Gray, in ibid.

17. PWD Resolution No. 374 C. W., 828 of 1883, in ibid.

18. PWD Resolution No. 230 C. W., 503 of 1884, dated 1 April, and PWD Resolution No. 70 C. W., 1549 of 1884, dated 23 October, both in ibid.

19. *Rast Goftar*, issues of 27 September 1885 and 21 February 1886, in *Report on the Native Newspapers of the Bombay Presidency*, Oriental and India Office Collections, British Library, London.

20. Shapoorjee, *A Chronicle*, pp. 33, 40–41.

21. Ashley-Cooper, 'Some Notes on Cricket in India'.

22. Quoted in Raiji, *India's Hambledon Men*, p. 16. Mehta's own abiding love for cricket is described in Homi Mody, *Sir Pherozeshah Mehta: A Political Biography* (second edn: Bombay, Asia Publishing House, 1963), pp. 3–4.

23. J. M. Framji Patel, *Stray Thoughts on Indian Cricket* (Bombay: The Times of India Press, 1905), pp. 33–7; Manekji Kavasji Patel, *History of Parsee Cricket*, pp. 25–7.

24. See Compilation No. 886, Vol. 72, PWD Records of 1890–97, Maharashtra State Archives, Mumbai.

25. Letter of 6 October 1886 in Compilation No. 4175, Vol. 713, PWD Records of 1890–97, Maharashtra State Archives, Mumbai.

26. Notes of 11 October and 18 October, ibid.

27. PWD Resolution No. 112 C. W., 323 of 1887, in ibid.

28. Framji Patel, *Stray Thoughts on Indian Cricket*, pp. 42–5; Manekji Kavasji Patel, *History of Parsee Cricket*, p. 32.

29. Manekji Kavasji Patel, *History of Parsee Cricket*, pp. 34–5; Framji Patel, *Stray Thoughts on Indian Cricket*, p. 51.

30. *Bombay Gazette*, 31 January 1890.

31. Ibid.

32. Ibid., 1 February 1890. The *Gazette* was here inaugurating a long and still active tradition of visiting English teams attributing cricket defeats in the sub-continent to the weather, the diet or the umpiring.

33. Framji Patel, *Stray Thoughts on Indian Cricket*, pp. 53–4.

34. Captain Philip Trevor, *The Lighter Side of Cricket* (London: Methuen and Co., 1901), pp. 269–70.

35. Framji Patel, *Stray Thoughts on Indian Cricket*, pp. 55, 59.

36. 'Dinner to the Parsee Cricketers', the *Times of India*, 10 February 1890, reproduced in ibid., 18 January 1992.

37. *Bombay Gazette*, 1 February 1890.

38. *Rast Goftar*, quoted in *Bombay Gazette*, 6 February 1890.

3. Claiming the Heartland

1. F. S. Ashley-Cooper, 'Some Notes on Early Cricket Abroad', *The Cricketer Annual*, 1922–3

2. M. Suryanarayana and P. N. Sundaresan, *Buchi Babu (Father of Madras Cricket) and His Sporting Clan* (Madras: published by the authors, 1993).

3. Interview with Bal J. Pandit, Poona, September 1999.

4. D. B. Deodhar, *The March of Indian Cricket* (Calcutta: Illustrated News, 1948), pp. 17–18.

5. Framji Patel, *Stray Thoughts on Indian Cricket* (Bombay: The Times of India Press, 1905), p. 134.

6. G. A. Canser, *My Cricket, 188?–1941* (Karachi: published by the author, 1941), pp. 1–4, 7, 9–10, 14–16, 34–5. See also J. Naoomal, 'Cricket in

Karachi', in Syed M. H. Maqsood, ed., *Who's Who in Indian Cricket* (Delhi: published by the author, 1940); C. B. Rubie and B. D. Shanker, *A History of the Sind Cricket Tournament and Karachi Cricket in General* (London: Edwin Forster and Co., 1928).

7. David Lelyveld, *Aligarh's First Generation: Muslim Solidarity in British India* (Princeton: Princeton University Press, 1978), pp. 256–61; also Taqui Imam, 'Aligarh's Contribution to Cricket', *Sport and Pastime* (Madras), 19 January 1957.

8. Habibullah, *Aligarh ka Cricket* (Aligarh: published by the author, 1951). The following paragraphs are also based on this source.

9. Raza Ali, quoted in S. K. Bhatnagar, *History of the MAO College, Aligarh* (Bombay: Asia Publishing House, 1968) p. 151. K. S. Ranjitsinhji, whose fuller acquaintance we shall make later in the book, was to be the ruler of Nawanagar, not Bhavnagar. Muhammad and Shaukat Ali were prominent nationalists and allies of Mahatma Gandhi in the Khilafat movement of 1919–22.

10. As told in F. S. Ashley-Cooper, 'Some Notes on Cricket in India', *The Cricketer*, Winter Annual, 1922–3

11. Akhtar Hasan, 'Cricket in Aligarh', in Maqsood, ed., *Who's Who in Indian Cricket* p. 56.

12. Framji Patel, *Stray Thoughts on Indian Cricket*, p. 31.

13. See David Gilmour, *The Long Recessional: the Imperial Life of Rudyard Kipling* (London: John Murray, 2002), chapter 5.

14. F. St. J. Gore, *Lights and Shades of Hill Life in the Afghan and Hindu Highlands of the Punjab: A Contrast* (London: John Murray, 1895), pp. 81–2.

15. In Manikaran, although the terrain is inhospitable to cricket the social structure is not. In these hills inequalities of status and property are much less marked than in the plains of India. Most farmers till the land registered in their names. Many Himalayan villages, indeed, are single-caste settlements of owner-proprietors. See Ramachandra Guha, *The Unquiet Woods: Ecological Change and Peasant Resistance in the Himalaya* (first published in 1989: second edn, Berkeley: University of California Press, 2000).

16. Quoted in Framji Patel, *Stray Thoughts on Indian Cricket*, pp. 37–8.

4. The Empire of Cricket

1. G. M. Trevelyan, *English Social History* (London: Longman, Green, and Co., 1945), p. 405.

2. Useful works on the history of British sport include Richard Holt, *Sport*

and the British: A Modern History (Oxford: Oxford University Press, 1990), and Tony Mason, ed., *Sport in Britain: A Social History* (Cambridge: Cambridge University Press, 1989). On cricket particularly, see Rowland Bowen, *Cricket: A History of Its Growth and Development throughout the World* (London: Eyre and Spottiswoode, 1970); David Underdown, *Start of Play: Cricket and Culture in Eighteenth Century England* (London: Penguin Books, 2000); and Derek Birley, *A Social History of English Cricket* (London: Aurum Press, 1999).

3. There was one well-known amateur football team, the Corinthians, which contained both public school and university men. This team was much written about precisely because it was so unusual. Cf. Tony Mason, 'Football', in Mason, ed., *Sport in Britain.*

4. The class dimensions of English cricket are engagingly treated in the works of Neville Cardus and, more recently, of Michael Parkinson.

5. A. A. Thomson, 'The Two Archbishops', in his *Pavilioned in Splendour* (London: Museum Press, 1956). Also James Bradley, 'The MCC, Society and Empire: A Portrait of Cricket's Ruling Body, 1860–1914', in J. A. Mangan, ed., *The Cultural Bond: Sport, Empire, Society* (London: Frank Cass, 1992).

6. S. R. Lushington, *The Life and Services of General Lord Harris, GCB, During his Campaigns in America, the West Indies and India* (London: John W. Parker, 1845); J. D. Coldham, *Lord Harris* (London: George Allen and Unwin, 1983).

7. Originally published in *Cricket*, December 1889, and quoted in Coldham, *Lord Harris*, p. 84.

8. Lord Willingdon, message to the Cricket Club of India, quoted in *The Hindustan Times*, 1 November 1933.

9. Thomson, 'The Two Archbishops', pp. 16, 14. Thomson is positively lyical in his effusions. Both Harris and his fellow Lord, Hawke, he says, 'were men of integrity and authority, men who did nothing common or mean, men who would have given their lives for the faith that was in them'.

10. Christopher Martin-Jenkins, ed., *World Cricketers: A Biographical Dictionary* (Oxford: Oxford University Press, 1996), p. 255.

11. Cecil Headlam, 'Cricket in India', in P. F. Warner, ed., *Imperial Cricket* (London: The London and Counties Press Association Ltd, 1912), pp. 353–4.

12. M. E. Pavri, *Parsi Cricket* (Bombay: J. B. Marzban and Company, 1901), p. 31.

13. W. D. Begg, *Cricket and Cricketers in India* (Ajmer: Begg and Co., 1929), p. 84.

14. N. S. Ramaswami, *From Porbandar to Wadekar* (New Delhi: Abhinav Publications, 1975), p. 21.

15. As reported in *Pratod*, 30 June 1890, in *Report on Native Newspapers for the Bombay Presidency* (hereafter RNNBP), 1890, Oriental and India Office Collections, British Library, London.

16. *Sudharak*, issues of 7 July and 8 August 1890, RNNBP, 1890.

17. Shapoorjee Sorabjee, *A Chronicle of Cricket Among Parsees and The Struggle: Polo versus Cricket* (Bombay: published by the author, 1897), pp. 109–10.

18. *Bombay Samachar*, 20 June 1891; *Jam-e-Jamshed*, 8 July 1891, both in RNNBP, 1891.

19. Shapoorjee, *A Chronicle of Cricket*, pp. 111–14.

20. *Kaiser-i-Hind*, 2 August 1891, in RNNBP, 1891.

21. Letter dated 24 September 1891, Compilation No. 571, Vol. 722, PWD Records for 1890–97, Maharashtra State Archives, Mumbai.

22. Handwritten note by Lord Harris, dated 14 July 1892, in ibid.

23. Letter in Compilation No. 866, Vol. 72, PWD Records for 1890–97, Maharashtra State Archives, Mumbai.

24. Harris to Cross, 18 July 1892, quoted in Richard Cashman, *The Myth of the Lokmanya* (Berkeley: University of California Press, 1975), p. 63.

25. *Jam-e-Jamshed*, 20 August 1892, in RNNBP, 1892.

26. Alan Gibson, *The Cricket Captains of India* (London: Cassell, 1979), pp. 90f. Winston Churchill had been F. S. Jackson's fag at Harrow. After his retirement from cricket Jackson entered politics, as a Conservative. In the late 1920s he served briefly as Governor of Bengal. He was shot at by an Indian revolutionary, but escaped unscathed. When asked about the incident he answered: 'Luckiest duck I ever made.'

27. E. H. D. Sewell, *Cricket Under Fire* (London: Stanley Paul and Co., 1942), p. 54.

28. *Native Opinion*, 22 January 1892, in RNNBP, 1892.

29. *Mahratta*, 25 December 1892, in ibid.

30. J. M. Framji Patel, *Stray Thoughts on Indian Cricket* (Bombay: The Times of India Press, 1905), pp. 73–6; Vasant Raiji, *India's Hambledon Men* (Bombay: Tyeby Press, 1986), pp. 38–40.

31. Harris to Wenlock, 31 December 1892, Mss Eur. D. 952/12, Baron Wenlock Papers, Oriental and India Office Collections, British Library, London.

32. Harris to Wenlock, letters of 5 January, 27 January and 13 February 1892, ibid.

33. Table reproduced from Harris to Wenlock, 31 December 1892, ibid.

34. *Jam-e-Jamshed*, 19 August 1893, in RNNBP, 1893.

35. *Gujarati*, 27 August 1893, in ibid.

36. *Native Opinion*, 27 August 1893, in ibid.

37. *Maharashtra Mitra*, 27 September 1894, in ibid., 1894.

38. This account of the Hindu Gymkhana opening ceremony is based on clippings from the *Times of India* and the *Bombay Gazette* contained in Compilation No. 866, Vol. 72, PWD Records for 1890–97, Maharashtra State Archives, Mumbai.

39. *Kaiser-i-Hind*, 3 February 1895, in *Opinions of the Indian Press on Lord Harris's Administration and the Hollowness of the Permanent Memorial in his Honour by his Friends and Admirers* (Bombay: Fort Printing Press, 1895).

40. *Mahratta*, 13 January 1895, in ibid.

41. Compare my analysis with, for instance, the series of unsubstantiated assertions in praise of Harris as cricketer and administrator contained in Coldham, *Lord Harris*. Harris's own, characteristically self-serving account of why he preferred cricket to governance in Bombay is contained in his 'Recreation and Cricket', in T. C. Collings et al., *Cricket* (London: T. Fisher Unwin, 1901).

42. Clement Scott, 'Cricket Etiquette in India' (1899), reproduced in David Rayvern Allen, ed., *Cricket's Silver Lining, 1864–1914* (London: Willow Books, 1987), pp. 89–91.

43. Lord Harris, *A Few Short Runs* (London: John Murray, 1921), pp. 234–5.

44. Cf. Sewell, *Cricket Under Fire*, pp. 49f.

45. Harris, *A Few Short Runs*, pp. 241–2.

46. *Rast Goftar*, 1 January 1893, in RNNBP, 1893.

47. Manekji Kavasji Patel, *History of Parsee Cricket* (Bombay: J. N. Petit Parsi Orphanage Press, 1892), pp. 48–9, 61–2.

48. Framji Patel, *Stray Thoughts on Indian Cricket*, pp. 165, 110, 25, 12.

49. Shapoorjee, *A Chronicle of Cricket*, pp. 121–2.

5. Working with Leather

1. As, for instance, Gail Omvedt, *Dalits and the Democratic Revolution* (New Delhi: Sage Publishers, 1994).

2. Marx, 'The Future Results of British Rule in India' (1853), reprinted in Karl Marx and Friedrich Engels, *The First Indian War of Independence, 1857–1859* (Moscow: Progress Publishers, 1976), pp. 29–34.

3. Geo W. Briggs, *The Chamars* (Calcutta: Association Press, 1920), pp. 241, 228, 58, 20.

4. The versions, respectively, of Baloo's nephew K. V. Palwankar (in an interview with me), and of an obituary in the *Times of India*, clipping in K. V. Gopalaratnam Collection, Sports Authority of India, New Delhi.

5. P. Vithal, *Maze Crida-Jivan* (Bombay: Bharati Publishers, 1948), pp. 11–12; Bal J. Pandit, *Khara Kheladu* (Poona: Vora and Company, 1959), p. 11; interview with K. V. Palwankar, Bombay, November 1996.

6. The original lease document was shown to me in July 1999 by the Secretary of the Poona Club, Colonel Sarkar.

7. Pandit, *Khara Kheladu*, pp. 11–12.

8. Benny Green, compiler, *The Wisden Book of Cricketers' Lives* (London: Queen Anne Press, 1986), p. 354; Vasant Raiji, *India's Hambledon Men* (Bombay: Tyeby Press, 1986), p. 61.

9. J. M. Framji Patel, *Stray Thoughts on Indian Cricket* (Bombay: The Times of India Press, 1905), p. 104.

10. Interview with Y. B. Palwankar, Poona, July 1999.

11. Vithal, *Maze Crida-Jivan*, pp. 10–13; interview with Bal J. Pandit, Poona, July 1999.

12. Pandit, *Khara Kheladu*, pp. 16–17; Vithal, *Maze Crida-Jivan*, p. 14; interview with K. V. Palwankar, Bombay, December 1996.

13. Pandit, *Khara Kheladu*, p. 17.

14. Dhananjay Keer, *Mahatma Jotirao Phooley: Father of Our Social Revolution* (Bombay: Popular Prakashan, 1964), pp. 210f.

15. Anon., 'Hindu Cricket', *Indian Social Reformer*, vol. 16, no. 25 (18 February 1906).

16. The information in this and the previous paragraph comes from contemporary newspaper accounts.

17. Interview with K. V. Palwankar, Bombay, December 1896.

18. Sir Chunilal V. Mehta, 'Beginnings of Hindu Cricket', in the *Diamond Jubilee Souvenir of Parmanandas Jivandas Hindu Gymkhana, 1894–1954* (Bombay: PJ Hindu Gymkhana, 1954).

19. M. E. Pavri, *Parsi Cricket* (Bombay: J. B. Marzban and Co., 1901), p. 164.

20. J. C. Maitra, writing in *The Sportsman*, Special Quadrangular Number, 30 November 1929.

21. H. C. Muckerjee, *The Indian Cricketers' Tour of 1911* (Calcutta: published by the author, 1911), p. 20.

22. Alan Ross, *Ranji: Prince of Cricket* (1983: reprint London: Pavilion Books, 1988); Simon Wilde, *Ranji: A Genius Rich and Strange* (London: the Kingswood Press, 1990). Cf. also Mario Rodrigues's forthcoming *Ranji: Pillar of Empire*, an exhaustively researched account of the cricketer as politician and ruler.

23. 'Rover', 'Prince Ranjitsinhji: A Character Sketch', in Prince Ranjitsinhji, *With Stoddart's Team in Australia* (London: James Bowden, 1898), p. 12.

24. Patrick Geddes, *On Universities in Europe and India, and a Needed Type of*

Research Institute, Geographical and Social: Five Letters to an Indian Friend (Madras: National Press, 1904 – based on articles published in 1901 and 1903), pp. 15–16.

25. K. S. Ranjitsinhji, *The Jubilee Book of Cricket* (Edinburgh: William Blackwood and Sons, 1897).

26. As told in the *Diamond Jubilee Souvenir of Parmanand Jivandas Hindu Gymkhana, 1894–1954.*

27. Vithal, *Maze Crida-Jivan*, pp. 29–32.

28. As related by Deodhar to Bal J. Pandit, who in turn told me the story when I interviewed him in Poona in July 1999.

29. Cf. Anthony de Mello, *Portrait of Indian Sport* (London: P. R. Macmillan and Co., 1959), pp. 17f.

30. These cricketers are described in Framji Patel, *Stray Thoughts on Indian Cricket* (Bombay: The Times of India Press, 1905), chapter 6.

31. Manekji Kavasji Patel, *History of Parsee Cricket* (Bombay: J. N. Petit Parsi Orphanage Captain Printing Press, 1892), pp. 13–14.

6. The Game Goes On

1. J. M. Framji Patel, *Stray Thoughts on Indian Cricket* (Bombay: The Times of India Press, 1905), pp. 70–71.

2. The details of these matches are provided in A. A. Fyzee, H. N. Contractor, D. P. Thanawala and Vijay Merchant, compilers, *Fifty Years of Bombay Cricket* (Bombay: Thacker and Co., 1946).

3. M. E. Pavri, *Parsi Cricket* (Bombay: J. B. Marzban and Company, 1901), p. 189.

4. Ibid., pp. 168–9.

5. Jamshed Dinshaw Antia, *Elphinstone College Tours* (Bombay: published by the author, 1913), p. 35.

6. Ibid., p. 24.

7. Cecil Headlam, *Ten Thousand Miles through India and Burma: An Account of the Oxford University Authentics' Cricket Tour with Mr K. J. Key in the Year of the Coronation Durbar* (London: J. M. Dent and Co., 1903), p. 36. See also Framji Patel, *Stray Thoughts on Indian Cricket*, pp. 149–50.

8. Headlam, *Ten Thousand Miles*, pp. 103–4, 131–2.

9. Ibid., pp. 168–9.

10. Ibid., pp. 226–8.

11. Ibid., pp. 216–17.

12. Framji Patel, *Stray Thoughts on Indian Cricket*, pp. 67–8.

13. Richard Cashman, *Patrons, Players and the Crowd: The Phenomenon of Indian Cricket* (New Delhi: Orient Longman, 1980), p. 29.

14. P. Vithal, *Maze Crida-Jivan* (Bombay: Bharati Publications, 1948), pp. 38ff.

15. As recalled in 'Vizzy', 'Cricketing Reminscences', *Dawn* (Lahore), 3 November 1952 (originally published in *The Pioneer* of Lucknow).

16. N. N. Langrana, 'I Gaze into the Fire', in *Cricket Association of Bengal Silver Jubilee Souvenir* (Calcutta: CAB, 1956).

17. Romesh Ganguly, 'The Spirit of Cricket', in ibid.

18. Prince Ranjitsinhji, *Cricket Guide and How to Play Cricket* (London: British Sports Publishing Company, 1906), pp. 101–2.

19. *Bombay Gazette*, 29 January 1906.

20. Sumit Sarkar, *The Swadeshi Movement in Bengal, 1903–1908* (Delhi: Peoples Publishing House, 1973). *Swadeshi* would translate as 'of one's own land'. The movement thus called for Indian dress and the use of Indian products generally, in preparation for *swaraj*, or self-rule.

21. *Kesari*, 2 February 1906, in *Report on Native Newspapers for the Bombay Presidency*, in Oriental and India Office Collections, British Library, London (hereafter RNNBP).

22. *Bhala*, 1 January 1906, in RNNBP.

23. *Mahratta*, 14 January 1906; *Kal*, 19 January 1906, both in RNNBP.

24. *Bombay Gazette*, 8 February 1906.

25. Ibid.

26. Ibid., 10 and 12 February 1906; *Madras Mail*, 15 February 1906.

27. *Bombay Gazette*, 12 February 1906.

28. *Indian Spectator*, 17 February 1906.

29. *Mahratta*, editorial of 11 February 1906.

30. *The Tribune*, 23 February 1906.

31. Captain Philip Trevor, *The Lighter Side of Cricket* (London: Methuen and Co., 1901), p. 270.

32. Anon., 'Hindu Cricket', *Indian Social Reformer*, vol. 16, no. 25 (18 February 1906).

33. *Bombay Gazette*, 11 February 1907.

34. Sir Chunilal V. Mehta, 'Beginnings of Hindu Cricket', in *Diamond Jubilee Souvenir of Parmanand Jivandas Hindu Gymkhana, 1894–1954* (Bombay: PJ Hindu Gymkhana, 1954).

35. *Mahratta*, 8 March 1907.

36. A useful discussion of these competing trends in the national movement, *c.* 1905–7, is contained in chapters 22 and 23 of B. R. Nanda's *Gokhale: The Indian Moderates and the British Raj* (Princeton: Princeton University Press, 1977).

37. *The Tribune*, 22 February 1906.

Histories of India often begin with Bengal, the region that was first exposed to British rule, and the region to which most of India's leading historians belong. Thus stories of Indian sporting triumphs usually begin with the victory of the Mohun Bagan football side over the East Yorkshire Regiment in the IFA Shield final of 1911. Even sporting-minded Indians do not know that twenty years before that the Parsis had defeated the British at cricket. As for the great Hindu victories of 1906 and 1907, however much they were talked of and written about at the time, they appear now to have been completely forgotten. They go unmentioned, for example, in the histories of Indian cricket written by Mihir Bose, Richard Cashman, E. L. Docker and N. S. Ramaswami.

38. 'The Negro Boxing Champion', the *Guardian*, 22 January 1914, reproduced in David Ayerst, ed., *The Guardian Omnibus, 1821–1971* (London: Collins, 1973), p. 313.

39. Cf. the thoughtful discussion of heavyweight boxing and racial politics in Lawrence Levine, *Black Culture and Black Consciousness* (Oxford: Oxford University Press, 1977), pp. 429–38.

40. See *Mahratta*, 2 February 1907.

41. Calculated from Fyzee et al., *Fifty Years of Bombay Cricket*.

42. As recalled in the *Bombay Chronicle*, 2 December 1941.

43. Cashman, *Patrons, Players and the Crowd*, pp. 117–8.

44. V. J. Divecha, 'The First Match', in *Official Souvenir of the Silver Jubilee of the Bombay Cricket Association, 1930–1954* (Bombay: BCA, n. d.).

45. Vithal, *Maze Crida-Jivan*, pp. 5–7.

46. P. N. Polishwalla, *Representative Matches in India from 1892 to 1919* (Bombay: published by the author, 1919), pp. 64–7.

47. H. C. Muckerjee, *The Indian Cricketers' Tour of 1911* (Calcutta: published by the author, 1911), pp. 24–5.

48. Patu Mukherjee, 'Bengali Cricket and Cricketers', in *Cricket Association of Bengal Silver Jubilee Souvenir* (Calcutta: CAB, 1956).

49. These figures are taken from S. K. Roy, compiler, *India–England Cricket Visits, 1911–1946* (Calcutta: Illustrated News, 1946).

50. Muckerjee, *The Indian Cricketers' Tour of 1911*, pp 153–4, 159, 109.

51. *The Indian Spectator*, 23 September 1911.

52. Vithal, *Maze Crida-Jivan*, pp. 17–18.

53. Eleanor Mae Zelliot, *Dr Ambedkar and the Mahar Movement*, unpublished PhD dissertation, University of Philadelphia, 1969, pp. 133, 252. Also interview with Professor Zelliot, Berkeley, March 1998.

7. Baloo's Struggle

1. F. S. Ashley-Cooper, 'Some Notes on Cricket in India', *The Cricketer*, Spring Annual, 1927.

2. Jamshed Dinshaw Antia, *Elphinstone College Tours* (Bombay: published by the author, 1913), pp. 194ff. There was actually a fifth brother, Krishna, who died very young. In deference to his memory P. Vithal titled a chapter of his memoirs 'Panch Palwalkar', a reference to the greatest of all Hindu brotherhoods, the five Pandavas, or 'Panch Pandeshwar'.

3. A. F. S. Talyarkhan, 'Before Memory Slams the Door', in *Official Souvenir of the Silver Jubilee of the Bombay Cricket Association, 1930–1954* (Bombay: BCA, 1954).

4. *Bombay Chronicle* (hereafter *BC*), 19 August 1915.

5. Illustrated article on 'Cricket in Bombay', *BC*, 2 June 1914.

6. Ibid., 11 May 1914.

7. The political orientation of the *Bombay Chronicle* is ably discussed in chapter 6 of Milton Israel's *Communication and Power: Propaganda and the Press in the Indian Nationalist Struggle, 1921–1947* (Cambridge: Cambridge University Press, 1994).

8. 'The Bombay Cricket Carnival', *BC*, 5 September 1913.

9. Extract from 'Cricket', reproduced in ibid., 11 December 1913.

10. Anon., 'Hindu Cricket', *Indian Social Reformer*, vol. 16, no. 25 (18 February 1906).

11. D. B. Deodhar, *I Look Back* (Madras: Sport and Pastime, 1966), p. 69.

12. *BC*, 1 October 1913.

13. Ibid., 2 June 1914.

14. Ibid., 7 July 1914.

15. See ibid., 29 May 1913.

16. Ibid., 3 September 1915.

17. Ibid.

18. Ibid., 4 September 1915.

19. There have been some successful bowler-captains in the history of cricket, such as Australia's Richie Benaud and Pakistan's Imran Khan. Yet the bias persists: bowlers who, like Baloo, have outstanding tactical minds are denied the captaincy simply because they are bowlers. One such case is that of the current Indian spin-bowler Anil Kumble, a cricketer of maturity and intelligence who has never been asked to lead his country.

20. *BC*, 17 September 1915.

21. Nayudu's background and formative years are described in Chandra Nayudu, *C. K. Nayudu: A Daughter Remembers* (Calcutta: Rupa and Co.,

1995). Also C. K. Nayudu, 'Lessons from a Long Innings', *MysIndia* (Bangalore), 25 November 1956.

22. Deodhar, *I Look Back*, p. 18.

23. *BC*, 9 September 1916.

24. Ibid., 11 September 1916.

25. This correspondence, carried out immediately after the Hindu–European match in the first week of September, was made public in the *Times of India*, 25 September 1916.

26. *BC*, 15 September 1916.

27. D. B. Deodhar, *The March of Indian Cricket* (Calcutta: Illustrated News, 1948), pp. 54–5.

28. P. Vithal, *Maze Crida-Jivan* (Bombay: Bharati Publications, 1948), pp. 77–8.

29. J. E. C. Welldon, *Recollections and Reflections* (London: Cassell and Co., 1915), p. 260.

30. *Kaiser-i-Hind*, 24 December 1916, in *Report on Native Newspapers in the Bombay Presidency*, Oriental and India Office Collections, British Library, London (hereafter RNNBP).

31. The Ilbert Bill was passed, but in a much watered-down version. See, for more details, David Gilmour, *The Long Recessional: The Imperial Life of Rudyard Kipling* (London: John Murray, 2002).

32. *Mahratta*, 18 October 1916, in RNNBP.

33. For a general overview of these protests see Judith M. Brown, *Gandhi's Rise to Power: Indian Politics, 1915–1922* (Cambridge: Cambridge University Press, 1972).

34. See Ravinder Kumar, ed., *Essays on Gandhian Politics: The Rowlatt Satyagraha of 1919* (Oxford: Clarendon Press, 1971).

35. Gail Minault, *The Khilafat Movement: Religious Symbolism and Political Mobilization in India* (New York: Columbia University Press, 1982).

36. See Jim Masselos, 'Some Aspects of Bombay City Politics in 1919', in Kumar, ed., *Essays on Gandhian Politics*.

37. *BC*, 2 December 1919.

38. Ibid., 4 December 1919.

39. Ibid., 9 December 1919.

40. *Collected Works of Mahatma Gandhi*, vol. 17, pp. 471, 534.

41. Ibid., vol. 18, p. 377.

42. Ibid., vol. 19, p. 8.

43. *BC* (Weekly Edition), 24 October 1920.

44. Talyarkhan, 'Before Memory Slams the Door'.

45. *BC*, 15 November 1920.

46. Ibid., 3 December 1920.

47. Vithal, *Maze Crida-Jivan*, p. 88.
48. See *BC*, 4 December 1920.
49. The statement was probably drafted by L. R. Tairsee, the reform-minded Congressman and industrialist who was to later become the President of the PJ Hindu Gymkhana.
50. *BC*, 4 December 1920. Govindji Vassanji used regularly to advertise in Gandhi's own journal, *Young India*.
51. *BC*, 7 December 1920.
52. Ibid., 9 December 1920.
53. Deodhar, *I Look Back*, p. 33.
54. C. L. R. James, *Beyond a Boundary* (London: Hutchinson, 1963).
55. As related in David Davies, 'Singh Carries the Torch of Sewgolum', the *Guardian* (London), 5 February 1998.

8. Vithal's Triumph

1. Mihir Bose, *A Maidan View: The Magic of Indian Cricket* (London: George Allen and Unwin, 1986), pp. 35–6.
2. Mohandas K. Gandhi, *An Autobiography, or the Story of my Experiments with Truth* (1927: reprint Ahmedabad: Navjivan Press, 1995), p. 37.
3. Harish S. Booch, 'He Played Cricket with Gandhiji', the *Sunday Standard*, 16 November 1958, reprinted in *Green Leaves* (Bombay: Harish S. Booch Memorial Volume Committee, 1966), pp. 205–8.
4. Ibid., p. 205.
5. *Collected Works of Mahatma Gandhi* (hereafter *CWMG*), vol. 19, pp. 149–50.
6. See D. G. Tendulkar, *Mahatma: Life of Mohandas Karamchand Gandhi, Volume Two, 1920–1929* (first published in 1951: second revised edn, 1961: reprint New Delhi: Publications Division, 1990), pp. 28ff; Stanley Wolpert, *Jinnah of Pakistan* (New Delhi: Oxford University Press, 1985), pp. 71–2.
7. This last quote comes from Tendulkar, *Mahatma, Volume Two*, p. 34; the rest of the paragraph is based on Sumit Sarkar, *Modern India, 1885–1947* (Delhi: Macmillan, 1983), pp. 204ff.
8. See, for instance, the article 'A Pertinent Question', *Young India*, 29 September 1921, in *CWMG*, vol. 21, pp. 216–18.
9. The next few paragraphs draw from the *Bombay Chronicle* (hereafter *BC*), issues of 28 October through 10 November 1921.
10. P. Vithal, *Maze Crida-Jivan* (Bombay: Bharati Publications, 1948), pp. 86–7.

11. Ravinder Kumar, 'From Swaraj to Purna Swaraj: Nationalist Politics in the City of Bombay, 1920–32', in Kumar, *Essays in the Social History of Modern India* (Delhi: Oxford University Press, 1983), pp. 258–60.

12. 'A Deep Stain', *CWMG*, vol. 21, pp. 462–5.

13. *BC*, 22 November 1922.

14. Letter from L. R. Tairsee, ibid., 7 November 1921.

15. Ibid., 24 August 1922.

16. D. B. Deodhar, *I Look Back: An Autobiography* (Madras: Sport and Pastime, 1966), p. 41; S. K. Roy, ed., *Bombay Pentangular* (Calcutta: Illustrated News, 1945), p. 100.

17. *BC*, 10 and 21 September 1922.

18. *Mahratta*, 24 September 1922.

19. Govind Chimnaji Bhate, *History of Modern Marathi Literature, 1800–1938* (Mahad, district Kolaba: published by the author, 1939), pp. 536–7; entry on Varerkar by S. G. Malshe in S. P. Sen, ed., *Dictionary of National Biography, Volume IV* (Calcutta: Institute of Historical Studies, 1974), pp. 383–4. *Kesari* was the influential Marathi counterpart to the *Mahratta* (which was published in English); both were founded by Bal Gangadhar Tilak.

20. 'Chambhar' is the Marathi variant of 'Chamaar'.

21. Bhargavram Vithal Varerkar, *Turungachya Darat* (Bombay: Lalitkaladarsha Natak Mandali, 1923).

22. As recalled by J. C. Maitra in *BC*, Sunday Edition, 17 October 1937.

23. Ibid., 11 December 1920.

24. Ibid., 13 December 1923; *Navakal* (Bombay), 13 December 1923.

25. Vithal, *Maze Crida-Jivan*, pp. 90–8.

26. Ibid., pp. 91–2.

27. C. K. Nayudu, 'Lessons from a Long Innings', *MysIndia*, 25 October 1953.

28. Vithal, *Maze Crida-Jivan*, pp. 98–9.

29. *BC*, 15 December 1923.

30. Ibid., 18 December 1923.

31. 'Inter-Racial Cricket in Bombay: A Traveller's Impressions', in P. N. Polishwalla, ed., *Indian Cricket Annual for 1923–24* (Bombay: published by the editor, 1924).

32. See W. D. Begg, *Cricket and Cricketers in India* (Ajmer: Begg and Co., 1929), pp. 278–9.

33. *BC*, 27 November 1924.

34. Ibid., 26 November 1924.

35. Quoted in Wolpert, *Jinnah of Pakistan*, p. 82.

36. See Hector Bolitho, *Jinnah: Creator of Pakistan* (London: John Murray, 1954), p. 5.

37. M. C. Chagla, *Roses in December: An Autobiography* (1973: reprint Bombay: Bharatiya Vidya Bhavan, 1994), pp. 63f.

38. Speech as reported in *BC*, 12 December 1924.

39. Vithal, *Maze Crida-Jivan*, pp. 117–18.

40. *BC*, 13 September 1926.

41. See the *Mahratta*, issues through September and October 1926.

42. Vithal, *Maze Crida-Jivan*, pp. 3–4, 61–2, 119; 'Cricket Then and Now: An Interview with Prof. D. B. Deodhar', *Frontline*, 17 January 1992.

43. *Mahratta*, 26 September 1926. Notably, the *Mahratta* did not mention the Hindu captain by name or caste.

44. *BC*, 4 December 1926.

45. Vithal, *Maze Crida-Jivan*, p. 156.

46. Ibid., p. 162.

47. Vijay Merchant, foreword, in ibid.

48. Dhananjay Keer, *Dr Ambedkar: Life and Mission* (third edn: Bombay: Popular Prakashan, 1971), pp 39–40, 86.

49. C. B. Rubie and B. D. Shanker, *A History of the Sind Cricket Tournament and Karachi Cricket in General* (Karachi: Edwin Forster and Co., 1928).

50. *The Hitavada* (Nagpur), 11 October 1922.

51. Ben Diqui, *A Visit to Bombay* (London: Watts and Co., 1927), pp. 31–4.

52. See S. K. Roy, ed., *India–England Cricket Visits, 1911–1946* (Calcutta: Illustrated News, 1946), pp. 306ff.

53. *BC*, 19 October 1926.

54. Ibid., 20 October 1926.

55. *The Indian National Herald* (hereafter *INH*), 28 November 1926.

56. *Navakal* (Bombay), 30 November 1926.

57. E. L. Docker, *History of Indian Cricket* (Delhi: Macmillan, 1976), p. 3.

58. Nayudu took 16 scoring strokes to reach his 50; another 17 to get to his century; and a further 16 to move to his final score, 153. These calculations, by the celebrated Bombay scorer Anandji Dossa, are reported in Raju Bharatan, 'Down Bombay Gym–Brabourne Lane', in *A Memento: The First Test 2000* (Mumbai: Sports Journalists' Association of Mumbai, 2000).

59. G. N. N., *C. K. Nayudu as I See Him* (Poona: Universal Sports Publications, 1941), p. 24.

60. Docker, *History of Indian Cricket*, p. 4.

61. Message sent by Wyatt for C. K. Nayudu's sixtieth birthday, copy in K. V. Gopalaratnam Collection, Sports Authority of India, New Delhi.

62. *INH*, 3 December 1926.

63. Ibid., 4 December 1926.

64. *BC*, 6 December 1926.

65. Ibid., 17 December 1926.

66. Ibid., 7 December 1926.
67. *INH*, 7 December 1926.
68. Ibid., 17 December 1926.
69. *BC*, 15 December 1926.
70. *INH*, 15 December 1926.
71. *BC*, 20 December 1926.
72. Ibid., 21 November 1927.
73. Ibid., 7 and 8 December 1927.
74. P. N. Polishwalla, ed., *The Indian Cricket Annual for 1926* (Bombay: published by the editor, 1926), p. 12.
75. *BC*, 13 December 1928.
76. Ibid., 20 November 1929.
77. Sir Chunilal V. Mehta, 'The Quadrangular Carnival: Whence and Whither?', *The Sportsman* (Bombay), 13 July 1929.
78. *The Sportsman*, 9 November 1929.
79. *BC*, 28 November 1929.
80. D. F. Karaka, 'This Is Cricket', *BC*, 25 November 1928.
81. *BC*, 28 November 1929.
82. Ibid., 29 November 1929.
83. Ibid., 6 December 1929.
84. Ibid., 9 December 1929.
85. The *Times of India*, 6 December 1929.
86. *BC*, 7 December 1929, emphasis added. Bukhari went on to become Director-General of Radio Pakistan.
87. Ibid., 11 December 1929.
88. See *Navakal*, issues of 21 and 24 November 1929; *BC*, issues of 7 and 23 November 1929.
89. 'R. V. M.', 'Hindu Cricket and Baloo Brothers', *BC*, 30 November 1929.

9. A Prodigal's Return

1. Wilfrid Thorley, *A Year in England: For Indian Students* (London: George Allen and Unwin, 1930), esp. pp. 32–8.
2. A. S. D'Mello, *Portrait of Indian Sport* (London: P. R. Macmillan and Co., 1959), p. 138.
3. Letter from K. P. Warden, Secretary, Bombay Cricket Union, *Bombay Chronicle* (hereafter *BC*), 11 December 1927.
4. E. L. Docker, *History of Indian Cricket* (Delhi: Macmillan, 1976), pp. 30–2.
5. As reported in *The Field* (Madras), June 1932, p. 19.

6. Sumit Sarkar, *Modern India, 1885–1947* (Delhi: Macmillan, 1983), p. 284.

7. Cf. Denis Dalton, *Mahatma Gandhi: Nonviolent Power in Action* (New York: Columbia University Press, 1993), chapter 6, 'The Salt Satyagraha'; Thomas Weber, *On the Salt March* (New Delhi: HarperCollins India, 1997).

8. Cf. *BC*, 27 October and 3 November 1930.

9. D. G. Tendulkar, *Mahatma: Life of Mohandas Karamchand Gandhi: Volume Three, 1930–1934* (second edn, 1961: reprint New Delhi: Publications Division, 1992), p. 128.

10. P. Vithal, *Maze Crida-Jivan* (Bombay: Bharati Publications, 1948), pp. 34–5.

11. *The Field*, July 1932, p. 18.

12. Quoted in A. C. Pradhan, *The Emergence of the Depressed Classes* (Bhubaneshwar: Bookland International, 1986), p. 179.

13. *Navakal* (Bombay), 15, 21 and 22 September 1932.

14. Pyarelal, *The Epic Fast* (Ahmedabad: Navjivan Press, 1932).

15. The *Times of India* (hereafter *TOI*), 3 November 1932.

16. Sir Pelham Warner, *Long Innings* (London: George G. Harrap and C. Ltd, 1950), p. 141.

17. J. H. Fingleton, *Cricket Crisis: Bodyline and Other Lines* (London: Collins, 1947); A. L. Le Quesne, *The Bodyline Controversy* (London: Martin Secker and Warburg, 1983).

18. D. R. Jardine, *Quest for the Ashes* (London, 1933).

19. *BC*, 12, 13 and 14 October 1933.

20. *TOI*, 23 October 1933.

21. Ibid., 26 October 1933.

22. *BC*, 11 and 16 October 1933.

23. *TOI*, 26 October 1933.

24. S. K. Roy, ed., *India–England Cricket Visits, 1911–1946* (Calcutta: Illustrated News, 1946).

25. Chandra Nayudu, *C. K. Nayudu: A Daughter Remembers* (Calcutta: Rupa and Co., 1995), pp 27, 29, 31, 34, 48.

26. Ramachandra Guha, *Wickets in the East* (New Delhi: Oxford University Press, 1992).

27. Clipping in K. V. Gopalaratnam Collection, Sports Authority of India, New Delhi.

28. See *National Sports*, May 1956.

29. Chandra Nayudu, *C. K. Nayudu*, p. 103.

30. *BC*, 16 September 1933.

31. *The Tribune* (Lahore), 2 November 1933.

32. Prithvi Raj, *Cricket: Indian and Universities* (Amritsar: M. M. Bhardwaja, 1938), pp. 48–9.

33. Prem Bhatia, *Of Many Pastures* (Delhi: Allied Publishers Ltd, 1989), p. 21.

34. *The Tribune*, 29 October 1933.

35. *TOI*, 8 November 1933.

36. *The Tribune*, 12 November 1933.

37. *TOI*, 18 November 1933.

38. Ibid., 22 November 1933.

39. 'G. R.', 'D. R. Jardine: An Appreciation', undated news clipping, probably from the 1950s, in K. V. Gopalaratnam Collection, Sports Authority of India, New Delhi.

40. *TOI*, 24 November 1933.

41. 'Vizzy', 'Cricketing Reminscences', *Dawn* (Lahore), 3 November 1952 (originally published in *The Pioneer* of Lucknow).

42. Willingdon to Florence Brooks, 27 November 1933, Eur. Mss. F. 237/4, Oriental and India Office Collections, British Library, London.

43. *BC*, 27 October, and 5 and 7 November 1933.

44. Ibid., 8 November 1933.

45. Ibid., 9 November 1934.

46. *TOI*, 1 and 8 December 1933.

47. Ibid., 15 December 1933.

48. *BC*, 13 December 1933.

49. Ibid., 18 December 1933.

50. *The Tribune*, 21 December 1933.

51. Ibid., 22 December 1933.

52. Ibid., 23 December 1933.

53. *TOI*, 19 December 1933.

54. *BC*, 26 December 1933.

55. E. H. D. Sewell, *An Outdoor Wallah* (London: Stanley Paul, 1945), pp. 109–10; *TOI*, 28 December 1933.

56. *TOI*, 6 January 1934.

57. See Rowland Ryder, *Cricket Calling* (London: Faber and Faber, 1995), p. 57.

58. *TOI*, 9 January 1934.

59. As told in 'G. R.', 'D. R. Jardine: An Appreciation'.

60. Cf. *TOI*, 17 January 1934.

61. Ibid., 20 December 1934.

62. Ibid., 12 February 1934.

63. The *Sind Observer*, quoted in *BC*, 14 February 1934.

64. See *BC*, 5 March and 10 March 1934.

65. *TOI*, 10 March 1934.

66. *BC*, 5 March 1934.
67. *TOI*, 22 December 1933.
68. C. K. Nayudu, 'A Great Cricketer', *Sport and Pastime*, 15 November 1958.
69. Quoted in Berry Sarbhadikary, 'C. K. Nayudu: An Appreciation', *Indian Cricketer Annual*, 1956.
70. *TOI*, 20 December 1933.
71. Quoted in Berry Sarbhadikary, *Indian Cricket Uncovered* (Calcutta: Illustrated News, 1945), p. 19.
72. Sir Lawrence Jones, appreciation in *The Times*, 24 June 1958, quoted in Ryder, *Cricket Calling*, p. 61.

10. Politics and Play

1. The *Times of India* (hereafter *TOI*), 14 December 1933.
2. *Bombay Chronicle* (hereafter *BC*), 21 December 1933.
3. M. E. Pavri, 'Reflections on the Test Matches Played in India in 1933–4 and Causes of the Failure of the Indian Team in Matches Played Against the MCC Team', in H. D. Darukhanawala, *Parsis and Sports* (Bombay: published by the author, 1934), p. 57.
4. See Sujit Mukherjee, 'From Paigah Nawab to Vazir Sultan', in his *An Indian Cricket Century* (Hyderabad: Orient Longman, 2002).
5. As described in E. L. Docker, *History of Indian Cricket* (Delhi: Macmillan, 1976), p. 85.
6. P. A. Kelly, Commissioner of Police, Bombay, to Home Secretary, Government of Bombay, 29 September 1932, in L/P and J/7/371, Oriental and India Office Collections, British Library, London.
7. G. N. Acharya, 'Syed Abdullah Brelvi', in *Some Eminent Indian Editors* (New Delhi: Publications Division, 1981), p. 50.
8. This discussion is based on Milton Israel, *Communications and Power: Propaganda and the Press in the Indian Nationalist Struggle, 1920–1947* (Cambridge: Cambridge University Press, 1994), esp. pp. 238–42.
9. *BC*, 2 December 1933.
10. See Stanley Wolpert, *Jinnah of Pakistan* (New Delhi: Oxford University Press, 1985), pp. 133f.
11. *The Sportsman*, inaugural issue, 13 July 1929.
12. *BC*, 28 September 1934.
13. *TOI*, 23 October 1934.
14. *BC*, 6 November 1934.
15. As reported in *TOI*, 12 November 1934.
16. Ibid., 8 and 14 November 1934.

17. *BC*, 13 November 1934.

18. Learie Constantine, *Cricket in the Sun* (London: Stanley Paul and Co., 1946), p. 88.

19. *BC*, 24 November 1934.

20. *TOI*, 26 November 1934.

21. K. N. Prabhu, 'He Raised the Tone of Sports Writing', ibid., 15 July 1990.

22. Quoted in Meher Dastur, 'A. F. S. T.', *The Illustrated Weekly of India* (Bombay), 20 May 1990.

23. Rustom Vakeel, 'The Joys of Cricket', *BC*, 2 December 1934.

24. *BC*, 30 November 1934.

25. *TOI*, 3 December 1934.

26. See *BC*, 1, 4 and 6 December 1934.

27. *BC*, 9 December 1934.

28. *BC* Weekly Edition, 10 November and 1 December 1935.

29. *Bombay Sentinel* (hereafter *BS*), 18 November 1935.

30. *BS*, 23 November 1935.

31. *BC*, 28 November 1935.

32. *BS*, 23 November 1935.

33. *BC*, 27, 28 and 29 November 1935.

34. Ibid., 7 November 1935.

35. Ibid., 30 November 1935. A year previously, another Parsi writer had suggested that it was a new-found passion for bridge that had led to a fall in the community's cricket: 'they exchanged the willow for the cards with the result that their play has now in a large measure deteriorated'. J. R. B. Jeejebhoy, 'The Sporting Parsi', in Darukhanawala, *Parsis and Sport*, pp 14–15.

36. *BC*, 27 November 1935.

37. There is an amusing account of this tour in Mike Coward, *Cricket Beyond the Bazaar* (Sydney: Allen and Unwin, 1990).

38. *BS*, 26 November 1935. Also, *Docker, History of Indian Cricket*, pp. 101f.

39. Docker, *History of Indian Cricket*, p. 115.

40. See Syed Mushtaq Ali, *Cricket Delightful* (Delhi: Rupa, 1967).

41. Quoted in Berry Sarbhadikary, *Indian Cricket Uncovered* (Calcutta: Illustrated News, 1945), p. 70.

42. Niket Bhushan, *Dhyan Chand: the Legend Lives on* (New Delhi: Wiley Eastern Ltd, 1992), pp. 44ff.

43. *BC*, 1 October 1936.

44. This paragraph is based on the daily reports in the *Bombay Chronicle*.

45. *BC*, 10 November 1936; *BC* Weekly Edition, 15 November 1936.

46. Ibid., 9 December 1936.

47. Rustom Vakeel, 'During the Cricket Carnival', *BC* Weekly Edition, 3 January 1937.

48. *BC*, 22 December 1936.

49. *BC*, 23 and 28 December 1936.

50. *TOI*, 31 December 1936.

51. Ibid., 19 October 1935; also A. C. Pradhan, *The Emergence of the Depressed Classes* (Bhubaneshwar: Bookland International, 1986), pp. 244–5.

52. Interviews with K.V. Palwankar, Mumbai, November 1996; and with Y. B. Palwankar, Pune, July 1999.

53. *BC* Weekly Edition, 17 January 1937.

54. *BC*, 18 January 1937.

55. For an elaboration of this argument see Ramachandra Guha, 'Gandhi's Ambedkar', in *An Anthropologist among the Marxists and other Essays* (New Delhi: Permanent Black, 2000).

56. *BC*, 7 July 1955.

57. *BC* Weekly Edition, 10 January 1937.

58. Ibid.

59. Interviews with K. V. Palwankar, Mumbai, November 1996, and with Y. B. Palwankar, Pune, July 1999.

60. Cf. L. R. Tairsee, 'The Harijan Problem', *BC* Weekly Edition, 29 December 1935.

61. *Navakal* (Bombay), 11 January through 17 February 1937.

62. *BC*, 5 February 1937.

63. *BS*, 8 February 1937.

64. *BC* Weekly Edition, 28 February 1937.

65. Joya Chatterji, *Bengal Divided: Hindu Communalism and Partition, 1932–1947* (Cambridge: Cambridge University Press, 1995).

66. Partha Chatterjee, *Bengal: the Land Question, 1920–1947* (Calcutta: K. P. Bagchi and Co., 1984).

67. Samar Sen, *A Babu's Tale*, translated by Asok Mitra (Calcutta: Papyrus, 1991), p. 45.

68. Moti Nandy, 'Calcutta Soccer', in Sukanta Chaudhuri, *Calcutta: the Living City, Volume 2* (New Delhi: Oxford University Press, 1990); Avijit Ghosh, 'The Sporting Mohammedan: Football, Community, Identity', *The Pioneer* (New Delhi), 27 July 1997.

69. *The Statesman*, 12 June 1937.

70. Ibid., 13 June 1937.

71. *Amrita Bazar Patrika*, 13 June 1937.

72. Ibid., 14 June 1937.

73. J. C. Maitra, 'Dangers of Communalism in Sport', *BC* Weekly Edition, 20 June 1937.

74. *BC*, 31 August 1937.
75. Ibid., 4 September 1937.
76. Vasant Raiji and Anandji Dossa, *CCI and the Brabourne Stadium, 1937–1987* (Bombay: The Cricket Club of India, 1987).
77. *BC* Weekly Edition, 17 October 1937.
78. *BS*, 5 October 1937.
79. Ibid., 6 October 1937.
80. Anon., 'Future of Indian Cricket', in *Official Souvenir of the Opening of the Brabourne Stadium*; 'Anon., 'How a Dream Developed', in the *Times of India, Brabourne Stadium Supplement*, both in Brabourne Papers, Oriental and India Office Collections, British Library, London (Mss. Eur. F. 97/77 and 97/78).
81. *TOI*, 7 December 1937.
82. *BC*, 27 November, 2 and 4 December 1937.
83. Ibid., 15 December 1937.
84. See *BS*, letters columns through December 1937.
85. Quoted in Chandra Nayudu, *C. K. Nayudu: A Daughter Remembers* (Calcutta: Rupa and Co., 1995), p. 54.
86. *TOI*, 27 December 1937.
87. *BC*, 27 December 1937.
88. Ibid.
89. Ibid., 28 December 1937.
90. Ibid., 18 December 1937.
91. This and the previous quote from Cardus are both taken from the K. V. Gopalaratnam Collection, Sports Authority of India, New Delhi.
92. M. N. M. Badruddin, 'India Must Give Up Cricket!', *BC* Weekly Edition, 14 March 1937.
93. 'N. J.', 'Is It Cricket?', *BC* Weekly Edition, 26 December 1937.
94. C. L. R. James, *Beyond a Boundary* (London: Hutchinson, 1963).

11. The Mahatma Is Called

1. P. H. Seervai, *Cricket Comments* (Bombay: published by the author, 1938), pp. 103–5.
2. Karaka, 'The Parsis: Their Present and Future', *Bombay Chronicle* (hereafter *BC*), 6 September 1938.
3. S. K. Roy, ed., *Bombay Pentangular* (Calcutta: Illustrated News, 1945), pp. 21–2.
4. *BC*, 7 December 1938.
5. Ibid.

6. P. Hardy, *The Muslims of British India* (Cambridge: Cambridge University Press, 1972), pp. 226ff.

7. *BC*, 1 September 1939; D. G. Dalvi, 'Tairsee as I Knew Him', ibid., 6 September 1939.

8. *The Star of India* (Calcutta), 16 November 1939.

9. *BC*, 23 November 1939.

10. *Bombay Sentinel* (hereafter *BS*), 23 November 1939.

11. *BC*, 25 November 1939.

12. See Vijay Merchant, 'The Quadrangulars', *Sportsweek Cricket Quarterly*, April–June 1974.

13. D. F. Karaka, 'This Is Cricket', *BC*, 25 November 1938.

14. Ibid., 28 November 1939.

15. Ibid., 30 November 1939.

16. Ibid., 2 December 1939.

17. Ibid., 28 November 1939.

18. See Nayantara Sahgal, ed., *Before Freedom: Nehru's Letters to his Sister* (Delhi: HarperCollins India, 2000), p. 321.

19. By D. G. Tendulkar in *Mahatma: Life of Mohandas Karamachand Gandhi: Volume Five, 1938–1940* (first published in 1954: revised edn., New Delhi: Publications Division, 1990), p. 263.

20. The text of Azad's speech is reproduced in Mushirul Hasan, ed., *India's Partition: Process, Strategy, and Mobilization* (Delhi: Oxford University Press, 1993), pp. 59–68. Hasan has, however, wrongly dated the speech as 'December, 1940'. It was actually delivered on 19 March.

21. Ayesha Jalal, *The Sole Spokesman: Jinnah, the Muslim League and the Demand for Pakistan* (Cambridge: Cambridge University Press, 1985), pp. 55ff.

22. See Hasan, *India's Partition: Process, Strategy, and Mobilization*, pp. 55–6.

23. *BC*, 20 July 1940.

24. Ibid., 22 July 1940.

25. Ibid., 12 August 1940.

26. BS, 15 August 1940.

27. Ibid., 20 August 1940.

28. The *Times of India* (hereafter *TOI*), 7 September 1940.

29. Ibid., 10 September 1940.

30. *BC*, 16 July 1940.

31. Sumit Sarkar, *Modern India, 1885–1947* (Delhi: Macmillan, 1983), p. 381.

32. 22 October 1940.

33. Ibid., 25 November 1940.

34. Ibid., 26 November 1940.

35. Ibid., 29 November 1940.

36. Ibid., 2 December 1940.

37. *BS*, 2 December 1940.

38. *BC*, 3 December 1940.

39. *BS*, 5 December 1940.

40. *BC*, 6 December 1940.

41. Ibid.

42. This is implied in a report in *BC*, 11 November 1940, as well as in Merchant, 'The Quadrangulars'.

43. Statement in *BC*, 7 December 1940. A somewhat abbreviated version, taken from *The Hitavada* of Nagpur, is printed in the *Collected Works of Mahatma Gandhi*, vol. 73, pp. 213–14.

44. A. F. S. Talyarkhan, 'The Future of Indian Cricket', in Syed M. H. Maqsood, ed., *Who's Who in Indian Cricket* (New Delhi: published by the author, 1940), pp. 21–2.

45. Interview with Talyarkhan in the *Sunday Standard*, printed sometime in December 1940, and reproduced in *A. F. S. T. Memorial Souvenir* (Bombay: A. F. S. T. Felicitation Committee, n.d.), pp 37–9.

46. *BC*, 7 and 10 December 1940.

47. *TOI*, 9 December 1940.

48. Ibid., 11 December 1940.

49. Ibid., 12 December 1940.

50. *BS*, 10 December 1940.

51. Ibid., 12 December 1940.

52. See *Collected Works of Mahatma Gandhi*, vol. 73, p. 232.

53. *BS*, 13 December 1940.

54. *BC*, 14 December 1940; *TOI*, 16 December 1940.

55. *BS*, 16 December 1940.

56. *BC*, 16 December 1940.

57. Ibid., 20, 21 and 25 December 1940; Ray, *Bombay Pentangular*, p. 37.

58. *BC*, 28 December 1940.

59. Ibid., 30 December 1940. Karaka seems to have taken as his model a famous *Sporting Times* obituary of 1882, mourning the death of English cricket.

12. Closing Time

1. Quoted in J. C. Maitra, *Indian Sports Flashback* (Bombay: published by the author, 1965), pp. 38–9.

2. *Bombay Chronicle* (hereafter *BC*), 7 October 1941.

3. The *Times of India* (hereafter *TOI*), 30 October 1941.
4. Ibid., 8 November 1941.
5. *BC*, 29 October 1941.
6. *Collected Works of Mahatma Gandhi*, vol. 74, p. 308.
7. *BC*, 28 November 1941.
8. K. G. Pardeshi, 'Communal Cricket: the Way Out', *BC*, 21 October 1941.
9. *TOI*, 8 November 1941.
10. Sir Chimanlal Setalvad, 'Communalism in Sport: Cricket and the Larger Issues', ibid., 20 November 1941.
11. Mukul Kesavan, *Secular Commonsense* (New Delhi: Penguin India, 2001).
12. *BC*, 24 November 1941.
13. Ibid., 1 December 1941.
14. Ibid.
15. *TOI*, 7 November 1941.
16. Ibid., 8 November 1941.
17. Ibid., 14 November 1941.
18. Letter by A. G. Mulgaokar, printed in *TOI*, 25 November 1941.
19. Ibid., 17 November 1941.
20. Ibid., 15 December 1941.
21. Richard Cashman, *Patrons, Players and the Crowd: The Phenomenon of Indian Cricket* (New Delhi: Orient Longman, 1980), p. 114.
22. *TOI*, 20 December 1941.
23. *BC*, 22 December 1941.
24. Ibid., 12 December 1941.
25. Sumit Sarkar, *Modern India 1885–1947* (Delhi: Macmillan, 1983), pp. 267–8.
26. See Gyanendra Pandey, ed., *The Indian Nation in 1942* (Calcutta: K. P. Bagchi and Company, 1988); Bejan Mitra and Phani Chakraborty, *Rebel India* (Calcutta: Orient Book Company, 1946).
27. *BC*, 5 October 1943.
28. Ibid., 1 November 1943.
29. *Bombay Sentinel* (hereafter *BS*), 15 November 1943.
30. *BC*, 1 and 23 November 1943.
31. Ibid., 24 November 1943.
32. *BS*, 29 November 1943.
33. Ibid., 1 December 1943.
34. A. F. S. Talyarkhan, *On With the Game!* (Bombay: Hind Kitabs, 1945), p. 38.
35. Ibid., 20 November 1943.
36. Ibid., 6 December 1943.
37. *TOI*, 24 November 1943.

38. *BC*, 7 December 1943.

39. *TOI*, 10 December 1943; *BS*, 9 December 1943.

40. *BC*, 8 December 1943.

41. 'Cricket and Unity', *Dawn*, 16 December 1943.

42. *BC*, 5 October 1944.

43. Berry Sarbhadikary, writing in *Amrita Bazaar Patrika*, 3 October 1944.

44. Reported in *Amrita Bazaar Patrika*, 14 November 1944.

45. *BC*, 15 November 1944.

46. Ibid., 8 November 1944.

47. *TOI*, 11 November 1944.

48. *BC*, 26 November 1944.

49. *TOI*, 30 November 1944.

50. Syed Mushtaq Ali, *Cricket Delightful* (Calcutta: Rupa and Co., 1967), pp. 145–6.

51. S. K. Roy, ed., *Bombay Pentangular* (Calcutta: Illustrated News, 1945), pp. 66–9.

52. *TOI*, 29 November 1944.

53. A. H. Kardar, *Memoirs of an All-Rounder* (Lahore: Progressive Publishers, 1987), pp. 40–6. In 1944 Kardar was entered in the scorebook as 'Abdul Hafeez': he added the surname later, when playing for Pakistan after 1947.

54. *The Hindu* (Madras), 20 February 1945.

55. *BS*, 26 February 1945.

56. Ibid., 27 February 1945.

57. Ibid., 28 February 1945.

58. Ibid., 2 March 1945.

59. *BC*, 2 March 1945.

60. *BS*, 9 March 1945.

61. Quoted in 'Eskari' (pseudonym of Berry Sarbhadikary) *C. K. Nayudu* (Calcutta: Illustrated News, 1945), pp. 91–2.

62. Cf. R. S. Whittington, *The Quiet Australian: The Lindsay Hassett Story* (Melbourne: Wren Publishing, 1969), chapter 6, 'Land of Ranji and Duleep'.

63. *BC*, 12 December 1945.

64. Quoted in *Amrita Bazaar Patrika*, 6 November 1945.

65. *TOI*, 5 January 1946.

66. Ibid., 16 and 21 January 1946.

67. For details see Sho Kuwajima, *Muslims, Nationalism and the Partition: 1946 Provincial Elections in India* (New Delhi: Manohar Publishers, 1998).

68. Denis Dalton, *Mahatma Gandhi: Nonviolent Power in Action* (New York: Columbia University Press, 1993), pp. 144ff.

69. *BC*, 1 October 1946.

70. Ibid., 6 September 1946.
71. Ibid., 12 September 1946.
72. Ibid., 23 September 1946.
73. *The Board of Control for Cricket in India: Annual Report, 1946–47* (Calcutta: BCCI, 1947), p. 12.
74. *BC*, 1 March 1947.

13. The Condemned Playground

1. Lawrence Le Quesne, *The Bodyline Controversy* (London: Martin Secker and Warburg, 1983), p. 6.
2. India Office Records numbers L/P and J/478, Oriental and India Office Collections, British Library, London.
3. Margaret Bourke-White, *Halfway to Freedom* (New York: Simon and Schuster, 1949), p. 18.
4. D. B. Deodhar, *The March of Indian Cricket* (Calcutta: Illustrated News, 1948), pp. 42–3.
5. C. B. Rubie and B. D. Shanker, *A History of the Sind Cricket Tournament and Karachi Cricket in General* (Karachi: Edwin Forster and Co., 1928), p. 3.
6. *Bombay Chronicle* (hereafter *BC*), 26 November 1940.
7. The *Times of India* (hereafter *TOI*), 14 November 1941.
8. Quoted in *BC*, 8 December 1939.
9. Alan Sillitoe, 'Sport and Nationalism', in his *Mountains and Caverns* (London: W. H. Allen, 1975), pp. 84–5.
10. Quoted in Donald Spivey, 'Black Consciousness and Olympic Protest Movement, 1964–1980', in Donald Spivey, ed., *Sport in America: New Historical Perspectives* (Westport, CA.: Greenwood Press, 1985), p. 246.
11. P. Vithal, *Maze Crida-Jivan* (Bombay: Bharati Publications, 1948), p. 60.
12. *BC*, 28 November 1935.
13. Russa Mehta, writing in ibid., 28 November 1941.
14. As told in S. Mushtaq Ali, *Cricket Delightful* (1967: reprint New Delhi: Rupa, 1981), pp. 147–8.
15. Nayudu, 'Through the Mist of Time', *Indian Cricketer Annual*, 1954, p. 132.
16. Hazare, *A Long Innings* (Calcutta: Rupa and Co., 1981), p. 28.
17. *TOI*, 17 December 1992.
18. Vijay Merchant, 'The Quadrangulars', *Sportsweek Cricket Quarterly* (Bombay), April–June 1974, pp. 67–8.
19. 'Get Ready. We Are Playing' (transcript of an interview given by Vijay

Merchant to Mridula Mukherjee, Aditya Mukherjee and Bipan Chandra in 1987), *The Telegraph* (Calcutta), 7 February 1988.

20. File No. 870 (12), Home (Special), Maharashtra State Archives, Mumbai.
21. *BC*, 27 December 1936.
22. Sir Lancelot Graham, quoted in Berry Sarbhadikary, *Indian Cricket Uncovered* (Calcutta: Illustrated News, 1945), p. 63.
23. *TOI*, 4 December 1943.
24. *BC*, 2 December 1944.
25. *Diamond Jubilee Souvenir of Parmanandas Jivandas Hindu Gymkhana, 1894–1954* (Bombay: PJ Hindu Gymkhana, 1954).
26. *BC*, 1 December 1935.
27. B. R. Kagal, 'Communal Cricket', in Syed M. H. Maqsood, ed., *Who's Who in Indian Cricket* (New Delhi: published by the author, 1941), p. 30.
28. *Bombay Sentinel* (hereafter *BS*), 24 November 1943.
29. D. B. Deodhar, *I Look Back: An Autobiography* (Madras: Sport and Pastime, 1966), pp 88–9.
30. *BC*, 27 November 1941.
31. TOI, 20 November 1941.
32. George Lobo, writing in *BC*, 27 July 1940.
33. V. H. Kamath, writing in *BS*, 4 December 1940.
34. *BS*, 12 December 1940.
35. Ibid., 16 December 1940.
36. Letter by Homi J. K. Taleyarkhan, *TOI*, 3 December 1943. This letter seems to have been, in part, the inspiration for the *Dawn* editorial quoted in the previous chapter.
37. 'G. N. N.', *C. K. Nayudu as I See Him* (Poona: Universal Sports Publications, 1941), pp. 68–9.
38. *BS*, 3 December 1936. Mahatma here refers not to Gandhi: the term is being used in its generic sense, i. e. 'saint'.
39. As reported to me by P. V. Varadarajan, a student in the 1940s at Central College, Bangalore.
40. Talyarkhan, *On With the Game!* (Bombay: Hind Kitabs, 1945), p. 61.
41. W. G. Archer, 'Football', unpublished note, *c.* 1934, in Mss Eur. F. 236/1, Oriental and India Office Collections, British Library, London.
42. *BC*, 24 November 1941.
43. 'Quadrangular Cricket: A Plea for its Abolition', *Indian Cricket* (Bombay), January 1938, p. 188.
44. Shapoorjee Sorabjee, *A Chronicle of Cricket Among Parsees and The Struggle: Polo versus Cricket* (Bombay: published by the author, 1897), p. 123.

14. The Commonwealth of Cricket

1. Balkrishna V. Keskar, 'Will Cricket "Quit India" with the British?', *Blitz* (Bombay), 13 July 1946.
2. Janaki Dass, 'Nationalize India Through Sports', *Bombay Chronicle*, 6 November 1946.
3. *Commonwealth Cricketers' Tour of India 1949–50: A Souvenir* (Madras: Sport and Pastime, 1949).
4. 'Axis' (pseud.), 'Willow-Wielding Envoys', *Mysindia*, 1 February 1953.
5. Extracts from this diary, from which this account draws, were published in the *Wisden Cricket Monthly* between 1981 and 1983.
6. R. K. Karanjia, 'Sport and Politics', in *Commonwealth Tour, 1949–50* (Bombay: Trades Publications, 1949).
7. Padmakar Davare, 'This Thing They Call Cricket' (a short story translated by Asha Bhalekar), *Illustrated Weekly of India* (hereafter *IWI*), 25 April 1971.
8. Vijay Barve, 'A Mania Called Cricket', ibid., 11 April 1971.
9. Mikes, 'Innocents at the Oval', essay of 1953, clipping in K. V. Gopalaratnam Collection, Sports Authority of India, New Delhi.
10. 'Bahuroope', 'The Bombay Beat', *IWI*, 1 January 1967.
11. R. Gopal Krishna, 'Today Is the Day', originally published in the *Times of India*, 27 November 1981, reprinted in his *Acute and Obtuse* (Bombay: Jaico Publishing House, 1994).
12. Pradeep Magazine, *Not Quite Cricket: The Explosive Story of How Bookmakers Influence the Game Today* (second edn: New Delhi: Penguin India, 2000), p. 89.
13. N. K. P. Salve, *The Story of the Reliance Cup* (New Delhi: Vikas Publishing House, 1987).
14. Rohit Brijnath, 'Hope and Glory: World Cup Special', *India Today*, 15 February 1996.
15. Mike Marqusee, *War Minus the Shooting: A Journey Through South Asia During Cricket's World Cup* (London: William Heinemann, 1996), pp. 189–97.
16. Chandra Nayudu, *C. K. Nayudu: A Daughter Remembers* (Calcutta: Rupa and Co., 1995), pp. 89–92.
17. *India Today*, 4 June 2001; the *Times of India*, 17 May 2001.
18. Sharda Ugra, 'Pinch Hitter', *India Today*, 28 May 2001.
19. Scruton, *England: An Elegy* (London: Chatto and Windus, 2000), pp. 14–15.
20. See, for example, Norman Yardley, *Cricket Campaigns* (London: Stanley Paul, 1950), pp. 58ff; Don Mosey, *The Best Job in the World* (London:

Pelham Books, 1985), pp. 118ff; Pete Davies, *Mad Dogs and Englishwomen* (London: Abacus, 1998); Jonathan Agnew, *Over to You, Aggers* (London: Victor Gollancz, 1997), pp. 118ff.

21. Scyld Berry, *Cricket Wallah: With England in India 1981–2* (London: Hodder and Stoughton, 1982), pp. 155–7.
22. Ed Smith, 'How I'm Trying to Put the Indian Sign on Spinners', *The Times* (London), 29 January 2001.
23. Rob Nixon, 'As American as Cricket', *The Atlantic Monthly*, July 2000.
24. Andre S. Markovits, 'The Other "American Exceptionalism": Why is There no Soccer in the United States?', *Praxis International*, vol. 8, no. 2, 1988.
25. 'Definitely Not Cricket', *The Times*, 2 January 1967, reproduced in Marcus Williams, editor, *Double Century: Cricket in The Times: Volume Two, 1935–1990* (London: Pavilion Books, 1990), pp. 163–4.
26. As described by Richard Cashman, *Patrons, Players and the Crowd: The Phenomenon of Indian Cricket* (New Delhi: Orient Longman, 1980), p. 79.
27. Cf. E. P. Thompson, 'The Nehru Tradition', in his *Writing by Candlelight* (London: Merlin, 1980), p. 138.
28. K. V. Gopalaratnam, 'A Cricketer among Philosophers', *Sport and Pastime* (Madras), 15 December 1962.
29. R. A. Fitzgerald, *Wickets in the West, or the Twelve in America* (London: Tinsley Brothers, 1873), pp. 292–3.
30. The *Daily Telegraph* (London), 4 March 2000.
31. Quoted in Shapoorjee Sorabjee, *A Chronicle of Cricket Amongst Parsees and The Struggle: Polo versus Cricket* (Bombay: published by the author, 1897), p. 21.
32. Yardley, *Cricket Campaigns*, p. 63.
33. V. S. Naipaul, 'London Newsletter', *IWI*, 28 July 1963.
34. In what follows I have selectively chosen only those Indian victories that seemed to have a wider social or political resonance. Valuable works that focus more sharply on the cricket and cricketers of independent India are Mihir Bose, *History of Indian Cricket* (London: André Deutsch, 1990), and Sujit Mukherjee, *Playing for India* (second edn: New Delhi, Orient Longman, 1987).
35. Clipping in K. V. Gopalaratnam Collection.
36. Ibid.
37. This account of Pataudi's election campaign is based on news reports in ibid.
38. Raju Bharatan, 'Home Are the Heroes', *IWI*, 25 April 1971.
39. This account is based on news reports in the K. V. Gopalaratnam Collection.
40. Clipping in ibid.

41. *Sportsweek*, 5 September 1971.
42. This account is based on clippings in the K. V. Gopalaratnam Collection.
43. Quoted in Cashman, *Patrons, Players and the Crowd*, p. 131.
44. *IWI*, 19 September 1971.
45. Ibid., 3 October 1971.
46. Ibid., 24 October 1971.
47. Interview in *Sportsweek*, 3 October 1971.
48. *India Today*, 15 July 1983.
49. *Indian Express*, 27 June 1983.
50. Ibid., 9 July 1983.
51. Raju Bharatan, *Indian Cricket: The Vital Phase* (New Delhi: Vikas Publishing House, 1977), pp 108–9.
52. The *Times of India*, 11 February 1952.
53. Quoted in W. F. Mandle, 'Cricket and Australian Nationalism in the Nineteenth Century', *Journal of the Royal Australian Historical Society*, vol. 59, part 4, 1973.
54. Thomas Keneally, 'The Cyclical Superiority of Australia in World Cricket', in Michael Meyer, ed., *Summer Days: Writers on Cricket* (Oxford: Oxford University Press, 1987), p. 115.
55. Cf. S. L. Price, *Pitching around Fidel: A Journey into the Heart of Cuban Sports* (New York: the Ecco Press, 2000).
56. Dan Goldberg, 'Caught in the Crossfire', the *Guardian Weekly*, 22 June 1997.
57. Negar Akhavi, 'Exile', *The New Republic*, 12 June 2000.
58. Günter Grass, *My Century* (New York: Harcourt, Inc., 1999), pp. 137–8.
59. Tony Mason, *Passion of the People? Football in Latin America* (London: Verso, 1995), p. 73. Cf. also Janet Lever, *Soccer Madness* (Chicago: University of Chicago Press, 1983).
60. C. P. Surendran, 'Would You Like to Be Reborn an Indian?', the *Sunday Times of India*, 26 April 1998.
61. I have written about the cricket and these cricketers in *Wickets in the East: An Anecdotal History* (New Dehli: Oxford University Press, 1992) and *Spin and Other Turns: Indian Cricket's Coming of Age* (New Delhi: Penguin India, 1994).
62. Cashman, *Patrons, Players and the Crowd*, Appendix IV.
63. J. C. Maitra, *Indian Sports Flashback* (Bombay: published by the author, 1965), pp. 22–3.
64. A. F. S. Talyarkhan, 'Shivaji Park: Breeding Ground for Promising Cricket Talent', in *Shivaji Park Gymkhana: Golden Jubilee Souvenir, 1909–1959* (Bombay: privately published, 1959).
65. Interview with Vasant Raiji, Bombay, June 2000.

66. Clipping in K. V. Gopalaratnam Collection.

67. *Bombay Chronicle,* 6 July 1955.

68. *Hindustan Times,* 6 July 1955.

69. *Indian Cricket Almanack for 1954–55* (Madras: Kasturi and Sons, 1955), pp. 198–9.

70. Both Merchant's letter and the *Times of India* clipping were shown to me by Vithal's son, K. V. Palwankar.

71. Interview with Bal J. Pandit, Poona, July 1999.

72. *Ravivar Sakal* (Poona), 10 January 1982.

73. The *New York Times,* 13, 15 and 16 April 1997.

74. Tygel, *Baseball's Great Experiment: Jackie Robinson and His Legacy* (second edn: New York, Oxford University Press, 1997), pp. 344f. Although few Americans now know of them, there had been some black baseball players who had played in the major leagues as far back as the 1880s. But after 1889 there was complete segregation in the sport until Robinson played his first major league game in 1947. See David W. Zang, *Fleet Walker's Divided Heart: The Life of Baseball's First Black Major Leaguer* (Lincoln: University of Nebraska Press, 1995).

75. Clippings in the K. V. Gopalaratnam Collection.

76. Quoted in the *Sunday Times* (London), 9 July 2000.

77. This paragraph is based on interviews with K. V. Palwankar, Bombay, November 1996; and with Y. B. Palwankar, Poona, July 1999.

78. The poem was given to me by Y. B. Palwankar.

15. Sibling Rivalry

1. 'New Ebor' (N. S. Ramaswami), writing in *Mysindia,* 23 November 1952.

2. A. H. Kardar, *Memoirs of an All-Rounder* (Lahore: Progressive Publishers, 1987).

3. *Dawn* (Karachi), 21 September 1952.

4. Quoted in ibid., 9 October 1952.

5. Ibid., 10 October 1952.

6. A. H. Kardar, *Inaugural Test Matches* (Karachi: Asad Ali and Sons, 1954), p. 2.

7. *Dawn,* 13 October 1952.

8. Ibid., 14 October 1952.

9. Kardar, *Inaugural Test Matches,* p. 11.

10. Hanif is the subject of a lovely word portrait by the Australian writer Ray Robinson: 'The Tilted Helmet', in his *The Glad Season* (London: The

Sportsmans Book Club, 1956); also reproduced in Ramachandra Guha, ed., *The Picador Book of Cricket* (London: Picador, 2001).

11. Valmiki Choudhary, ed., *Dr Rajendra Prasad: Correspondence and Select Documents: Volume Sixteen* (New Delhi: Allied Publishers, n.d.), pp. 334f.

12. *Dawn*, 17 October 1952.

13. Ibid., 18 October 1952.

14. Ibid., 25 October 1952.

15. Kardar, *Inaugural Test Matches*, p. 24.

16. Akhtar, 'Pakistan Cricketers in India', *Dawn*, 2 December 1952.

17. Kardar, *Inaugural Test Matches*, p. 31.

18. *Hitavada* (Nagpur), 30 October 1952.

19. Ibid., 30 October 1952.

20. *Dawn*, 31 October 1952.

21. *Hitavada*, 31 October 1952.

22. Kardar, *Inaugural Test Matches*, p. 32.

23. Ibid., pp. 85–6.

24. *Dawn*, 3 December 1952.

25. Ibid., 16 November 1952.

26. *Amrita Bazar Patrika* (Calcutta), 9 December 1952.

27. Ibid., 12 December 1952.

28. Ibid., 13 December 1952.

29. Ibid.

30. *Dawn*, 3 December 1952.

31. *Amrita Bazar Patrika*, 16 December 1952.

32. Kardar, *Memoirs of an All-Rounder*, pp. 157–8.

33. *Dawn*, 2 January 1955.

34. Ibid., 15 January 1955.

35. Ibid., 16 January 1955.

36. Ibid., 27 and 29 January 1955.

37. Hamid Jalal, 'Afterword', in Saadat Hasan Manto, *Kingdom's End and Other Stories*, translated from the Urdu by Khaild Hasan (New Delhi: Penguin India, 1989), pp. 249–50.

38. *Dawn*, 29 January 1955.

39. Ibid., 30 January 1955.

40. S. K. Gurunathan, 'No Gain, No Loss in Pakistan', *Indian Cricket Almanack for 1954–55* (Madras: Kasturi and Sons, 1955).

41. *Dawn*, 2 and 4 February 1955.

42. Ibid., 3 February 1955.

43. Clipping in K. V. Gopalaratnam Collection, Sports Authority of India, New Delhi.

44. *Dawn*, 2 February 1955.

45. Ibid., 9 and 10 February 1955.

46. Ibid., 26 February 1955.

47. Ibid., 23 February 1955.

48. Gurunathan, 'No Gain, No Loss in Pakistan'.

49. *Dawn*, 6 March 1955.

50. Ibid., 4 March 1955.

51. Copies of these souvenirs are kept in the K. V. Gopalaratnam Collection.

52. Thackeray, *Cricketers in Cartoon: Pakistan v/s India* (Bombay: Marmik Publications, 1960).

53. *Dawn*, 24 November 1960.

54. Ibid., 15 December 1960.

55. Quoted in the *Pakistan Times*, 23 January 1961.

56. *Dawn*, 28 November 1960.

57. The *Pakistan Times*, 3 February 1961.

58. Interview in *Current*, reproduced in *Dawn*, 1 December 1960.

59. 'Jayee', 'The End of a Dreary Series', *The Illustrated Weekly of India* (hereafter *IWI*), 5 March 1961.

60. Kardar, *Memoirs of an All-Rounder*, p. 159.

61. Ajit Wadekar, 'My Tour of Pakistan', *IWI*, 2 January 1977.

62. I owe this story to Kishore Bhimani, former cricket correspondent of *The Statesman*.

63. Khushwant Singh, 'India–Pakistan: First Test', *IWI*, 19 February 1978.

16. Kashmir Comes to the Pennines

1. Krishna Prasad, 'Circle of Deceit' and 'Mr X Makes Cricket a Gambling Game', both in the *Sunday Observer*, (Bombay), 26 February 1995.

2. Minu Jain, 'Cricket to be a Great Leveller', *The Telegraph* (Calcutta), 14 February 1996.

3. Sumit Mukherjee, 'India, Pak Forget Bitterness to Call Australia's Bluff', ibid.

4. The *Times of India* (Bangalore), 13 March 1996; *Deccan Herald* (Bangalore), 11 March 1996.

5. *The Telegraph*, 13 March 1996.

6. Swapan Dasgupta, 'Unsavoury Calcutta', *Indian Express* (Delhi), 15 March 1996.

7. *The Telegraph*, 16 December 1995.

8. Mukherjee, 'Original Sin at Eden', ibid., 15 March 1996.

9. Z. A. Suleri, quoted in Mike Marqusee, *War Minus the Shooting: A Journey*

Through South Asia During Cricket's World Cup (London: Heinemann, 1996), p. 263.

10. *The Asian Age*, 16 and 18 September 1997.

11. *The Telegraph*, 26 September 1997.

12. 'A Pitch for Diplomacy', *India Today*, 6 October 1997.

13. *The Telegraph*, 4 November 1998; *The Hindu*, 21 November 1998.

14. Cf. interview with Thackeray in the *Times of India*, 11 June 1999.

15. Thackeray, interviewed by R. Padmanabhan in *Frontline*, 21 April 1995.

16. As quoted in Sharda Ugra, 'New Delhi, Old Scores', *The New Ball, Volume Two* (Edinburgh: Mainstream Publishing, 1999).

17. Quoted in the *Sunday Times of India*, 22 November 1998.

18. *Mid-Day* (Bombay), 2 December 1998.

19. Report by the Press Trust of India, printed in *Deccan Herald*, 10 January 1999.

20. 'Sena Men Spoil Kotla Pitch on Thackeray's Fiat', *The New Indian Express*, 7 January 1999.

21. Richard Cashman, *Patrons, Players and the Crowd: The Phenomenon of Indian Cricket* (New Delhi: Orient Longman, 1980), p. 111.

22. Soumya Bhattacharya, 'Passions, All But Bottled Up', *The Telegraph*, 20 February 1999.

23. Ugra, 'New Delhi, Old Scores'.

24. Bhattacharya, 'Passions, All But Bottled Up'.

25. Quoted in Tim Heald, *The Character of Cricket* (first published 1985: reprint London: Faber and Faber, 1989), pp. 88–9.

26. Neville Cardus, *Autobiography* (London: Collins, 1949), p. 179; idem, *The Summer Game: A Cricketer's Journal* (1925: revised edn London: Rupert Hart-Davis, 1948), p. 138.

27. 'Yorkshire', in Neville Cardus, *Good Days* (London: Jonathan Cape, 1934).

28. *Autobiography*, p. 155.

29. Richard Binns, *Cricket in Firelight* (London: Selwyn and Blount, 1935), p. 115.

30. A. A. Thomson, *Cricket: The Wars of the Roses* (London: Pelham Books, 1967), pp. 11, 14, etc.

31. Some of these cricket riots have been described in Ray Robinson, *The Wildest Tests* (London: Pelham Books, 1972).

32. *The Times*, 8 June 1999: *Daily Express*, 9 June 1999.

33. *Autobiography*, p. 179.

34. Harsha Bhogle, *Azhar: The Authorized Biography of Mohammad Azharuddin* (New Delhi: Penguin India, 1996).

35. As reported in *The Asian Age*, 5 December 1997.

36. Aslam Sher Khan, *To Hell with Hockey* (New Delhi: Allied Publishers, 1982), p. 73.

37. Geoffrey Moorhouse, *To the Frontier* (London: Hodder and Stoughton), p. 95. In fact, four Christians as well as two Hindus have played Test cricket for Pakistan.

38. This analysis is inspired, in part, by the treatment of the 'good' and 'bad' black boxers in David Remnick, *King of the World: Muhammad Ali and the Rise of an American Hero* (New York: Random House, 1998).

39. Bhogle, *Azhar*, p. 118.

40. The *Times of India*, 21 May 1999.

41. All issues of newspapers mentioned in this paragraph were dated 9 June 1999.

42. *Times Literary Supplement*, 2 July 1999.

43. *The Asian Age*, 21 June 1999.

44. *The Telegraph*, 22 June 1999.

45. This paragraph draws on reports in the *New Indian Express*, 21 and 25 June 1999; *The Scotsman*, 22 June 1999.

46. Clipping in K. V. Gopalaratnam Collection, Sports Authority of India, New Delhi.

47. Quoted in Ugra, 'New Delhi, Old Scores'.

48. As told to me by Rajsingh Dungarpur, former President of the Board of Control for Cricket in India.

49. Pradeep Vijayakar, 'India Pull Off a Thrilling Win', the *Times of India*, 19 January 1998.

50. K. Shankar Bajpai, 'Blame It on India', ibid., 27 April 1999.

51. Rajiv Rao, 'Take the Long Way Home', *Man's World*, July 2000.

52. The *Times of India*, 29 May 2001; *The Hindu*, 26 April 2001.

53. As I write these words in August 2001, the Indian Government has just confirmed its ban on bilateral cricket ties with Pakistan.

54. The *Guardian*, 7 June 1999.

55. Editorial in *Pravada*, vol. 6, no. 4, 1999.

Epilogue

1. *Indian Express* (New Delhi), 20 February 1992.

2. M. S. Golwalkar, 'Be Men with Capital "M"', in his *Bunch of Thoughts* (Bangalore: Vikrama Prakashan, 1966), p. 393.

3. R. Gopal Krishna, 'Cricket, Cricket', originally published in the *Times of India*, 6 September 1979, reprinted in his *Acute and Obtuse* (Bombay: Jaico Publishing House, 1994). Cf. also Dhundiraj Ganorkar, *We Go to*

the Lingiad (Amravati: Hanuman Vyayam Prasarak Mandal, 1951), pp. 28, 258–9, etc.

4. From Prem Bhatia, *Of Many Pastures* (New Delhi: Allied Publishers, 1989), pp. 175–6. Mr Bhatia was the editor of *The Tribune*.

5. Aslam Sher Khan, *To Hell with Hockey* (New Delhi: Allied Publishers, 1982), pp. 74–5.

6. Aniruddh Bahal and Krishna Prasad, 'Cricket's Dirty Games', *Outlook*, 11 June 1997; also Pradeep Magazine, *Not Quite Cricket: the Explosive Story of How Bookmakers Influence the Game Today* (second edn: New Delhi: Penguin India, 2000); G. Rajaraman, *Match-Fixing: the Enemy Within* (New Delhi: Har-Anand, 2001).

7. These stories are too numerous to list, but for an example see 'People Power: Cricket has been Given Undue Importance', the *Sunday Times of India* (Bangalore), 24 September 2000.

8. *The Hindu* (Chennai), 24 July 2000.

9. *Outlook*, 22 May 2000.

10. Sunil Khilnani, 'India Delivers the Last Rites for the Raj in an American Accent', the *Sunday Times* (London), 8 June 1997.

11. Robert Blackwill, 'A Test for US', *The Asian Age* (Bangalore), 5 September 2001.

12. 'New Ebor' (pseudonym of N. S. Ramaswami), 'Cricket Is Part of the Indian Scene', *Indian Express*, 1959, clipping in K. V. Gopalaratnam Collection, New Delhi.

13. This story was told to me by one of Dr Lohia's associates, Shri Arun Kumar of Delhi. Cf. also 'Cricket, British Journalism and Fair Play' (1959), in Rammanohar Lohia, *Interval During Politics* (second edition: Hyderabad: Rammanohar Lohia Samata Vidyalaya Trust, 1985).

Index

NOTE: unless otherwise stated, all italicized entries refer to newspapers and periodicals.